KIERKEGAARD'S PSEUDONYMOUS AUTHORSHIP

A Study of Time and the Self

KIERKEGAARD'S PSEUDONYMOUS AUTHORSHIP

A Study of Time and the Self

MARK C. TAYLOR

Princeton University Press
Princeton, New Jersey

For Dinny

PREFACE

Søren Kierkegaard is a captivating figure. His probings drive the reader ever more deeply into himself. This feature of Kierkegaard's work is what makes him so fascinating, and yet what makes writing about him so difficult. It is a great temptation to listen to Kierkegaard, to talk with him, but to refuse to write about him. However, his works are not so easily dismissed. They demand a close examination and a serious reply. Through his pseudonyms, Kierkegaard creates a Socratic dialogue in which the reader is invited to participate. In this book, we enter his dialogue for the purpose of clarifying his understanding of the problems of time and of the self. As active participants in this dialogue, we must question Kierkegaard, asking him to explain in detail his views on the central issues of time and the self, and to make explicit the implications of his position. But we must always recognize that Kierkegaard is also questioning us, demanding that we clarify our viewpoint. Therefore, our task cannot be simply one of analyzing his works in an effort to grasp his understanding of temporality and of selfhood. After engaging Kierkegaard, we must turn our reflection back upon ourselves, and offer a response to his arguments.

The peculiarly powerful nature of Kierkegaard's personality has greatly influenced books written about him. Many secondary studies are little more than eulogies to a writer who opens our eyes to our own inwardness. However, since the initial infatuation with Kierkegaard has begun to subside, a more serious scholarly consideration of his writings has become possible. In recent years, several important works have been published that seek to grapple with the intellectual issues he raised. The contribution I seek to make to this ongoing research is described in some detail in the first chapter of the book. Hopefully, by continuing our Socratic dialogue with and about Kierkegaard, we will be led to a deeper understanding of his rich insight and to a more profound comprehension of ourselves.

A study such as this is not possible without generous support from various institutions and persons. I would like to thank Harvard University for a fellowship that enabled me to study in Denmark, and Williams College for assistance during the final stages of my work. The lives and minds of many of my friends and teachers are woven into this book. I am sure they will see themselves in the following pages. For debts so deep, a formal acknowledgment seems rather superficial. Nevertheless, there are several persons to whom I would like publicly to express my gratitude: To Professor Stephen Crites of Wesleyan University for sparking my interest in Kierkegaard and for constantly kindling my enthusiasm through our friendship and many long conversations. To Professor Richard R. Niebuhr of Harvard University for his persistent confidence in my work. To Professor Gordon Kaufman of Harvard University for his numerous insightful criticisms. To Professor Niels Thulstrup of the University of Copenhagen for his encouragement and for his warm hospitality during our stay in Denmark. To Professor James Collins of Saint Louis University for his many helpful suggestions. To Ms. Lisa Forrow of Williams College for her help with the final details of the manuscript. To Ms. Carol Orr and Ms. R. Miriam Brokaw of Princeton University Press for their invaluable assistance. To my parents, Noel and Thelma Taylor, for making so many opportunities available to me. And to my wife, Dinny, for . . .

M. C. T.

Williams College
September 1973

TABLE OF CONTENTS

CONTENTS

CHRONOLOGY OF KIERKEGAARD'S WRITINGS

Because of the thematic nature of this essay, it might be helpful for the reader to note the chronology of Kierkegaard's writings at the outset of the investigation.[1] I have listed bibliographical information for the English texts used throughout the study, and have specified the way in which these works are indicated in the footnotes of the essay.

Sept. 7, 1837   *From the Papers of One Still Living* (not translated)

Sept. 16, 1841   *The Concept of Irony, with Constant Reference to Socrates*, trans. by Lee N. Capel, Bloomington: Indiana University Press, 1968. (*The Concept of Irony*)

Feb. 20, 1843   *Either-Or*, vol. I trans. by David F. and Lillian M. Swenson, vol. II trans. by Walter Lowrie, Princeton: Princeton University Press, 1971. (*Either-Or*, I; *Either-Or*, II)

May 16, 1843   *Two Edifying Discourses*[2]

Oct. 16, 1843   *Repetition*, trans. by Walter Lowrie, New York: Harper Torchbooks, 1964. (*Repetition*)

Fear and Trembling, trans. by Walter Lowrie, Princeton: Princeton University Press, 1970. (*Fear and Trembling*)

---

[1] Howard and Edna Hong's table at the beginning of the first volume of their *Søren Kierkegaard's Journals and Papers* (Bloomington: Indiana University Press, 1967) has been helpful in arranging this list.

[2] Kierkegaard's Edifying Discourses are collected in a four-volume series: *Edifying Discourses*, trans. by David F. and Lillian M. Swenson (Minneapolis: Augsburg Publishing House, 1943ff.).

Oct. 16, 1843   *Three Edifying Discourses*
Dec. 6, 1843   *Four Edifying Discourses*
March 5, 1844   *Two Edifying Discourses*
June 8, 1844   *Three Edifying Discourses*
June 13, 1844   *Philosophical Fragments*, trans. by David F. Swenson, revised by Howard V. Hong, Princeton: Princeton University Press, 1967. (*Philosophical Fragments*)
June 17, 1844   *The Concept of Dread*, trans. by Walter Lowrie, Princeton: Princeton University Press, 1957. (*The Concept of Dread*)
   Prefaces (not translated)
Aug. 31, 1844   *Four Edifying Discourses*
April 29, 1845   *Three Discourses on Imagined Occasions*, trans. by David F. Swenson, Minneapolis: Augsburg Publishing House, 1941.
April 30, 1845   *Stages on Life's Way*, trans. by Walter Lowrie, New York: Schocken Books, 1967. (*Stages on Life's Way*)
May 29, 1845   *Eighteen Edifying Discourses*
Feb. 27, 1846   *Concluding Unscientific Postscript*, trans. by David F. Swenson and Walter Lowrie, Princeton: Princeton University Press, 1941. (*Postscript*)
March 30, 1846   *A Literary Review* (not translated)
March 13, 1847   *Edifying Discourses in Various Spirits*, partially translated as: *Purity of Heart Is To Will One Thing*, trans. by Douglas V. Steere, New York: Harper Torchbooks, 1948.
Sept. 29, 1847   *Works of Love*, trans. by Howard and Edna Hong, New York: Harper Torchbooks, 1962. (*Works of Love*)
April 26, 1848   *Christian Discourses*, trans. by Walter Lowrie, New York: Oxford University Press, 1962. (*Christian Discourses*)

PART I
METHODOLOGICAL
CONSIDERATIONS

CHAPTER ONE

THE SCOPE AND SETTING
OF THIS STUDY

A. The Temporal Self

Ever since Plato's *Timaeus* and *Parmenides* and Aristotle's *Physica*, the problems of time and of the self have been central concerns of human reflection. Although the way in which the questions are posed varies from age to age, there has been a persistent effort to plumb the depths of selfhood and to fathom the mystery of temporality. For many persons who have examined these issues, time and the self remain independent problems. However, for other thinkers, they cannot be separated. Each is implied in the other.

The brooding reflections recorded in Augustine's *Confessions* represent the first clear evidence of a perception of the close relationship between time and the self. In the tenth book, Augustine poses the problem with which he is wrestling. "What then am I, my God? What is my nature? A life various, manifold, and quite immeasurable."[1] The more Augustine probes, the more enigmatic his own self becomes. As he tries to solve the riddle of his self by recollecting and reconstructing his personal history, his attention invariably turns to the problem of time. Perhaps the key to unlocking the self lay in understanding the relationship among the past, the present, and the future. But when temporality is subjected to penetrating analysis, Augustine finds it as puzzling as the self: "What then is time? Who can find a quick and easy answer to that question? Whoever in his mind can grasp the subject well enough to be able to make a statement on it? Yet in ordinary conversation we use the word 'time' more often and

[1] Augustine, *Confessions*, trans. by Rex Warner (New York: Mentor-Omega Books, 1963), Book x, Chapter 17, p. 227.

more familiarly than any other. And certainly we understand what others mean by it when we hear the word from them. What then is time? I know what it is if no one asks me what it is; but if I want to explain it to someone who has asked me, I find that I do not know."[2]

The circle seems closed. The exploration of the self drives Augustine to consider the problem of time. But time proves to be as perplexing as the self. The way out of this impasse emerges only when Augustine realizes the positive relation between time and the self: "All this I do inside me, in the huge court of my memory. There I have by me the sky, the earth, the sea, and all things in them which I have been able to perceive—apart from what I have forgotten. There too I encounter myself; I recall myself—what I have done, when and where I did it, and in what state of mind I was at the time. There are all the things I remember to have experienced myself or to have heard from others. From the same store too I can take out pictures of things which have either happened to me or are believed on the basis of experience; I can myself weave them into the context of the past, and from them I can infer future actions, events, hopes, and then I can contemplate all these things as though they were in the present."[3]

At this point, Augustine recognizes that time and selfhood cannot finally be separated. On the one hand, apart from man's self-conscious remembering, attending, and expecting, there is no time. On the other hand, the self is inherently temporal. The discovery of the temporality of selfhood provides Augustine with the fundamental answer to the question of the nature of the self, and marks a major turning point in the history of Western thought.

Strangely enough, however, many of Augustine's most suggestive insights about the nature of time and of the self lay dormant for nearly fourteen hundred years. With the work of Søren Kierkegaard, the problems of time and the self again

[2] *Ibid.*, Book XI, Chapter 14, p. 267.
[3] *Ibid.*, Book X, Chapter 8, pp. 218-219.

emerge as primary foci of reflection.[4] Kierkegaard, as Augustine, feels a need to explore the depths of selfhood. Kierkegaard's understanding of nineteenth-century Denmark makes such "anthropological contemplation" all the more urgent. In his Journals, he insists that in his age, "what it means to be a human being has been forgotten."[5] Individuality was constantly consumed by the crowd, and concern with "world historical" events blinded people to the subtle dynamics of individual selfhood. In this situation, Kierkegaard seeks to turn people from self-forgetfulness to self-awareness. His personal life and writings are a persistent quest for authentic selfhood. Though indirectly, he constantly entreats his reader to undertake a similar journey.

For Kierkegaard, as for Augustine, selfhood is preeminently temporal. Therefore, he believes that time and the self must be studied together. In developing his analysis, he creates an intricate series of pseudonymous writings. The vari-

[4] Other thinkers in the modern period of philosophical reflection recognize a connection between time and selfhood. Most notable in this regard are Pascal, Leibniz, and Kant. What distinguishes Kierkegaard's analysis from the comments of these writers is the centrality of the temporality of selfhood for all of his thought. As will become apparent, Kierkegaard sees a more profound relationship between time and the self than any author since Augustine. See: Georges Poulet: *Studies in Human Time*, trans. by Elliott Coleman (Baltimore: Johns Hopkins Press, 1956).

[5] *Journals and Papers*, no. 649; *Papirer*, VIII² 81. It is necessary to add a word about translations. For the most part, English translations of Kierkegaard's works are rather responsible. There are, however, instances in which the translations are somewhat misleading. Furthermore, often one is not able to notice the multiple meanings of the words with which Kierkegaard constantly plays. For these reasons, at many points it has been necessary to supplement and to correct current English translations. Where significant alterations are involved, the Danish phrases are usually indicated parenthetically. In all instances, the Danish text is cited along with the English translation. The Danish editions that I have used are: *Søren Kierkegaards Samlede Værker*, eds. A. B. Drachmann, J. L. Heiberg, and H. O. Lange (København: Gyldendalske Boghandel, 1901ff.) and *Søren Kierkegaards Papirer*, eds. P. A. Heiberg and V. Kuhr (København: Gyldendalske Boghandel, 1912).

5

ous pseudonyms represent different points of view (or "stages of existence")[6] and present widely contrasting writings. The purpose of this book is to examine the correlative themes of time and of the self as Kierkegaard unfolds them in his pseudonymous writings. Our study will make evident the richness of his exploration of the temporality of selfhood. His insights are of interest to the theologian, the philosopher, and the psychologist. In the course of our inquiry, we will endeavor to indicate the import of his pseudonymous authorship for seemingly divergent disciplines. In short, we will try to do justice to the depth of Kierkegaard's writings by approaching them from a cross-disciplinary perspective. No single viewpoint is broad enough to encompass his vision.

Three fundamental theses inform our investigation. First, all of Kierkegaard's pseudonymous works form a coherent whole whose unifying theme is the consistent effort to delineate the temporality of the self. Second, a most effective way in which to understand his writings is to focus on the dramatic presentation of time and of the self that appears at each stage of existence. Third, the doctrines of Christianity that Kierkegaard selects for detailed consideration can be understood by examining the ways in which he uses them to develop his analysis of human existence.[7] Christianity establishes the possibility of resolving the dilemma of the self that Kierkegaard defines in the pseudonymous writings.

Kierkegaard plainly states the centrality of time for the different stages of existence when he writes: "The significance attached to time is in general decisive for every standpoint up to that of the paradox, which paradoxically accentuates

[6] Kierkegaard defines three principal "stages of existence": the aesthetic, the ethical, and the religious. There are, however, further divisions within this overall structure. For an analysis of the stages, see chapter two, sections C and D.

[7] Hong points out that in the Danish language there are two words for "exist": *existere*, "to exist as a striving person," and *være til*, "to be there in time and space, *Dasein* in German." *Journals and Papers*, vol. 1, p. 535. The difference is not, however, always as clear as Hong indicates.

time. In the same degree that time is accentuated, in the same degree we go forward from the aesthetic, the metaphysical, to the ethical, the religious and the Christian-religious."[8] However, we have noted that Kierkegaard regards time and selfhood as inseparable problems. He argues that the self is a delicate synthesis of diverse components: possibility/actuality; infinitude/finitude; eternity/temporality; freedom/actuality; and dependence upon God. In developing his analysis of the self, he makes it clear that time is the form of *human* existence. Temporality is the process of actualizing possibilities through the free exercise of one's will. To be in time is to be faced with the either-or of decision. The present, the moment of decision, differentiates past and future. Thus selves are "tensed"—they live in memory, anticipation, and decision. The modalities of time are directly related to the different dimensions of the self. The past is the self's actuality, the future is its possibility, and the present is the moment in which freedom can be exercised by actualizing possibilities.

The synthesis of the different components of the self is not, however, a given, but must be achieved by the self. As a matter of fact, one of the self's principal tasks is to bring about the proper "equilibrium" [*Ligevægt*] among these components. Each way of existing that fails to attain such an equilibrium is a form of despair. The different stages of existence are efforts to establish an equilibrium within the self. The various forms of existence represented by the stages are not randomly selected. A movement of increasing individuation informs Kierkegaard's arrangement of the three stages as well as his interpretation of the movement within each particular stage.

At the aesthetic stage of existence, decision is absent as a result of the participation in sensuous inclination, the identification of oneself with the social-natural environment, or the evaporation of the either-or of decision in infinite reflection. Furthermore, since Kierkegaard understands decision to be constitutive of selfhood, those persons who live at the

[8] *Postscript*, p. 265; S.V., vii, p. 256.

aesthetic stage cannot properly be called selves. The aesthete's experience of time is characterized by an emphasis on any one of the three tenses of time to the exclusion of the other two. One can, therefore, be immersed in the sensual pleasure of the present moment, oblivious to the past and to the future; one can be wrapped up in reflection on the past, forgetful of the present and the future; or one can be so occupied with anticipation of the future that one has no regard for the present and the past. Whereas the existence of the aesthete is marked by the lack of decision and therefore by the lack of individuality,[9] at the ethical stage one becomes a self through decisions by which one forges a personal history. For the ethical self, time becomes a medium of self-expression. By committing oneself to ethical ideals, one assumes the obligation of remaining loyal to those goals throughout temporal duration. Such a decision bestows a continuity both upon the self and upon otherwise discontinuous segments of time. Through decisions in time, the self defines itself by establishing a thread of continuity that passes through temporal flux.

The Christian religious stage is the culmination of Kierkegaard's analysis of human existence. As such, it poses the possibility of the most complete realization of selfhood, and discloses most thoroughly the significance of time for the life of the individual. While Christianity's doctrine of sin manifests the extreme to which the self is rooted in time and is cut off from eternal blessedness,[10] the doctrine of the incarnation establishes the possibility of resolving this dilemma by the faithful response to the temporal presence of God. Kierkegaard indicates this dual emphasis of Christianity in the

[9] Following Kierkegaard's lead, I use "individual" and "self" interchangeably in this context.

[10] The word "blessedness" is one about which translators have been highly misleading. The Danish word is "*Salighed*." This is consistently translated "happiness." "Blessedness" or even "salvation" is a much more accurate rendering of the Danish term, and is more in keeping with Kierkegaard's intention. For this reason, "blessedness" will be used throughout the book.

8

course of defining the difference between Christian and Socratic religiousness:

"But the more difficult it is made for him [the existing in-
dividual] to take himself out of existence by way of recollection [*erindrende*], the more profound is the inwardness that
his existence may have in existence; and when it is made impossible for him [as Christianity, with its doctrine of sin,
holds it is], when he is held so fast in existence that the back
door of recollection is forever closed to him, then his inwardness will be the most profound possible. . . . Forward he must,
backward he cannot go. . . . Let us now go further, let us suppose that the eternal essential truth is itself a paradox [as
Christianity, with its doctrine of the incarnation, holds it to
be]. How does the paradox come into being? By putting the
eternal essential truth into juxtaposition with existence.
Hence when we posit such a conjunction within the truth itself, the truth becomes a paradox. The eternal truth has come
into being in time: this is the paradox. If in accordance with
the determinations just posited, the subject is prevented by
sin from taking himself back into the eternal, now he need not
trouble himself about this; for now the eternal essential truth
is not behind him but is in front of him, through its being in
existence or having existed, so that if the individual does not
existentially and in existence lay hold of the truth, he will
never lay hold of it. Existence can never be more sharply accentuated than by means of these determinations."[11]

The point that Kierkegaard makes in this text is that from
the Christian point of view, man sins in the course of his self-
development. This sin disrupts one's relationship with God,
the source of his eternal blessedness. The recognition of this
disruption emphasizes the importance of the decisions by
which the self defines itself. Through its own decisions, the
self is alienated from God. But Christianity's stress on the significance of temporal development does not stop here. The
possibility of reestablishing a relationship to God arises as the

[11] *Postscript*, pp. 186-187; S.V., VII, 175.

result of the self's relationship in time to something historical —to the God who has become incarnate in time. This relationship between the temporal individual and the temporalized deity occurs in the moment. But the moment must be understood in two ways. First, the moment is the moment of the incarnation of God in Christ. This established the possibility of the second moment—the moment of faith. What characterizes both of these moments is that there is a coincidence of the temporal and of the eternal. There is, however, an important distinction. In the moment of the incarnation, God (the eternal) becomes temporal. In the moment of faith, the sinner (the temporal self) is saved (becomes eternal). Faith is, thus, the inverse image of the incarnation. In the incarnation the Eternal becomes temporal but remains eternal; in the moment of faith, the sinner realizes the possibility of eternal blessedness (immortality), but remains temporal. If eternal blessedness is not realized in time, it will never be realized. Kierkegaard argues that "existence can never be more sharply accentuated than by means of these determinations."[12]

As the *telos* of Kierkegaard's authorship, Christianity is the point at which one sees most clearly what it means to be a temporal self, and thereby recognizes that all forms of existence other than Christianity are modes of despair in which there is a failure to achieve genuine selfhood. By accepting responsibility for one's sin and by faithfully responding to God's act of forgiveness in the incarnation, one is able to establish a proper equilibrium among the manifold components of the self. All of Kierkegaard's authorship points to such an individual salvation or self-integration. Only at the final stage of existence, Christianity, is this goal attained.

In the following pages, these claims will be developed and supported. But before a detailed examination of Kierkegaard's understanding of time and of the self can begin, it is necessary to turn our attention to the methodological problems created by the complexity of Kierkegaard's writings and

[12] *Ibid.*, p. 187; S.V., VII, 175.

by the vast body of secondary literature that has grown up around them. The remainder of this chapter is concerned with the methodological problems confronting Kierkegaard scholarship. After considering some of the obstacles that have inhibited a sufficient understanding of Kierkegaard's works, we will give an explicit statement of the method that will be employed in developing our argument. Finally, the method of the present study will be compared with alternative approaches to Kierkegaard's writings. Certain methodological problems involved in the study of Kierkegaard's works will be examined in chapter one. Chapter two will be devoted to exploring the methodological problems within Kierkegaard's authorship.[13] The consideration of these issues prepares the way for the analysis of Kierkegaard's argument in the second part of the essay. Part III is an evaluation of Kierkegaard's position.

B. PROBLEMS CONFRONTING KIERKEGAARD SCHOLARSHIP

There are four primary factors that make arriving at a satisfactory interpretation of Kierkegaard's work so difficult: the diversity of his writings; the relationship between his personal life and his works; the use of the pseudonymous method; and his historical influence.

Seldom has an author penned as wide a variety of works as did Kierkegaard. Both in style and in content, his writings range from seemingly lighthearted aesthetic essays to the most sober Christian discourses. Each work is undertaken with a specific purpose in mind, and all of the works fit together to further his overall goal as a religious author. Kierkegaard presents the interpreter with four primary kinds of writings. The first major part is the "pseudonymous authorship," which consists of nine works written under various

[13] The term "authorship" has a technical use in Kierkegaard scholarship. It refers particularly to the pseudonymous works. I shall use it in this manner throughout the essay.

names between 1841 and 1850. The pseudonymous works include: *Either-Or, Fear and Trembling, Repetition, Philosophical Fragments, The Concept of Dread, Stages on Life's Way, Concluding Unscientific Postscript, The Sickness Unto Death,* and *Training in Christianity.*[14] The first seven of these works make up the chief part of the authorship. *Concluding Unscientific Postscript* was originally intended to complete Kierkegaard's authorship. Furthermore, in the *Postscript* he first publicly acknowledges that he is the author of the other pseudonymous works.[15] This admission does not come, however, until the end of the book, and throughout the text itself Kierkegaard treats the other works as if he were not their author. The last two pseudonymous works, *The Sickness Unto Death* and *Training in Christianity,* were written later and are both under the pseudonym of Anti-Climacus (*vs.* Johannes Climacus, who is supposed to be the author of *Philosophical Fragments* and of the *Postscript*). These works are characterized by a more explicit Christian position than the first seven.

The second major portion of Kierkegaard's works consists of a series of Religious Discourses. It was Kierkegaard's custom to accompany each of the pseudonymous works with one or more religious works published under his own name. He frequently complained that while his pseudonymous works attracted rather widespread attention, his explicitly religious works went virtually unnoticed. But even the Religious Discourses are not all of a piece. There are two distinct sorts of discourses: the Ethical Discourses, which are concerned with ethical religiosity,[16] and the Christian Discourses, which are directly concerned with Christian religious categories.[17]

[14] For a chronology of these works, see the listing at the beginning of the book.

[15] See "A First and Last Declaration," *Postscript,* pp. 551-554; S.V., VII, 545-549.

[16] The Ethical Discourses number eighteen (nine of which were published in 1843 and nine of which were published in 1844).

[17] The more specifically Christian Discourses include: *Edifying Discourses in Various Spirits, Works of Love, Christian Discourses, The*

Though often overlooked by commentators, this distinction is important to keep in mind if confusion is to be avoided. The Ethical Discourses quite self-consciously exclude Christian categories. Kierkegaard himself notes the difference between the two types of discourses when he says that "whatever is decisive for the Christian-religious mode of existence is not to be found in the Edifying Discourses. . . ."[18] There is, moreover, a general chronological distinction between the two sorts of discourses. The point of division between the Ethical and the Christian Religious Discourses is a book entitled *Three Speeches on Imagined Occasions*, published in 1845.[19] Ethical Discourses are more common prior to this work, and Christian Discourses after it.

The third major category of Kierkegaard's writing is the collection of articles that he published attacking the Danish church. These articles were presented in two principal places: a publication of the day entitled the *Fatherland*, and *The Instant* [*Øieblikket*], a publication that Kierkegaard himself issued.[20] These writings are in a popular style and are extremely polemical.

The fourth, and final, major part of Kierkegaard's writing is his Journal. Throughout his life Kierkegaard kept a detailed Journal that he knew would be published after his death. The Journal contains a wealth of information concerning Kierkegaard's personality and his writings. In many instances preliminary drafts of works are included in the Journal. There are also frequent comments on the works that he

---

Lilies of the Field and the Birds of the Air, Three Discourses at the Communion on Fridays, Two Discourses at the Communion on Fridays, For Self-Examination, and *Judge for Yourselves!*

[18] *Postscript*, p. 242; S.V., VII, 230.

[19] English edition: *Thoughts on Crucial Situations in Human Life: Three Discourses on Imagined Occasions*, trans. by David F. Swenson (Minneapolis: Augsburg Publishing House, 1941).

[20] These writings are collected in vol. XIV of the *Samlede Værker*. Water Lowrie has translated them under the title of *Attack Upon "Christendom"* (Princeton: Princeton University Press, 1968).

did publish. Furthermore, in his Journal he carries on debates both with many of his contemporaries and with thinkers in the philosophical-theological tradition. The Journals offer helpful insights for the interpretation of his works.[21]

If a coherent understanding of Kierkegaard's work is to be developed, one must decide how these highly different writings are related. Their diverse nature forces the analyst to focus attention on one part of the Kierkegaardian corpus, and to understand the rest of the writings in relation to this primary body of material.

The second obstacle to arriving at a satisfactory understanding of Kierkegaard has been noted to be the relationship between his life and his works. Not only does his work present the reader with a bewildering variety of approaches, but the life of the author also bears an extremely problematic relationship to the works. The last mentioned type of writing—Kierkegaard's Journals—leads directly to the problem of the connection between his life and his works. Although the Journals are never fully revelatory of Kierkegaard's personal life, significant aspects of his personality are disclosed.[22] The life that is exposed in these Journals is exceedingly complex. The reader's fascination is heightened by his constant self-analysis

[21] In the Danish edition, Kierkegaard's Journals number twenty volumes, *Søren Kierkegaards Papirer*, eds. P. A. Heiberg and V. Kuhr (København: Glydendalske Boghandel, 1912). There is no English translation of all of the Journals. The following are selections from them: *Journals*, trans. and edited by Alexander Dru (New York: Oxford University Press, 1938); *Journals and Papers*, *op.cit.*; *The Last Years: Journals 1853-1855*, trans. and edited by Ronald Gregor Smith (New York: Harper and Row, 1965). It should also be noted that there are five works important for understanding Kierkegaard, but which do not exactly fit the categories that have been used to divide his writings: *Af En Endu Levendes Papirer; The Concept of Irony, with Constant Reference to Socrates; Johannes Climacus or, De Omnibus Dubitandum Est;* and *The Point of View of My Work as an Author: A Report to History.*

[22] Because he was certain that his Journals would be published after his death, Kierkegaard intentionally remains enigmatic about several key aspects of his personal life.

throughout the Journals. When one moves from the Journals to the published writings (particularly to the pseudonymous works) many parallels between Kierkegaard's own life and the problems with which he concerns himself in the published works are evident. In addition to this, there are many similarities between his biography and the lives of the pseudonyms. This has led to the temptation to reduce the pseudonymous works to covert presentations of his own life.[23] Scholarship then becomes an elaborate detective game of trying to discern which passages of the pseudonyms actually refer to Kierkegaard himself. In such investigations, the theological and philosophical ideas are virtually forgotten.

Kierkegaard's pseudonymous method forms the third problem that confronts the investigator of his works. As has been indicated, one major part of his writings is a series of works written under various pseudonyms. Each of the pseudonymous authors is quite distinct from the others, and each presents writings that are very different. When taken at face value, the writings form a series of contradictory viewpoints. The interpreter must come to terms with these writings and reach some understanding of Kierkegaard's motives for using such a method. Interpretations have ranged from the claim that Kierkegaard uses the pseudonyms to hide his "skeptical and melancholy" personality[24] to sophisticated considerations of his dialectical method of communication in the pseudonymous works.[25] The interpretive task is further complicated by the fact that Kierkegaard claims none of the views of the pseudonyms as his own:

"So in the pseudonymous works there is not a single word that is mine, I have no opinion about these works except as a third person, no knowledge of their meaning except as a

[23] This way of approaching Kierkegaard's work is developed in more detail, and is criticized in section E of this chapter.

[24] Edward John Carnell, *The Burden of Søren Kierkegaard* (Grand Rapids: William B. Eerdmans Publishing Co., 1965), p. 41.

[25] For example, Hermann Diem, *Kierkegaard's Dialectic of Existence*, trans. by Harold Knight (London: Oliver and Boyd, 1959).

reader, not the remotest private relation to them, since such a thing is impossible in the case of a doubly reflected communication. One single word of mine uttered personally in my own name would be an instance of presumptuous self-forgetfulness, and dialectically viewed it would incur with one word the guilt of annihilating the pseudonyms."[26]

The relationship among the different pseudonyms, the relationship between Kierkegaard's own views and the ideas of the pseudonyms, and his intention in using the pseudonymous method must be determined before a satisfactory understanding of his authorship can be reached.

Kierkegaard's historical influence is the final obstacle to understanding his works. As is well-known, his philosophical and theological ideas exerted almost no influence either during his own lifetime or throughout the remainder of the nineteenth century.[27] During the twentieth century, with its world wars, theologians and philosophers have been more inclined to turn away from the liberalism that marked most of the nineteenth century and to turn toward a theological and philosophical vision that is more congenial to the ideas of Kierkegaard. But Kierkegaard bears a peculiar relationship to those whom he influences so deeply. It seems that while he frequently serves as a catalyst to the creative energies of twentieth-century writers, once these energies have been released, the authors soon forget the one from whom they have learned so much.[28]

Let us take two examples to illustrate this point—one from theology (Karl Barth) and one from philosophy (Martin

[26] *Postscript*, p. 551; S.V., VII, 545.

[27] Part of the reason is that it was not until the twentieth century that most of Kierkegaard's works were translated from Danish. Although there were some translations into German in the nineteenth century, most of his works were untranslated until this century. In this country the work of Walter Lowrie and in France the work of Paul-Henri Tisseau made Kierkegaard available to a wide audience.

[28] One often has the feeling that part of the reason for such "forgetfulness" is that the later authors learned more than they would like to admit from Kierkegaard.

Heidegger). The impact of Kierkegaard on Barth is evident on every page of his epoch-making book, *The Epistle to the Romans* (1918). In this work Barth frequently adopts Kierkegaard's categories without indicating their source. The influence of Kierkegaard is more or less acknowledged through 1930. At this time Barth's thinking is supposed to have undergone a fundamental shift that is thought to place him in a theological position opposed to Kierkegaard. Certainly after 1930 Barth's theological method changes significantly and this change is in a direction away from Kierkegaard. By claiming that the starting point of theological investigation always must be God's Word and can never be the self, Barth moves in a way opposed to Kierkegaard, who concerns himself with an analysis of human existence.[29] Nevertheless, even in the later Barth there remain significant similarities between the content of his theological position and that of Kierkegaard, though their methods of approach are different.

It is also interesting to note that Barth is quite reluctant to speak of his debt to Kierkegaard.[30] The most striking example of this is the omission of Kierkegaard from his study of nineteenth-century thought.[31] However, even when Barth does speak of Kierkegaard directly, his comments are brief and in no way indicative of the actual theological issues between himself and Kierkegaard.[32] The result of this situation was that while many of Kierkegaard's ideas were being used in theological circles, little effort was expended to study the works of Kierkegaard. Kierkegaard's ideas became involved in twentieth-century debates to the degree that his own presentation of the issues was overlooked.

[29] Surely one of the major factors influencing the sharpness of Barth's shift, and hence his increasing disaffection with Kierkegaard, was his developing polemic against Bultmann. Kierkegaard bears too many similarities to Bultmann to permit Barth to acknowledge his own kinship to Kierkegaard.

[30] This again is closely related to Barth's differences with Bultmann.

[31] *From Rousseau to Ritschl* (New York: Simon and Schuster, 1969).

[32] See "Kierkegaard and the Theologians," *Canadian Journal of Theology*, vol. 13, Jan. 1967, pp. 64-65.

There was a similar situation in the field of philosophy. Martin Heidegger's *Being and Time* (1926) was as influential both in philosophy and theology as Barth's *The Epistle to the Romans.* For Heidegger, as for Barth, the debt to Kierkegaard was profound but the acknowledgment of this debt was slight. Many of the major ideas in *Being and Time* can be found in nascent form in Kierkegaard's writings. Yet in the entire text there are but three brief references to Kierkegaard. Again the result was that Kierkegaard's ideas were used, but his works were not the subject of scholarly inquiry.[33]

Heidegger's philosophical use of Kierkegaard had its impact on theology. In working out his theological position, Bultmann appropriated many of Heidegger's insights. Thus often the ideas that Kierkegaard had formulated (and Heidegger had developed) entered the theological mainstream by way of Heidegger, and not by way of Kierkegaard himself.

The principal point to be underscored is that the two major trends of thought to which Kierkegaard gave rise—Neo-Orthodoxy and Existentialism—have more often than not inhibited rather than advanced an adequate understanding of Kierkegaard's own ideas.

These are the major factors that make a sufficient understanding of Kierkegaard so difficult. In the pages that follow, it will be necessary to propose ways in which these problems can be met.

C. Method To Be Followed

In light of the complexities of interpreting Kierkegaard's works, an explicit statement of the method to be followed is required. Furthermore, this method must be distinguished from other possible approaches to the material.

[33] There are two competent English treatments of the relations between Kierkegaard and Heidegger: Michael Wyschogrod, *Kierkegaard and Heidegger: The Ontology of Existence* (London: Routledge and Kegan Paul, Ltd., 1954) and Calvin O. Schrag, *Existence and Freedom: Towards an Ontology of Human Finitude* (Evanston: Northwestern University Press, 1961). Schrag's study is particularly perceptive.

The first methodological decision that has to be made concerns the relationship between Kierkegaard's life and his works. Is one to give primary emphasis to his writings, to his biography, or to the relationship between the two? In this study we shall be chiefly concerned with his *writings*. This is an important decision and it distinguishes the present approach from a whole body of Kierkegaard literature. Adopting this procedure is not intended to deny that there are significant connections between the life and the work of an author. To do so, especially in Kierkegaard's case, would be foolish. Neither is it meant to deny the value of studies that either examine his biography or focus on the connections between his life and his writings. It is intended to affirm that such investigations can be of only limited usefulness in understanding Kierkegaard. This affirmation has two bases: First, Kierkegaard is fundamentally a *religious* author who is concerned with theological and philosophical ideas. Second, his method and intention as an author are directly opposed to any study that concerns itself primarily with his life.[34]

Having stated that we shall be concerned with Kierkegaard's works and not directly with his biography only advances us a short distance, for, as we have seen, Kierkegaard's works vary greatly. To which kind of work should we give priority, or are they to be regarded equivalently? In this essay it will be argued that the pseudonymous authorship forms the most important part of his corpus. In the pseudonymous works Kierkegaard most carefully articulates his ideas and accomplishes his purpose of clarifying what it means to be an existing individual. The other three kinds of writing should be understood in relation to the pseudonymous authorship. At certain points they are very useful in interpreting the pseudonymous works. For example, many of the Christian Discourses explore more deeply (and in a different spirit) categories that are discussed in the pseudonymous works. The Journals are also often helpful in explaining in more detail the

[34] This argument is developed below in section E. Some of the issues raised in chapter two also bear on this problem.

purpose and meaning of the published pseudonymous writings. It is not proposed to exclude writings other than the pseudonymous ones from consideration, but priority will be given to the pseudonymous works, and the other works will be used only insofar as they illuminate these.

To claim that the pseudonymous works are the most important for understanding Kierkegaard sets this method apart from three other approaches to Kierkegaard. First, there are those studies which contend that his attack upon Christendom, which was presented in the popular publications of the day, was the logical culmination of his work, and offers the key to understanding other aspects of his writings.[35] Such discussions, however, usually fail to notice that almost everything that is presented in the attack is also present in the Journals. Furthermore, these commentators are not sufficiently aware of the tensions between many points raised in the attack and the major ideas of Kierkegaard's earlier writings. Finally, there is not an adequate recognition of the fact that his popular style and increasingly violent polemic in these more occasional writings prevent him from carefully formulating his ideas. The result is repeated obscurity and contradiction.

Second are those studies that regard Kierkegaard's extensive Journals as the key to his writings and his life. Often analyses that regard his biography as essential for understanding his works follow this course. Some authors even contend that the pseudonymous writings can *only* be understood in light of the insights disclosed in the Journals. Kierkegaard's Journals are often quite difficult to interpret. His remarks are frequently cryptic and undeveloped. To build arguments on such fragmentary comments, as many analysts do, is to base one's discussion on a very problematic foundation. To say that the Journals can be helpful in understanding Kierke-

---

[35] See Conrad Bonifazi, *Christendom Attacked: A Comparison of Kierkegaard and Nietzsche* (London: Rockliff, 1963) and John A. Gates, *Christendom Revisited: A Kierkegaardian View of the Church Today* (Philadelphia: Westminster Press, 1963).

gaard's views is quite correct. But to hold that they are the key to all of his writings or that his pseudonymous works can be understood only through the Journals is belied by both his own claims and the works themselves.

Finally, there are those studies which hold that the Religious Discourses (both the Ethical and the Christian) are the most important kind of writing in which Kierkegaard engages. The pseudonymous works are sometimes called "profane"[36] and are said not to contain the central theological ideas most important to Kierkegaard. Such arguments are simply incorrect. It is apparent that from the outset of his writing, Kierkegaard claims to be a religious author. Furthermore, the entire pseudonymous authorship is designed with religious purposes in mind. It is here that he tries to establish what it means to be a Christian, and endeavors to clarify the mind of the reader concerning the reader's relationship to the Christian mode of existence. To hold that the Religious Discourses present Kierkegaard's religious ideas while the pseudonymous works represent non-religious interests is to misunderstand the entire point of the authorship.

It is our conclusion, then, that many of the problems encountered by Kierkegaard interpretation can be overcome by centering our attention on the pseudonymous works. His other kinds of writing are helpful in understanding his pseudonymous authorship, but they should not be regarded as the central part of the corpus.

However, even the resolution to concentrate on Kierkegaard's works, and more particularly on his pseudonymous works, meets problems. Within the pseudonymous works themselves there is a wide variety of style and of content. Do these writings have any fundamental coherence, or do they represent an array of conflicting points of view? Scholarly

[36] Theodor Haecker, *Søren Kierkegaard*, trans. by Alexander Dru (New York: Oxford University Press, 1937), p. 55. Compare pp. 17 and 56ff. Another example of this approach is Vernard Eller, *Kierkegaard and Radical Discipleship: A New Perspective* (Princeton: Princeton University Press, 1968).

opinion is also divided on this question. There are those who argue quite emphatically that within both the pseudonymous authorship, and Kierkegaard's work as a whole, there is no basic coherence. Torsten Bohlin is an example of the interpreter who argues against the coherence of Kierkegaard's work. Bohlin identifies two tendencies in Kierkegaard's thought that stand in tension: "the paradox line" and "the personal experience line." The first trend, found in *Philosophical Fragments, Concluding Unscientific Postscript,* and *Training in Christianity,* borrows concepts and language from Hellenistic thought. The second tendency, present in the Religious Discourses, *The Concept of Dread,* and *Sickness Unto Death,* stresses the personal experiences of sin and of grace and issues in ideas that are more in keeping with the Judaic-Christian tradition.[37] Quite opposed to this argument is the contention that Kierkegaard's works are in some fundamental way unified. Valter Lindström, who directly opposes Bohlin, is among those thinkers who stress the unity of Kierkegaard's authorship.[38] The manner in which this unity is to be defined, and the extent to which it is evident, are both subject to a wide range of interpretation. Lindström, for example, defines the unifying theme as "the unavoidability of the God relationship."

Earlier remarks make it clear that our study allies itself with those critics who hold that there is a coherence in Kierkegaard's authorship. Certain qualifications and explanations are, however, necessary. The word "coherence" is carefully

---

[37] See *Kierkegaards dogmatiska aaskaadning i dess historiska sammanhang* (Stockholm: Svenska Kyrkans Diakonistyrelses, 1925). Compare Per Lønning, "Kierkegaard's Paradox," *Kierkegaard Symposion* (København: Munksgaard, 1955), pp. 158-159, and Paul Sponheim, *Kierkegaard on Christ and Christian Coherence* (New York: Harper and Row, 1968), pp. 39-42.

[38] *Stadiernas Teologi, en Kierkegaard Studie* (Lund: Haakan Ohlssons, 1943). See also George Price, *The Narrow Pass: A Study of Kierkegaard's Concept of Man* (New York: McGraw-Hill Book Co., 1963), p. 26; and T. H. Croxall, *Kierkegaard Studies* (New York: Roy Publishers, n.d.), p. 81.

chosen. "Coherence" is intended to indicate a middle ground between those authors who hold that Kierkegaard's works are disunited and those who argue that they are "systematic."[39] To say the former is to say too little; to say the latter is to say too much. The essay as a whole is an effort to refute the thesis that Kierkegaard's pseudonymous works are disunited and contradictory. But by denying this we do not necessarily affirm that the writings are rigidly systematic. That would be a peculiar argument for a system-hater like Kierkegaard. The point that we shall try to establish is that throughout the diversity of the pseudonymous authorship there is a basic vision of the nature of the self and of what it means to attain authentic selfhood. There is also a singular intention of the authorship, and that is to lead the reader to actualize genuine selfhood in his personal existence.

As has been stated, the stages of existence are not randomly selected and ordered, but are arranged so that as one moves from one to another stage there is an increasing emphasis on time and a further delineation of the self. It would be a misunderstanding of Kierkegaard's method and his works to think that he had merely tried to clothe a naked and an abstract conception of the self in concrete examples. Kierkegaard takes as his point of departure a detailed consideration of concrete personalities.[40] From these observations, he thinks that he can discern both a general structure of selfhood and different points of view that characterize the lives of many people. The personalities that the pseudonymous authorship portrays are ideal representations of different stances that a person can assume. The ideality of the representation excludes the pseudonymous characters from real life. For example, in actual life one never encounters as pure a representation of an aesthetic person as one meets in the first volume of *Either-Or*. It is, moreover, Kierkegaard's understanding of

[39] Despite the title of his book, this is the claim that Sponheim makes. *Kierkegaard on Christ and Christian Coherence, op.cit.*, Part I, pp. 3-50.

[40] This comment indicates the extent to which Kierkegaard is a precursor of more recent phenomenological methods.

the general structure of selfhood that informs his interpretation of the different stages of existence that he defines. Without such an understanding of the structure of the self, he would have no basis upon which to criticize different life-views and to contend that genuine selfhood is only attained in Christianity. Finally, the fact that Kierkegaard, for the most part, presents his views by way of pseudonymous characters should not blind us to his more abstract considerations of selfhood. These discussions are primarily in *The Concept of Dread* and *The Sickness Unto Death*, two works that will play an important part in our analysis. Thus we shall try to show that the different views of time and of the self that characterize the various stages of existence form a motif enabling the investigator to see a coherence among the apparently disparate works.

Another qualification that must be made concerning the contention that there is a coherence in Kierkegaard's works is that it is of the *pseudonymous authorship* that this claim is made. Although the Religious Discourses are *generally* compatible with the arguments of the pseudonymous works, there are many points in the Journals and in the writings attacking the church that stand in considerable tension with the insights of the pseudonymous literature. The writings that create this tension come primarily from the last period of Kierkegaard's life (1853-1855). During this time, central ideas such as "faith" and "suffering" undergo significant changes. Authors who try to argue that *all* of Kierkegaard's writings are self-consistent are forced to overlook many important distinctions when they are confronted by the relationship between the pseudonymous works and these later writings.[41] In

[41] Gregor Malantschuk's *Indførelse i S. Kierkegaards Forfatterskab* (København: Munksgaard, 1953) is an example of a work that meets such a problem. Malantschuk holds that the theory of the stages is the unifying theme in *all* of Kierkegaard's writings. He is, however, faced with a serious dilemma when he tries to extend this argument beyond the pseudonymous works to the attack on the church. Compare Sponheim, *Kierkegaard on Christ and Christian Coherence*, pp. 41-43, for another example of this line of interpretation.

the final analysis, many comments from the later years cannot be made to cohere with those of earlier years. For this reason, it seems more accurate to restrict the argument for coherence to Kierkegaard's pseudonymous works.

It should be mentioned in support of the contention that there is a coherence in Kierkegaard's pseudonymous authorship that Kierkegaard himself intends such a unity. In a Journal entry he comments: "My contemporaries can form no idea of my work as a whole. *Either-Or* divided into four or six parts and published separately so that it occupied six years; that would have been suitable. But that each part of *Either-Or* should only be part of the whole, and then again *Either-Or* only a part of a whole, that is enough to make one take leave of one's senses, says the bourgeois age in which we live."[42] This assertion is developed in his short work, *The Point of View for My Work as An Author*, which was written for posthumous publication. Here Kierkegaard repeatedly insists that he was from the beginning a religious author whose intention had remained constant: "The contents of this little book affirm, then, what I truly am as an author, that I am and was a religious author, that the whole of my work as an author is related to Christianity, to the problem of 'becoming a Christian,' with a direct or indirect polemic against the monstrous illusion we call Christendom, or against the illusion that in such a land as ours all are Christians of a sort."[43]

Critics of the view that there is a coherence in Kierkegaard's authorship often argue, against such statements by Kierkegaard, that the claims made in *The Point of View* are the result of hindsight. In the works themselves, they contend, no such unity can be noticed. It is certainly true that at times Kierkegaard overstates the explicitness of the unity.[44] Never-

[42] *Journals*, trans. by Dru, *op.cit.*, number 597; *Papirer*, VIII A 118. See also no. 795; *Papirer*, IX A 175.

[43] *The Point of View*, pp. 5-6; S.V., XIII, 517. Compare p. 12; S.V., XIII, 523 and p. 18; S.V., XII, 526.

[44] That Kierkegaard is himself aware of this is indicated by his remarks in *The Point of View*, pp. 72-74; S.V., XIII, 561-563.

theless, a coherence does pervade the works. Furthermore, such critics invariably overlook the fact that it is not only in *The Point of View* that Kierkegaard insists that the pseudonymous works form a consistent whole. In addition to various Journal comments, there is a very revealing remark made in the *Postscript*. In the course of commenting upon all of the pseudonymous works up to the *Postscript*, Kierkegaard, under the pseudonym of Johannes Climacus notes, ". . . I mention these books only in so far as they constitute stages in the realization of an idea that I had conceived, but that I was ironically absolved from realizing."[45] Both his own comments about his pseudonymous authorship and the authorship itself support the view that the pseudonymous works form a coherent whole.

D. Alternative Approaches

As has become apparent, when one studies Kierkegaard, one not only engages a highly complex author, but one also must concern oneself with an enormous body of secondary material. In this section of the essay, alternative approaches to Kierkegaard's work will be examined and contrasted to the method that we will follow.

There are three major approaches to Kierkegaard's works: biographical-psychological, historical-comparative, and descriptive-thematic. Clearly it is both impossible and of limited usefulness to try to survey all, or even a major portion, of the secondary studies of Kierkegaard. An efficient way of proceeding, therefore, would seem to be to take a single example of each approach. Since this study is primarily a contribution to English Kierkegaard scholarship, it seems appropriate to select the examples from recent English studies. For these reasons the works to be examined are: Josiah Thompson's *The Lonely Labyrinth: Kierkegaard's Pseudonymous Works* (the biographical-psychological approach); Stephen Crites' *In the Twilight of Christendom: Hegel vs. Kierkegaard on*

[45] *Postscript*, pp. 240-241; S.V., vii, 228.

Faith and History (the historical-comparative approach); and Paul Sponheim's *Kierkegaard on Christ and Christian Coherence* (the descriptive-thematic approach). It is to be emphasized that the intention here is not to undertake a detailed analysis of these works, but to examine the method employed, so that the distinctiveness of our study becomes apparent.

The biographical-psychological treatment has dominated much of the secondary material.[46] This line of argument holds that the principle of unity in Kierkegaard's writings lies in the development of his own life rather than in the theological-philosophical ideas of the works themselves. Such studies usually center on Kierkegaard's biography, trying to discern his physical and psychological maladies,[47] or to analyze the way

[46] This approach to Kierkegaard's life and works was pioneered by P. A. Heiberg (1864-1926) in the following works: *Bidrag til et psykologist Billede af Søren Kierkegaard i Barndom og Ungdom* (København, 1895); *En Episode i Søren Kierkegaards Ungdomsliv* (København, 1912); *Et Segment af Søren Kierkegaards religiøse Udvikling 1835 1 Juni til 1838 19 Mai: Psykologisk Studie* (København, 1918); and *Søren Kierkegaards religiøse Udvikling: Psykologist Mikroskopi* (København, 1925).

[47] The number of physical and psychological illnesses that has been attributed to Kierkegaard is both astounding and ridiculous. For example: "Masochism-sadism," Eric Danois, *Mennesket i Myreperspektiv*; "masochism," Fredrich Brandt, *Den Unge Søren Kierkegaard*; "schizophrenia," Rudolf Friedmann, *Kierkegaard: Analysis of Psychological Personality*; "neurosis of obedience," S. Naesgaard, *En Psykoanalyse af Søren Kierkegaard*; "epilepsy," Fr. Hallager, *Sindssygdom, Forbrygdelse, Genialitet*; "manic-depressant," H. I. Schou, *Religiostet og Sindstilstande*; "pathological melancholy," Hjalmar Helweg, *Søren Kierkegaard: En Psykiatrisk-psykologisk Studie*; "homosexuality," W. Lange-Eichbaum, *Genie-Irrsinn und Ruhm*; "venereal disease," A. Vetter, *Frümmigkeit als Leidenschaft: Eine Deutung Kierkegaards*; "sexual impotence," A. Gemmer and A. Messer, *Sören Kierkegaard und Karl Barth*. For responsible summaries of various psychological and physiological analyses of Kierkegaard, see: Marguerite Grimault, *La Mélancholie de Kierkegaard* (Paris: Aubier Montaigne, 1965) and Aage Henriksen, *Methods and Results of Kierkegaard Studies in Scandinavia: A Historical and Critical Study* (Copenhagen: Ejnar Munksgaard, 1951), pp. 66-128.

in which the writings reflect the development of his life.[48] Thompson's book is an example of the latter tendency.

The opening words of Thompson's study leave no doubt about the method that he intends to follow or about the results to which he will be led: "IS THE PHILOSOPHER a 'sick' man and his philosophy a 'symptom' of his sickness? In one form or another this question haunts every page of the following study of Kierkegaard. For if any single thesis is to emerge from the study, it is that Kierkegaard was a profoundly sick man and that the character of his sickness established a privileged perspective for the understanding of his work."[49]

One gains access to the "privileged perspective" through Kierkegaard's Journals. Thompson devotes the first part of his book to diagnosing Kierkegaard's illness by an examination of the Journals. Unlike many other authors who follow this method, Thompson does not conclude that Kierkegaard's malady is either psychological or physiological. Rather, the source of his illness is "universal"; it is none other than "consciousness itself."[50] Having defined Kierkegaard's sickness in Part I, Part II of Thompson's study consists of an interpretation of the pseudonymous works up to the *Postscript* in light

[48] Walter Lowrie's *Kierkegaard* (New York: Oxford University Press, 1938) is another outstanding example of this method.

[49] Josiah Thompson, *The Lonely Labyrinth: Kierkegaard's Pseudonymous Works* (Carbondale, Ill.: Southern Illinois Press, 1967), p. xiii. The following remarks concerning Thompson's understanding of Kierkegaard must be qualified. In subsequent publications, most notably his contribution to *Kierkegaard: A Collection of Critical Essays*, ed. Josiah Thompson (New York: Doubleday Anchor, 1973) and in *Kierkegaard* (New York: Knopf, 1973), Thompson makes it clear that he does not simply want to reduce Kierkegaard's works to his life, but seeks to use his biography to illuminate his published works. This approach seems to be more satisfactory, but represents a notable shift from the method of his earlier book. The qualifications that emerge from Thompson's more recent work notwithstanding, *The Lonely Labyrinth* offers a lucid example of the problems that the biographical-psychological approach to Kierkegaard's writings invariably encounters.

[50] *Ibid.*, p. 46. Compare p. 209.

of the privileged perspective. Thompson goes so far as to claim that without the insights of the privileged perspective, one cannot understand the pseudonymous authorship. One of the reasons that Kierkegaard's contemporaries misunderstood him was that they did not have access to the Journals. Viewed from the privileged perspective the pseudonymous works become his effort to overcome his illness and to attain health: "Against the background of Kierkegaard's life-world, these works turn out to be, not abstruse theological-philosophical treatises or mysterious aesthetic essays, but successive moves in a complicated dialectic of therapy."[51] The desired "health" is acquired when Kierkegaard no longer seeks to escape the suffering that plagued his life, but is able to appropriate his suffering as the necessary condition of future happiness.

The method that Thompson follows and the conclusions to which it leads him must be criticized at three major points. First, he misunderstands Kierkegaard's motivation in writing the pseudonymous works. He argues, "The motivating force behind Kierkegaard's work is always an interest in his own existence, and we have seen how his interest becomes finally an interest in his own *healthy* existence."[52] This is a prime example of the most basic misunderstanding of the biographical-psychological approach. It is simply incorrect to regard the pseudonymous works as fundamentally concerned with Kierkegaard's own existence. His interest is rather the existence of the *reader*. In an effort to express this concern, he self-consciously withdraws his own person behind the pseudonyms. The effect of this is to turn the reader away from Kierkegaard's personality toward his (the reader's) own self.[53] This leads directly to the second misunderstanding of Thompson and of the biographical-psychological ap-

[51] *Ibid.*, p. xiii. [52] *Ibid.*, p. 62.

[53] For a similar criticism of Thompson's study on this point, see Stephen Crites, "The Author and the Authorship: Recent Kierkegaard Literature," *Journal of the American Academy of Religion*, vol. xxxviii, no. 1, March 1970.

proach. Kierkegaard's pseudonymous method is consistently misinterpreted. The different stages of existence are understood by Thompson as the different life-views that Kierkegaard tried on "in the hope of finding one which protects."[54] An effort is then made to correlate the stages of existence with different phases of Kierkegaard's life. The fact that Kierkegaard intends to present to the reader ideal representations of different life-views so that the reader can clarify his own understanding of himself is fully overlooked.[55] Finally, by contending that the pseudonymous works are not "theological-philosophical treatises" this approach misinterprets some of Kierkegaard's most important categories. Thompson's understanding of Kierkegaard's use of "suffering" serves as an example of this tendency. Thompson seems to assume that Kierkegaard means by "suffering" either physical or psychological suffering.[56] Although the term often has such connotations in Kierkegaard's later Journals, this definitely is not his meaning in the pseudonymous works, the writings upon which Thompson builds his case. Here "suffering" indicates the inward relationship between the sinful individual and his desire for salvation. To identify "suffering" with physical or psychological suffering is to fail to grasp the meaning of Kierkegaard's argument in the pseudonymous works.

Thompson's book is, therefore, a good example of the way in which the biographical-psychological approach frequently leads to a misunderstanding of Kierkegaard's motivation, method, and use of categories in the pseudonymous works.

The historical-comparative approach takes as its main task the placement of Kierkegaard's work within the context of the history of theology and philosophy by the explicit comparison of Kierkegaard with one or another major thinker. Such

[54] Thompson, *The Lonely Labryinth: Kierkegaard's Pseudonymous Works, op.cit.*, p. 58.

[55] Kierkegaard's method is considered in detail in the following chapter. This discussion clarifies the incompatibility between his method and the biographical-psychological approach.

[56] Pp. 176ff.

studies seek to delineate the historical influences exerted on or by Kierkegaard,[57] or attempt to define a major theological or philosophical problem with which Kierkegaard and the one to whom he is compared are concerned. Crites' study takes the latter approach to the material.

Crites' essay is one of the most profound analyses of Kierkegaard to have appeared in recent years. The problems this study encounters are inherent in the historical-comparative approach. In the preface to his work, Crites defines the central issue between Hegel and Kierkegaard as "the reaction to Christendom."[58] Crites contends that although Hegel's early theological reflection results in a negative evaluation of Christianity and of Christendom, in his later work Hegel interprets them both positively. In fact, Hegel becomes the philosopher of Christendom. Kierkegaard, on the other hand, constantly holds a negative view of both Christendom and of its philosophy, Hegelianism. Crites points out that Kierkegaard's repeated criticism of Hegel and his attack on the church are of a piece. It soon becomes evident, however, that there is another closely related problem that guides Crites' inquiry: the ethical implications of Hegel's and Kierkegaard's positions. He considers this issue in the "Introduction" in which Hegel's and Kierkegaard's different views of marriage are taken as paradigms of their understandings of ethical obligation and of the relation of the religious to the ethical.

[57] An outstanding example of this method is Niels Thulstrup's *Kierkegaards forhold til Hegel og til den spekulative idealisme indtil 1846* (København: Gyldendale, 1967).

[58] *In the Twilight of Christendom: Hegel vs. Kierkegaard on Faith and History* (Chambersburg, Pa.: American Academy of Religion, no. 2, 1971). See my review of Crites' monograph: *Union Seminary Quarterly Review*, vol. xxvii, no. 4, summer 1972, pp. 243-245. As with Thompson, these remarks about Crites' method must be qualified. Although this work is an example of the historical-comparative approach to Kierkegaard, a recent essay, "Pseudonymous Authorship as Art and as Act," *Kierkegaard: A Collection of Critical Essays, op.cit.*, pp. 183-229, makes it clear that Crites does not hold to this method exclusively. The orientation of the later essay indicates more aesthetic interests.

Crites contends that for Hegel the social bond of family life is itself religious, while for Kierkegaard the religious lies decisively beyond any ethical-social relationship.[59]

After briefly considering the different ways in which Hegel and Kierkegaard interpret Kant's practical reason, Crites proceeds to an examination of Hegel and of Kierkegaard in turn. In connection with the central issue of the study—the response to Christendom—Crites points out that while Hegel initially argues that it is impossible for Christianity to be a proper *Volksreligion*,[60] in his mature philosophy Christianity is regarded as the *Volksreligion par excellence*. The course of Christendom (particularly the Protestant Reformation) is seen as the necessary condition for the possibility of speculative philosophy. Hegel's speculative philosophy, in turn, brings to conceptual clarity the truth that was implicit in the incarnation and that had developed throughout the history of Christendom—the identity of the human and the divine. So regarded, Christendom is seen as necessary to the current stage of the spirit.

Part III, the most interesting for our purposes, is devoted completely to Kierkegaard. Crites argues that while Kierkegaard agrees with Hegel that Christian history involves the increasing "domestication" of Christianity, he disagrees with Hegel's evaluation of this process. Kierkegaard offers an alternative "phenomenology of spirit"[61] in which he examines the dynamics of individual selfhood in the movement toward faith. Against Hegel, who sees the incarnation as the dissolution of God's transcendence, Kierkegaard views the incarnation as indicating the absolute transcendence of God. It is with this paradoxical event that the individual must come to terms if despair is to be overcome and faith is to be attained. The intervening history of Christendom is of no help, and is actually a hindrance to the individual's appropriation of the Christ event.

[59] See p. 20. Crites has hit upon a crucial issue. It will be considered in some detail in chapters seven and eight.
[60] *Ibid.*, p. 35ff.   [61] *Ibid.*, p. 66.

In Crites' treatment of some of the central Kierkegaardian categories, the shortcomings of this method become apparent. Kierkegaard is such a complex author (or complex of authors) on his own terms that comparison with another thinker is quite difficult. We have already seen the way in which the different pseudonyms represent alternative viewpoints. What often happens when comparisons with other thinkers are made is that certain of Kierkegaard's arguments are abstracted from the overall authorship. This leads to considerable distortion. Thus, for example, while Crites' identification of the relationship between religious faith and ethical obligation as central in the Hegel-Kierkegaard debate is accurate from the Christian perspective, it is not completely correct from the point of view of the ethical stage of existence. As a matter of fact, Kierkegaard's ethical pseudonym presents an outlook similar to that expressed by Hegel in the *Philosophy of Right*.[62] Crites' discussions of time and eternity are further instances of this problem.[63] For example, when Crites tries to define Kierkegaard's use of "eternal" he argues that the eternal "always in some sense implies infinite possibility."[64] While this interpretation explains *part* of what is involved in the concept of the "eternal," the precise manner in which this term is defined at each of the stages of existence varies considerably. The same is true of the notion of "time." At each stage, time is understood and experienced differently.

It becomes apparent that the major difficulty with the historical-comparative approach is that it frequently forces the writer to abstract Kierkegaard's ideas, or the meaning of his concepts, from the totality of the works, a procedure that creates major problems. If one is to arrive at an adequate understanding of Kierkegaard, one's inquiry must be conducted in light of the various stages of existence and of the different meanings that terms have at these stages.

---

[62] See especially: Hegel, *Philosophy of Right*, trans. by T. M. Knox (New York: Oxford University Press, 1969), paragraphs 158-180, pp. 110-120.

[63] See pp. 59ff.   [64] *Ibid.*, p. 79.

The descriptive-thematic approach seeks to interpret Kierkegaard's writings on their own terms, rather than by an examination of the influence of his life upon his works or by a comparison of his arguments with other thinkers. As the name of this type of study indicates, there are two major subdivisions: descriptive studies and thematic studies. The former usually give a summary of Kierkegaard's works with a minimum of interpretive and analytical comment.[65] The latter attempt to define and to analyze a major theme with which Kierkegaard concerns himself. This essay is such a thematic study. Therefore it will be useful to note some of the pitfalls to which this procedure can succumb. Paul Sponheim's *Kierkegaard on Christ and Christian Coherence* manifests certain methodological problems that must be kept in mind when this approach is followed. Although Sponheim's work is long and involved, we can treat it briefly by considering only those issues which bear on the method he employs.

As has been noted, unlike the present book, which restricts its argument for coherence to the pseudonymous works, Sponheim extends his argument for "systematic unity" to all of Kierkegaard's writings. Sponheim states what he sees as the unifying theme when he claims that "Kierkegaard's religious thought moves between two poles formed by his affirmations concerning God and man."[66] Sponheim directs his argument against views of Kierkegaard's works that hold there is a sharp separation between God and man, Christ and Jesus, or faith and history. He identifies two "rhythms" that pervade Kierkegaard's discussions of God and of man. The first, "diastasis," stresses the separation of God and man and is balanced by the second, "synthesis," which emphasizes their interrelationship:

[65] For example, Hermann Diem, *Kierkegaard, An Introduction*, trans. by David Green (Richmond: John Knox Press, 1966); Louis Dupré, *Kierkegaard as Theologian* (New York: Sheed and Ward, 1958); Regis Jolivet, *Introduction to Kierkegaard*, trans. by Barber (London: Frederick Muller, Ltd., 1950); and Reidar Thomte, *Kierkegaard's Philosophy of Religion* (Princeton: Princeton University Press, 1948).

[66] Paul Sponheim, *Kierkegaard on Christ and Christian Coherence*, *op.cit.*, p. 7.

"On the one hand, there is discernible a centrifugal current by which the opposition between the two poles is ensured and enhanced. That opposition may be defined in widely differing ways, but in every case the emphasis is on disengagement— on withdrawal to stress the separateness of God and man. We may call this movement *diastasis*. On the other hand, the diastatic current is balanced by a centripetal one which perceives and emphasizes the relatedness, the co-involvement of God and man. We shall speak of this movement as synthesis."[67] Sponheim's study traces these two "rhythms" throughout Kierkegaard's works.

The details of Sponheim's argument need not concern us here. However, we must examine the possible problems that the descriptive-thematic approach can encounter. Sponheim's work exhibits these problems. In the first place, as has already been observed, Sponheim contends that Kierkegaard's writings are "systematic." He overstates his case, making Kierkegaard more rigidly systematic than he ever would have thought himself to have been. An effective study must walk the fine line between viewing the pseudonymous works as a chaotic array of perspectives and a strictly systematic whole. Sponheim's first error leads him further astray. Because he is interested to show the "systematic" aspect of Kierkegaard's thought, he organizes his study according to what he regards as the most important systematic problems in Kierkegaard's works rather than organizing his analysis according to the writings themselves. The result of this method is that Sponheim randomly abstracts his arguments from Kierkegaard's different works, and does not pay sufficient attention to the principle of the stages of existence. Statements from all of the works are treated in the same manner without regard for the pseudonym through whom they are spoken, and hence without regard for the point of view that they represent. This oversight finally proves to be the undoing of Sponheim's analysis. The rhythms of diastasis and of synthesis, which form the heart of Sponheim's argument, represent two differ-

[67] *Ibid.*, p. 9.

ent stages of existence in Kierkegaard's analysis. The synthesis motif characterizes the ethical stage of existence and the diastasis motif characterizes the Christian religious stage of existence. To include the kind of ethical obligation and the sort of God-relationship that characterize the ethical stage within Christianity is to misapprehend Kierkegaard's argument and to overlook many of the shortcomings of his interpretation of Christianity.

Finally, Sponheim's "systematic" analysis cannot comprehend the intention that leads Kierkegaard to employ the pseudonymous method. This again results from the tendency to abstract Kierkegaard's arguments from the pseudonymous proponents of those arguments.

If the descriptive-thematic approach is to be followed, as we propose to do, the errors that Sponheim has committed must be corrected. The argument for a coherence within Kierkegaard's pseudonymous authorship cannot be extended to all of his writings. Furthermore, coherence cannot signify "systematic" unity. The interpretation must keep in mind Kierkegaard's purpose in the authorship, and hence his reasons for using the pseudonymous method. Finally, arguments must always be presented within the framework of Kierkegaard's understanding of the stages of existence.

E. Conclusion

In the course of analyzing secondary treatments of Kierkegaard's work, Aage Henriksen comments, "A point of view which neither violates the totality nor the separate parts [of the authorship] does not seem to have been attained by anybody."[68] This book is an attempt to help to rectify this situation. The aim is to present the coherence of the pseudonymous writings in a way that does not do an injustice to the uniqueness of each work. In this chapter we have explored

[68] Aage Henriksen, *Methods and Results of Kierkegaard Studies in Scandinavia, op.cit.*, p. 10. Although this judgment was voiced in 1951, it still obtains.

some of the methodological problems involved in the study of Kierkegaard. By offering a brief preview of the analysis to be developed and a summary of the method to be used, and by contrasting this method with other approaches to the material, we have both set our study within the context of current Kierkegaard scholarship and have indicated the distinctiveness of the contribution to understanding Kierkegaard that we seek to make.

Having examined the methodological problems in the study of Kierkegaard, we must now turn our attention to the method that Kierkegaard himself employs in writing the pseudonymous works. We shall try to discern his motivation in using the pseudonymous method, and thereby to discover both his intention as an author and the structure of the authorship with which he presents the interpreter.

CHAPTER TWO

THE STRATEGY OF THE
AUTHORSHIP

A. Religious Truth as Subjectivity

Kierkegaard's use of the pseudonymous method depends upon his conception of the nature of religious truth. Therefore if we are to understand his pseudonymous authorship and his purpose in these writings, we must begin by examining the way in which he views religious truth.

For Kierkegaard religious truth is subjectivity. Although this dictum is well-known, it is frequently misinterpreted. In holding that religious truth is subjectivity, Kierkegaard certainly is not arguing that religious truth is solipsistic or that it is the function of the capricious desire or interest of the individual. We can begin to understand what he means by comparing subjectivity with its opposite, objectivity.

Kierkegaard argues that one can be concerned with the problem of truth either from an objective or a subjective point of view. "*The objective accent falls on* WHAT [*hvad*] *is said, the subjective accent on* HOW [*hvorledes*] *it is said*."[1] When one seeks truth objectively, he adopts the standpoint of objective apprehension. His attention is turned away from himself and toward a certain object (the "what"), which he attempts to understand. "*When the question of truth is raised in an objective manner, reflection is directed objectively to the truth, as an object to which the knower relates himself*."[2] The person involved in this pursuit of truth is fundamentally an observer to whom objects become manifest.[3] The ideal to-

---

[1] *Postscript*, p. 181; S.V., viii, 196.

[2] *Ibid.*, p. 178; S.V., vii, 166.

[3] In the introduction to his translation to *Crisis in the Life of an Actress and Other Essays on Drama* (New York: Harper Torchbooks,

ward which such knowledge is directed is the correspondence between one's idea and the object of that idea. Truth is regarded as the identity of thought and being. In cognition one endeavors accurately to re-present the object with which he is concerned. To attain the desired unity of thought and being, the inquirer must remove as far as possible his own subjectivity and become fully receptive to the object:

"The way of objective reflection makes the subject accidental, and thereby transforms existence into something indifferent, something vanishing. Away from the subject the objective way of reflection leads to the objective truth, and while the subject and his subjectivity become indifferent, the truth also becomes indifferent, and this indifference is precisely its objective validity; for all interest [*Interessen*], like all decisiveness, is rooted in subjectivity. The way of objective reflection leads to abstract thought, to mathematics, to historical knowledge of different kinds; and always it leads away from the subject, whose existence or non-existence, and from the objective point of view quite rightly, becomes infinitely indifferent [*uendelig ligegyldig*]."[4]

Thus when truth is pursued objectively, attention is directed to the "what," or to the object of inquiry. The aim is to attain a knowledge, i.e., a correspondence of thought (idea) and being (object), which is valid independent of the particular knower conducting the investigation. This intention is only hindered by subjectivity and its interests.

Kierkegaard criticizes such an approach to truth. In the first place, there is a contradiction directly built into the ideal of objective truth. Because an objective approach to truth requires that subjectivity be excluded as far as is possible, the ideal would seem to be the complete elimination of subjectivity so that the object can be accurately known. But this would

---

1967), pp. 20-26, Stephen Crites points out that this use of "objectivity" by Kierkegaard is very similar to Kant's view of the "theoretical" employment of reason.

[4] *Postscript*, p. 173; S.V., vii, 161.

mean the elimination of the thinker himself, and therefore the end of the process of cognition. "As its maximum this way will lead to the contradiction that only the objective has come into being, while the subjective has gone out; that is to say, the existing subjectivity has vanished...."[5]

In the second place, and more importantly, Kierkegaard holds that although it is correct to view truth as the conformity of thought and being, it is necessary to define the sort of being with which one is concerned.[6] The being that objective contemplation deals with is *conceptual being.* Although objective contemplation may be directed to empirical reality, it can never arrive at that empirical reality. One reason for this is that while empirical reality is irreducibly particular, thought is fundamentally general. Thought always deals with concepts that abstract from the particularities of empirical existence, and not immediately with that existence itself. Thus the object with which such objective contemplation comes into relation is, in the final analysis, a conceptual object; the being with which it deals is conceptual being. Kierkegaard surely does not deny that such being, in a certain sense, "is." "That the content of my thought *is* in the conceptual sense needs no proof, or needs no argument to prove it, since it is proved by my thinking it."[7] However, since the being with which such objective contemplation is concerned is conceptual being, the truth at which it arrives (truth, it will be recalled, is the conformity of thought and being) is completely tautologous. Such thought constantly relates itself to concepts that abstract from concrete reality, and does not treat that reality itself. These concepts certainly "are," and insofar as the thinker's thoughts correspond to these concepts, there is a conformity of thought and being. But this conformity is between thought and *conceptual* being. This is only another way of saying that there is a conformity of thought with itself.[8]

[5] *Ibid.*, p. 173; S.V., vii, 161.   [6] *Ibid.*, p. 169; S.V., vii, 157.
[7] *Ibid.*, p. 172; S.V., vii, 161.
[8] This is one of the bases upon which Kierkegaard forms his criticism

The fact that empirical reality is particular and thought is general is not, however, the only reason that objective reflection cannot break away from itself and become related to concrete existence. We have seen that for Kierkegaard, one who argues that truth is the conformity of thought and being must always be aware of the nature of the being with which he is concerned. If the being involved is not conceptual being, but is empirical being, a conformity of thought and being is possible only as an ideal toward which one strives. The reason for this lies in the very nature of empirical being: "If being . . . is understood as empirical being [*empiriske Væren*], truth is at once transformed into a desideratum, and everything must be understood in terms of becoming; for the empirical object is unfinished and the existing cognitive spirit is itself in the process of becoming. Thus the truth becomes an approximation [*Approximeren*] whose beginning cannot be posited absolutely, precisely because the conclusion is lacking, the effect of which is retroactive."[9]

Because the nature of empirical reality is to be in the process of becoming, it never is, but always becomes. Truth, as the conformity of thought and *being*, could, therefore, be attained only when the process of becoming had stopped. But this would mean that truth could be achieved only after empirical being had ceased to be what it fundamentally is. Kierkegaard thinks that such an alteration of empirical reality takes place in objective reflection. When this procedure is followed, there is an abstraction from the process of becoming that is indigenous to empirical reality. Again, it is apparent that such reflection deals with a constructed conception (a mental object) and not with the empirical object: ". . . for the correspondence between thought and being is, from the abstract point of view, always finished. Only with the concrete does becoming enter in, and it is from the concrete that ab-

---

of speculative philosophy of Hegel's sort. He contends that such thought deals only with thought itself, and not with existing reality.

[9] *Postscript*, p. 169; S.V., vii, 157.

stract thought abstracts."[10] Such an abstraction from the process of becoming negates concrete reality. However, if the process of cognition so changes that which it cognizes that it ceases to be what it is, one can hardly say that he attains the truth of what he had been examining. Therefore, Kierkegaard thinks that objective reflection is unable to grasp the truth of empirical reality.

The implications, for his understanding of religious truth, of Kierkegaard's contention that empirical being is a process of becoming become more evident when the exact form that becoming takes in the life of the self is examined. While the general character of all becoming is, for Kierkegaard, a process of moving from potentiality to actuality, the peculiar feature of human becoming is that here this process is self-directed. In order for such a self-directed actualization of possibility to occur, two things are necessary: first, one must be able to imagine possibilities, and, second, one must be able to realize what has been imagined. Let us consider each of these conditions of human becoming. For the self, imaginative thought is the means by which possibilities are apprehended. "Knowledge places everything in possibility, and to the extent that it is in possibility, it is outside the actuality of existence."[11] Kierkegaard elaborates this important issue in somewhat more complex terms when he says: "Abstract thought considers both possibility and actuality, but its understanding of actuality is a false reflection, since the medium within which the concept is thought is not actuality but possibility. Abstract thought can get hold of actuality only by nullifying [*ophæve*] it, but to nullify actuality is to transform it into possibility."[12]

To clarify the point that Kierkegaard is making in this obscure passage, let us take an example from interpersonal relationships. Suppose one person, *A*, says to another person,

[10] *Ibid.*, p. 170; S.V., vii, 158.

[11] *Works of Love*, p. 218; S.V., ix, 221.

[12] *Postscript*, p. 279; S.V., vii, 270. Compare p. 280: "All knowledge about actuality is possibility." S.V., vii, 287.

B, "Would you please do X for me?" B must first hear A and comprehend what A has requested. In this process, B translates the request of A into a possibility for himself. Whether explicitly or implicitly, B says to himself, "It is possible for me either to do what A has asked or to refuse to do it." The grasping of possibility through the thought process is not, however, the actualization of possibility. It is quite evident that, in this instance, thought and being do not conform to each other. To *think* a possibility is not to *be* the one who has accomplished that possibility by translating it into actuality. Therefore Kierkegaard argues, "Man thinks and exists, and existence separates thought and being, holding them apart from one another in succession."[13] If this were not the case, then to think of doing X would be the same as doing X. This Kierkegaard certainly does not allow.

If we turn from the first to the second condition of human becoming, it is apparent that while thought is the means by which possibilities are apprehended, imagined possibilities are actualized through the will. Between conceiving a possibility (thought) and the actualization of that possibility (being) lies the will. In brief, possibilities are actualized by the assertion of the individual's will. Returning to our previous example, after B has recognized the possibilities posed to him by A's request, he must decide which of the possibilities he will realize. On the basis of this insight, Kierkegaard claims that "reality is an *inter-esse* between the moments of that hypothetical unity of thought and being that abstract thought presupposes."[14] By this Kierkegaard means that reality—here human existence—is a "being between," or is a being that moves between potentiality and actuality. In other words, concrete existence is a process of becoming. It is also important to note in this context that there is another nuance to "*inter-esse*" with which Kierkegaard plays. For Kierkegaard it is "interest" that motivates the will, and hence commences the process of becoming. When one is moved to actualize po-

---

[13] *Ibid.*, p. 296; S.V., VII, 271.   [14] *Ibid.*, p. 279; S.V., VII, 270.

tentialities, it is the result of one's own subjective interest. Therefore, the "being between" actuality and potentiality is the exertion of the will, moved by interest, to realize possibilities.[15] This, Kierkegaard argues, is reality.

For the existing individual, thought and being can never fully coincide. As long as one exists, one is in a process of becoming in which one seeks to enact that about which one has thought, thereby striving to effect a unity of one's thought and being. The conclusion of Kierkegaard's argument is that *the unity of thought and being is a task that is posed to the existing individual and is not an accomplished fact.*

We are now in a position to understand what Kierkegaard means when he says that "religious truth is subjectivity." He defines religious truth as follows: "Here is such a definition of truth: *An objective uncertainty held fast in an appropriation-process [Tilegnelse] of the most passionate inwardness is truth,* the highest truth attainable for an *existing* individual."[16] The important phrase in this definition for our present purpose is "an appropriation-process." Because the existing individual is in a state of becoming, his life is a constant approximation of the ideals that he conceives. "Subjectivity" indicates the process by which an individual appropriates what he thinks, or constitutes his actuality by realizing his possibilities.[17]

Kierkegaard proceeds to identify subjectivity (the process of appropriating what one has conceived) with truth for the existing individual: ". . . the truth consists in nothing else than the self-activity of personal appropriation. . . ."[18] Kierkegaard's argument at this juncture is not intended to deny the general notion of truth as the conformity of thought and being. However, due to the fact that the existing individual is

---

[15] It will be recalled that it is precisely "subjective interest" that objective contemplation excludes.

[16] *Postscript,* p. 182; S.V., VII, 170.

[17] Compare Louis Mackey, "Kierkegaard and the Problem of Existential Philosophy, II," *The Review of Metaphysics,* vol. 9, 1956, p. 572.

[18] *Postscript,* p. 217; S.V., VII, 203.

in a process of becoming, Kierkegaard holds that such a conformity is never reached as long as existence continues, but remains an ideal that is asymptomatically approximated: "Not for a single moment is it forgotten that the subject is an existing individual, and that existence is a process of becoming, and that therefore the notion of truth as identity of thought and being is a chimera of abstraction, in its truth only an expectation of the creature; not because truth is not such an identity, but because the knower is an existing individual for whom the truth cannot be such an identity as long as he lives in time."[19]

Therefore, after defining religious truth as subjectivity, Kierkegaard elaborates his meaning in terms of the process by which an individual appropriates what he thinks. We have considered two aspects of this process. While thought grasps the possibilities with which actuality confronts the individual (i.e., thought moves from *esse* to *posse*), the will actualizes these possibilities (i.e., moves from *posse* to *esse*).[20]

As will become increasingly apparent as the argument progresses, the process by which possibilities are actualized results in an alteration of the self's actuality. Upon the basis of such insights, Kierkegaard proceeds to extend the implications of his argument one step further by holding that to say "truth is subjectivity" is to say that "truth is the subject's transformation in himself."[21] The following passage is one of Kierkegaard's clearest statements about the subjectivity of truth:

"Truth in its very being is not the simple duplication of being in terms of thought, which yields only the thought of being, merely ensures that the act of thinking shall not be a cobweb of the brain without relation to reality, guaranteeing

---

[19] *Ibid.*, p. 176; S.V., vii, 279.   [20] *Ibid.*, p. 288; S.V., vii, 279.

[21] *Ibid.*, p. 38; S.V., vii, 27. Compare Carnell's comment: "The Subjective is character change." *The Burden of Søren Kierkegaard, op.cit.,* p. 111; and Thomte's point when he says that for Kierkegaard, "truth was consigned to the realm of personality." *Kierkegaard's Philosophy of Religion, op.cit.*, p. 205.

the validity of thought, that the thing thought actually is, i.e., has validity. No, truth in its very being is the duplication [*Fordoblelse*] in me, in thee, in him, so that my, that thy, that his life, approximately in the striving to attain it, is the very being of truth, is a *life*, as the truth was in Christ, for he was the truth. And hence, Christianly understood, the truth consists not in knowing the truth but in being the truth."[22]

As this quotation makes clear, truth, when considered subjectively, is not identified with the accuracy of certain propositions, but is the quality of an individual's *life*. The English phrases "he is true to . . ." or "he is faithful to . . ." express the way in which Kierkegaard understands religious truth.

Kierkegaard frequently points to the identification of truth with the life of the individual. The following is a concise example: ". . . only then do I truly know the truth when it becomes a life in me. Therefore Christ compares truth with food, and the appropriation of it with eating; for just as food, corporally by being appropriated [*Tilegnes*] (assimilated) becomes the sustenance of life, so also is truth, spiritually, both the giver of life and its sustenance; it is life."[23] The logic of the identification of truth with the life of an individual is implicit in what has gone before, and forms a convenient summary of our argument about the nature of religious truth.

1. Human reality is a "being between" possibility and actuality, or is a process in which one constitutes his actuality by realizing that which he has conceived.

2. Subjectivity is "the process by which an individual appropriates what he thinks."

3. Therefore, subjectivity is the reality of the self (a reality that the self defines by the realization of possibility through decision).

Because Kierkegaard identifies religious truth with subjectivity, religious truth refers to the processive or dynamic

[22] *Training in Christianity*, p. 201; S.V., xii, 189.

[23] *Ibid.*, p. 202; S.V., xii, 190. It is interesting to note in this context that the Danish *"at tilegne"* can also be translated "to dedicate."

life of the individual.[24] A person reaches truth when he is true to the ideal to which he pledges his loyalty. Kierkegaard stresses that in religious matters, truth does not concern intellectual assent to propositions, but entails volitional commitment to ideals. Religious truth must always be embodied in the life of the individual, and this can be accomplished only by the consistent and disciplined assertion of the will. Kierkegaard does not, however, intend to set the intellect and the will in opposition. Rather, they are closely related. Through the intellectual capacity to use language and reason, the individual is enabled to articulate goals and to specify possibilities. Once these ideals have been established, they pose a task for the individual. Here thought and being do not coincide; i.e., to think about an ideal is not to have realized what one has thought. Through the will, the imagined possibilities can be actualized. In this instance, truth is not the duplication of being in thought, but the duplication of thought in being (in the individual's personal being). To put this in other terms, in the actualization of possibility, the existing individual defines the truth of his own self.

Two important consequences of the view that religious truth is subjectivity must be noted here. In the first place, one's attention is turned toward the subject and the subject's striving to realize his potentialities: "For a subjective reflection the truth becomes a matter of appropriation, of inwardness, of subjectivity, and thought must probe more and more deeply into the subject and his subjectivity."[25] This movement is exactly opposite that of objective reflection, which, as we saw, directs itself away from the subject. Secondly, by contending that the locus of truth is the individual's life, Kierke-

[24] For this reason, Kierkegaard calls subjective truth "edifying" [opbygge]. Literally translated, "opbygge" means to build (bygge) up (op). This is precisely what is accomplished in the subjective pursuit of truth. The personality of the individual is built up insofar as he appropriates the truth with which he is concerned, or as he strives to achieve his ideals. See *Works of Love*, pp. 199-212; S.V., IX, 201-215.

[25] *Postscript*, p. 171; S.V., VII, 159-160.

gaard gives more importance to the quality of the relationship to one's goal, or his possibility, than to the nature of that goal or possibility. This raises a rather startling possibility that Kierkegaard is fully prepared to acknowledge: "If one who lives in the midst of Christendom goes up to the house of God, the house of the true God, with the true conception of God in his knowledge, and prays, but prays in a false spirit; and one who lives in an idolatrous community prays with the entire passion of the infinite, although his eyes rest upon the image of an idol: where is there most truth? The one prays in truth to God though he worships an idol; the other prays falsely to the true God, and hence worships in fact an idol."[26]

On the basis of this passage, some critics argue that by his view that religious truth is subjectivity Kierkegaard, in effect, denies the objective (i.e., extra-subjective) existence of God.[27] Although there are a few points at which Kierkegaard seems to suggest such a view, most notably in the Journals,[28] this certainly is not his intention. He never doubts that God exists apart from the subjectivity of the believer.[29] To contend that

[26] *Ibid.*, pp. 179-180; S.V., VII, 168.

[27] Karl Löwith offers the most striking instance of this line of argument. He presents his views in the context of pointing out certain similarities between Feuerbach's analysis of Christianity in terms of subjective feeling and Kierkegaard's principle of subjectivity. Löwith, however, overstates the similarities between the two thinkers. See *From Hegel to Nietzsche* (New York: Doubleday and Co., 1967), pp. 357ff. Compare his argument in "On The Historical Understanding of Kierkegaard," *Review of Religion*, 1943, pp. 234ff., esp. p. 241.

[28] See *Journals*, ed. Dru, *op.cit.*, no. 605; *Papirer*, VII A 139.

[29] For support of this interpretation, see Paul Holmer, "Kierkegaard and Theology," *Union Seminary Quarterly Review*, vol. XII, 1957, pp. 21-31; Valter Lindström, "The Problem of Objectivity and Subjectivity in Kierkegaard," *A Kierkegaard Critique*, edited by Howard A. Johnson and Niels Thulstrup (Chicago: Henry Regnery Co., 1961), pp. 228-243; David F. Swenson, *Something About Kierkegaard*, ed. Lillian M. Swenson (Minneapolis: Augsburg Publishing Co., 1956), pp. 126ff.; James Brown, *Kierkegaard, Heidegger, Buber, and Barth: Subject and Object in Modern Theology* (New York: Collier Books, 1962), p. 90.

Kierkegaard's proposal that truth is subjectivity restricts the being of God to the believer's belief in God is to misapprehend the import of his argument. What he intends to stress is that religious faith is not to be identified with the cognitive assent to propositions, but must be related to the assertion of the individual's will, or to the transformation of one's life.

This is the appropriate place to clarify another of Kierkegaard's terms that bears on the subjectivity of truth: reduplication. At times it seems as if he unnecessarily complicates this category. For example, he offers the following comment on the nature of reduplication: "However, coming into existence may present a reduplication, i.e., the possibility of a second coming into existence within the first coming into existence. Here we have the historical in the stricter sense, subject to a dialectic with respect to time. The coming into existence that in this sphere is identical with the coming into existence of nature is a possibility, a possibility that for nature is its whole reality. But this historical coming into existence in the stricter sense is a coming into existence within a coming into existence."[30]

Here reduplication is defined as "a coming into existence within a coming into existence." Furthermore, it seems to have a special relationship to time. Kierkegaard's point is that reduplication is the actualization of possibilities. The first coming into existence is the conceptualization of possibility. Possibility, as will become evident in chapter three, is fundamentally related to the *future* as that toward which the individual moves. The second coming into existence is the realization of possibilities. This takes place, as we have seen, through one's *present* decisions, which thereby come to constitute his *past*. Kierkegaard's most concise definition of "reduplication" is: ". . . to reduplicate [*at redupplicere*] is to 'exist' in what one understands."[31] Reduplication is, therefore, another way of indicating the process by which an individual strives to embody in his life that which he has understood. It

[30] *Philosophical Fragments*, p. 94; S.V., IV, 240.
[31] *Training in Christianity*, p. 133; S.V., XII, 125.

is another way of pointing to the fact that, for an existing individual, religious truth is subjectivity.

By holding that religious truth is subjectivity, Kierkegaard feels that he is fully in line with what he regards as the two most authoritative sources of the Christian tradition: the Bible and Luther.[32] *The Letter of James* is Kierkegaard's favorite book of the Bible, and from this source he draws the biblical justification for his stance with respect to religious truth.[33] The particular text, to which Kierkegaard frequently refers in this connection, is James 1:22-25: "But be doers of the word, and not hearers only, deceiving yourselves. For if any one is a hearer of the word and not a doer, he is like a man who observes his natural face in a mirror; for he observes himself and goes away and at once forgets what he was like. But he who looks into the perfect law, the law of liberty, and perseveres, being no hearer that forgets but a doer that acts, he shall be blessed in his doing."[34]

[32] There are certain anticipations of Kierkegaard's view of religious truth in Hegel's work. See Crites, *In the Twilight of Christendom, op.cit.,* part i; Karl Löwith, "On the Historical Understanding of Kierkegaard," *op.cit.,* p. 243; and Jean Wahl, *Études Kierkegaardiennes* (Paris: Fernard Aubier, n.d.). J. Heywood Thomas notes anticipations in Von Braeder, Schelling, Hamann, and Lessing. *Subjectivity and Paradox* (New York: Macmillan Co., 1957), pp. 44-59. Finally, there are evident parallels between Kierkegaard's "subjectivity" and Kant's "practical reason." See Crites, *In the Twilight of Christendom, op.cit.,* part i; "Introduction," *Crisis in the Life of an Actress,* pp. 19-28; Jerry H. Gill, "Kant, Kierkegaard, and Religious Knowledge," *Essays on Kierkegaard,* ed. J. H. Gill, (Minneapolis: Burgess Publishing Co., 1969), pp. 58-73; Louis Mackey, "Kierkegaard and the Problem of Existential Philosophy, ii," *op.cit.,* pp. 575, 608; H. Richard Niebuhr, *The Responsible Self* (New York: Harper and Row, 1963), p. 92; Günter Rohrmoser, "Kierkegaard und das Problem der Subjektivität," *Neue Zeitschrift für Systematische Theologie und Religionsphilosophie,* vol. 8, no. 3, pp. 289-310, esp. p. 292.

[33] Kierkegaard could never quite forgive Luther for his dismissal of *The Letter of James.* He tried to explain it by holding that Luther's historical situation demanded that grace and not works be stressed. See *Journals,* ed. Dru, *op.cit.,* nos. 88 and 1008; *Papirer,* i a 328 x² a 244.

[34] See *Edifying Discourses,* vol. ii, pp. 84-85.

Kierkegaard finds the issue of personal appropriation raised in Luther's writings, especially in the theme of *pro me* or *pro nobis*. Kierkegaard writes: "Take away from the Christian determinations the factor of personal appropriation, and what becomes of Luther's merit? But open to any page of his writings, and note in every line the strong pulse-beat of personal appropriation. Note it in the entire trembling propulsive movement of his style, which is as if it were driven from behind by the terrible thunderstorm that killed Alexius and created Luther. Did not the papacy have objectivity enough, objective determinations to the point of superfluity? What then did it lack? It lacked appropriation, inwardness."[35]

Kierkegaard argues, therefore, that his thesis that religious truth is subjectivity grows out of the biblical and the Lutheran tradition. It refers to the process by which an individual appropriates what he has conceived as a possibility. In so doing, the individual himself becomes true and "truth exists for the particular individual only as he himself produces it in action."[36]

B. Socratic Midwifery:
Method and Intention of the Authorship

Our purpose in taking up the foregoing discussion of Kierkegaard's notion of religious truth was to arrive at an understanding of his use of the pseudonymous method. We must now turn our attention to the relationship between the view of truth just examined and the method of the authorship.

[35] *Postscript*, pp. 327-328; S.V., VII, 317. Compare his remark in his Journal: "Formally the category of 'for thee' (Subjectivity, Inwardness) with which *Either-Or* ended (only the truth that edifies is the truth for thee) is exactly Luther's." *Papirer*, VII A 465.

[36] *The Concept of Dread*, p. 123; S.V., IV, 405. It should be noted that many writers give special emphasis to the way in which the theme of *imitatio Christi* develops in Kierkegaard's later works. But, as Lindström correctly observes ("The Problem of Objectivity and Subjectivity in Kierkegaard," *op. cit.*, p. 240), this is only another form of the view that truth is subjectivity.

According to Kierkegaard, the nature of truth affects the mode of communication appropriate to that truth.[37] We might begin here, as we did above, by briefly examining the way in which objective reflection and truth must be communicated. Objective reflection, it will be recalled, is directed away from the subject and toward an object that one seeks to know. This object can be something as concrete as a rock or as abstract as a mathematical formula. In all cases, however, the primary concern is with the object and not with the subject. Furthermore, one is chiefly interested in the *results* of the inquiry, and not in the intrinsic value of the investigation itself. This is not to imply that the method followed in arriving at the result is unimportant. It is necessary to pursue a correct procedure if proper results are to be attained. But once these results are reached, the method becomes a matter of indifference. A second person need not necessarily go through all of the steps in the method to obtain the result. Rather, the result can be directly communicated from one person to another. This communication takes place through the medium of ideas. Appropriation entails one person's understanding another person and giving assent to what he understands.

An example from the natural sciences clarifies this point. Suppose a physicist wished to arrive at a mathematical formula that would express the motion of an electron. It would be necessary for him to spend much time developing a method to measure the activity of the particle. Elaborate equipment might have to be constructed, and many experiments would have to be conducted. Suppose, however, that the investigator were successful. After years of labor he arrived at a relatively simple mathematical formula to express the motion of the electron. He is able to communicate this result directly to his colleagues and to his students. They do not need to go through all of the steps in the method that had led

[37] *Postscript*, p. 68; S.V., vii, 56. "The difference between subjective and objective thinking must express itself also in the form of communication suitable to each."

to this result, but are able to grasp the result independent of the manner in which it was attained. Although the procedure might have taken the researcher years, others could reap the result within a few hours. This is a plain example of what Kierkegaard means by his contention that objective reflection and objective truth can be communicated directly. Through the interchange of ideas and assent to those ideas, one person can understand what the other person proposes without passing through all of the stages that led to the result.

The discussion of religious truth as subjectivity should lead us to suspect, however, that when truth is subjectivity, the mode of communication will be quite different: "Suppose a man wished to communicate the conviction that it is not the truth but the way that is the truth, i.e. that the truth exists only in the process of becoming, in the process of appropriation, and hence that there is no result."[38] If this is correct—and it is Kierkegaard's view that in ethical-religious matters it is correct—there must be a sharp distinction between the modes of communicating objective and subjective truth. "While objective thought is indifferent to the thinking subject and his existence, the subjective thinker is as an existing individual essentially interested in his own thinking, existing as he does in his thought. His thinking has therefore a different type of reflection, namely the reflection of inwardness, of possession, by virtue of which it belongs to the thinking subject and to no one else. While objective thought translates everything into results, and helps all mankind to cheat, by copying these off and reciting them by rote, subjective thought puts everything in process and omits the result; partly because this belongs to him who has the way, and partly because as an existing individual he is constantly in the process of coming to be. . . ."[39] If truth is subjectivity, or if it is "the way that is the truth," the communicator must both employ a different method of communication and must have a different intention in communicating.

[38] *Ibid.*, p. 72; S.V., vii, 59.   [39] *Ibid.*, pp. 67-68; S.V., vii, 55.

The method that must be used when truth is subjectivity is an *indirect*, as opposed to a direct method of communication. The meaning of "indirect communication" begins to become evident by considering a related term—"double reflection." Kierkegaard comments: "The reflection of inwardness gives to the subjective thinker a double reflection [*Dobbelt-Reflexion*]. In thinking, he thinks the universal; but as existing in this thought and as assimilating it in his inwardness, he becomes more and more subjectively isolated."[40]

It might be said that the foregoing discussion of the subjectivity of religious truth was concerned with the second aspect of "double reflection." Truth, it was seen, is the process by which an individual reduplicates his thought in his life by realizing possibilities. In connection with the term "double reflection," this means that truth is the reflection of conceived possibilities in the life of the individual through the determination of the will.

However, the previous analysis has made it apparent that this second aspect of double reflection depends upon an earlier reflection—the reflective apprehension of possibility.[41] Before one can effectively actualize possibilities, he must recognize those possibilities. Reflecting on one's possibilities is the first aspect of "double reflection." It is the necessary condition of the second aspect, the reflection (or reduplication) of the imagined possibilities in the life of the individual.

Within this dual aspect of "double reflection" we can see both Kierkegaard's reason for using the pseudonymous method and his intention in the authorship. Kierkegaard's pseudonymous works present various possibilities to the reader (the first dimension of "double reflection"). He intends that the reader, through his confrontation with these different possibilities, will be led to a clarification of his own situation and will be moved to actualize one of the possibilities that he has met (the second aspect of "double reflection").[42]

[40] *Ibid.*, p. 68; S.V., VII, 56.   [41] See above pp. 42ff.
[42] Compare Paul Holmer, "Kierkegaard and Religious Propositions,"

54

Further examination of the way in which Kierkegaard presents possibilities to the reader is required. Kierkegaard comments on his method: "A pseudonym is excellent for accentuating a point, a stance, a position. It creates a poetic person. . . ."[43] Each of the different pseudonyms is an ideal representation of a certain "life-view."[44] They might be regarded as ideal personality types. By "ideal" Kierkegaard means that these life-views are never found in as pure a form in actual existence as they are in their pseudonymous representatives. The pseudonymous authors present imaginative constructions or "poetic persons." The works are supposed to be understood as the creation of the pseudonymous author and not as the creation of Kierkegaard, the author of the authors. Each pseudonymous writing represents the point of view of its author both in style and in content. The pseudonymous author tries to portray a particular way of looking at the world in as ideal a form as possible. The work, therefore, presents the reader with a *possible* way of regarding the world—it creates a possibility for the reader.

As we have noted, Kierkegaard's purpose in employing the complex pseudonymous method is to clarify the reader's mind about his own situation in existence, and to move the reader to realize the possibilities with which the pseudonyms confront him. Kierkegaard repeatedly insists that a single overriding concern informs his authorship. His aim is to clarify "how to become a Christian."[45] He regards this as "an undertaking that means neither more nor less than proposing to

---

Journal of Religion, 1955, pp. 135-146; "On Understanding Kierkegaard," *A Kierkegaard Critique, op.cit.*, pp. 40-54; and E. D. Klemke, "Some Insights for Ethical Theory from Kierkegaard," *Philosophical Quarterly*, vol. x, 1960, pp. 322-330.

[43] *Papirer*, x¹ 510, in *Armed Neutrality and An Open Letter*, trans. and ed. by Howard V. and Edna Hong (New York: Simon and Schuster, 1969), p. 88.

[44] The Danish word is *"Livs-Anskuelse."* Compare the German *Weltanschauung.*

[45] *The Point of View*, p. 13; S.V., xiii, 523.

reintroduce Christianity . . . into Christendom."[46] It is Kierkegaard's conviction that, although the age in which he lived regarded itself as "Christian," in fact very few Christians were
to be found. The whole understanding of what it means to be
a Christian had undergone such a change that Christianity,
as the New Testament had presented it, was nowhere evident. If Christianity were to be "reintroduced into Christendom," people would first have to become aware of the kind
of life they were leading, and would then have to comprehend accurately what it means to become a Christian. In order to accomplish this, an author must start where his reader
is:

"It is an illusion that all are Christians—and if there is anything to be done about it, it must be done indirectly, not by
one who vociferously proclaims himself an extraordinary
Christian, but by one who, better instructed, is ready to de-
clare that he is not a Christian at all. That is, one must approach from behind the person who is under an illusion. Instead of wishing to have an advantage of being oneself that
rare thing, a Christian, one must let the prospective captive
enjoy the advantage of being the Christian, and for one's own
part have resignation enough to be the one who is far behind
—otherwise one will certainly not get the man out of his illusion, a thing which is difficult enough in any case."[47]

This is Kierkegaard's peculiar affirmation of the principle
of Socratic ignorance. As Socrates had proclaimed his own
ignorance, while letting others affirm their knowledge, in order to expose their actual ignorance, so Kierkegaard affirms
his own non-Christianity, while letting others assert that they
are Christians, in order to expose the fact that they actually
are not Christians. For Kierkegaard, this is a justified deception, because its final aim is to lead the reader to truth.[48]

[46] *Ibid.*, p. 23; S.V., XIII, 530.   [47] *Ibid.*, pp. 24-25; S.V., XIII, 513.
[48] It should be noted that Kierkegaard carried this deception over into
his personal life. Thus during the period of his pseudonymous production, he was constantly at pains to create the impression that he was
a pleasure-seeking dandy. He tried to impress his fellow Copenhageners

If one proposes to destroy such an illusion, Kierkegaard does not think that he should begin directly with Christian categories. After acknowledging that the reader is a Christian, he begins by depicting the actual form of life which the supposed Christian represents: ". . . one does not begin thus: I am a Christian; you are not a Christian. Nor does one begin thus: It is Christianity I am proclaiming; and you are living in purely aesthetic categories. No, one begins thus: Let us talk aesthetics. The deception consists in the fact that one talks thus merely to get to the religious theme."[49]

The aesthetic style of life is, therefore, presented in all of its ideality.[50] The goal of this effort is to have the reader recognize himself in the work. The preface to *Stages on Life's Way* could serve as an epigram for the entire pseudonymous authorship: "*Such works are mirrors: when a monkey peers into them, no Apostle can be seen looking out.*"[51] In the first instance the pseudonymous works offer the reader a mirror in which he can see himself, a map on which he can locate his place in existence.

The recognition of one's actual situation in existence is, however, only a prerequisite for Kierkegaard's more important purpose: the elucidation of other possibilities of existence. After one has become clear about his own life-view, he can entertain those life-views which he does not share. For example, when one realizes that his style of life is not Christian, but is aesthetic, he is in a position to consider what the

---

with his frivolity by all sorts of wild schemes, some of which are recounted in *The Point of View*. For example, he used to appear at the Royal Theatre at the beginning and end of a performance as well as during the intermission. In between he would rush home and feverishly devote himself to his writing. *The Point of View*, ch. II, pp. 44-63; S.V., XIII, 543-575.

[49] *Ibid.*, p. 41; S.V., XIII, 541.

[50] The meaning of "aesthetic" is discussed in chapter four.

[51] *Stages on Life's Way*, p. 26; S.V., VI, 14. Kierkegaard indicates that this is quoted from Lichtenberg. Recall the use of the image of the mirror in one of Kierkegaard's favorite biblical texts, James 1:22-25.

Christian life-view entails.[52] Kierkegaard proceeds to multiply the possible life-views throughout the pseudonymous works. Each form of existence presents the reader with a possibility that he might actualize. In an especially revealing remark, Kierkegaard says, "A communication in the form of a possibility compels the recipient to face the problem of existing in it...."[53]

The appropriateness of the image of the mirror in connection with the pseudonymous works should now be evident. We have already seen that this method entails double *reflection*. As the image of the mirror suggests, the movement of the pseudonymous works is always away from the author and toward the reader. In writing the pseudonymous works Kierkegaard seeks to withdraw his own person as far as possible from his works:[54] "When in reflection upon the communication the receiver is reflected upon, then we have ethical communication. The maieutic. The communicator disappears, as it were, makes himself serve only to help the other to become."[55] The intention is: first, that the reader will see his present situation reflected in one of the life-views in the pseudonymous writings; second, that he will reflect on the other life-views presented; and, third, that he will reflect these possibilities in his own life through personal appropriation. Kierkegaard is not, of course, indifferent to which life-view his reader appropriates. As will be seen below, the arrangement

---

[52] Stanley Cavell has pointed out that Kierkegaard's work can be understood in a way analogous to the work of current linguistic analysts. Kierkegaard is involved in the clarification of concepts. Much of the problem with Christendom was, on his terms, that the meaning of Christian concepts had been lost. His work is an effort to remove some of the confusion. See "Kierkegaard's *On Authority and Revelation*," *Must We Mean What We Say?* (New York: Charles Scribner's Sons, 1969), pp. 163-179.

[53] *Postscript*, p. 320; S.V., VII, 310.

[54] These comments further illustrate the problems with the biographical-psychological approach to Kierkegaard's work. It goes exactly counter to his purpose in the pseudonymous works.

[55] *Journals and Papers*, no. 657; *Papirer*, VIII[2] B 89.

of the possibilities of existence is designed to lead the individual to genuine selfhood, which can be reached only through the Christian mode of existence.

In his understanding of indirect communication and his use of the pseudonymous method to achieve this communication, Kierkegaard is quite indebted to Socrates. In many ways he views his task and his method as analogous to those of Socrates: "Although ever so many parsons were to consider this method unjustifiable, and just as many were unable to get it into their heads (in spite of the fact that they all of them, according to their own assertion, are accustomed to use the Socratic method), I for my part tranquilly adhere to Socrates."[56]

Kierkegaard's method, adopted from Socrates, is thoroughly dialectical. "Dialectical" is here to be understood in connection with its origin as a philosophical term—as a dramatic dialogue.[57] But Kierkegaard's use of "dialectic" or the "dramatic dialogue" cannot be understood simply. The authorship is dialogical in two senses: first, within itself, and, second, between the whole authorship and the reader. The pseudonymous authors can be understood as participants in one long dialogue among themselves and with the reader.[58] Kierkegaard's pseudonymous authors are not presented in isolation from one another, but are engaged in an intricate debate among themselves. One author constantly comments on the ideas of another. This can be seen both within particular works and among different writings. For example, Judge William offers extended comments to the aesthete, Johannes, in

[56] *The Point of View*, p. 41; S.V., XIII, 541.

[57] David F. Swenson makes this point. *Something About Kierkegaard, op.cit.*, pp. 117-118.

[58] See Hermann Diem, *Kierkegaard's Dialectic of Existence, op.cit.*, pp. 41-42. As our discussion should make clear, although it is indisputable that Kierkegaard's method is of central importance for his authorship, it would seem to be an error to claim, as Diem does elsewhere, that Kierkegaard "had no doctrine, but only a method." "Methode der Kierkegaard Forschuung," *Zwischen den Zeit*, 1928, pp. 140ff.

the second volume of *Either-Or*, and *Fear and Trembling* and *Repetition*, published on the same day, treat the same problem from two different points of view.

Perhaps the most fascinating example of the kinship between Kierkegaard's pseudonymous writings and the Socratic dialogues is the first part of *Stages on Life's Way*, "*In Vino Veritas.*" This work is a self-conscious parallel to Plato's *Symposium* and *Phaedo*.[59] The similarity is illuminated by examining Kierkegaard's treatment of the Platonic dialogues in *The Concept of Irony*.[60] When one compares "*In Vino Veritas*" with the way in which Plato's *Symposium* and *Phaedo* are here interpreted, the parallels are even more striking. The topic of Kierkegaard's discourse, like the *Symposium*, is love. Each of the participants in turn offers comments on the nature of woman and of marriage. Although all of the speakers remain within Kierkegaard's aesthetic stage, each represents a particular feature of that stage.

However, as has been indicated, not only do the pseudonymous authors engage in dialogue with each other, but they also attempt to draw the reader into the dialogue. If the pseudonymous works are properly understood, the reader becomes a participant in the dialogue, and Kierkegaard becomes a Socratic midwife who interrogates his interlocutor. Again Kierkegaard takes Socrates as his model: "He [Socrates] entered into the role of midwife [*Gjordemoder*] and sustained it throughout; not because his thought "had no positive content," but because he perceived that this relation is the highest that one human being can sustain to another."[61] The midwife seeks to bring to birth truth in the reader. It is, however, the reader, and not the midwife, who must effect the birth. The nature of religious truth itself makes this

[59] Note the repeated references to the Platonic dialogues throughout the text. For example, pp. 45, 46, 48, and 49; S.V., VI, 33, 34, 37, and 38.

[60] *The Concept of Irony*, pp. 65-89 and 98-115; S.V., XIII, 123-147 and 156-171.

[61] *Philosophical Fragments*, p. 12; S.V., IV, 180.

method necessary. As we have seen, religious truth is subjectivity, or an appropriation process in which one actualizes imagined possibilities. Because the end product of religious truth is the transformation of a personal life, such truth cannot be communicated directly to another person. The most one can do is to communicate indirectly. He can offer to another person possible life-views in which the other person can recognize himself, and which he can strive to realize. The realization, or the result, however, is not within the power of the communicator, but lies with the recipient of the communication:

"But this result is not in my power; it depends upon so many things, and above all it depends upon whether he will or not. In all eternity it is impossible for me to compel a person to accept an opinion, a conviction, a belief. But one thing I can do: I can compel him to take notice. In one sense this is the first thing; for it is the condition antecedent to the next thing, i.e. the acceptance of an opinion, a conviction, a belief. In another sense it is the last—if that is, he will not take the next step."[62]

This is the basis for Kierkegaard's repeated contention that his authorship offers the reader no "results."[63] In speaking of Plato's dialogues, Kierkegaard illuminates his own works: "The reason why several of Plato's dialogues end without result is far more profound than I used to think. It is an expression of Socrates' maieutic art that makes the reader, or the hearer, himself active, and so does not end in a result but in a sting. It is an excellent parody of the modern method of learning by rote which says everything as quickly as possible and all at once, and does not have the effect of making the reader take an active part, but makes him hear it like a parrot."[64]

[62] *The Point of View*, p. 35; S.V., xiii, 538.

[63] This is, of course, quite contrary to the earlier example of the natural scientist who is engaged in objective reflection, and who seeks to communicate primarily the *results* of his inquiry.

[64] *Journals*, ed. Dru, no. 578; *Papirer*, vii A 74. Compare *The Concept of Irony*, p. 91; S.V., xiii, 149.

Kierkegaard's dialectical method of indirect communication is constantly saying to the reader, "Your move!" It prepares the way for personal commitment by helping the reader to clarify his situation through illustrating an individual's possibilities. But the decision itself must come from the reader.

The possible life-views are not, however, randomly selected and presented. They are very carefully articulated as progressively ordered *stages* of existence. In light of the preceding remarks on the similarities between Kierkegaard's method and his understanding of Socrates' method, the following comment that Kierkegaard makes about the *Symposium* might be applied to his entire pseudonymous authorship: "All the discourses are therefore like sections in a telescope, with the one account terminating ingeniously in the next. . . ."[65] The precise way in which "the sections" of Kierkegaard's "telescope," the stages of existence, are to be regarded, and the manner in which "one account terminates ingeniously in the next," is, however, subject to a variety of interpretations. In the last two sections of this chapter we will examine the different ways in which the stages of existence can be understood, and outline the overall structure of the dialectic of existence in the pseudonymous authorship.

C. The Stages of Existence

The multiplicity of interpretations to which Kierkegaard's stages of existence can be subjected is usually not recognized by commentators. They accept one or another view without considering the alternatives. There are four basic ways in which the stages[66] can be understood: (1) as stages in Kier-

---

[65] *The Concept of Irony*, p. 79; S.V., XIII, 137.

[66] It should be underscored that the term "stages" is consistently used throughout the book. This is a translation of the Danish "*Stadier.*" Kierkegaard also uses the word "*Sphære*" (English: "sphere"). "Stages" is used in this book because it is felt that it gives more emphasis to the developmental character of Kierkegaard's dialectic. The nature of this development will become evident in what follows.

kegaard's own development; (2) as stages in the development of world history; (3) as ideal personality types; (4) as
the stages in the development of the individual self. We must
consider each of these in turn.

One of the most common ways of regarding the stages of
existence is to view them as the different stages through
which Kierkegaard personally passed during his lifetime.
Quite evidently this interpretation is most popular among
those authors who accept the biographical-psychological approach to the authorship.[67] The stages are supposed to chart
the development of Kierkegaard from a rather dissipated
youth (his university years), through the recognition of the
importance of ethical obligation (the period of his engagement to Regina Olsen), to mature Christianity (the later
years of his life). Elaborate efforts are made to discern parallels between the Journals and the pseudonymous writings. It
is important to acknowledge that there is a certain justification for this procedure in some of Kierkegaard's comments.
The following would be a clear instance of this: "The fact is
that in the works under my own name or that of pseudonyms
I have treated and described fundamentally, as I always do,
the various stages through which I passed before reaching
the point where I now am."[68] The limitations of the biograph-

[67] Josiah Thompson's book which was discussed above (chapter one,
section E) is an illustration of this approach. For other examples, see
James Collins, *The Mind of Kierkegaard, op.cit.*, p. 37; Aage Henrik-
sen, *Methods and Results of Kierkegaard Studies in Scandinavia, op.cit.*,
p. 11; Paul Holmer, "Kierkegaard and Ethical Theory," *Ethics*, vol.
LXII, p. 158; Regis Jolivet, *Introduction to Kierkegaard, op.cit.* Chapter
II; Walter Lowrie, *Kierkegaard, op.cit.*, pp. 289-290; Winfield Nagley,
"Kierkegaard's Irony in the 'Diapsalmata,'" *Kierkegaardiana*, vol. VI,
ed. Niels Thulstrup (København: Munksgaard, 1966); Jean Wahl,
Études Kierkegaardiennes, op.cit., pp. 44ff.

[68] *Attack on Christendom*, p. 52. From the *Fatherland*, Friday, May
15, 1855. Compare: ". . . thus the productivity has also been my own
development and I have learned progressively to understand that I
have gone the right way." *Papirer*, IX B 64 (1848); translated in *Armed
Neutrality and An Open Letter*, p. 79.

ical-psychological approach in general are evident in this understanding of the stages. While it should not be denied that Kierkegaard's personal experience is reflected in his pseudonymous writings, it is quite misleading to view the stages as *fundamentally* Kierkegaard's own phases of development.

The second way of interpreting the stages is far less common. There are places in Kierkegaard's works where he indicates that the stages of existence can be understood as stages in the development of the world historical process.[69] A certain stage of history can exemplify a particular stage of existence. This might seem to be most Hegelian, and not at all Kierkegaardian. Certainly it must be acknowledged that it is. But one cannot forget that despite his constant polemic against Hegel (and perhaps more basically against the Danish Hegelians of the day), Kierkegaard learned an immense amount from him. Just how much will become increasingly evident as the essay proceeds.

Given the problematic nature of the claim that Kierkegaard's stages of existence can be regarded as stages of world history, some support must be offered. Kierkegaard does not only cryptically indicate from time to time that there are certain parallels between the stages of existence and the world historical process. In *The Concept of Irony*, he goes so far as to indicate an outline of these stages.[70] The stages trace the emergence of man's recognition of the nature of his own self. Both the pre-Sophists and the Sophists of the ancient Greek world Kierkegaard describes as aesthetic. The period of the pre-Sophists is generally characterized by a full participation in sensual pleasures that paved the way for the downfall of

[69] As a matter of fact, Gregor Malantschuk is the only commentator of whom I am aware who has detected this tendency in Kierkegaard's thinking. He argues that the aesthetic view of life was generally characteristic of the pagan world, but began to break down with Socrates, Job, and finally with Christ. See *Kierkegaard's Way to the Truth* (Minneapolis: Augsburg Publishing Co., 1963), pp. 25ff. and pp. 46ff.; *Frihends Problem I Kierkegaards Begrebet Angest* (København: Roskenkilde og Bagger, 1971), esp. Chapter II.

[70] See pp. 222-240; S.V., XIII, 279-297.

the Athenian state.[71] A longing for the immediate satisfaction of sensual desire drove this epoch of world history. What marks the Sophists as an important turning point in the historical process is that with them "reflection begins":[72] "The Sophists represent knowledge in a condition of confused multiplicity [*brogede Mangfoldighed*] tearing itself loose from the substantial ethic through awakening reflection. They represented a detached culture for which everyone felt a need, that is, everyone for whom the enchantment of immediacy had vanished."[73]

The Sophists, therefore, began a process that reached a crucial juncture in Socrates—the emergence of self-consciousness. For the pre-Socratics, the individual self had not been differentiated from the environment. Persons remained immediately subject to determination by sensual pleasures and by factors external to the self such as the state. There was no *self*-determination. With the reflection that started with the Sophists, individuals began to differentiate themselves from their surroundings. As the above passage indicates, here the self remains in "a condition of fragmented multiplicity tearing itself loose from the substantial ethic through dawning consciousness."

Upon these bases Kierkegaard proceeds to make a most illuminating comment summarizing the significance of Socrates: "The expression 'know thyself' means: separate [*adskil*] yourself from the 'other.' Inasmuch as prior to Socrates the self did not exist, so the pronouncement of the oracle in turn corresponded to Socrates' own consciousness commanding him to know himself."[74] Socrates discovered the self as a subjective reality independent of its external determinations. He

[71] *Ibid.*, pp. 222-224; S.V., XIII, 279-289. As will become apparent in chapter four, there are two poles of the aesthetic stage: the immediate and the reflective. The pre-Sophists represent the immediate pole of the aesthetic stage.

[72] *Ibid.*, p. 225; S.V., XIII, 282. The Sophists represent the reflective pole of the aesthetic stage.

[73] *Ibid.*, pp. 225-226; S.V., XIII, 282-283.

[74] *Ibid.*, pp. 202-203; S.V., XIII, 260.

discovered the self as self-determining, or as *will*.[75] And yet while Socrates was an historical turning point, his discovery remained a potentiality that had to be realized in the course of later historical development: "He [Socrates] was not the one to introduce the new principle in its fullness, for in him it was only present cryptically . . . ; instead, he must render its appearance possible. This intermediate state, which is and is not the new principle, which is potentially but not actually the new principle (*potentia non actu*), is irony."[76] Therefore, Socrates stood at the border between the aesthetic and the ethical stages; his standpoint was irony.

It was left for Judaism, and finally for Christianity, to elaborate the conception of the self as willful. Judaism represents the ethical stage of existence and is the first step in the elaboration of the understanding of the self as volitional. From the point of view of Judaism, the law and the individual's willful submission to the law are the primary foci of attention. However here, in a way analogous to the Sophists, problems arise. "And as irony resembles the Law, so the Sophists resemble the Pharisees, for the latter operated in the province of the will exactly like the Sophists in the sphere of knowledge."[77] The individual's exercise of his will in obedience to the law becomes a form of self-righteous self-assertion. Something similar to Socrates' criticism of the Sophists had to take place for a further development in the world process to be

[75] This interpretation of the significance of Socrates for the development of world history is, of course, fully consistent with the way in which Hegel understands Socrates. See, for example, Hegel's discussion of Socrates in *Lectures on the History of Philosophy*, trans. by Elizabeth S. Haldane and Francis Simson (London: Kegan Paul, Trench, Trübner and Co., 1892-1896).

[76] *The Concept of Irony*, p. 234; S.V., xiii, 291. Compare: "Now it is certainly true that subjectivity in its fullness, inwardness with its infinite richness, may also be designated by the words: 'know thyself'; but in the case of Socrates this self-knowledge was scarcely so full of content, for it properly contained no more than the separation and differentiation of that which only subsequently became the object of knowledge." *Ibid.*, p. 202; S.V., xiii, 260.

[77] *Ibid.*, p. 236; S.V., xiii, 292.

66

reached: "What Socrates did for the Sophists was to confront them with the next moment [*øieblik*], a moment wherein their momentary truth dissolved itself into nothingness, that is to say, he allowed infinitude to swallow up finitude."[78]

With Christianity, the final "moment" in man's recognition of the nature of his own self takes place: "With respect to the chosen people, the Jews, it was necessary for the skepticism of the Law to prepare the way, by means of its negativity to consume and burn away the natural man, as it were, in order that grace should not be taken in vain."[79] Christianity represents the religious stage of existence. Through the doctrines of sin and of the incarnation, man becomes aware of the eternal significance of his decisions. Furthermore, because he recognizes his sin, man becomes conscious of his dependence upon God. If the dilemma posed by man's sinfulness is to be resolved, a prior act of God is necessary. As will become apparent as we proceed, Kierkegaard does not think that the recognition of sin and the correlative awareness of the significance of the incarnation minimize the importance of the role of the will in human life, but rather stress it all the more.

In light of these comments, it might be said that when Kierkegaard's stages of existence are understood as stages in the world historical process, they can be interpreted as indicating the development of man's self-consciousness. For Kierkegaard, unlike Hegel, Christianity is the *telos* of this developmental process, and is not transcended in a speculative philosophy.[80] It does, therefore, seem that there is evidence in Kierkegaard's writings to support a view of the stages of

[78] *Ibid.*, p. 236: S.V., XIII, 293. Note the Hegelian overtones of this passage.

[79] *Ibid.*, pp. 235-236; S.V., XIII, 292.

[80] Kierkegaard, of course, does not mean to establish sharp boundaries in this view of world history. In keeping with Hegel, he does not think that a previous stage is fully replaced by a later stage in world history. The later stage takes up into itself the previous stage. Therefore Kierkegaard can still argue that during his own time aesthetic categories dominated the lives of most persons.

existence as epochs of world history.[81] Furthermore, it seems that there is a close connection between this view and the understanding of the stages of existence as the phases in the development of the individual self. Kierkegaard states: "What has been briefly indicated with reference to universal history is repeated within Christianity in individualities."[82]

The third way to interpret the stages of existence is as ideal personality types[83] or as ideal representations of possible life-views that an individual can appropriate.[84] This approach has

[81] Although the argument that has just been rehearsed is developed in *The Concept of Irony*, this tendency in Kierkegaard's thought cannot be explained away by saying that this first work was written before he decisively broke with Hegel. Such arguments generally stem from the failure of the critic to see the way in which Kierkegaard uses Hegel's insights throughout the authorship. At any rate, the conception of the stages as phases of world history can be found at many points in Kierkegaard's writings. See *The Concept of Irony*, pp. 248-249; S.V., XIII, 306; *Either-Or*, pp. 45, 60, 71, 87-88, and 141; S.V., I, 31, 44, 54, 69-70, and 121; and *The Concept of Dread*, pp. 38-39, 58ff., and 84; S.V., IV, 314-315, 334ff., and 364ff.

[82] *The Concept of Dread*, p. 93; S.V., IV, 373.

[83] In this connection, Friedrich C. Fischer has pointed to antecedents of Kierkegaard's view of the stages. Particularly he examines Selon's poem, *"Die Lebensalter"* and some of Goethe's insights. *Existenz und Innerlichkeit: eine Einführung in Gedankenwelt Sören Kierkegaards, op.cit.*, pp. 19ff. Samuel Taylor Coleridge's idea of the development of the self (*Biographia Literaria*, ed. J. Shawcross, New York: Oxford University Press, 1954) and Schleiermacher's comments on the three stages of the development of the self and of religion (*The Christian Faith*, trans. by H. R. Mackintosh and J. S. Stewart, Edinburgh: T. and T. Clark, 1960) should also be mentioned. Anticipations of this view of the stages can be seen in Kierkegaard's own reflections on "the three great ideas: Don Juan, Faust, and the Wandering Jew." See *Journals and Papers*, no. 795; *Papirer*, I A 150. Stanley Cavell (as Paul Holmer) has pointed out various similarities between Kierkegaard and Wittgenstein on this issue. With respect to the way in which Kierkegaard's stages are to be understood, Cavell says: "The religious is a Kierkegaardian stage of life, and I suggest that it should be thought of as a Wittgensteinian form of life." "Kierkegaard's *On Authority and Revelation*," *op.cit.*, p. 172.

[84] When one accepts this view of the stages, he sees that there is a strong similarity between a Kierkegaardian stage and the notion of

been developed in the context of our discussion of Kierkegaard's method and intention as an author. Although this view of the stages is relatively common,[85] the precise manner in which the different life-views are characterized varies greatly. A frequent way of describing each stage is to accept one of Kierkegaard's statements at its face value: "But back to the *Stages* [*On Life's Way*]. It is obviously differentiated from Either-Or by its tripartite division. There are three stages: an aesthetic, an ethical, and a religious. But these are not distinguished abstractly, as the immediate, the mediate and the synthesis of the two, but rather concretely, in the existential determinations, as enjoyment-perdition; action-victory; and suffering."[86] Accordingly the stages are regarded as hedonistic, ethical, and Christian. But such a view greatly oversimplifies Kierkegaard's insights. As has been indicated, we shall analyze the different stages in light of their characteristic views of time and of the self.

The fourth, and final, way to regard the stages is as the phases through which the developing self passes in coming to mature selfhood. This line of interpretation is somewhat more complex than the foregoing views, and has been vir-

---

"world" or of "significance structure" as later developed by Husserl and Heidegger. The relevant portion of *Being and Time* (trans. by John Macquarrie and Edward Robinson, New York: Harper and Row, 1962) is Part One, Chapter iii, paragraphs 14-24. For analysis, see Magda King, *Heidegger's Philosophy: A Guide to His Basic Thought* (New York: Macmillan Co., 1964) and Calvin Schrag, *Existence and Freedom, op.cit.*

[85] For examples the reader is referred to: James Collins, *The Mind of Kierkegaard, op.cit.*, p. 38; F.C. Fischer, *Existenz und Innerlichkeit: eine Einführung in die Gedankenwelt Sören Kierkegaards, op.cit.*, p. 17; Martin Heinecken, *The Moment Before God* (Philadelphia: Muhlenberg Press, 1956), p. 247f.; Perry LeFevere, "An Interpretation of Kierkegaard's Life and Thought," *The Prayers of Kierkegaard* (Chicago: University of Chicago Press, 1963); R. Thomte, *Kierkegaard's Philosophy of Religion, op.cit.*, p. 200; David F. Swenson, *Something About Kierkegaard, op.cit.*, chapter iii, esp. pp. 145 and 158.

[86] *Postscript*, p. 261; S.V., vii, 252.

tually overlooked in secondary literature.[87] Let us first examine the more common way of seeing the development of the self in Kierkegaard's stages of existence. The general understanding of the stages as representations of possible life-views is accepted. But it is recognized that these life-views are arranged so that there is a successive movement from the pleasure-seeking life of the aesthete to the devout life of the Christian. The stages are the different stances that a self assumes in moving toward Christianity.

There is, however, another way in which the stages of existence can be seen as descriptive of the phases of the self's development. They can be viewed as the stages through which the self passes in moving from infancy to mature personhood. According to this viewpoint, each stage is particularly characteristic of a certain period in the individual's life: "Life is divided into two parts: the period of youth belongs to the aesthetical; the latter age to religion—but speaking honestly, we all would prefer to remain young."[88] The following rather long quotation is one of the most lucid examples of this aspect of the stages. It should be noted in considering this passage that Kierkegaard uses the words "self" and "spirit" interchangeably.[89]

"And yet child-life and youth-life is dream-life, for the innermost thing, that which in the deepest sense is man, slumbers. The child is completely turned outward, its inwardness

[87] The only critics that I know who have even suggested such an interpretation are: Frithiof Brandt, *Søren Kierkegaard: His Life—His Works* (Copenhagen: Det Danske Selskab, 1963), pp. 29-30; J. Preston Cole, *The Problematic Self in Kierkegaard and Freud* (New Haven: Yale University Press, 1971); Bradley R. Dewey, *The New Obedience: Kierkegaard on Imitating Christ* (Cleveland: Corpus Books, 1968), p. 6; and Libuse L. Miller, *In Search of the Self: The Individual in the Thought of Kierkegaard* (Philadelphia: The Muhlenberg Press, 1962), pp. 152 and 156.

[88] *The Point of View*, p. 31; S.V., XIII, 535. Also note: *Journals*, ed. Dru, no. 754; *Papirer*, VIII A 650.

[89] Support for this contention will be given in the examination of the structure of the self in chapter three.

is extraversion, and to that extent the child is wide awake. But for a man, to be awake means to be eternally turned inward in inwardness, and so the child is dreaming, it dreams itself sensuously at one with everything [*drømmer sig sandseligt sammen med Alt*], almost to the extent of confounding itself with the sense impression [*forvexler sig selv med Sandse-Indtrykket*]. In comparison with the child, the youth is more turned inward, but in imagination [*Indbildningen*]; he dreams, or it is as though everything about him were dreaming. On the other hand, he who in the sense of eternity is turned inward perceives only what is of the spirit, and for the rest, he is like a sleeper, an absentee, a dead man, with respect to the perceptions of flesh and blood, of the temporal, of the imaginative—in him the spirit is awake, the lower functions sleep; hence he is awake. Dream-life is so denominated with a view to the nobler part—in the waking man the spirit wakes, whereas there is doubtless something which sleeps, namely, the lower part. In the child and in the youth it is the spirit that sleeps, the lower part is awake; nevertheless, as it is the determining characteristic of spirit to be awake, this is called dream-life [*Drømmeliv*]."[90]

This is an extremely rich passage and requires some discussion.[91] What Kierkegaard is saying here is that the child, the infant, is fully determined by sensuous inclination, and constantly seeks the gratification of pleasure. In this condition, the spirit, or the self, "is dreaming, it dreams itself sensuously at one with everything, almost to the extent of confounding itself with the sense-impression." In other words, there is no differentiated self at this stage. It will be recalled that in the course of examining the view of the stages as historical epochs it was noted that Kierkegaard argues that "universal history is repeated within Christianity in individualities."

[90] "The Joy of It—That Affliction Does not Bereave of Hope, But Recruits Hope," *Christian Discourses*, p. 113; S.V., x, 113.

[91] The full implications of this text can become apparent only as we proceed. We will have to return to it frequently in coming to terms with each of the stages.

71

Here one sees in the development of the individual self the parallel to the pre-Sophistic stage of world history in which there is an immediate identification of self and not-self. This identification begins to break down when the infant acquires the capacity to use language and to cognize. Through reflection, the child differentiates himself from his surroundings, and *self*-consciousness gradually begins to emerge. This stage parallels the stage in world history represented by the Sophists, in whom the self begins "tearing itself loose from the substantial ethic through dawning reflection." As reflection develops further in the child, he begins to imagine goals and to envision alternative roles that might be appropriated. At this point, the child is more turned inward, for self-consciousness has developed. Yet all remains "in imagination; he dreams, or it is as though everything about him were dreaming." Both sensual immediacy and imaginative reflection remain at the aesthetic stage. Although self-consciousness has begun to emerge, the self remains in a state of potentiality. Just as world historically "prior to Socrates the self did not exist," so up to this stage in the individual's development, properly speaking, there is as yet no actual self.

For the emergence of the actual self to take place, the will must be activated. The self must decide to actualize its imagined possibilities; the child or youth must strive to attain imagined goals. The emphasis on the will that develops world historically with Judaism takes place for the developing self at the ethical stage of existence. However, Kierkegaard thinks that it is only with Christianity that the eternal significance of the individual's decisions is perceived. By an awareness of one's own sin and of the possibility of faith and forgiveness that the incarnation establishes, one gains a clear recognition of the structure of his self. Authentic selfhood can be reached only when one lives within the categories of Christianity. In the progressive development of the stages so interpreted, we can see the movement of the self from an undifferentiated identity with the environment to the stage of authentic selfhood that, according to Kierkegaard, consists of the individual in a private relationship to God.

We have noted that the understanding of Kierkegaard's stages as epochs of world history shows some remarkable similarities to Hegel's view of historical development. Furthermore we have demonstrated that the world historical epochs can be correlated with the stages in the individual's personal development. From the combination of these insights, we can see that part of Kierkegaard's procedure entails the application of many of the insights garnered from his understanding of Hegel's dialectic of the historical process to the development of the individual self. Upon this basis, one sees the justification for Stephen Crites' comment: "In fact, though Kierkegaard never directly claimed any such thing, the development of the so-called stages or spheres of existence through his pseudonymous writings amounts to the construction of a new 'phenomenology of the spirit' alternative to Hegel's."[92]

For anyone acquainted with twentieth-century psychological theories of selfhood, the preceding interpretation of Kierkegaard's doctrine of the stages must be quite striking. What we see in him is a significant anticipation of some of the insights of Sigmund Freud and his followers. The analysis begins with the self in a state of undifferentiated immediacy, ruled by sensual desire. This parallels Freud's oral stage of development in which the "pleasure principle" dominates. The chief characteristics of Freud's anal stage are analyzed by Kierkegaard in the reflective-aesthetic and the ethical stages of development. The reflective-aesthetic stage marks the emergence of the ability to use language, and hence of consciousness, and the ethical stage marks the development of the will as a formative factor in the life of the self. It is also important to stress that another characteristic of the ethical stage is important in Freud's late anal and early genital stage. This is the development of a strong sense of morality (the

---

[92] Stephen Crites, *In The Twilight of Christendom, op.cit.,* p. 6.

law) that Freud indicates by arguing that at this point in the individual's life the superego develops.[93] Kierkegaard's Christian stage of existence represents a phase of development beyond the point traced by Freud, but not beyond that defined by some of his most influential followers. At the Christian stage of existence Kierkegaard argues that the self achieves the balance within itself that has been the goal of the entire quest of the self. The psychological phenomenon that he here isolates for consideration is what later students of personality called "ego integration." It is the achievement of a genuine stability within the personality system that accompanies the development of a mature self. The psychologist calls this the achievement of a healthy self; the theologian, Kierkegaard, calls it the attainment of salvation.[94] But the phenomenon being described is the same.

These are the four ways in which Kierkegaard's stages of existence can be interpreted. But which one is the most accurate representation of Kierkegaard's analysis? First it must be underscored that there is some validity in each interpretation. Hopefully the analysis of the different approaches has made such validity evident. However, it does seem that the most adequate view of Kierkegaard's theory of the stages of existence is attained by combining the last two interpretations—the stages seen as ideal personality types (or as ideal representations of various life-views) and as the stages of the development of the individual self.[95] The basis of the possibility

[93] There are, of course, very important differences between Kierkegaard and Freud on the issue of the development of the self. These will become more evident as we progress. In the present context, it is sufficient to recognize that Kierkegaard's stages can be seen as the phases through which the developing self passes, and that, when the stages are so regarded, certain characteristics of each phase bear important similarities to distinctive features of the stages of the self's development as described by later psychological theories.

[94] For a further development of this argument, see chapter five.

[95] Our misgivings with the other two views of the stages are implicit in the discussion of them. The criticism of the biographical-psychological approach to Kierkegaard's work can likewise be applied to an argument

of integrating these two interpretations of the stages lies in Kierkegaard's conviction that the characteristics which dominate any particular phase of the self's development can become determinative for the entire world-view of the adult self. A person can live his whole life according to the principles of pleasure, or he can live his entire life without ever making a genuine decision, constantly letting others decide for him. Though old in years, such a person would, for Kierkegaard, remain a child. Furthermore, one could not properly call such a person a self. Or, one could live his entire life in the self-reliance and self-assertion that is representative of the first emergence of selfhood. If one goes through life without coming to the realization of one's ontological dependence on God, and without recognizing that one's very self-reliance has severed one's relation with the ground of being, one never comes to a full realization of selfhood.

Kierkegaard seeks to explore the dynamics of individual selfhood in the movement to authentic existence. He is keenly aware of the developmental character of selfhood. But he is also conscious of the fact that the development of the self can be retarded short of genuine selfhood. Kierkegaard is interested in diagnosing the forms of existence that he thinks fail to establish a proper equilibrium within the individual self. As we have seen, the pseudonymous authorship presents a series of ideal representations of various world-views in a manner that enables the reader to recognize his own life in them, and to perceive the shortcomings of all forms of existence that fall short of the final stage in which full individuation is achieved. Thus the interpretation of the stages as both phases of the development of the individual self and as ideal

---

that sees the stages as phases of his own development. As for the view of the stages as epochs of world history, although present in some of the writings, it is not Kierkegaard's dominant argument. As his thinking progressed, he was increasingly concerned to apply the insights of Hegel's argument about historical development to his analysis of the individual self.

personality types is fully in keeping with Kierkegaard's intention as an author. His pseudonymous authorship attempts to establish a dialogue with the reader in which the reader is prompted to move through the different stages of development to genuine selfhood. He attempts to prod the reader to work out his own salvation in "fear and trembling."

D. The Structure of Kierkegaard's Dialectic

A last comment about the doctrine of the stages remains to be made. The stages of existence have a very definite structure. Since the stages delineated in the pseudonymous writings analyze the development of the self, it will be helpful in understanding these works to note briefly the bare structure of the dialectic.

As has become evident, there are three major stages of existence: the aesthetic, the ethical, and the religious. The structure of the stages is, however, quite a bit more complex than this. The aesthetic stage is divided into two poles: the immediate and the reflective. The immediate pole is further divided into three stages. Here at the beginning of the dialectic there is a microcosm of the dialectic as a whole. The immediate pole of the aesthetic stage is characterized by the domination of desire. As one moves through its three stages, there is a gradual differentiation of the principle of desire and the object desired. Furthermore, there is a progressive movement that culminates in the third stage of the immediate pole. The second pole of the aesthetic stage—reflection—disrupts and stands in tension with immediacy. Unlike the immediate pole, it is not further divided. The second major stage is the ethical. It is not subdivided as is the aesthetic stage, but serves as a transition to the religious stage. The religious stage, like the aesthetic stage, is bi-polar. It is constituted by religion *A* and religion *B* (Christianity). Christianity is the *telos* of the dialectic, and represents the point at which an equilibrium within the self is established. One

76

might depict the structure of Kierkegaard's dialectic of the stages in the following manner:

Aesthetic *Stage*	*Ethical* *Stage*	*Religious* *Stage*

Immediate   Reflective
Pole   Pole
Immediate
  Stages of
  the Erotic
1. 2. 3.
		Religion *A* Religion *B*
		(Christianity)

These stages are dialectically related insofar as each succeeding stage displaces its predecessor from a position of centrality while at the same time taking it up within itself, giving the former stage a relativized status:[96]

"By posing as a task the scientific process instead of the existential simultaneity [*Samtidighed*], life is confused. Everywhere the succession is obvious, as in the case of the different ages in the individual's life, the task is to achieve simultaneity. It may be a genial observation that the world and the human race have grown older; but is not everyone still born in infancy? In the life of the individual the task is to achieve an ennoblement of the successive within the simultaneous. To have been young, and then to grow older, and finally to die, is a very mediocre form of human existence; this merit belongs to every animal. But the unification of the different stages of life in simultaneity is the task set for human beings. And just as it is an evidence of mediocrity when a human be-

[96] The Danish word that Kierkegaard uses to indicate this process is *"ophæve."* It should be noted that this is the Danish translation of the German *"aufheben,"* which is so important for Hegel's dialectic.

Certainly the structural similarities between Kierkegaard's and Hegel's dialectics are apparent. For comments on these similarities, see Wilhelm Anz, *Kierkegaard und der deutsch Idealismus* (Tübingen: J. C. B. Mohr, 1956). For a consideration of the dissimilarities, see James Collins, *The Mind of Kierkegaard, op.cit.*, esp. Chapter III.

ing cuts away all communication with childhood, so as to be a man merely fragmentarily, so it is also a miserable mode of existence for a thinker who is an existing individual to lose imagination and feeling, which is quite as bad as losing his reason."[97]

Such, in outline form, is the structure of Kierkegaard's stages of existence. The task of Part II of this book is to fill in this ouline. In Part I we were occupied with methodological considerations.

[97] *Postscript*, p. 311; S.V., VII, 301-302.

PART II

THE STAGES OF
EXISTENCE

CHAPTER THREE

TIME AND THE STRUCTURE
OF SELFHOOD

Before we engage in a detailed consideration of each stage of existence, it is necessary to examine in more general terms the two phenomena with which we will be concerned at each of the stages—time and the self. Therefore, in this chapter we will: first, endeavor to indicate what Kierkegaard means by time; second, examine his view of the structure of selfhood; and, third, specify the close connection between the problems of time and of the self.

A. SPATIALIZED TIME

Kierkegaard holds the understanding of time presented in much of the philosophical tradition to be inadequate for explaining human existence. It might be helpful to begin by considering the view of time that he regards as unsatisfactory. The conception of time of which Kierkegaard is critical can be called spatialized time. The term "spatialized time" is intended to indicate that time so understood refers primarily to *objects*. This is to be distinguished from "life-time," which Kierkegaard thinks is a more appropriate way of conceptualizing time in relation to *subjects* or *selves*. This distinction should not be reduced to the difference between externality (objective time) and inwardness (subjective time). The point to be stressed is that in the consideration of time, spatialized time is based on an examination of objects, while life-time is based on a study of subjects or selves. Because much philosophical reflection on the problem of time had been conducted under the category of spatialized time, Kierkegaard thinks that those aspects of the problem which are most important for subjects or selves are usually left untouched.

Kierkegaard argues that spatialized time actually identifies time and space: "Precisely here the practiced reader will see the proof of my representation [*Fremstilling*], since for abstract thinking time and space are absolutely identical (*nacheinander* and *nebeneinander*), and they become so for visualization [*Forestilling*]. . . ."[1] But when one considers the argument more carefully, it becomes clear that Kierkegaard does not think that this identification is between equals. In the final analysis, spatialized time gives priority to the concept of space, and derives the view of time from the understanding of space. In the context of criticizing the conception of spatialized time, he comments: "But just because every moment, like the sum of moments, is a process (a going-by) [*en Gaaen-forbi*] no moment is a present, and likewise there is neither past, present, nor future. If one thinks it possible to maintain this division, it is because we *spatialize* [*spatierer*] a moment, but thereby the infinite succession comes to a standstill, and that is because one introduces a visualization, visualizing time instead of thinking it."[2] According to Kierkegaard, a spatial understanding of time "visualizes" it. Unfortunately he nowhere develops these comments in much detail. It is, therefore, incumbent upon us to try to grasp more completely what he means by "spatialized" time.

The best place to begin to see the import of Kierkegaard's argument concerning spatialized time is by a consideration of Aristotle's definition of time in the *Physica*. In book four, Aristotle gives what was to become the normative definition of time for much of the history of philosophy: "It is clear, then, that time is 'number of movement in respect of before and after,' and is continuous since it is an attribute of what is continuous."[3] What is important to recognize for the present

---

[1] *The Concept of Dread*, p. 77; S.V., IV, 356.

[2] *Ibid.*, pp. 76-77; S.V., IV, 355.

[3] Aristotle, *Physica*, Book IV, 11, p. 220ᵃ. Page references are to: *The*

discussion is that Aristotle establishes an indissoluble connection between time and motion. As Aristotle remarks at another point, "The time marks the movement, since it is its number, and the movement the time."[4] According to this line of argument, time is the means by which the motion of objects through space is measured. The perception of the movement of objects is prior to, and the necessary condition of, the formation of the concept of time: "For it is by means of the body that is carried along that we become aware of the 'before and after' in the motion, and if we regard these as countable we get the 'now.' "[5]

Quite evidently Aristotle has in mind the movement of an object along a straight line. It is from the movement of an object through space that one derives the concepts of before and after. The space that the object has traversed is the "before," the past, and the space yet to be traversed is the "after," the future. If the observer thinks that he can count the movements of the object, he arrives at the "now," the present. Understood according to the model of an object moving through space, time is a line composed of an infinite series of points. The points represent the successive presents that divide the past from the future. It is this understanding of time that we have called "spatialized time" and that Kierkegaard argues commits the error of "visualizing time instead of thinking it."[6] Several important consequences follow from such a view of time.

In the first place, all of the moments of time are homogeneous and equivalent. Each moment is identified with a point

---

Works of Aristotle Translated Into English, trans. by R. P. Hardie and R. K. Gaye (Oxford: The Clarendon Press, 1970).

[4] Ibid., Book IV, 12, p. 220[a].   [5] Ibid., Book IV, 11, p. 219[b].

[6] For further discussion of the aspects of Aristotle's view of time, see: John F. Callahan, Four Views of Time in Ancient Philosophy (Cambridge: Harvard University Press, 1948); and John E. Smith, "Time, Times, and the 'Right Time,'" The Monist, vol. 53, no. 1, January 1969, pp. 1-13.

in space, and there is no essential difference among the various points. Closely related to this is a second factor: the quantitative aspect of spatialized time. Time is intended to measure the quantity of motion. According to Kierkegaard's understanding of the matter, such quantification would seem to exclude all qualitative differentiations.

Thirdly, spatialized time is universal; i.e., it applies to all objects irrespective of their character.[7] That spatialized time is regarded as homogeneous, quantitative, and universal points to the fact that time so understood is viewed as a grid upon which occurrences can be plotted.[8] The fact that objective time derives from the perception of the motion of objects does not prevent this understanding of time from being used in connection with persons. When this is done, however, persons are treated in a manner similar to objects. In this instance, spatialized time becomes primarily concerned with chronology. An effort is made to locate events by means of spatial and temporal coordinates. Although this approach to the event may be able to locate the occurrence with respect to "before and after" in relation to other events, it cannot concern itself with human purposes or with the importance of the events. This aspect of spatialized time has led some thinkers to regard it as external time as opposed to the internal time that characterizes human action.[9]

Fourth, according to the analysis of spatialized time, only the present has reality. In other words, only the present is, for the past has been but now is not, and the future will be, but is not yet. This feature of spatialized time is already apparent in Aristotle's argument: "One part of it [time] has been and

[7] For a criticism of this aspect of spatialized time, see William Earle, "Inter-Subjective Time," *Process and Divinity* (La Salle, Illinois: Open Court Publishing Co., 1964), pp. 285-298.

[8] See John E. Smith, *op.cit.*, p. 3.

[9] See, for example, Tillich's discussion of *"Chronos"* and *"Kairos"* in *The Protestant Era*, trans. by James Luther Adams (Chicago: University of Chicago Press, 1957), pp. 32-54; and H. Richard Niebuhr, *The Meaning of Revelation* (New York: Macmillan Co., 1967), pp. 44-53.

is not, while the other is going to be and is not yet . . . if the 'now' which is not, but formerly was, must have ceased-to-be at some time, the '*nows*' too cannot be simultaneous with one another, but the prior 'now' must always have ceased to be."[10] It becomes apparent that for this understanding of time, the present is a point that is isolated from the past and the future. Kierkegaard comments on this characteristic of spatial time when he argues that according to such a view, the present is ". . . the instant [that] remains a silent atomistic abstraction [*en lydløs atomistisk Abstraktion*] which is not any further explained when one ignores it."[11]

By labeling the instant (i.e., the now), as presented according to a spatial view of time, an "atomistic abstraction," Kierkegaard is pointing to its abstraction from the past and the future. There is no interpenetration or coinherence of the tenses of time. It should be noted that this is a direct result of basing the concept of time on the view of space. For a spatial understanding of time, which derives from the observation of objects, time is correlated with the movement of an object along a line. In such movement, the object always maintains its definite boundaries. When movement is represented as a straight line that the object traverses, the points represent the different positions of the object. The points, like the object they represent, retain definite boundaries; they do not overlap.[12] When the points of the line are taken to represent moments, there is likewise no interrelationship. Past, present, and future remain discrete, non-interrelated "atomistic abstractions."[13]

[10] Aristotle, *Physica, op.cit.*, Book IV, 10, p. 218ª.

[11] *The Concept of Dread*, p. 75; S.V., IV, 353.

[12] Compare Cornelius A. Benjamin, "Ideas of Time in the History of Philosophy," *The Voices of Time*, ed. J. T. Fraser (New York: George Braziller, 1966), p. 24.

[13] It should be mentioned by way of anticipation that when pushed to its logical conclusion this view of time creates problems for the unity of the self. It is no accident that Hume, who did carry out this view of time, was the one who declared the self to be a "bundle of sensations." See below section B.

A final consequence follows from this argument concerning the nature of the present and its relation to the past and the future. It is not clear that it is possible to speak of the three tenses of time from within the standpoint of spatialized time. If only the present is, and the past and future are consistently excluded from the present, it is difficult to see how one could become aware of the past and of the future.[14] The only way for such a recognition to take place would seem to be from a standpoint that is outside of the time continuum from which the moving present, and hence the past and the future, could be viewed. But such a standpoint outside the temporal process is precisely that "Archimedean point" that Kierkegaard thinks an existing individual can never attain.

This, then, is what is meant by the term "spatialized time." Furthermore, some of the consequences of this conception of time and Kierkegaard's criticism of time so regarded have been indicated. Against this unsatisfactory view of time, Kierkegaard sets life-time, which is inextricably related to the lives of selves. Therefore, to understand life-time, we must first understand how he interprets the structure of selfhood.

B. THE STRUCTURE OF SELFHOOD

1. The Problem

Understanding Kierkegaard's view of the structure of selfhood is one of the most difficult problems in all of Kierkegaard interpretation. This fact is testified to by the conspicuous absence of adequate discussions of the issue in secondary literature. Part of the reason for this lies in Kierkegaard's works themselves. His argument on this issue is even more intricate than his other perplexing views. This difficulty is compounded by his very inconsistent use of terms. Furthermore, at this point his debt to Hegel is very apparent. It should be noted that in examining Kierkegaard's view of the *structure*

---

[14] Kierkegaard presents the existential correlate of this conception of time in his consideration of the aesthete, Don Juan, in *Either-Or*. See chapter four, section B.

of the self we are not forced to abstract artificially from his presentation of particular personalities. At several points, most notably in *The Concept of Dread* and in *The Sickness Unto Death*, he gives explicit structural analyses of selfhood. Unfortunately, these passages are among the most obscure in the whole corpus. This situation is not helped by the deficiencies of English translations at several important points. In order to come to terms with this complex set of issues, we will first state the problem of the structure of selfhood according to Kierkegaard's point of view. Then, in an effort to clarify some of the terms that he uses, we will briefly look at the historical context in which he poses this problem. Finally, we will try to state clearly Kierkegaard's own interpretation.

It will be helpful first to get before us the texts in which Kierkegaard explicitly states his views on this problem. One of the best-known passages in which he defines the self is the one that opens *The Sickness Unto Death*:

"Man is spirit [*Aand*]. But what is spirit? Spirit is the self [*Selvet*]. But what is the self? The self is a relation [*Forhold*] which relates itself to its own self [*der forholder sig til sig selv*], or it is that in the relation which relates itself to its own self; the self is not a relation, but [the self is] that the relation relates itself to its own self. Man is a synthesis [*Synthese*] of the infinite [*Uendelighed*] and the finite [*Endelighed*], of the temporal [*Timelige*] and the eternal [*Evige*], of freedom [*Frihed*] and necessity [*Nødvendighed*], in short, a synthesis. A synthesis is a relation between two [components]. So regarded, man is not yet a self. In the relation between two, the relation is the third as a negative unity, and the two relate themselves to the relation, and in the relation to the relation; such a relation is that between soul [*Sjel*] and body [*Legeme*], when man is determined as soul. If, on the contrary, the relation relates itself to its own self, the relation is then the positive third, and this is the self."[15]

[15] *The Sickness Unto Death*, p. 146; S.V., xi, 127. A comment about my translation of "*Sjel*" should be made. This is a very difficult word

Here Kierkegaard defines man as spirit, and then identifies spirit with the self. To avoid confusion, it is necessary to recognize that in the texts under consideration Kierkegaard employs the term "self" in a more restricted way than is usual. Rather than referring to the overall personality, "self" designates one component of the personality. For this reason, it will be helpful throughout the analysis to use the term "self system" to describe the total structure of the personality. In addition to defining man as spirit, or self, Kierkegaard argues that man is a synthesis, and offers different statements of the elements of this synthesis: infinite/finite; temporal/eternal; freedom/necessity;[16] and soul/body. At another point, he makes it clear that spirit, or the self, is the means by which the synthesis of these components is accomplished: "But a synthesis is unthinkable if the two are not united in a third. This third is the spirit [*Aanden*]."[17] In these passages, Kierkegaard defines two aspects of the self system. The first he calls spirit, or the self. The second he designates by different elements of a synthesis. These two dimensions of the self system are related insofar as spirit (the self) is the means by which the synthesis of the various elements is achieved.

In order to make further progress in unraveling Kierke-

---

to render accurately in English. I have used "soul" as the translation. This should not, however, imply strictly religious connotations, though these are involved. The word refers more to the essential psychic and mental aspects of the individual's personality. As such, it might also be rendered "mind." This broader meaning of "*Sjel*" must be kept in mind if the following argument is to be comprehensible.

[16] Kierkegaard's use of the polarity "freedom and necessity" in this context misrepresents his own meaning. When he discusses these terms, he shifts usage to "possibility and necessity." The latter statement is more accurate. As a matter of fact, if one retains "freedom and necessity," his argument cannot be rendered intelligible. It should also be recognized that, for the most part, Kierkegaard uses necessity [*Nødvendighed*] and actuality [*Virkelighed*] interchangeably. This polarity is, therefore, most precisely stated as possibility and necessity, or as possibility and actuality.

[17] *The Concept of Dread*, p. 39; S.V., IV, 315.

gaard's understanding of the structure of selfhood, certain distinctions among the different dimensions of the self system must be examined. In the initial definition of the self system, the two components that he defines seem to be clearly distinguished, and the four expressions of the elements to be synthesized are apparently fully parallel. However, as Kierkegaard's argument unfolds, the distinction between the two aspects of the self system becomes less clear as it becomes evident that the four statements of the synthesis are not identical. Kierkegaard argues that: "The synthesis of the soulish and the bodily[18] is to be posited by the spirit, but *spirit is the eternal*, and therefore this is accomplished only when the spirit posits along with the former synthesis the other synthesis of the temporal and the eternal."[19] In this text, Kierkegaard equates a term that he had used to designate one of the components of the self system (spirit) with one of the terms used to specify the synthesis that characterizes the other component of the self system (eternal). At this juncture an apparent problem emerges. Spirit was said to be the third through which the other components of the self system were synthesized. Now Kierkegaard identifies spirit with one of the elements to be synthesized — with the eternal. It would seem impossible for spirit (the self or the eternal) to be both the synthesizing third and that which is synthesized. This impression is supported when it is recognized that Kierkegaard thinks that two things can be synthesized only through a third. By the identification of spirit with one of the elements to be synthesized, the third necessary for the synthesis seems to have disappeared.

The problem encountered here can be resolved by clearly distinguishing the expression of the synthesis within the self's structure in terms of temporality and eternity from the other expressions. The following text is illuminating in this connec-

---

[18] The implications of this passage (as well as several to follow) are more apparent when it is recalled that soul/body, infinite/finite, and possibility/necessity are different expressions for the same polarity.

[19] *The Concept of Dread*, p. 81; S.V., IV, 360-361.

tion: "... man was said to be a synthesis of soul and body; but he is also a *synthesis of the temporal and the eternal.* . . . As for the latter synthesis, it evidently is not fashioned in the same manner as the former. In the former instance, the two moments [*Momenter*] were soul and body, and the spirit was the third, but was the third in such a sense that there could not properly be any question of a synthesis until the spirit was posited. The other synthesis has only two moments: the temporal and the eternal."[20]

This distinction should not, however, be thought to define two different and separate syntheses. All four sets of terms taken together define one complex synthesis that is the self system: "The synthesis of the eternal and the temporal is not a second synthesis but is the expression for the first synthesis in consequence of which man is a synthesis of soul and body sustained by spirit."[21] What the recognition of the distinction noted here does establish is that it is by virtue of the fact that man is a synthesis of the temporal and the eternal that he can be regarded as a synthesis of soul and body, of the infinite and the finite, and of possibility and necessity.

Yet the various expressions of the synthesis are even more complexly related. The three pairs of terms that are different expressions for the same aspect of selfhood (infinitude/finitude, possibility/necessity, and soul/body) disclose dimensions of one of the elements in the other pair of terms — temporality. It must be stressed that with respect to the self, no sharp separation of temporal and eternal is possible in Kierkegaard's terms. They are dialectically related. A deeper comprehension of his analysis of the structure of selfhood can

[20] *Ibid.*, p. 76; S.V., IV, 355. Lowrie repeatedly translates "*Moment*" as "factor." This is an extremely misleading translation. Particularly, it obscures certain similarities between Kierkegaard's analysis and that of Hegel. This will become evident in the discussion of Kierkegaard's dependence on Hegel for his understanding of the structure of selfhood.
[21] *Ibid.*, p. 76; S.V., IV, 355. It will be seen that the necessary third for the synthesis of the temporal and the eternal is the "moment" [*Øieblikket*].

be achieved by investigating the meaning of "temporal" and "eternal" with reference to the self system.

Arriving at a satisfactory understanding of Kierkegaard's definition of "temporal" and of "eternal" is most difficult, for his use of both of these terms is rather confusing. In many instances, he employs language of the philosophical tradition, but gives the words meanings that are quite different from their usual definitions. To understand Kierkegaard's argument and to comprehend the innovation of his view of the structure of selfhood, we are forced to take account of the historical context within which he was working. A beginning can be made by considering the term "eternal."

Kierkegaard uses the word "eternal" in a bewildering variety of ways. It is essential to note that he uses "eternal" both of God and of man. The oversight of this fact leads to serious misinterpretation. Kierkegaard is able to say that God is the Eternal, and that the human self is the eternal. Especially in light of such well-known characterizations of Kierkegaard's God as infinitely and qualitatively different from man, such comments seem confusing. It will become evident that he means different things when he uses "eternal" of man and of God. There is, however, a formal consistency in his use of "eternal." "Eternal" always refers to unchangeability and to possibility. These two aspects of the eternal are related but for the moment we must focus our attention on the first dimension of eternity, its unchangeability. In this chapter we are concerned with Kierkegaard's use of "eternity" with reference to *man*. The meaning of "eternity" in relation to God will become apparent in chapter seven.

When eternity is understood to involve unchangeability, it is usually set in polar tension with temporality. Temporality, as distinguished from eternity, is the realm of change, the sphere of becoming. Within this world all is in perpetual flux. This distinction between time and eternity dates back to the Greeks, and it is within this framework that Kierkegaard develops his argument: "This characteristic of existence recalls the Greek conception of Eros, as found in the *Symposium*, and which Plutarch in his work on Iris and Oris (57) interprets correctly . . . when Plutarch reminds us that Hesiod has assumed Chaos, Earth, Tartarus, and Love as cosmic principles, it is quite proper in this connection to recall Plato. For love is here evidently taken as identical with existence, or that by virtue of which, life is lived in its entirety, the life which is a synthesis of the infinite and the finite. According to Plato, Wealth and Poverty conceived Eros, whose nature partook of both. But what is existence? Existence is the child that is born of the infinite and the finite, the eternal and the temporal, and is therefore a constant striving. This was Socrates' meaning. It is for this reason that Love is constantly striving; or to say the same thing in other words, the thinking subject is an existing individual. . . . The Socratic principle is naturally not to be understood in a finite sense, about a continued and incessant striving toward a goal without reaching it. No, but however much the subject has the infinite within himself, through being an existing individual, he is in the process of becoming."[22] The eternal, in contradistinction from the temporal, is that which is, and does not become,[23] the unchanging as opposed to the changing. This is Kierkegaard's point when he says that ". . . it is the perfection of the Eternal to have no history, and of all that is, the Eternal alone has absolutely no history."[24]

Another way of expressing the fact that the eternal is the un-

---

[22] *Postscript*, p. 85; S.V., VII, 73.

[23] Compare Søren Holm, "L'être comme catégorie de l'éternité," *Kierkegaard Symposion* (København: Munksgaard, 1955), pp. 84-92; Jens Himmelstrup, *Terminologisk Ordbog, Søren Kierkegaard Samlede Værker*, eds. Drachmann, Heiberg, Lange, vol. xx (København: Gyldenal, 1964), pp. 64-65; and Michael Wyschogrod, *Kierkegaard and Heidegger: The Ontology of Existence, op.cit.*, pp. 42-51.

[24] *Philosophical Fragments*, p. 94; S.V., IV, 239. Compare: "Likewise in the eternal there is not to be found any division of the past and the future, because the present is posited as the annulled succession." *The Concept of Dread*, p. 77; S.V., IV, 356.

changeable is to say that the eternal is that which is self-identical—that which remains the same throughout change. In what has gone before, it has become clear that Kierkegaard understands the self to be in the process of becoming, or of change. Furthermore, we have seen that he contends that the self is a synthesis of the temporal and the eternal. Unchangeability has been noted to be a primary characteristic of eternity. This would mean that the self is both changeable and unchangeable, a view that seems to be self-contradictory. However he insists that such a paradoxical conception of the self is both correct and necessary. Being and becoming, or unchangeability and changeability, are dialectically related; each presupposes the other. The analogy that Kierkegaard uses to make this point, again borrowing from Greek arguments, is that of the relationship between motion and rest.

"In so far as existence consists in movement there must be something that can give continuity to the movement and hold it together, for otherwise there is no movement. Just as the assertion that everything is true means that nothing is true, so the assertion that everything is in motion means that there is no motion. The unmoved mover is therefore a constituent of the motion as its measure and its end. Otherwise the assertion that everything is in motion, and, if one also wishes to take time away, that everything is always in motion, is *ipso facto* the assertion of a state of rest. Aristotle, who emphasizes movement in so many ways, therefore says that God, Himself unmoved, moves all. Now while pure thought either abrogates motion altogether, or meaninglessly imports it into logic, the difficulty facing an existing individual is how to give his existence the continuity without which everything simply vanishes. An abstract continuity is no continuity, and the very existence of the existing individual is sufficient to prevent his continuity from having essential stability; while passion gives him a momentary continuity, a continuity that at once and the same time is a restraining influence and a moving impulse. The goal of movement for an existing individual is to arrive at a decision, and to renew it. The eternal is the factor of continuity...."[25]

This passage has been quoted at length because it is important to recognize the way in which Kierkegaard argues that for the existing individual, *the eternal is the factor of continuity.* To be in existence is to be in the process of becoming. Becoming is change, and is dialectically related to being, or unchangeability. Therefore, when Kierkegaard states that the individual is a synthesis of the temporal and the eternal, he is arguing that the individual is a synthesis of being and becoming, or of unchangeability and changeability. In this synthesis, the eternal is the factor of continuity.

To have defined "eternal" as the unchangeable is not, however, to have exhausted Kierkegaard's argument. When Kierkegaard contends that man is a synthesis of the temporal (the changing) and the eternal (the unchanging), he is using language that had a long history in philosophical reflection. But his meaning is not the same as much of that tradition. Further specification of what he means by "a synthesis of the temporal and the eternal" is, therefore, required. In an effort to clarify his argument, it will be helpful to look at the historical context in which he develops his thoughts.

2. *The Historical Context*

The way in which the problem that Kierkegaard's foregoing reflections address was formulated in the history of philosophy might be stated as the problem of the one and the many with respect to the self. How can one talk about both the unity of the self and recognize that the self constantly experiences changing states? How can one express the apparent experiential fact that the self is simultaneously one and many? To put it explicitly in Kierkegaard's terms, what sense does it make to argue that the self is both changing and unchanging?

[25] *Postscript,* p. 277; S.V., VII, 267-268.

A common way of resolving this problem has been to argue that the self is a *substance* in which accidents inhere.[26] "Substance" is taken to be that which exists in and through itself, or that which does not depend on anything else for its existence. "Accidents" are what exist in and through something else, or what depend on something else for existence. Substance is that which is self-identical, and which underlies accidents. The accidents are identified with the changing states of the self. Substance holds together these otherwise disparate experiences or changing states.

In the first part of this chapter, we saw that spatialized time is derived primarily from an analysis of objects. It should be evident that the understanding of the self in terms of substance and accidents likewise derives chiefly from the analysis of objects. The model that informs this view of the self is that of an object with certain attributes. For example, when describing a table, one might say that it is large, brown, old, scratched, four-legged, etc. However, it is always the table that we are describing. We may be able to give an exhaustive list of the table's attributes, but it is not to be thought that these attributes taken together comprise the table. The attributes are predicated of the table, and the table is, in a certain sense, something more than or independent of the sum of its attributes. Furthermore, this "table" of which the attributes are predicated serves the function of holding together different attributes. In this instance, table, or tableness, is the substance of which large, brown, old, scratched, four-legged, etc., are attributes. When this analysis is applied to persons, the self is regarded as composed of substance and attributes. Although the experiences of the self are constitutive of its being, the self is not exhausted by these experiences. "Substance" refers to that which underlies and unites the various experiences of the self. While the particular experiences change, the substance remains the same. Thus one

---

[26] H. J. Paton gives a good statement of this position and its implications. "Self-Identity," *Mind*, vol. 38, 1929, pp. 312-329.

is enabled to undergo different experiences while remaining the same self.

The parallels between this way of presenting the problem of the unity and the diversity of the self, or of explaining the fact that the same self has different experiences (i.e., that the self is both unchanging and changing), with Kierkegaard's argument should be evident. Substance, as Kierkegaard's eternal, is that which does not change. Attribute, as his temporal, is that which changes. It is, furthermore, substance, as Kierkegaard's eternal, that is the factor of continuity in the otherwise changing self.

During the seventeenth and eighteenth centuries, however, the view of the self as a substance underwent critical reevaluation. On the one hand, the notion of substance was extended from individual selves to the whole of being until all that is became a single substance of which everything was a mode. On the other hand, the conception of substance was criticized as a figment of the imagination, and was dismissed. It is not possible to develop these trends of thought in detail in the present context. We must limit ourselves to a brief statement of these two tendencies as the background for Hegel's consideration of the problem, because it is on Hegel's analysis that Kierkegaard's argument depends.

Spinoza extends the notion of substance to include all being within a single substance. This move is, however, implicit in the traditional view of substance. Spinoza draws the logical consequence. He defines substance as ". . . that which is in itself and is conceived through itself; in other words, that, the conception of which does not need the conception of another thing from which it must be formed."[27] According to this definition, substance is that which is self-sufficient. But it is usually thought that God alone is self-sufficient, while all of creation is dependent on God. Thereby a dualism is set up between the self-sufficient Creator and the fully dependent cre-

---

[27] Spinoza, *Ethics*, trans. by W. H. White (London: Trübner and Co., 1883), "Of God," First Part, Definition, III.

ation. Spinoza rejects such a dualism for a monism in which all of reality is of a piece. He does this by defining God in terms of substance: "By God, I understand Being absolutely infinite, that is to say, substance consisting of infinite attributes, each of which expresses eternal and infinite essence."[28] Only God is, and all else is a mode of this one reality. In Spinoza's language, God is that single, self-sufficient substance of which all else is a mode. Here is an extension of the idea of substance to the whole of being until all that is becomes a single substance expressed in infinite modes.

In the development of thought from Locke, through Berkeley to Hume, there is a criticism of the notion of substance, and of the particular application of substantial language to the self. Locke initiates this criticism. Locke's argument is, however, posed less in opposition to Spinoza and more in opposition to Descartes' definition of the self as an "immaterial substance" ("*une substance immaterielle*").[29] Because Locke has Descartes and not Spinoza in mind, there is a slightly different meaning attached to the notion of substance than we noted in Spinoza. Rather than understanding substance primarily as "that which is in itself and is conceived through itself," Locke regards substance as "that which supports accidents."

Although Locke begins the critical evaluation of the notion of substance, his position on the issue is not consistent.[30] While Locke discerns many of the problems with the idea of substance, he is unable to divest himself of the category. For example, on the one hand, Locke argues that the concept of substance is "an uncertain supposition"[31] that is derived by abstracting common elements from different "simple ideas." Given Locke's empirical epistemology, he often seems unwill-

---

[28] *Ibid.*, Definition vi.

[29] For Descartes' consideration of this issue, see *Discourse on Method*, Part iv, and *Metaphysical Meditations*, "Third Meditation."

[30] See *An Essay Concerning Human Understanding* (New York: Meridan Books, 1968), esp. book ii.

[31] *Ibid.*, book i, chapter iii.

ing to acknowledge the intelligibility of the idea of substance. Because substance is never experienced, the concept must be regarded as questionable. On the other hand, Locke indicates that the notion of substance is a logical necessity: ". . . there is substance, *because we cannot conceive how qualities should subsist by themselves.*"[32] It is difficult, if not impossible, to make the two positions presented in Locke's writings consistent. The problem stems from his inability to divest himself completely of substantialism, and to accept the implications of his empiricism. He tries to render his argument coherent by drawing a distinction between the idea of substance and the being of substance, claiming to call into question the former, but not the latter. This formulation does not, of course, overcome the problems of his position.

It is important for the present discussion to notice that when considering the problem of personal identity[33] Locke's uneasiness with the idea of substance becomes especially apparent. Unlike many of his predecessors who had solved the problem of the continuity of the self by the postulation of a substance that joins together accidents, Locke, drawing on a Cartesian emphasis on the centrality of consciousness for the self, argues that personal identity is a function of consciousness. We cannot develop Locke's argument and its implications at this point. The important thing to recognize is that Locke brings the problem of substance to the forefront of philosophical reflection. While his arguments do not establish a consistent view on the problem of using the category of substance in relation to the self, they do set the terms in which the debate will be carried on by later thinkers.

[32] From "Third Letter to Stillingfleet," quoted by Risieri Frondizi, *The Nature of the Self: A Functional Interpretation* (New Haven: Yale University Press, 1953), p. 31. Frondizi's summary of the development of the problem of the self from Locke to Hume has been quite helpful in constructing this argument. My interests and intentions are, however, very different from those of Frondizi.

[33] "Personal Identity" is here to be understood in the philosophical sense of the term, as the unity of the self at any given time, and as the continuity of the self through time.

Berkeley, in a sense, forms a bridge between Locke's and Hume's views of substance. In some ways he is more consistent than Locke, drawing the logical conclusions from Locke's analysis, while in other ways he is more inconsistent than Locke. Berkeley destroys the notion of material substance but retains the idea of spiritual substance. For Berkeley, as for Locke, substance is understood as that which supports accidents. Berkeley argues that substance is an "abstract general idea," which he describes as follows:

"By abstract idea, genera, species, universal notions, all which amount to the same thing, as I find these terms explained by the best and clearest writers, we are to understand ideas which equally represent the particulars of any sort, and are made by the mind, which observing that the individuals of each kind agree in some things and differ in others, takes out and singles from the rest, that which is common to all, making thereof one abstract general idea; which contains all those ideas wherein the particulars of that kind agree, separated from and exclusive of all those other concomitant ideas, whereby they are distinguished from one another. To this abstract general idea thus framed the mind gives a general name, and lays it up and uses it as a standard whereby to judge what particulars are and what are not to be accounted of that sort, those only which contain every part of the general idea having a right to be admitted into that sort and called that name."[34]

Berkeley thinks that such "abstract general ideas" are hypotheses not grounded in concrete reality. He places material substance in the same category as dreams or illusions—a figment of one's imagination that is not actual. In fact, corporeal bodies are nothing other than a combination of sensible qualities; there is no supporting substratum of which qualities are accidents.

Berkeley does not, however, apply the same analysis to spiritual substance, or to the self. He equates the terms "spir-

[34] Berkeley, *The Works of George Berkeley*, ed. A. C. Fraser (Oxford: Clarendon Press, 1901), p. 360. Quoted by Frondizi, *op.cit.*, p. 50.

it," "soul," "self," "mind," and "spiritual substance," and defines this phenomenon as "that indivisible, unextended *thing* which thinks, acts and perceives."[35] He continues: "But it has been shown that there is no corporeal or material substance: it remains therefore that the cause of ideas is an incorporeal active substance or Spirit."[36] It is not possible to examine the reasons for Berkeley's position on this issue. Suffice it to recognize that by working out the implications of some of Locke's views on the problem of substance, Berkeley dissolves the notion of material substance. He is, however, unable to give up the idea of spiritual substance. Here he does not even show the ambiguity we observed in Locke's position. Berkeley's understanding of material substance (it is denied) is consistent, as is his understanding of spiritual substance (it is affirmed). What is inconsistent is the relation of these two arguments. While material objects are a combination of sensible qualities, selves are spiritual substances.

It was left for Hume to apply the kind of analysis to which Berkeley subjected material substance to spiritual substances or to selves. Hume denies that it is proper to speak of either material objects or of selves in terms of substance. The epistemological basis of his criticism of the notion of substance is evident in the following sentence: "As every idea is derived from a precedent impression, had we any idea of the substance of our minds, we must also have an impression of it, which is very difficult, if not impossible to be conceived."[37] Hume proceeds to specify the implications of this position for his understanding of the self when he adds: ". . . nor have we any idea of *self.* . . . For from what impression could this be derived?"[38]

[35] "Dialogues," III, *The Works of George Berkeley, op.cit.*, I, p. 448. Italics added.

[36] "A Treatise Concerning the Principles of Human Knowledge," *The Works of George Berkeley, op.cit.*, III, section 25.

[37] David Hume, *A Treatise on Human Nature* (London: John Noon, 1739), vol. III, p. 405. Compare Locke, *An Essay Concerning Human Understanding, op.cit.*, vol. I, book II, chapter XXVII.

[38] *Ibid.*, p. 437.

Hume accepts empirical verification as the criterion of truth. Since the idea of substance cannot be empirically verified, it must be denied. He agrees with Berkeley that the conception of substance is imaginatively constructed to hold together what is otherwise different (be that attributes of an object, or experiences of a self).[39] But, unlike Berkeley, Hume extends his criticism of substance from material objects to selves. Berkeley had been right, Hume thinks, in holding objects to be a combination of sensible qualities. However it was wrong for Berkeley not to apply his analysis of material substance to spiritual substance. Neither for material objects nor for selves is there an underlying substratum that supports properties or accidents. As objects are combinations of sensible qualities, so selves are "bundles of sensations":[40] "A mind is a kind of theatre, where several perceptions successively make their appearance, pass, repass, glide away, and mingle in an infinite variety of postures and situations. There is properly no simplicity in it at one time, nor *identity* in different times."[41] According to Hume's analysis, the self is a ceaseless flux of sensations with no continuity through time and no unity at a given time. From the perspective within which Hume and his predecessors work, the denial of substance means the denial of the unity of the self. For Hume, any unity predicated of the self is an imaginative illusion that is not rooted in experience.[42]

Thus, on the one hand, it was argued that selves are modes of the single substance, God, and, on the other hand, that selves are bundles of disunited sensations. Hegel finds both of these alternatives unacceptable. He tries to resolve the

[39] *Ibid.*, pp. 440-441.   [40] *Ibid.*, see "Appendix."

[41] *Ibid.*, p. 439.

[42] Our discussion of the development of thought on this issue has been necessarily abbreviated. For responsible summaries of the problem that go into more detail, see Anthony Flew, "Locke and the Problem of Personal Identity," *Philosophy*, vol. 26, 1951, pp. 53-68; Risieri Frondizi, *The Nature of the Self: A Functional Reinterpretation, op.cit.*; and Sydney Shoemaker, *Self-Knowledge and Self-Identity* (Ithaca: Cornell University Press, 1963).

problem by reworking the concept of substance in terms of the idea of subject.

In the "Preface" to his *Phänomenologie Des Geistes*, Hegel comments: "In my view — a view which the developed exposition of the system itself alone can justify — everything depends on grasping [*aufzufassen*] and expressing the truth not as Substance [*Substanz*] but as Subject [*Subjekt*] as well."[43] In this quotation one can see Hegel's dissatisfaction with those metaphysical positions in the history of philosophy that employ the Greek ideas of substance and accident. In place of these categories, which are drawn from the natural sciences, Hegel proposes to interpret reality in terms of social metaphors. Reality should be understood not as substance but as subject. Much of Hegel's argument is posed in opposition to that of Spinoza. Against Spinoza's single substance, Hegel places his Absolute, which is self, a move Hegel regards as one of the fundamental philosophical advances of his system. Many of Hegel's arguments are directed to reality as a whole, and not simply to individuals that make up that totality. Thus, the Absolute, the totality of all that is and has been, is interpreted as Subject. However, Hegel's arguments also apply to individual selves. This fact is important to recognize for, as we have seen, much of Kierkegaard's argument can be understood as the application of Hegel's comments about the Absolute Self to individual selves. For this reason we will consider Hegel's argument in connection with individual selves.

Hegel directly attacks the understanding of the subject[44]

---

[43] My quotations from Hegel's *Phenomenology* are taken from John Baillie's translation: *The Phenomenology of Mind* (New York: Harper Torchbooks, 1967). In some instances it has been necessary to correct Baillie's translations or to indicate the German phrase. When this has been required, I have worked from the German text edited by Johannes Hoffmeister: *Phänomenologie Des Geistes* (Hamburg: Felix Meiner, 1952). This quotation is from Baillie, p. 80; Hoffmeister, p. 19.

[44] As is perhaps evident, "subject" and "self" can be used interchangeably in discussing Hegel's argument. Support for this is given by the fact that Hegel himself so uses the terms (subject — *Subjekt*, and self — *Selbst*). *Phenomenology*, Baillie, p. 118; Hoffmeister, p. 49.

in terms of substance and attributes as it has been presented above, when he writes: "The subject is taken to be a fixed point, and to it as their support the predicates are attached, by a process falling within the individual knowing about it, but not looked upon as belonging to the point of attachment itself; only by such a process, however, could the content belong to the subject; but when the point of support is fixed to start with, this process cannot be otherwise constituted, it can only be external [*äusserlich*]. The anticipation that the Absolute is subject is therefore not merely the realization of this conception; it even makes realization impossible. For it makes out the concept [*Begriff*] to be a static [*ruhenden*] point, while it is actually self-movement [*Selbst-bewegung*]."[45]

According to Hegel's argument, when the subject is taken to be a substance, it is seen as a static substratum (a "fixed point") to which predicates are "externally attached." It is as if one simply postulates a substance of which nothing more can be said than that it holds together accidents. Such a conception is, for Hegel, empty. He argues that this view of the subject or of the self is derived, in part, from the grammar of statements that refer to the self in which the subject is linked to a predicate by the copula "is." For example: X is A. From this grammatical structure emerges the notion that the subject, X, is something independent of its descriptive predicate, A. According to this line of interpretation, Hegel notes that ". . . self is an ideally presented subject to which the content is related as an accident and predicate."[46] Such an understanding of the self in terms of substance and accident is, for Hegel, quite unsatisfactory. He thinks that the very structure of grammar that encourages this misunderstanding makes a proper view of the self difficult to grasp. Therefore, Hegel argues that ". . . the nature of the judgment or proposition, which involves the distinction between subject and predicate, is destroyed by the speculative position."[47] The subject does not exist independently of the predicates, but the predicates

[45] *Phenomenology*, Baillie, pp. 84-85; Hoffmeister, p. 23.
[46] *Ibid.*, p. 118; p. 49.   [47] *Ibid.*, p. 120; p. 51.

themselves express the subject: "Beginning with the subject, as if this remained the basis, one finds, because the predicate is really the substance, that the subject has moved into the predicate and has thus been taken up [*aufgehoben*]."[48]

The denial of the actuality of a subject or of a substance independent of the attributes or predicates, and the affirmation of the sole reality of the predicates, sound very similar to the position of Hume as described above. Hegel would agree with Hume insofar as Hume offers a criticism of the empty notion of substance. Yet Hegel cannot accept the Humean interpretation of the self. By denying substance while affirming accidents, Hume remains within a generally substantialistic understanding of the issue. Hegel seeks to give a more adequate interpretation of the self by moving away from the categories of substance and accident.

In attempting to present a satisfactory view of selfhood, Hegel consistently regards the self in the dynamic terms of purposive activity.[49] In the following quotation, Hegel offers a definition of the self. This text is especially important because it is quite similar to Kierkegaard's definition of the self in *The Sickness Unto Death*:[50]

"The result is the same as the beginning only because the beginning is purpose [*Zweck*]. In other words, the actual is the same as its Concept [*Begriff*] only because the immediate, being purpose, contains the self or pure actuality in itself. The executed purpose or the actual as existent is movement [*Bewegung*] and unfolded becoming [*entfaltates Werden*]; but precisely this unrest [*Unruhe*] is the self. And it is like the immediacy and simplicity of the beginning because it is the

[48] *Ibid.*, p. 119; p. 50.

[49] This argument is not undercut by Hegel's emphasis on the importance of reason as definitive of man, for he argues that "reason is purposive activity." *Phenomenology*, Baillie, p. 83; Hoffmeister, p. 22.

[50] Crites also notes the significance of the similarity of these passages. See *In the Twilight of Christendom, op.cit.*, p. 70 note. Other commentators suggest that the opening lines of *The Sickness Unto Death* are a parody of Hegel. The latter view will be refuted as the argument proceeds.

result, that which has returned into itself [*das in sich Zurück-gekehrte*] — and that which has returned into itself is the self and the self is the identity and simplicity that relates itself to itself [*und das Selbst die sich auf sich beziehende Gleichheit und Einfachheit ist*]."[51]

The actuality of the self is the function of "executed purpose" (*ausgeführte Zweck*), which develops through "unfolded becoming" (*entfaltetes Werden*). Hegel argues that the unrest (*Unruhe*), the activity, the movement (*Bewegung*) by which purposes are executed is the self. Mediation is the name of the process by which the self actualizes itself: "For mediation [*Vermittlung*] is nothing but self-identity [*Sichselbstgleichheit*] working itself out through an active self-directed process; or, in other words, it is reflection into self, the aspect in which the ego [*Ich*] is for itself, objective to itself."[52]

Hegel is arguing that the self becomes objective to itself in the form of a purpose to be carried out, or a goal to be achieved. The self is that self which it intends to become through its purposive activity, but initially it is that self in an immediate or a potential form. Before the self actually is the self that it now is only potentially, the immediate must be mediated, the possible must be actualized. The self must strive to realize the potentialities that have been envisioned. In the process that Hegel is analyzing, the self first posits the ideal self as objective to, and distinguished from, the real self, and then seeks to actualize the potentiality envisioned in the ideal self.

These insights enable us to understand more fully some of the language of a text previously cited from Hegel (p. 104 above). It is important to grasp this language, for Kierkegaard uses almost identical terms. It will be helpful to quote again part of this passage: "The executed purpose or the actual as existent is movement and unfolded becoming; but precisely this unrest is the self. And it is like the immediacy and

---

[51] *Phenomenology*, Baillie, pp. 84-85; Hoffmeister, p. 22.
[52] *Ibid.*, p. 82; p. 21.

simplicity of the beginning because it is the result, that which has returned into itself — and that which has returned into itself is the self and the self is the identity and simplicity that relates itself to itself." The self establishes an internal opposition by setting goals for itself. In this process, the real and the ideal selves are at once distinguished, and yet remain part of a single self. In establishing a purpose, or in envisioning an ideal self, one passes away from his actual self. In the realization of that ideal, one returns to his self. This movement by which the ideal self is actualized, or by which purposes are executed, is an activity in which the self "relates itself [its ideal self] to itself [its real self]." The self, properly so-called, is this process of self-relation — the self is the active process by which potentialities are actualized:

"The living substance, further, is that being which is truly subject, or, what is the same thing, is truly realized and actual solely in the process of positing itself [*Sichselbstsetzens*], or in mediating with its own self its transitions from one state or position to the opposite. As Subject it is pure and simple negativity [*Negativität*], and just on that account a process of duplicating [*Verdopplung*] and setting factors in opposition which [process] in turn is the negation of this indifferent diversity and of the opposition of factors it entails. True reality is merely this process of reinstating self-identity, or reflecting into its own self in and from its other, and is not an original and primal unity as such, not an immediate unity as such. It is the process of its own becoming, the circle which presupposes its end as its purpose, and has its end for its beginning; it becomes concrete and actual only by being carried out, and by the end it involves."[53]

[53] *Ibid.*, pp. 80-81; p. 20. Kojève's comment is helpful: ". . . he [man] cannot be a *being* that is eternally *identical* to itself, that is self-*sufficient*. Man must be an emptiness, a nothingness, which is not a pure nothingness [*reines Nichts*], but something that *is* to the extent that it *annihilates* Being, in order to realize itself at the expense of Being and to nihilate in Being. Man is negating *Action*, which trans-

Hegel's understanding of the manner in which possibilities are realized should be specified, for again we will note striking similarities with Kierkegaard's argument. According to Hegel (and Kierkegaard would agree), the will, motivated by interest, is the means by which possibilities are actualized: "Purposes, principles, and the like, are at first in our thoughts, our inner intention. They are not yet in actuality [*Wirklichkeit*]. That which is in itself is a possibility, a faculty. It has not yet emerged out of its implicitness into existence. A second element must be added for it to become an actuality, namely, activity, actualization. The principle of this is the will, man's activity in general. It is only through this activity that the concept and its implicit determinations can be realized, actualized; for of themselves they have no immediate efficacy. The activity which puts them in operation and existence is the need, the instinct, the inclination, and passion of man."[54]

Furthermore, the will, moved to actualize certain potentialities through interest or passion, is constitutive of one's personality. In a statement that is quite contrary to the mood of the speculative philosopher who has forgotten the existing individual, the caricature of Hegel usually presented by Kierkegaard, Hegel writes: "This particular objective is so bound up with the person's will that it alone and entirely determines

---

forms given Being, and by transforming it, transforms itself. Man *is* what he is only to the extent that he *becomes* and he *becomes*, he *is* History only in and by *Action* that negates the given, the Action of Fighting and of Work — of the Work that finally produces the table on which Hegel writes his *Phenomenology*, and of the Fight that is finally the Battle of Jena whose sounds he hears while writing the *Phenomenology*." *Introduction to the Reading of Hegel*, trans. by James H. Nichols, ed. by Allan Bloom (New York: Basic Books, 1969), p. 38.

[54] Hegel, "Reason in History: A General Introduction to the Philosophy of History," trans. by Robert S. Hartman (New York: Bobbs-Merrill Co., 1953), pp. 27-28.

its direction and is inseparable from it. It is that which makes the person what he is. For a person is a specific existence. He is not man in general — such a thing does not exist — but a particular human being."[55]

According to Hegel, the self is the purposive activity in which possibilities are actualized. It is the self-relating activity in which the real self is related to the ideal self. As the ideal self is realized, the real self is negated. This constant unrest, or incessant striving, is the self. The motor of the process is the will, which is driven by desire or interest. Only in such dynamic and developmental terms does Hegel think that selfhood, and in the final analysis, the whole of reality, can be understood.

The consideration of Hegel's effort to rework the idea of substance in terms of subject or of the self brings us to the conclusion of the examination of the historical context within which Kierkegaard develops his view of the structure of the self. As we proceed, we shall see the way in which he both appropriates and reinterprets the insights and the categories of his predecessors to articulate his own notion of the self.

[55] *Ibid.*, p. 29. Kojève's analysis is again illuminating: "This I, which 'feeds' on desires, will itself be Desire in its very being, created in and by the satisfaction of its Desire. And since Desire is realized as action negating the given, the very being of this I will be action. This I will not, like the animal 'I,' be 'identity' or equality to itself, but 'negating negativity.' In other words, the very being of this I will be becoming, and the universal form of this being will not be space, but time. Therefore, its continuation in existence will signify for this I: 'Not to be what it is (as static and given being, as natural being, as innate character) and to be (that is, to become) what it is not.' Thus, this I will be its own product: it will be (in the future) what it has become by negation (in the present) of what it was (in the past), this negation being accomplished with a view to what it will become. In its very being this I is intentional becoming, deliberate evolution, conscious and voluntary progress; it is in the act of transcending the given that is given to it and that it itself is. This I is a (human) individual, free (with respect to the given real) and historical (in relation to itself). And it is this I and only this, that reveals itself to itself and to others as Self-Consciousness." *Op.cit.*, p. 5.

3. Kierkegaard's Analysis

We can begin where we left off Kierkegaard's consideration of the problem of the structure of selfhood — by further
clarifying the temporal-eternal polarity. We have seen that,
in general terms, eternity refers to the component of the self
that does not change, while temporality denotes the aspect of
the self that is constantly changing, or is always becoming. It
will be helpful to reconsider Kierkegaard's most complete
statement of the structure of the self. After the analysis of the
foregoing section, we can read this passage with Hegel's arguments in mind.

"Man is spirit. But what is spirit? Spirit is the self. But what
is the self? The self is a relation which relates itself to its own
self; or it is that in the relation which relates itself to its own
self; the self is not a relation, but [the self is] that the relation
relates itself to its own self. Man is a synthesis of the infinite
and the finite, of the temporal and the eternal, of freedom
and necessity, in short, a synthesis. A synthesis is a relation
between two [components]. So regarded, man is not yet a
self. In the relation between two, the relation is the third as
a negative unity, and the two relate themselves to the relation, and in the relation to the relation; such a relation is that
between soul and body, when man is determined as soul. If,
on the contrary, the relation relates itself to its own self, the
relation is then the positive third, and this is the self."[56]

As has been noted previously, in this text, Kierkegaard
identifies "spirit" with "self." At another point, he equates
"spirit" with the "eternal" in man.[57] Kierkegaard is arguing
that it is nothing other than the *self* (or spirit) that is the
eternal in man.

[56] *The Sickness Unto Death*, p. 146; S.V., xi, 127. See above, p.
87. An important etymological parallel should be noted at the
outset. The Danish word that is translated "spirit" in this passage is
"*Aand.*" This is the Danish translation of the German "*Geist.*" "*Geist,*"
of course, is Hegel's central concern in the *Phenomenology.*

[57] See above p. 88.

We can begin to recognize the implications of the argument on this issue by establishing that, for Kierkegaard, the eternal, the spirit, or the self is "that in the relation which relates itself to its own self." As should be apparent by now, Kierkegaard views the self system as a complex set of relationships. The self is the component of the self system that accomplishes these relationships. In full agreement with Hegel, Kierkegaard stresses that the self is not a static *entity* (as the substantialistic notion of selfhood might imply), but a *dynamic activity*. For this reason he continues, "the self is not a relation, but [the self is] that the relation relates itself to its own self." The self is the dynamic activity of self-relating. Kierkegaard's argument at this point directly parallels Hegel's contention that ". . . that which has returned into itself is the self and the self is the identity and simplicity that relates itself to itself."[58] The precise meaning of Kierkegaard's confusing characterization of the self as an activity that "relates itself to it own self" needs further clarification.

To understand this, it is necessary to turn to the other three sets of terms that Kierkegaard uses to describe the self system: soul/body, infinitude/finitude, and possibility/necessity.[59] Two claims have been made about these terms that now need to be supported. First, it has been stated that the three sets of terms are different expressions for the same dimension of selfhood.[60] Second, it has been asserted that the three sets of terms are efforts to disclose certain aspects of one component of the other expression of the synthesis — temporality.[61] Let us consider each of these in turn.

[58] *Phenomenology*, Baillie, pp. 84-85; Hoffmeister, p. 22.

[59] The reader must bear in mind several terminological clarifications that have been made earlier. First, the polarity specified as "freedom and necessity" is more accurately expressed as "possibility and necessity." Second, Kierkegaard uses "necessity" (*Nødvendighed*) and actuality (*Virkelighed*) interchangeably. Third, "soul" (*Sjel*) refers to the essential psychic and mental aspects of the individual's personality. (See above p. 88 for the prior definitions.)

[60] Carnell makes the same point. *The Burden of Søren Kierkegaard*, *op.cit.*, p. 48.

[61] See above pp. 89-90.

In the text in which Kierkegaard delineates the different components of the self system, he offers three sets of terms in addition to temporal and eternal: infinite/finite, possibility/ necessity, and soul/body. It is important to notice that within the context of his initial definition of the self system, Kierkegaard does not include soul/body. This set of terms is added in the second paragraph. Although he tends to use soul/body more frequently in other contexts, most notably in *The Concept of Dread,* in this text, his primary focus is on infinite/ finite and possibility/necessity. Nothing is lost by this limitation for, as becomes evident, each set of terms is the functional equivalent of the other two. The centrality of infinite/ finite and possibility/necessity is underscored by the fact that when Kierkegaard turns to a detailed consideration of the various polarities, soul/body is eliminated. It is, therefore, justifiable to limit our analysis to the other two dichotomies.

Both infinite/finite and possibility/necessity refer to the fact that man is conditioned by his historical situation and is free to act within the limits of that situation.[62] The terms "finitude" and "necessity" designate man's determination, and the terms "infinitude" and "possibility"[63] refer to man's capacity to act. According to Kierkegaard's analysis, selfhood always includes these two components that stand in tension. A person always finds himself historically situated in a certain place and at a certain time. This situation conditions the possibilities open to the individual. One's historical epoch, spatial location, parents, natural abilities, etc., are all components of one's being that affect what the individual can do. It is not true for Kierkegaard, as it is for some of his Existentialist followers, that man is radically free and is unconditioned by his situation

[62] The same analysis of human experience is presented in Heidegger's phrase, "*Dasein* is a thrown projection." See *Being and Time, op.cit.,* par. 44, p. 265.

[63] The following passage is an instance of Kierkegaard's equation of possibility and infinity: "He who is educated by possibility, and only the man who is educated by possibility is educated in accordance with his infinity. Possibility is, therefore, the heaviest of all categories." *The Concept of Dread,* pp. 139-140; S.V., IV, 422.

and by his past. Kierkegaard never holds that man has *liberum arbitrium*:

"That abstract freedom of choice (*liberum arbitrium*) is a phantasy, as if a human being at every moment of his life stood continually in the abstract possibility, so that consequently he never moves from the spot, as if freedom were not also an historical condition — this has been pointed out by Augustine and many moderns. It seems to me that the matter can be illuminated simply in the following way. Take a weight, even the most accurate gold weight — when it has been used only a week it already has a history. The owner knows this history, for example, that it leans towards off-balance one way or the other, etc. This history continues with use. So it is with the will. It has a history, a continually progressive history."[64]

Infinitude and finitude or possibility and necessity are dialectically related in concrete human existence: "The self is the conscious synthesis of infinitude and finitude which relates itself to itself, whose task it is to become itself, a task that can be performed only by means of a relationship to God. But to become one's self means neither to become finite nor infinite, for that which is to become concrete is a synthesis. Accordingly, the development consists in moving away from oneself infinitely by the process of infinitizing oneself, and in returning to oneself infinitely by the process of finitizing."[65]

"Finitude" designates the temporally situated and determined aspect of the self system (i.e., the self's actuality). It is that which is necessary or which is given to the self, and from which the self must necessarily proceed in any further development. "Infinitude" indicates the capability of the individual so situated to envision various alternative courses of action. It is the capacity of the historically conditioned individual to entertain different *possibilities*.[66] That "finitude-

---

[64] *Journals and Papers*, no. 1268; *Papirer*, x⁴ A 175.

[65] *The Sickness Unto Death*, pp. 162-163; S.V., XI, 143.

[66] Heidegger's terms "facticity" and "being-ahead-of-itself-in-already-being-in-a-world" refer to Kierkegaard's "finitude" and "necessity";

infinitude" and "necessity-possibility" are parallel terms referring to the same dimension of human experience is indicated by Kierkegaard's analysis of the latter expression:

"Just as finitude is the limiting factor in relation to infinitude, so in relation to possibility it is necessity that serves as a check. When the self as a synthesis of finitude and infinitude is once constituted, when already it is κατὰ δύναμιν, then in order to *become* it reflects itself in the medium of imagination [*Phantasiens Medium*], and with that the infinite possibility comes into view. The self κατὰ δύναμιν is just as possible as it is necessary; for though it is itself, it has to become itself. Inasmuch as it is itself, it is the necessary, and inasmuch as it has to become itself, it is a possibility."[67]

The reference to the imagination [*Phantasie*] in this passage raises another important point. The reflective imagination is, for Kierkegaard, the capacity by which an individual recognizes his infinitude, or envisions his possibilities: "Generally speaking, imagination is the medium of the process of infinitizing; it is not one faculty on a par with others, but, if one would so speak, it is the faculty *instar omnium*. What feeling, knowledge, or will a man has, depends in the last resort upon what imagination he has, that is to say, upon how these things are reflected, i.e. it depends upon the imagination. Imagination is the reflection of the process of infinitizing. . . ."[68]

In another context Kierkegaard makes even clearer the function of the reflective imagination in a way that indicates parallels with views of Hegel which have been discussed: "Every man possesses in a greater or lesser degree a talent that is called imagination [*Indbildningskraften*], the power

---

"potentiality for being" and "anticipatory resoluteness" parallel Kierkegaard's "infinitude" and "possibility."

[67] *The Sickness Unto Death*, p. 168; S.V., xi, 148. Fredrick Sontag has given a brief but good analysis of the dialectical relationship between possibility and actuality in the self. See "Kierkegaard and the Search for a Self," *Essays on Kierkegaard, op.cit.*, pp. 158ff.

[68] *Ibid.*, pp. 163-164; S.V., xi, 144.

that is the first condition of determining what a man will turn out to be; for the second condition is the will [*Villen*], which in the final resort is decisive [*afgjørende*]. Memory is strongest in childhood and decreases with years.[69] We will now think of a youth. With his imagination he constructs one or another picture (ideal) [*Ideal*] of perfection, whether it be one handed down by history, that is, belonging to a time past, so that it has been actually, has possessed the actuality of being, or whether it be formed by the imagination alone, so that it has no relation to time or place and receives no definition by them, but has only the actuality of thought [*Tanke-Virkelighed*]. To this picture (which—since for the youth it has existence only in imagination, that is, in imagination's endless remoteness from actuality—is the picture of completed perfection, not of striving and suffering perfection), to this picture the youth is now drawn by his imagination, or his imagination draws this picture to him; he falls in love with this picture, or the picture becomes the object of his love, of his enthusiasm, becomes his more perfect (ideal) self [*hans fuldkomnere (idealere) Selv*]. . . ."[70]

By means of the imagination, an individual constructs an ideal self distinguished from his real or actual self. The ideal self presents to him his possibility (his infinitude), and the real self confronts him with his actuality (his finitude). These two aspects of the individual's self system are always dialectically related. The real self conditions the ideal self, and vice versa. Having imagined an ideal self, one endeavors to actualize the potentialities there envisioned. This is the identical process to which Hegel points in his argument that has been discussed above (see especially p. 105). Furthermore, it was seen that Hegel identifies the self, properly so-called,

[69] For some unexplainable reason, Lowrie has omitted this important phrase from his English translation of the text.

[70] *Training in Christianity*, p. 185; S.V., xii, 173. Kierkegaard uses "*Phantasie*" and "*Indbildningskraft*" interchangeably. Both can be translated by the English "imagination."

with the active interrelationship between the real self and ideal self.

We are now in a position to see that Kierkegaard makes the same identification. We have noted that he argues that "the self is a relation which relates itself to its own self." In light of the foregoing analysis, this can be understood to mean: "the self is a relation which relates itself [its ideal self, its potentiality, its infinitude] to its own self [its real self, its actuality, its finitude]." For Kierkegaard, as for Hegel, the self is the dynamic process by which potentialities are actualized.

However, as is well known, one of the main points in Kierkegaard's argument is that the self develops (i.e., actualizes potentialities) through free decision. For this reason, he makes the final move of identifying the self with freedom. The two following quotations make this point quite clearly:

"The self is composed of infinity and finiteness. But the synthesis is a relationship, and it is a relationship which, though it is derived, relates itself to itself, which means freedom. *The self is freedom* [*Selvet er Frihed*]. But freedom is the dialectical element in terms of possibility and necessity."[71]

"But what, then, is this self of mine: If I were required to define this, my first answer would be: It is the most abstract of all things, and yet at the same time it is the most concrete — *it is freedom*."[72]

The careful reader should have noticed that with the equation of the self with freedom we have added another (and the final) term to several equivalent categories that we have previously discussed. At the outset it was seen that Kierkegaard identifies spirit with the self, and proceeds to equate the self with the eternal element of the self system. Now it becomes apparent that the self is also identified with freedom. There

[71] *The Sickness Unto Death*, p. 162; S.V., xi, 142. Italics added.

[72] *Either-Or*, ii, p. 218; S.V., ii, 192. Italics added. It must, of course, be kept in mind that the freedom here in question is not an absolute freedom but is related to and conditioned by the actuality of the individual's situation in existence.

are four terms that Kierkegaard uses to designate the aspect of the self system that is under investigation: spirit, eternal, freedom, and self. The recognition of the equivalence of these terms enables us to clarify what Kierkegaard means when he says that the self is a synthesis of the temporal and the eternal.

Earlier in this chapter, it was argued that one of the fundamental meanings of "eternal" for Kierkegaard is that which is unchangeable, while one of the basic characteristics of the "temporal" is its changeability. Such use of language was noted to have a long history in the philosophical consideration of the problem of the self. What makes understanding Kierkegaard's argument at this point so difficult is that he persists in using the language of the philosophical tradition to express an understanding of the structure of selfhood that stands in tension with much of the tradition. When Kierkegaard contends that the self is a synthesis of the temporal (changeable) and the eternal (the unchangeable), he does not mean, as had many of his predecessors, that the self is comprised of a self-identical (unchanging) substratum (substance) in which constantly changing experiences (accidents) inhere. As we have seen, his view of the structure of selfhood is much more congruent with Hegel's understanding of the self as the dynamic process by which possibilities are actualized than it is with substantialistic notions of selfhood. With this qualification in mind, we can understand Kierkegaard's idiosyncratic use of the categories "temporal" and "eternal" in his claim that the self is a synthesis of the temporal and the eternal. The eternal component of the self system is nothing other than the self itself. But we have seen that he uses the term "self" in a restricted sense when analyzing the self system: he equates the self properly so-called with freedom. Therefore, we can say that the eternal aspect of the self system is freedom. Recalling the general characterization of the eternal as unchanging, we arrive at the conclusion that the unchanging component of the self system is freedom. That which does not change within the self system is the fact of the self's freedom. In this context, "unchanging" carries the specific connotation of "constant." The eternal or unchanging dimension of the self system is the constant capacity of the self to relate itself (its ideal self, its possibilities, its infinitude) to itself (its real self, its actuality, its infinitude). The eternal component of the self does not refer to an unchanging substratum or to a static substance, but designates the constant ability of the self to act, or to resolve to strive to actualize certain possibilities in any given situation.

Temporality, as has been noted, is characterized by its changeability — it is the realm of becoming. Becoming, however, arises from the interrelationship of possibility and actuality. For Kierkegaard, this interrelationship is the result of the exercise of freedom, an activity he calls the self. Therefore, spirit (or the self) is the means by which the various components of the self system are synthesized. The self is the necessary third through which the synthesis of possibility and necessity, infinitude and finitude, soul and body, the ideal self and the real self, takes place.

When Kierkegaard claims that "temporality" refers to those aspects of the self system that are constantly changing, his intention is to stress that the possibilities and the actuality of the self are always changing as the self continues to exist. These changes, which can be accomplished either by actions of others upon the self, or by the self's own actions, mutually condition one another. Although the concrete actuality and possibilities of the self constantly change, what does not change is the fact that the self is free to act in each and every situation. The particular course of action open to the individual will not be the same, but the fact of one's freedom, and hence the capacity to take some course of action, is the unchanging factor in the self system. It is in this sense that Kierkegaard's claim that the self is both temporal and eternal, both changing and unchanging, is to be understood.

Although we have made considerable progress in untangling Kierkegaard's complex notion of the structure of selfhood, a major problem remains. We have seen that for Kierkegaard a synthesis between two elements must always be accomplished through a third. For the polarities of infinitude/finitude, possibility/necessity, and soul/body, the self (spirit, the eternal, or freedom) has been seen to be the synthesizer. But the self cannot be the means by which the temporal and the eternal components of the self system are synthesized, for Kierkegaard identifies the self with one of these two components, the eternal. He is aware of this dilemma. A more complete consideration of a text cited earlier makes this evident: "As for the latter synthesis [temporal and eternal], it evidently is not fashioned in the same way as the former [soul and body]. In the former case, the two moments were soul and body, and spirit was a third term, but was a third term in such a sense that there could not properly be any question of a synthesis until the spirit was posited. The other synthesis has only two factors: the temporal and the eternal. Where is the third term? And if there be no third term, there is really no synthesis. . . ."[73]

In other words, while infinite/finite, possibility/necessity, and soul/body are brought together through the self (spirit, or freedom), through what third term are temporality and eternity brought together? Kierkegaard attempts to solve this problem by the introduction of the category *Øieblikket* — the moment or the instant.[74] In this context, the instant refers to the situation in which the individual is confronted with a choice — it is the moment of decision. In the moment of decision, the

---

[73] *The Concept of Dread*, p. 76; S.V., IV, 355.

[74] The Danish word "*Øieblik*" (spelled *øjeblik* in modern Danish) is a compound of "*øie*," which means "eye," and "*blik*," which means "look" or "glance." A literal translation of the word might be "a glance of the eye." Kierkegaard recognizes that such a reading of the word calls to mind Paul's phrase, "in an instant, in the twinkling of an eye." See *The Concept of Dread*, p. 79, note; S.V., IV, 358. At some points, Kierkegaard uses the word "*Moment*" instead of "*Øieblik*." Although Kierkegaard has a propensity to use *Øieblik* more frequently in connection with Christianity, no consistent distinction is made between this term and "*Moment*." I intend no systematic distinction in my use of "instant" and of "moment."

eternal and the temporal dimensions of the self are brought together. This argument is clarified by remembering that Kierkegaard equates the eternal with the self, with spirit, and with freedom, and that he indicates the central dimensions of the temporal component of the self system by the polar terms infinitude/finitude, possibility/necessity, and soul/body. He proceeds to argue that human becoming is generated by bringing together these two aspects of selfhood (i.e., the temporal and the eternal) in the moment of decision. In this moment, one faces one's possibilities in full recognition of one's actuality, and with a complete awareness of one's freedom (limited though it is) to act to realize these possibilities. The decision that one makes constitutes a further definition of one's actuality. While Kierkegaard holds that there are aspects of the self's actuality that are given and are not a function of the individual's own choice, he also argues that a person's actuality is more definitely constituted by his own decisions. On the basis of one's given actuality, he strives to realize those possibilities that are commensurate with his actuality. The realization of these possibilities, however, further defines one's actuality, and correlatively conditions one's possibilities. This complex process takes place in *Øieblikket*, in which all of the major components of the self system are brought together, resulting in the development of the self.

Even this complex analysis does not, however, fully exhaust Kierkegaard's understanding of the self system. One further element must be added: the dependence of the self system upon God. Kierkegaard contends that the entire self system either constitutes itself, or is constituted by another. Given the "Christian" premise of the authorship, he thinks that the self system is established by another, and this other is God: "Such a relation which relates itself to its own self, that is to say a self [*et Selv*], must either have constituted itself [*have sat sig selv*] or have been constituted by another. If this relation which relates itself to its own self is constituted by another, the relation doubtless is the third, but this relation (the third) is in turn a relation relating itself to that which constituted the whole relation. Such a derived [*derivert*], constituted, relation is the human self, a relation which relates itself to its own self, and in relating itself to its own self relates itself to another. . . . This formula is the expression of the total dependence [*hele Afhængighed*] of the relation (that is, of the self), the expression for the fact that the self cannot of itself attain and remain in equilibrium [*Ligevægt*] and rest by itself, but only by relating itself to that[75] which constituted the whole relation."[76]

Our foregoing discussion illuminates this aspect of the self system. Part of the actuality of the self is to be constituted by God. Insofar as the self is, it is necessarily dependent upon God for its being. When one entertains possibilities, it must always be with a recognition of one's total dependence upon God. From Kierkegaard's point of view, to have a full awareness of the structure of selfhood, there must be an acknowledgment of the ontological dependence of the self upon God.

With these comments, we have indicated the major features of Kierkegaard's understanding of the components of the self system and their relationship to one another. The discussion has, however, been long and involved. If we are to be able to trace Kierkegaard's analysis of selfhood and of time throughout the different stages of existence, a summary of the argument that has been presented is required. The diagram on page 121 might be of some help in this regard.

For the sake of simplification, the different components of the self system that Kierkegaard defines can be expressed by four terms: possibility, actuality, freedom, and the moment. The rationale for this abbreviation lies in the argument of this chapter. We have seen that three of his sets of terms (possibility/necessity, infinitude/finitude, and soul/body) are func-

---

[75] Lowrie misleadingly inserts the word "Power" at this point. I suspect he takes his justification for this from Kierkegaard's use of *Magt* later in this paragraph and in the following paragraph. At any rate, it seems incorrect to use it here. The sentence contains only the pronoun "*Det*," which refers to "that which has constituted the whole relation."

[76] *The Sickness Unto Death*, pp. 146-147; S.V., XI, 127-128.

The Self System

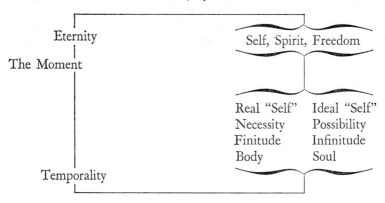

	Self, Spirit, Freedom	
Eternity		
The Moment		
	Real "Self"	Ideal "Self"
	Necessity	Possibility
	Finitude	Infinitude
	Body	Soul
Temporality		

tionally equivalent. For analytical purposes, the terms "possibility" and "necessity" are the most useful. Furthermore, it should be stressed that Kierkegaard more often designates the aspects of the self system to which the terms "possibility" and "necessity" refer by the terms "possibility" and "actuality." "Necessity," when used with respect to the self system, refers to the actuality of the self. Therefore, we can reduce his multiple use of terms at this point to two: possibility and actuality. In addition to his confusing use of terms to designate the individual's possibility and actuality, Kierkegaard has a variety of words to point to another important part of the self system. We have seen that "eternal," "spirit," "freedom," and "self" are functionally equivalent. Rather than use all of these terms in the remainder of the essay, it will be helpful if one is selected. The most useful of these four terms is "freedom," and it alone will be used to designate this part of the self system. The fourth category related to Kierkegaard's view of the structure of selfhood that will be used throughout the remainder of the essay is the "moment." In the moment, the other three components of selfhood are brought together, insofar as *possibility* is related to *actuality* through the *freedom* of decision.

Finally, it will be helpful to discontinue the use of the term "self system." This expression was necessitated by Kierkegaard's idiosyncratic equation of "self" with "spirit," "eternal," and with "freedom." This is a somewhat limited use of the term, and does not include all of the elements that Kierkegaard understands to be constitutive of selfhood. However, since we have selected "freedom" from among these equivalent terms, the word "self" is freed for a more general use. Throughout the rest of the essay, "self" will be used in place of "self system." This is a more common use of the term, and it should help to avoid confusion. The self, therefore, refers to the totality of the existing individual's personality. The major components of the self are: possibility, actuality, and freedom. This gives us a very much simplified, yet fully accurate form of the above diagram of the structure of selfhood.

The Self

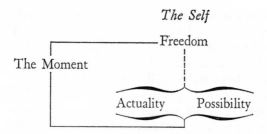

Of course, the self remains fully dependent upon God for its initial constitution and continued existence.

C. Life-time

In the first part of this chapter, we examined Kierkegaard's interpretation of spatialized time. We saw that Kierkegaard contends that spatialized time, which derives from a consideration of objects, is unable to comprehend human existence. Against this unsatisfactory view of time, he sets life-time, which is closely related to his understanding of the structure of selfhood. Having analyzed his interpretation of the structure of selfhood, we are in a position to consider the view of time that he thinks is able to comprehend human existence.

Kierkegaard argues that each of the three tenses of time is correlated with one of the components of the self. The past refers to the self's actuality, or to that which the self has become through sufferings and actions. The future is correlative with the possibility of the person. It is that which one can yet become, or that toward which one moves. The present is associated with the activity of the spirit, or with the engagement of freedom in the effort to actualize one's possibilities.

Because Kierkegaard sees such a close connection between the tenses of time and the structure of selfhood, he thinks that the tenses of time are not implied in the concept of time itself, and cannot be established by the examination of objects: "When one correctly defines time as infinite succession [*uendelige Succession*], it seems plausible to define it also as the present, the past, and the future. However this distinction is incorrect if one means by it that it is implied in time itself; for it first emerges with the relation of time to eternity and the reflection of eternity in it. If in the infinite succession of time one could in fact find a foothold, i.e., a present, which would serve as a dividing point, then this division would be quite correct. But precisely because every moment, like the sum of the moments, is a process (a going-by), no moment is a present, and in the same sense there is neither past, present, nor future."[77]

In this puzzling passage, Kierkegaard makes two important points. The first is a logical point, and the second is related to his understanding of the structure of selfhood. Concerning the logical point, he argues that if time is understood simply as infinite succession, it is impossible to speak of the tenses of time. There would be only incessant flux, or perpetual "going-by." However, "If in the infinite succession of time one could in fact find a foothold, i.e., a present, which would serve as a dividing point, then this division would be quite correct."[78] To attain such a "foothold" or "present" that would differen-

[77] *The Concept of Dread*, pp. 76-77; S.V., IV, 355.
[78] *Ibid.*, pp. 76-77; S.V., IV, 355.

tiate the past and the future, there would have to be duration. Kierkegaard seems to think that the infinite succession that he describes excludes any such duration, and therefore renders impossible the establishment of the tenses of time. For time to be tensed, there must be duration in addition to the continued alteration of infinite succession. Accordingly, time is not an incessant flux, a perpetual "going-by," or an unchanging presence, but a combination of mutability and duration. In other words, Kierkegaard holds that time is a synthesis of persistence and change. He tries to specify his awareness of the paradoxical union of alteration and duration in the temporal process by arguing that time is a synthesis of two heterogeneous factors — the unchanging and the changing, eternity and temporality.[79] Insofar as the unchanging (eternity) is brought into relation with the changing (infinite succession), a foothold or a present is established that differentiates the past and the future. Time always retains this paradoxical character for Kierkegaard.

Kierkegaard's second point in arguing that the distinction of the tenses of time "first emerges with the relation of time to eternity" is related to his understanding of the structure of selfhood. In his consideration of the components of the self, he equates eternity with freedom, and argues that the polar terms soul/body, infinitude/finitude, and possibility/necessity indicate aspects of the individual's temporality. Temporality and eternity are brought together in the self through the instant that is the moment of choice, or the moment in which freedom is exercised by relating possibilities and actuality. If these points are kept in mind, the above passage is more intelligible. The three tenses of time first emerge when freedom (eternity) is brought into relation with one's finitude and infinitude, or with one's actuality and possibility. The point that Kierkegaard is making here is very important. Time, understood as tensed, emerges *only* in connection with

[79] For a competent discussion of this issue, see Paul Dietrichson, "Kierkegaard's Concept of the Self," *Inquiry*, vol. VIII, 1965, pp. 6-7.

man's purposeful activity. As far as the non-human world is concerned, time remains a perpetual flux in which there is no differentiation of past, present, and future. Furthermore, it is impossible to derive an adequate conception of time from the observation of objects. It is the present, the moment in which freedom can be exercised, that differentiates the past (one's actuality) from the future (one's possibility). So understood, time is a reality that grows out of, and is related to, the lives of selves in the stance of purposeful activity. For Kierkegaard, time is properly grasped as life-time.

Kierkegaard's concern in developing his analysis of life-time is to arrive at a view of temporality in which time is not subordinated to the concept of space. He believes that his argument establishes an understanding of time that is able to comprehend human existence. For this reason, he thinks that his interpretation of time overcomes many of the shortcomings of the notion of time that had dominated much of Western philosophy.

D. Equilibrium

The purpose of this chapter has been to examine in general terms the two phenomena with which we will be concerned at each of the stages of existence — time and the self. By way of conclusion, we should note that from Kierkegaard's point of view, the very structure of selfhood poses the most fundamental task of human existence. The existing individual must seek to establish an equilibrium (*Ligevægt*)[80] or a balance among the various components of the self. Kierkegaard often makes this point by drawing attention to the etymology of the word "*Ligevægt.*" "*Ligevægt*" is a compound of "*lige,*" meaning like or equal, and "*vægt,*" meaning weight.[81] The problem

---

[80] See *The Sickness Unto Death*, pp. 146-147; S.V., XI, 127-128.

[81] See *The Gospel of Our Sufferings*, pp. 112-113; S.V., VIII, 386. Two other words that are used frequently in passages we have discussed are also interesting. "*Forhold*" (verb: "*forholde*") is the Danish word for "relation." But it can also be translated "proportion." In the relating activity that Kierkegaard calls the self, it is precisely the proper *propor-*

for the existing individual is to achieve a like weight, or a balance among the different dimensions of his self. Any form of existence that does not reach such an equilibrium is despair. Kierkegaard's understanding of the structure of selfhood and of the relationship among the components of the self informs his consideration of each of the stages of existence. For him, selves, as time itself, are tensed — they live in memory, in decision, and in hope. The problem for the temporal individual is to establish the appropriate relationship among the past, the present, and the future, i.e., among memory, decision, and hope. Kierkegaard's analysis of each of the stages of existence seeks to discern the various ways in which the components of the self are related to one another at each stage. He attempts to delineate the increasing realization of selfhood and the more complete recognition of the significance of time for the life of the self in the movement from the aesthetic through the ethical to the Christian stage of existence. Only at the final stage, Christianity, is it possible to establish an equilibrium among the components of the self, and to become fully aware of the importance of one's life-time. Having considered time and the self in general terms, we must now examine the specific characterizations of these phenomena at each stage of existence.

---

tion among the parts of the self system that is sought. *"Sygdom"* is the Danish word for "sickness." This can also be translated "disorder." Despair is the *sickness* unto death. As we have seen, despair is a *disorder* in the self, or a misordering of the different components of the self.

CHAPTER FOUR

THE AESTHETIC STAGE
OF EXISTENCE

A. General Features of Aestheticism

The aesthetic stage is, perhaps, the most misunderstood of the three Kierkegaardian stages of existence. Many commentators characterize aesthetic existence as the life of pleasure seeking. The aesthete, it is argued, is one who lives primarily for the purpose of gratifying his desires.[1] In the egoistic quest for pleasure, the aesthete is oblivious to moral obligation and to religious concerns. Another way of characterizing the aesthetic stage that finds support in secondary literature, is as the stance of theoretical speculation. A person is regarded primarily as an observer to whom objects become manifest. The aim of such a perspective is objective comprehension, rather than moral action or religious devotion.[2] These two views of the aesthetic stage seem to stand in tension with one another. On the one hand, the aesthetic stage is seen as a form of life in which one is governed by sensuous inclination, and, on the other hand, as a mode of existence dominated by objective thought. The interpretative task is further complicated when one recognizes that it is within his consideration of the aesthetic stage that Kierkegaard develops his criticisms of two of the major trends of thought during his time: romanticism and Hegelianism.

It must be acknowledged that there is an element of truth in each of these understandings of the aesthetic stage. The

[1] F. C. Fischer, *Existenz und Innerlichkeit: eine Einführung in die Gedankenwelt Sören Kierkegaards, op.cit.*, p. 17; and Martin Heinecken, *The Moment Before God, op.cit.*, pp. 247f.

[2] For an instance of this line of argument, see Stephen Crites, "Introduction," *Crisis in the Life of an Actress, op.cit.*, pp. 19-28.

problem with secondary interpretations has been that they have stressed either the dominance of sensuous inclination or of theoretical speculation to the exclusion of the other. As a matter of fact, the aesthetic stage is composed of two poles: immediacy and reflection. The failure of analysts to recognize the bipolarity of the aesthetic stage, and the propensity to analyze only one of the two poles,[3] has necessarily resulted in the failure to arrive at a satisfactory view of the stage that encompasses both sensual immediacy and theoretical cognition. The possibility of discerning what Kierkegaard regards as the common element in sensual immediacy and in theoretical reflection is established by recognizing that *the most fundamental characteristic of the aesthetic stage of existence is the absence of decision.* At the aesthetic stage, freedom is not exercised through the individual's personal decision:[4] "But what is it to live aesthetically, and what is it to live ethically? What is the aesthetical in man, and what is the ethical? To this I would reply: the aesthetical in man is that by which he is immediately what he is; the ethical is that whereby he becomes what he becomes. He who lives in and by and of and for the aesthetical in him lives aesthetically."[5]

To understand this quotation, and hence to begin to grasp the general character of the aesthetic stage, it is necessary to understand the word "immediate(ly)." In the simplest terms, Kierkegaard means by immediacy: "that which is not mediated." But immediacy can take different forms: the immediate can be that which is not mediated either by reflection, or by decision, or by both. The immediate pole of the aesthetic stage is, as will be seen in more detail, governed by the absence of both decision and its necessary (but not sufficient) condition, reflection. At the reflective pole, reflection is evi-

---

[3] Crites' consideration of the aesthetic stage cited above does not succumb to this error.

[4] Reidar Thomte quite incorrectly holds that the aesthete's domain is that of action, while that of the Hegelian philosophers is contemplation. *Kierkegaard's Philosophy of Religion, op.cit.*, p. 33.

[5] *Either-Or*, II, p. 182; S.V., II, 161.

dently present. However, there remains a lack of decision. Therefore at neither pole of the aesthetic stage is there decision. This is what Kierkegaard means when he says that the aesthetic "is that by which [a person] is immediately what he is." What a person is "immediately" (i.e., un-mediatedly) is a function of that which does not result from his own decisions. One's body, mental ability, physical talents, family, etc. would be examples of such aspects of the self. The aesthete, therefore, is what he is by virtue of circumstances that lie outside the realm of his self-determination. He cannot "become what he becomes" because it is precisely decision that issues in such becoming.

A serious consequence follows from the absence of decision at the aesthetic stage. Those who live at the aesthetic stage of existence cannot properly be called actual selves. Kierkegaard's argument at this juncture rests upon his conviction that self-conscious decision is the means by which the actuality of the self is constituted. As will become apparent, one must even accept responsibility (through decision) for what is suffered. Surely one could go through life relying on his natural endowments, but if one never came to a clear understanding of these endowments and acknowledged and accepted them as one's own, one could never be called a self on Kierkegaard's terms. This is the point of one of Kierkegaard's general statements about the aesthetic stage:[6] "Great as the difference within the aesthetic domain may be, all the stages have this similarity, that spirit is not determined as spirit, but is immediately determined. The differences may be extraordinary, all the way from complete stupidity [*Aandløshed*] to the highest degree of cleverness [*Aandrighed*], but even at the stage where cleverness is evident, the spirit [*Aanden*] is not determined as spirit, but as talent [*Gave*]."[7]

Because there is no exercise of the will in self-determining

[6] It will be recalled from the third chapter that Kierkegaard uses "spirit" (*Aand*) and "self" interchangeably. In this text, substitute "self" for "spirit" and the argument will be clearer.

[7] *Either-Or*, ii, p. 185; S.V., ii, 163-164.

decision at the aesthetic stage, there is, for Kierkegaard, no actual self. Rather, the self is determined as "talent." Here Kierkegaard plays on the nuances of the Danish word for talent, "*Gave.*" "*Gave*" is related to the past tense of "to give," "*gav.*" Furthermore, "*Gave*" can also be translated as "present," "gift," "endowment," or "donation." "*Gave*" refers to the dimension of the self that is given, and that has not developed through the individual's own decisions.

At two points in *The Sickness Unto Death*, Kierkegaard makes it especially clear that the failure freely to exercise one's will issues in the absence of the actuality of the self: "The more consciousness, the more the self; the more consciousness, the more will, and the more will, the more self. A man who has no will at all is no self; the more will he has, the more consciousness of self he also has."[8] "Insofar as the self does not become itself, it is not its own self. . . ."[9] As should be apparent, Kierkegaard understands decision to be the self-conscious exercise of the will. Therefore, self-consciousness is necessary for decision to be possible. Because self-consciousness has not yet developed at the immediate aesthetic stage, decision is impossible. At the reflective pole, self-consciousness has begun to emerge, but the will still has not been engaged. Kierkegaard claims, "Insofar as the self does not become itself, it is not its own self."

It is, therefore, the absence of decision that links the two seemingly contradictory poles of the aesthetic stage. However, as the names of the poles indicate, there are different ways in which one can forego decision: either through the immersion in sensuous inclination, through immediate identification with the social-natural environment, or through the evaporation of the either-or of decision in infinite reflection. In the conclusion of the last chapter, we saw that Kierkegaard thinks a fundamental task of selfhood is the maintenance of an equilibrium among the different components of the self. At each pole of the aesthetic stage, a disequilibrium within

[8] *The Sickness Unto Death*, p. 162; S.V., xi, 142.
[9] *Ibid.*, p. 163; S.V., xi, 143.

the self persists. When one is primarily governed by sensuous desire or is not differentiated from the social-natural environment, there is an overemphasis on the component of actuality within the self. When one is ensnared in ceaseless reflection, there is too great a stress on the element of possibility within the self. It is necessary to examine each of these poles of the aesthetic stage.

B. Immediacy: Life in Actuality

As we begin our analysis of the stages of existence, two important points must be recalled. In the first place, we have argued that the stages are best understood both as representations of ideal personality types and as the phases through which the developing self passes. In this section of the chapter, we will consider the immediate pole of the aesthetic stage first as one of the phases through which the self passes on its way to maturity, and then as an ideal personality type. In the second place, it has been claimed that Kierkegaard arranges the stages of existence so that there is an increasing individuation or further realization of individual selfhood as one moves both from one to another stage, and as one moves through any single stage. In addition to this, as one passes from the aesthetic through the ethical to the religious stage, there is a deeper recognition of the significance of time for the life of the self. If this analysis is correct, it would follow that at the first stage of existence there would be the least emphasis on time, and the least realization of the self, or minimal individuation.

All selves begin their development at the immediate pole of the aesthetic stage. It is possible for one never to advance beyond this point, but to live his entire life within the categories that characterize immediacy.[10] Kierkegaard points to the fact that all persons begin life at the immediate pole by his repeated identification of childhood with immediacy.[11]

[10] The general nature of such a person will be discussed below.
[11] See *De Omnibus Dubitandum Est*, p. 147; *Papirer*, IV, 145; *Either-*

The immediate pole of the aesthetic stage is to be understood in the first instance as descriptive of the initial stage of the development of the child.[12] Immediacy antedates the development of reflection in the infant. At this stage one is fundamentally governed by natural desire, seeking pleasure and avoiding pain. The infant is not an individuated self, for differentiation between the self and the environment has not yet taken place. In an important passage that we have previously noted, Kierkegaard argues:

"And yet child-life and youth-life are dream-life, for the innermost thing, that which in the deepest sense is man, slumbers. The child is completely turned outward, its inwardness is extraversion, and to that extent the child is wide awake. But for a man, to be awake means to be eternally turned inward in inwardness, and so the child is dreaming, it dreams itself sensuously at one with everything [*drømmer sig sandseligt sammen med Alt*], almost to the extent of confounding itself with the sense impression [*forvexler sig selv med Sandse-Indtrykket*]. In comparison with the child, the youth is more turned inward, but in imagination; he dreams, or it is as though everything about him were dreaming. On the other hand, he who in the sense of eternity is turned inward perceives only what is of the spirit, and for the rest he is like a sleeper, an absentee, a dead man, with respect to the perceptions of flesh and blood, of the temporal, of the imaginative — in him the spirit is awake, the lower functions sleep; hence he is awake. Dream-life is so denominated with a view to the nobler part — in waking man the spirit wakes, whereas there is doubtless something which sleeps, namely, the lower part. In the child and in the youth it is the spirit that sleeps, the

---

Or, i, pp. 69, 146; S.V., i, 53, 126; *The Point of View*, p. 81; S.V., xiii, 567; *The Sickness Unto Death*, pp. 238-39; S.V., xi, 211-212; *Stages on Life's Way*, p. 59; S.V., vi, 48; and *Works of Love*, pp. 199-200; S.V., ix, 201.

[12] Croxall mentions in passing the parallel between the immediacy of the aesthete and the life of the infant. See *Kierkegaard Studies, op.cit.*, p. 68.

lower part is awake; nevertheless, as it is the determining character of spirit to be awake, this life is called dream-life."[13]

The initial phase of the self's development is called "dream-life" because "that which in the deepest sense is man [i.e., the self] slumbers." The child "dreams itself sensuously at one with everything, almost to the extent of confounding itself with sense-impression." This is one of Kierkegaard's clearest statements concerning the undifferentiated character of the self in the state of immediacy. One is purely dominated by desire at this stage. The identification with desire is so strong that one virtually "confounds himself with the sense-impression." But such a condition in man is markedly different from an animal existence, for the self is present, though in a dreaming or an undifferentiated state. Within the context of elaborating his understanding of the fall, Kierkegaard makes the following point: "In the state of innocence man is not merely an animal, for if at any time of his life he were merely an animal, he would never become a man. So then the spirit is present, but in a state of immediacy, a dreaming state."[14]

During the first phase of life, the world is experienced as a ceaseless flux of sense impressions. One cannot distinguish various perceptions clearly, and is unable to separate one's self from the world that one experiences. Both self and world (not-self) are fully indefinite: "How then is the child's consciousness to be described? It is essentially quite indefinite, a fact we can also state by saying that it is 'immediate.' *Immediacy is indefiniteness [Umiddelbarheden er netop Ube-*

---

[13] "The Joy of It — That Affliction Does not Bereave of Hope, But Recruits Hope," *Christian Discourses*, p. 113; S.V., x, 113. As in other cases, this text is clarified by remembering that "spirit" and "self" can be used interchangeably.

[14] *The Concept of Dread*, p. 39; S.V., IV, 315. Compare: ". . . even though man is spirit from the moment of birth he first becomes conscious as spirit later, and therefore prior to this he has lived for a certain time within sensuous-psychic categories. The first portion of life shall not, however, be cast aside when the spirit awakens . . . The first portion is taken over by spirit, and is thus used, thus laid at base, it *becomes transferred [overførte]*." *Works of Love*, p. 199; S.V., IX, 201.

stemmetheden]. In immediacy relationships are absent; for as soon as relationships exist, immediacy is annulled."[15] At the immediate pole of the aesthetic stage, all is "indefinite" because the self is as yet undifferentiated. Since there is no differentiated self, there can be no relationships. For relationships to be possible, there must be two clearly distinguished selves who can come together.

In addition to the lack of a clearly differentiated self, there is another important characteristic of the immediate aesthetic. In immediacy, one is fully determined by desire, or by sensuous inclination. There is, in fact, no exercise of freedom, for the infant is the reflex of desire.[16] Pleasure and pain are dominant categories in this mode of life. In specific terms, the infant has a spontaneous affinity for pleasurable experiences and an aversion to painful ones. Life is governed by desire, or guided by the principle of pleasure. For Kierkegaard, however, desire is a complex phenomenon that he subjects to a detailed examination. The recognition of the sophistication of his understanding of desire makes it evident that we have not indicated sufficiently the intricacy of his analysis of the immediate pole of the aesthetic stage. Up to this point, we have spoken of immediacy as if it were a single, undivided stage of development. But this is not accurate. As Kierkegaard makes clear in his essay in the first volume of *Either-Or* entitled "The Immediate Stages of the Erotic," there are

[15] *Johannes Climacus or, De Omnibus Dubitandum Est*, p. 147; *Papirer*, IV, 145.

[16] Compare Hegel: "In the same way, Spirit is only that into which it makes itself, and it makes itself actually into that which it is in itself (potentially). The development of the organism proceeds in an immediate (direct, undialectic), unhindered manner. Nothing can interfere between the concept and its realization, the inherent nature of the germ and the adaptation of its existence to its nature. It is different with spirit. The transition of its potentiality into actuality is mediated through consciousness and will. These are themselves first immersed in their immediate organic life; their first object and purpose of this natural existence as such. But the latter, through its animation by Spirit becomes itself infinitely demanding, rich, and strong." "Reason in History," *op.cit.*, p. 69.

actually three sub-stages within the immediate pole. Furthermore at the point of departure for the entire dialectic of the stages, he presents a stage which in structure and in the general direction of its movement is a microcosm of the entire dialectic.

The three sub-stages within the immediate aesthetic are very closely related, for they have no independent existence, but together comprise the larger whole that is called "immediacy." Within these closely related stages, each leads directly to the next and all culminate in the third stage, which is the most complete expression of immediacy: "The different stages taken together constitute the immediate stage, and from this we may perceive that the individual stages are rather a revelation of a predicate, so that all the predicates rush down into the wealth of the last stage. The other stages have no independent existence; in and of themselves they exist only as parts of a conceptual scheme, and from this one may see their accidental character as over against the last stage...."[17]

In very general terms, this represents the tripartite structure of the whole dialectic. There are three stages of existence that are very closely related. Each stage consistently (though not necessarily) leads to the next. Only at the third stage — Christian religion — are the full implications of selfhood adequately explicated, and is a genuine equilibrium of the components of the self achieved. However, it is important to recognize another similarity between the dialectic as a whole and the dialectic of the immediate aesthetic. We have seen that one way in which the progression of the stages of existence can be characterized is as the movement of increasing

---

[17] *Either-Or*, I, p. 73; S.V., I, 56. By "accidental" [*Tilfældighed*] Kierkegaard emphasizes that the stages of the aesthetic do not have independent existence, but persist only as parts of the larger whole that he calls the immediate aesthetic.

Certainly one should not overlook the Hegelian overtones of this passage, or when extrapolated from the immediate aesthetic to the whole dialectic of existence, the Hegelian overtones of the entire dialectic.

individuation (or differentiation) in which the self moves from the undifferentiated identification with the environment to full individuation as a responsible individual standing before God. The movement within the three stages of the immediate aesthetic is also characterized by a progressive differentiation. In these stages, a gradual distinction is established between the principle of desire and the object desired. It is necessary to look at this process in more detail.

We have seen that domination by desire is a general characteristic of the immediate aesthetic. But Kierkegaard presents a detailed analysis of human desire. He argues that there can be no desire in the proper sense of the word unless there is a distinction between desire and what is desired: "This impulse with which desire [*Attraaten*] awakens, this trembling, separates the desire and its object, affords desire an object. This is a dialectical qualification that must be kept sharply in mind — only when the object exists does desire exist, only when the desire exists does the object exist; desire and its object are twins, neither is born a fraction of an instant before the other."[18] The distinction between desire and the object of desire emerges only gradually. As a matter of fact, it is just the lack of a clear distinction between these two factors that is the primary feature of the first stage of the immediate aesthetic. Kierkegaard uses three of Mozart's musical compositions to indicate each of the three stages of the immediate aesthetic.[19] In order they are: *Figaro, The Magic Flute*, and *Don Juan*.

At the first stage of the immediate aesthetic, desire is not properly determined as desire. In keeping with passages examined above, Kierkegaard holds that at this stage "desire is *dreaming*."[20] Interestingly enough, he repeatedly uses sexual language when describing this condition. In discussing the Page in Mozart's *Figaro*, he states: "In harmony with the

[18] *Ibid.*, p. 78; S.V., I, 61.

[19] The reason for Kierkegaard's consistent use of music to indicate the immediate aesthetic will become apparent in what follows.

[20] *Either-Or*, I, p. 79; S.V., I, 62.

description of the first stage given here, we shall find it very significant that the Page's part is so arranged musically that it always lies within the range of a female voice. The contradictory in this stage is, as it were, suggested by this contradiction, the desire is so indefinite, its object so little separated from it, that the object of desire rests androgynously [*androgynisk*] within the desire, just as in plant life the male and the female parts are both present in one blossom. Desire and its object are joined in this unity, that they both are of neuter gender."[21]

At this stage of development there is the least differentiation between the self and the not-self. Even the most basic distinction of sexuality has not yet emerged. The infant is, as it were, carried along in a stream of sensuality. But there is as yet no desiring, for there has not even been enough differentiation to enable a distinction between desire and the object of desire to be made: "Desire possesses what will become its object, but possesses it without having desired it, and so does not possess it. . . . Its pain lies not in there being too little, but rather in there being too much. The desire is quiet desire, the longing quiet longing, the ecstasy quiet ecstasy, wherein the object of desire is dawning, and is so near that it is within the desire."[22]

At the second stage of the immediate aesthetic, the distinction between desire and what is desired develops. The initial distinction between these two is experienced as a keen sense of separation from that to which one wishes to be united. The response is, of course, to seek reunion with the object of desire. With this development, the "quiet longing" of the first stage becomes a restless quest to secure what has been lost:

[21] *Ibid.*, pp. 75-76; S.V., I, 58-59.
[22] *Ibid.*, p. 74; S.V., I, 57. Compare: "Hence the desire, which in this stage is present only as a presentiment about itself, is without movement, without disquiet, only gently rocked by an unclarified inner emotion. As the life of the plant is bound to the earth, so is desire lost in a present quiet longing, buried in contemplation, and yet cannot evacuate its object, because essentially in a deeper sense, there is no object," p. 75; S.V., I, 58.

"But this movement of the sensuous, this earthquake, splits the desire and its object infinitely asunder for the moment; but as the moving principle appears a moment separating, so it again reveals itself as wishing to unite the separated. The result of this separation is that desire is pulled out of its substantial repose within itself, and consequently the object no longer falls under the qualifications of substantiality, but disperses itself in a manifold [*Mangfoldighed*]."[23]

The important points to note in connection with the second stage of the immediate aesthetic are two: first, there is a differentiation between desire and its object; second, the object of desire has not been clearly defined, but remains a "manifold." The latter point leads Kierkegaard to contend that desire is still not properly present at this stage. Rather, desire is here qualified as "seeking" [*søgende*]:[24] "It [desire] does not find the precise object of this search, but discovers the manifold, as it seeks therein the object it would discover."[25] This phase of the development of the self designates the juncture at which the infant has begun to distinguish himself from the flow of sense impressions. There is a dawning awareness of a difference between self and other, but such self-differentiation has only begun. In the first place, there is as yet no *self*-consciousness. Indeed, there is no consciousness at all. Furthermore, there is no differentiation made within the stream of experience itself. There cannot, therefore, be any specific object of desire. The mode in which the difference between self and other is experienced is not cognitive but affective. It comes about through the development of desire as a consequence of the absence of the desired.

At the third stage of immediacy, desire is fully determined as "desiring" [*attraaende*][26] by the consolidation of the manifold into a concrete object of desire. In highly Hegelian terms, Kierkegaard offers what is at once an able summary of the relationship among the three stages of immediacy and a clear characterization of the third stage: "The contradiction

---

[23] *Ibid.*, pp. 78-79; S.V., i, 62.   [24] *Ibid.*, p. 79; S.V., i, 62.
[25] *Ibid.*, p. 79; S.V., i, 62.   [26] *Ibid.*, p. 79; S.V., i, 62.

of the first stage lay in the fact that desire could acquire no object, but without having desired was in possession of its object, and therefore could not reach the point of desiring. In the second stage, the object appears in its manifold, but as desire seeks its object in this manifold, it still has, in a deeper sense, no object, it is not yet posited as desire. In *Don Juan*, on the other hand, desire is absolutely determined as desire, it is, in an intensive and extensive sense, the immediate synthesis of the two preceding stages. The first stage desired the one ideally, the second stage desired the particular under the qualification of the manifold; the third stage is a synthesis of these two. Desire has its object in the particular, it desires the particular absolutely."[27] At this stage the manifold, in which the desired object had been sought at the second stage, is refined into a particular, concrete object. Now the necessary conditions for desire properly so-called have been met. Desire and its object are distinguished. One might understand this stage in the development of the self as the point at which the infant becomes aware of the specific object of his desire. He now wants the mother's breast or the bottle.

Two important qualifications must be added. In the first place, at none of the three stages of immediacy does consciousness develop. The immediate aesthetic in its entirety is pre-reflective. Kierkegaard comments on the stages of immediacy: "Above all, however, one must avoid considering them as different degrees of consciousness, since even the last stage has not yet arrived at consciousness. I have always to do only with the immediate in its sheer immediacy."[28]

With the development of consciousness, one progresses to the reflective pole of the aesthetic stage. Moreover, as will be seen, it is precisely the development of reflection that annuls immediacy. Secondly, even at the third stage of the immediate aesthetic, it is incorrect to say that there has emerged an autonomous individual who stands in relation to a concrete object of desire. Kierkegaard's primary concern is to understand the phenomenon of desire. At this stage the person re-

[27] *Ibid.*, p. 83; S.V., I, 66-67. [28] *Ibid.*, p. 73; S.V., I, 56.

mains an embodiment of the force that is called desire. The dialectic of the immediate aesthetic discloses the developing distinction between the power of desire and the object desired. The self at this stage has not been differentiated from the desire whose embodiment it is. For such differentiation to take place, both reflection and decision must develop. These are reached only at later stages. While the stages of immediacy are necessary to the gradual differentiation of the self, a full differentiation is not yet accomplished.

When Kierkegaard's immediate aesthetic is understood as a stage through which the developing self passes, and is characterized in the preceding manner, significant parallels between his argument and later psychological theories of personality are apparent. The phase of development that Kierkegaard is describing is what Freud and his followers call the oral stage.[29] There are two primary characteristics of the oral stage that are important for our purposes. In the first place, at this stage the id is the dominant force in the personality. The infant is ruled by desire or, in Freud's terms, the "Pleasure Principle" has ascendancy. The child naturally seeks to maximize pleasure and to minimize pain. In the second place, initially there is no differentiation between the infant and his world. Both prior to and immediately after birth, the child remains closely identified with its surroundings. For the fetus, there is no fundamental distinction from the organism of the mother; the self and the not-self are one. But even after birth, the differentiation of the child from the environment progresses only slowly. Freud, as Kierkegaard, sees that the first break in the immediate identity of the child and its world is the consequence of the frustration of desire. In the pre-

[29] The only other authors of whom I am aware who even hint at parallels between Kierkegaard and Freud on this issue are: J. Preston Cole, "The Function of Choice in Human Existence," *Journal of Religion*, vol. 45, pp. 196-210, and *The Problematic Self in Freud and Kierkegaard* (New Haven: Yale University Press, 1972); and James E. Loder, *Religious Pathology and Christian Faith* (Philadelphia: The Westminster Press, 1966). The argument of this book, however, differs substantially from these works.

natal stage, the desires of the fetus are instantly gratified; desire and its object are unseparated. With birth, however, such gratification of desire ceases, and an interval between desire and fulfillment is established. In this "earthquake," the process of individuation begins. Desire is separated from its object, and longs to restore the lost unity. The pain incurred by the separation of desire is expressed in crying and other manifestations of displeasure. It should be noted that the infant is not yet clearly aware of what it desires. The child does not know that it wants the mother's breast or the bottle. This awareness develops gradually. From the previously undifferentiated sensational flux emerges the particular object of desire. For Freud, as for Kierkegaard, even at this juncture, the infant remains under the control of id forces and has not yet advanced to the state of self-consciousness.[30]

We have seen, however, that the stages of existence are not only to be understood as the phases through which the developing self passes, but also should be interpreted as ideal personality types, or as descriptive of different life-views. Furthermore, these two understandings of the stages are related insofar as Kierkegaard believes that the self's development can be retarded at any stage. While this certainly does not mean that a person might actually remain an infant for his whole life, it does mean that a grown person can be childlike. Those features which characterize the life of the child can dominate the life of an adult. For example, an adult's entire life can be governed by the search for pleasure, or he can live his whole life without ever becoming fully conscious of his own individuality as distinguished from and opposed to the social matrix of which he is a part. In both instances no true *self*-consciousness has emerged, and no genuine decisions are

---

[30] For the development of these issues, see Freud, *The Ego and the Id*, trans. by Joan Riviere (New York: W. W. Norton and Co., 1960); Erik Erikson, *Childhood and Society* (New York: W. W. Norton and Co., 1963); *Identity and the Life Cycle* (New York: International Press, Inc., 1968); and *Identity, Youth, and Crisis* (New York: W. W. Norton and Co., 1968).

made. The person remains a reflex of either the force of desire or his social environment. Let us look at each of these alternatives in turn.

Don Juan, as presented in Mozart's opera by the same name, is Kierkegaard's ideal type of person whose life is governed by the effort to satisfy pleasure. He is what Kierkegaard calls the "sensuous-erotic genius."[31] In dealing with the figure of Don Juan, however, Kierkegaard encounters problems. The basis for most of the difficulties lies in the fact that for Kierkegaard, Don Juan is not an individual, but an ideal expression of the power of sensuousness: "Here we do not hear Don Juan as a particular individual, nor his speech, but we hear a voice, the voice of sensuousness, and we hear it through the longing of womanhood. Only in this manner can Don Juan become epic, in that he constantly finishes, and constantly begins again from the beginning, for his life is the sum of repellent moments that have no coherence, his life as moment is the sum of the moments, as the sum of the moments it is the moment."[32]

Certainly Don Juan, and those who live according to the principles ideally represented by Don Juan, appear within the opera as particular individuals. But Kierkegaard thinks it incorrect to call such persons selves, for they have no clear self-consciousness and they make no definite decisions. They are not self-determining, but are embodiments of a force, or of a power, that fully determines them. As Kierkegaard says of Don Juan, he "is, then, if I dare say so, flesh incarnate, or the inspiration of the flesh by the spirit of the flesh":[33] "If I imagine a particular individual, if I see him [Don Juan] or hear him speak, then it becomes comic to imagine that he has seduced 1,003; for as soon as he is regarded as a particular individual, the accent falls in quite another place. When, on the contrary, he is interpreted in music, then I do not have a

---

[31] *Either-Or*, I, p. 86; S.V., I, 69.   [32] *Ibid.*, p. 95; S.V., I, 77.

[33] *Ibid.*, p. 87; S.V., I, 70. Compare: "His [Don Juan's] power to deceive lies in the essential genius of his *sensuousness, whose incarnation he really is.*" P. 99; S.V., I, 73. Italics added.

particular individual, but I have the power of nature, the demonic, which as little tires of seducing or is done with seducing as the wind is tired of blowing, the sea tired of billowing, or a waterfall of tumbling downward from the heights."[34]

By understanding Don Juan as "flesh incarnate" or as a "power of nature," one is enabled to comprehend his association with women. As distinguished from a seducer, who will be discussed under the reflective aesthetic, Don Juan does not lay elaborate plans for the conquest of women. To do so would require detailed reflection, and this is just what Don Juan lacks. Don Juan simply overpowers women through the natural force whose embodiment he is. Therefore, even those with whom Don Juan comes into contact are not self-conscious persons so far as Don Juan's awareness goes, but are extensions of the natural power ideally present in Don Juan.[35]

It is important for our purposes to stress that for Don Juan it is the moment of sensual pleasure that is of concern. He is interested in neither preparations nor consequences, but focuses all of his efforts on the climactic moment: "To see her and to love her is the same thing; it is in the moment, in the same moment everything is over, and the same thing repeats itself endlessly."[36] As quickly as one erotic adventure has culminated, Don Juan abandons the seduced and seeks another outlet for his sensuous energy. His life manifests no continuity, but constantly seeks the new, or the different: "Psychical love is a continuance in time, sensuous love a disappearance in time, but the medium which exactly expresses this is music. Music is excellently fitted to accomplish this,

[34] *Ibid.*, p. 91; S.V., I, 73-74.

[35] Stephen Crites makes this point: "But the hero of the immediate is Don Juan, whose eroticism is frequently referred to as a force of nature, guileless, direct, and overpowering. The characters in the opera, including even the particular figure of Don Juan, himself, are not so much consciously self-determined individuals as satellites whirled about in the magnetic field of Juan's sheer erotic power, which is expressed in the music." "Introduction" to *Crisis in the Life of an Actress, op.cit.*, p. 35.

[36] *Either-Or*, I, p. 93; S.V., I, 75-76.

since it is far more abstract than language, and therefore does not express the individual but the general in all its generality, and yet it expresses the general not in reflective abstraction, but in the immediate concrete."[37]

The reference to music in this passage raises an important point. It is no accident that Kierkegaard selects Mozart's *Don Juan* as representative of immediacy. Kierkegaard believes that the only medium that can adequately express the immediate aesthetic is music. This view rests on his basically Hegelian theory of aesthetics according to which each medium has one particular idea that it can most perfectly express.[38] Because music is the medium from which reflection is the farthest removed, it ideally embodies the idea of the sensuous erotic genius. Moreover, music is able to express movement. It can capture the successiveness in which a Don Juan abruptly moves from one sensual adventure to another, but never experiences a continuity either within his own self, or among the various experiences of which he is a part:

"The most abstract idea conceivable is sensuous genius. But in what medium is this idea expressible? Solely in music. It cannot be expressed in sculpture, for it is a sort of inner qualification of inwardness; nor in painting, for it cannot be apprehended in precise outlines; it is an energy, a story, impatience, passion, and so on, in all their lyrical quality, yet so that it does not exist in one moment but in a succession of moments, for if it existed in a single moment, it could be modeled or painted . . . it has not yet advanced to words, but moves always in immediacy."[39]

[37] *Ibid.*, p. 94; S.V., I, 76.

[38] For a very good brief summary of Kierkegaard's aesthetic theory, see Stephen Crites, "Introduction" to *Crisis in the Life of an Actress, op.cit.*, section iii, pp. 28-36.

[39] *Either-Or*, I, p. 55; S.V., I, 40. Compare: "In *Don Juan* the keynote is nothing other than the primitive power in the opera itself; this is Don Juan, but again — just because he is not character but essentially life — he is absolutely musical," p. 118. It is important to recognize the connection between these remarks and the foregoing comments about the

Don Juan is, therefore, Kierkegaard's ideal representation of a person who lives his life entirely within the categories most prevalent during the initial phase of the development of the self — pleasure and pain. Neither self-consciousness nor self-determination through free decision has yet emerged. Although desire has been distinguished from its object, the self remains in an undifferentiated state, a reflex or embodiment of sensuousness, a force of nature. Life is lived fully within the necessary, or the actual component of the self.

Kierkegaard's analysis of the immediate aesthetic is not, however, exhausted by his consideration of Don Juan. There is another important type of personality that he includes within this general category — the crowd-man.[40] The crowd-man is one who lives his whole life without ever becoming fully conscious of his own individuality as distinct from the social and natural environment of which he is a part. Given the character of the immediate aesthetic as developed above, it might seem problematic to include a person such as the crowd-man within this category. Some explanation is, therefore, in order.

Certainly the crowd-man represents a very different sort of person from Don Juan. He is, as a matter of fact, an ideal representation of the average citizen — the established member of the bourgeois world in Kierkegaard's Copenhagen. He is the person who is born into a family of adequate circumstance, and who diligently follows the rules laid down by society so that he will become a well-respected bourgeois citizen. A person such as this is surely far removed from the

---

immediate aesthetic as descriptive of infancy. Kierkegaard writes ". . . the child's first babbling syllables are musical," p. 68; S.V., I, 51.

[40] The word that Kierkegaard consistently uses for "crowd" is "*Mængde.*" The term "crowd-man" is selected to draw to mind Heidegger's category of "*das Man.*" Here, as in so many other places, Kierkegaard's analysis substantially anticipates Heidegger's. It is Heidegger, however, who is more commonly associated with the perception of this phenomenon.

pleasure-seeking dilettante depicted by Don Juan. However, in Kierkegaard's view, there are important similarities between the two.

The most fundamental characteristic of the aesthetic stage as a whole has been seen to be the absence of decision. As long as one remains at the aesthetic stage of existence, there is no clear recognition of one's self as a concrete center of consciousness distinct from all else that is, and capable of initiating purposeful activity. How this is so for a figure like Don Juan is relatively apparent. Because sensuous inclination dominates his life, self-consciousness and self-determination never find expression. The matter is somewhat more complicated with the crowd-man. Such a person might be, for example, a powerful businessman who is daily engaged in making important financial "decisions." But according to Kierkegaard, these deeds are not necessarily decisions. For the most part, the crowd-man represents an extension of the social and natural world of which he is a part. He has not clearly distinguished himself from that matrix, and therefore his conduct is less a function of free self-determination than the reflex of his given environment. An example of the type of person Kierkegaard has in mind is the young man who had always wanted to be a doctor because his father had been a doctor. Although he might have labored hard throughout high school and college to get into a good medical school, and thereby to enter the medical profession, one could not properly say that he had decided to become a doctor. Kierkegaard's comment about another example could aptly be applied to this instance: "He now acquires some little understanding of life, he learns to imitate the other men, noting how they manage to live, and so he too lives after a sort. In Christendom he too is a Christian, goes to church every Sunday, hears and understands the parson, yea, they understand one another; he dies; the parson introduces him into eternity for the price of $10 — but a self he was not, and a self he did not become."[41] Such conduct is

[41] *The Sickness Unto Death*, p. 186; S.V., xi, 165.

not, for Kierkegaard, free and self-conscious decision, but is the determination of the self by external forces. This, he believes, is the death of the self.[42]

Another way of putting this point is to say that the crowd-man and Don Juan are similar in that for both there is a preponderance of the actuality or the necessity of the self. For Don Juan this actuality is experienced as a domination by given, natural impulses. For the crowd-man, this actuality or necessity is the constant control of his life by powers external to himself, most notably his social world. For the crowd-man, no less than for Don Juan, there is no self-conscious decision. As a matter of fact, for the crowd-man too, *self*-consciousness has not developed. It might seem strange to argue that the well-known bourgeois citizen is not self-conscious, but Kierkegaard insists that this is the case. The crowd-man has not come to a clear consciousness of himself as distinguished from his surroundings. Therefore his self has not become individuated, but remains in a state of undifferentiation.[43]

[42] To understand Kierkegaard's point more clearly, compare the following passage to one from Heidegger. "If he forgets to take account of the headway, there comes at last an instant when there no longer is any question of an either/or, not because he has chosen but because he has neglected to choose, which is equivalent to saying, because others have chosen for him, he has lost his self." *Either-Or*, II, p. 168; S.V., II, 149.

"The 'they' always kept *Dasein* from taking hold of these possibilities of Being. The 'they' even hide the manner in which it has tacitly relieved *Dasein* of the burden of explicitly *choosing* these possibilities. It remains indefinite who has 'really' done the choosing. So *Dasein* makes no choice, gets carried along by the nobody, and thus ensnares itself in inauthenticity." *Being and Time, op.cit.*, p. 312.

[43] As will become evident in what follows, many of Kierkegaard's views regarding the crowd-man bear a relation to Hegel's arguments. Compare the following comment from Hegel to Kierkegaard's position: "Hence, further, the individual, as he immediately finds his existence in the actual objective social order in the life of his nation, has a solid imperturbable confidence; the universal mind has not for him resolved itself into its abstract moments, and thus, too, he does not think of

In the context of Kierkegaard's discussion of Hegel's conception of Socrates in his early work, *The Concept of Irony,* one can see the beginnings of Kierkegaard's analysis of the crowd-man.[44] The following remark is made in the course of his discussion of Hegel's view of Socrates: "In older Hellenism the individual was not at all free in this sense, but was implicated in the substantial concrete ethic; he had not yet taken himself, not yet separated himself from this condition of immediacy, did not yet know himself."[45] This comment can be applied to the crowd-man. The crowd-man is not free in the sense of being a self-conscious center of self-determination because he has not yet "taken himself out, not yet separated himself" from his identification with his environment. Such identity with the social and natural matrix represents a form of "immediacy." Thus he does "not yet know himself." "The expression 'know thyself' means: separate yourself from the 'other.' Inasmuch as prior to Socrates this self did not

himself as existing in singleness and independence. When however he has once arrived at this knowledge, as indeed he must, this immediate unity with mind, this undifferentiated existence in the substance of mind, his naive confidence, is lost. Isolated by himself he is himself now the central essential reality — no longer universal mind. The element of this singleness of self-consciousness is no doubt in universal mind itself, but merely as a vanishing quantity, which, as it appears with an existence of its own, is straightway resolved within the universal, and only becomes consciously felt in the form of that confidence. When the individual gets fixity in the form of singleness (and every moment, being a moment of the essential reality, must manage to reveal itself as essential), the individual has thereby set himself over against the law and customs. These latter are looked on as merely a thought without absolutely essential significance, an abstract theory without reality; while he, qua this particular ego, is in his own view the living truth." *Phenomenology,* p. 379. As can be seen in the lines immediately following this text, Hegel thinks this development took place historically in the person of Socrates.

[44] Some of these points were considered in chapter two in the demonstration that one of the ways in which Kierkegaard's stages could be understood is as descriptions of historical epochs.

[45] *The Concept of Irony,* p. 248; S.V., xiii, 306.

exist, so the pronouncement of the oracle in turn corresponded to Socrates' own consciousness in commanding him
to know himself. It was nevertheless reserved for a later age
to immerse itself in this self-knowledge."[46] For there to be
self-knowledge, the self must first be distinguished from what
is not the self. The crowd-man, however, remains immediately identified with his natural abilities, his family, the state,
etc. In such a situation, "Man [does] not yet have the condition of reflecting into himself, of determining himself."[47]

Since there is a lack of self-determination, the crowd-man
constantly feels himself to be acted upon by forces over
which he has little or no control.[48] His life is expressed in
categories such as "fortune," "misfortune," and "fate." The
crowd-man, like the sensuous erotic genius, is the embodiment of forces that constantly determine him from without,
rather than a free agent. The following text draws the distinction between these two forms of conduct rather clearly:
". . . the ancient world did not have subjectivity fully self-
conscious and reflective. Even if the individual moved freely,
he still rested in the substantial categories of state, family,
and destiny. The substantial category is exactly the fatalistic
element in Greek tragedy, and its exact peculiarity. The hero's
destruction is, therefore, not only a result of his own deeds,
but is also a suffering, whereas in modern tragedy, the hero's
destruction is really not suffering, but is action. In modern
times, therefore, situation and character are really predomi-
nant. The tragic hero, conscious of himself as a subject, is
fully reflective, and this reflection has not only reflected him
out of every immediate relation to state, race, and destiny,
but has often even reflected him out of his own preceding
life."[49] The crowd-man has not distinguished himself from the

---

[46] *Ibid.*, pp. 202-203; S.V., XIII, 248.

[47] *Ibid.*, p. 190; S.V., XIII, 248. Quoted from Hegel's *Lectures on the History of Philosophy.*

[48] ". . . *the view of life natural to immediacy* is one based on fortune."
Postscript, p. 388, S.V., VII, 376.

[49] *Either-Or*, I, p. 141; S.V., I, 121. As should be apparent from com-

state, race, and destiny. He is not, therefore, "conscious of himself as a subject," as a self-determining actor: "For the immediate man does not recognize his self, he recognizes himself only by his dress, he recognizes (and here again appears the infinitely comic trait) he recognizes that he has a self only by externals. There is no more ludicrous confusion, for a self is just infinitely different from externals."[50]

Although he may appear to act deliberately and freely, in fact, the crowd-man is constantly determined by the world around him. The result of such a life is, according to Kierkegaard, nothing less than the loss of selfhood: "The worldly view always clings fast to the difference between man and woman, and naturally it has no understanding of the narrowness and meanness of mind which is exemplified in having lost one's self — not by evaporation in the infinite, but by being entirely finitized, by having become, instead of a self, a number, just one man more, one more repetition of this everlasting *Einerlei*."[51]

Before we move to the reflective pole of the aesthetic, it will be useful to stress several important points about the self and time as they are presented at the immediate aesthetic. Let us begin with the self. When the stages of existence are

---

ments in chapter two, and as will become clearer in chapter five, ancient and modern tragedy err in opposite directions. Ancient tragedy conceives the self primarily in terms of necessity; the hero is a *sufferer*. Modern tragedy conceives the self fully in terms of possibility, and the freedom to actualize possibility; the hero is an *actor*. As a matter of fact, both elements, necessity and possibility, must be acknowledged in the self's constitution. The self is *both* a sufferer and an actor. To stress either factor to the exclusion of the other is to present an unbalanced view of selfhood.

[50] *The Sickness Unto Death*, p. 187; S.V., xi, 165.

[51] *The Sickness Unto Death*, p. 166; S.V., xi, 146. Compare: "This is pure immediacy, or else an immediacy that contains a qualitative reflection. — Here there is no infinite consciousness of the self, of what despair is, or of the fact that the condition is one of despair; the despair is passive, succumbing to the pressure of outward circumstance, it by no means comes from within as action." P. 184; S.V., xi, 162-163.

regarded as phases through which the developing self passes, the immediate aesthetic represents the first stage of development — the stage of infancy. When regarded as an ideal personality type, the immediate aesthetic represents those persons whose lives are controlled by the effort to satisfy their desires or those persons who unreflectively follow the course laid down for them by their society. In all instances there is an overemphasis on the necessary, or the actual, component of the self. Freedom is not exercised in purposeful decision. Furthermore, self-consciousness has not yet developed. At this stage, the self remains in a state of undifferentiated identity with its surroundings, be those surroundings natural forces or social influences. The self, understood as a conscious center of free decision, has not yet emerged. By the domination of the self's actuality or necessity, a disequilibrium is set up within the self.

A further aspect of life at the immediate aesthetic is important to notice. At this stage, there is no unity of the self.[52] The person simply moves from one momentary experience to another without establishing any continuity among them. His activity thereby becomes mindless, unreflective motion. We have seen that Kierkegaard says of Don Juan: ". . . his life is the sum of repellent moments that have no coherence [*Sammenhæng*], his life as moment is the sum of the moments, as the sum of the moments, is the moment."[53] In another context, Kierkegaard puts this important point in more general terms: "When an individual regards his self aesthetically, he becomes conscious of this self as a manifold concretion very variously characterized; but in spite of the inward diversity

[52] Johannes Sløk has explored some of the aspects of the multiplicity of the self in an excellent book, *Die Anthropologie Kierkegaards* (København: Rosenkilde und Bagger, 1954), esp. pp. 21ff. Rohrmoser has also noted that man is not actually a self, and that life lacks continuity at the aesthetic stage. Unfortunately, he has not discerned the immediate-reflective distinction within the aesthetic. "Kierkegaard und das Problem der Subjectivität," *Neue Zeitschrift für Systematische Theologie und Religionsphilosophie*, vol. 8, no. 3, pp. 296f.

[53] *Either-Or*, I, p. 95; S.V., I, 77.

[*Forskjellighed*], all of it taken together, is, nevertheless, his nature; each component has just as much right to assert itself, just as much right to demand satisfaction. His soul is like a plot of ground in which all sorts of herbs are planted, all with the same claim to thrive; his self consists of this multifariousness, and he has no self which is higher than this."[54]

Here is a view of the self similar to that of Hume discussed above. The self is a bundle of disconnected sensations.[55] The momentary conduct of one who lives in immediacy results from the exertion of external forces upon him. The moment of sensual enjoyment is all-encompassing, and when that moment has passed it is immediately forgotten in the quest of another such moment. There is no coherent history of development, but only a succession of discrete moments.

These insights concerning the self at the immediate pole of the aesthetic stage lead directly to the view of time present in this mode of existence. We have seen that Kierkegaard argues that the immediate aesthete cannot properly be called an actual self. We must now recognize that neither is it possible for Kierkegaard to speak of time, in the strict sense of the word, in immediacy. In the foregoing chapter, we have argued that he understands the notion of time appropriate for comprehending human existence as life-time, which emerges in relation to man's purposeful activity. As has become apparent, however, at the immediate pole of the aesthetic, there is no such intentional action. Therefore, time, understood as life-time, cannot be present in immediacy. Rather, for the immediate aesthete, time is what Kierkegaard calls "a perpetual going-by," or an undifferentiated succession of disconnected moments. Time is an infinite series of unrelated "nows."[56]

---

[54] *Either-Or*, II, p. 229; S.V., II, 202.

[55] Sikes' comment is helpful: "Since the determinant of life at this level is instinctual pleasure-seeking of the passing moment, the person is not yet a self but only a kaleidoscopic movement." *On Becoming the Truth* (St. Louis: The Bethany Press, 1968), p. 49.

[56] This mode of experiencing time is very similar to the way in which Heidegger argues the Greeks understood time. See *Being and Time, op.cit.*, Division Two, Chapter four. Helen Weiss' article, "The Greek

Kierkegaard offers a general comment about time at this stage: "This is in its generality the essential aesthetic principle, namely, that the moment is everything, and insofar again essentially nothing; just as the sophistic proposition that everything is true means that nothing is true."[57] What we have in immediacy is the experiential analogue of the spatial conception of time. We have seen that one result of basing the notion of time on the model of an object moving along a line is that only the present is viewed as having reality. Past and future are excluded from the passing "now."[58] At the immediate pole of the aesthetic stage, life is concentrated in the passing moment, and has no intrinsic relation to, or interest in, past and future: "For the sensual is the momentary. The sensual seeks momentary satisfaction, and the more refined it is, the better it knows how to make the moment of enjoyment a little eternity."[59]

It is not accidental that this view of time dominates the immediate aesthetic, for the nature of immediacy demands it: "But for an aesthetic representation there always is required a concentration in the moment, and the richer this concentration in the moment, the greater is the aesthetic effect. Now it is only by this concentration that the happy, the indescribable moment, the moment of infinite significance, in short, *the* moment, acquires its true value."[60] In order to be fully immersed in the pleasure of the passing moment, there must be a consistent effort to exclude both the past and the future. From

---

Conceptions of Time and Being in Light of Heidegger's Philosophy," *Philosophy and Phenomenological Research*, vol. 2, no. 2, Dec. 1961, pp. 173-187, is most helpful in understanding Heidegger's analysis of this point. Time so experienced is identical to Heidegger's notion of "inauthentic time," Part II, Paragraph 65.

[57] *Postscript*, p. 265; S.V., VII, 256.

[58] See above chapter three, section A.

[59] *Either-Or*, II, p. 22; S.V., II, 20. Compare: "The more the personality disappears in the twilight of mood, so much the more is the individual in the moment, and this again, is the most adequate expression for aesthetic existence: it is in the moment." P. 234; S.V., II, 206.

[60] *Ibid.*, II, p. 135; S.V., II, 121.

the viewpoint of the immediate aesthete, remembrance of the past and anticipation of the future can only detract from the enjoyment of the present.

A convenient way of summarizing this conception of time is to look at the setting and the circumstances of the banquet discussed in the first part of *Stages on Life's Way*. Kierkegaard's elaborate description of the way in which the party came about is not needless embellishment but is descriptive of experience at the immediate aesthetic stage. At one of the frequent meetings of five Copenhagen gentlemen, the possibility of holding a banquet was raised. The comrades entered a discussion about the ideal conditions for such an occasion. The following is the most important part of that conversation:

"However, if this [i.e., the banquet] were to be taken seriously, he [Johannes][61] proposed one condition, that it should be so arranged as to be accomplished all of a sudden. To this all were agreed. The surroundings should be fashioned anew, and everything subsequently destroyed, indeed one might well be pleased on rising from the table to hear the preparations for destruction. Nothing should remain over; 'not so much,' said the Ladies' Tailor, 'as there remains of a gown when it is made over into a hat'; 'nothing at all should remain,' said Johannes, 'for nothing is more unpleasant than a piece of sentimentality. . . .' "[62]

The five left one another, and for some time nothing more was said about the banquet. Then one day, when most of the friends had forgotten the conversation, Constantine sent them all an invitation to a banquet to be held the very same night. The banquet fulfilled the conditions laid down in the above passage. First of all, the invitation came suddenly. It had not been expected by any, and the party was proposed for that very night. There was no time for long anticipation. Secondly, the banquet was to be held in a hall that was some distance from Copenhagen, and that had been redecorated for the oc-

[61] This is the same person who is the author of "The Diary of a Seducer," which will be discussed below.

[62] *Stages on Life's Way*, p. 38; S.V., vi, 26-27.

casion so that it was "rendered entirely unrecognizable."[63]
Finally, there was a group of workers "ready to act at the decisive moment as a demolition corps."[64] The password for the
evening was "*In Vino Veritas*." Speeches would be permitted
only on the condition that the speaker was under the sway of
wine. It is also interesting to note in the light of our earlier
discussion that the music playing in the hall was Mozart's
Don Juan.

The conditions here established for the banquet are, in
fact, the conditions for immediate aesthetic experience in
general. What is sought is momentary pleasure. The moment
of enjoyment must be isolated from both the past and the future. It is for this reason that the invitation for the party must
come *suddenly*, without expectation, and that the banquet
must be held away from familiar surroundings, in a hall that
has been newly decorated and that will be destroyed immediately after the festivities are over. But even such elaborate
preparations cannot insure the success of the banquet, or the
arrival of immediate aesthetic experience: "A banquet in and
for itself [*i og for sig selv*][65] is a difficult business, for even
though it be arranged with all possible taste and talent, there
is still something else essential to it, namely luck [*Lykke*]."[66]
We have noted that the categories of "fortune," "misfortune,"
"fate," and now "luck" dominate the immediate aesthetic. Because there is no self-determination, the success of an occurrence does not lie within one's own power.

This concludes our analysis of the immediate aesthetic. As
has been seen, at this stage the self remains in an undifferentiated identification with its surroundings either through the
domination by desire or through the control of social forces.
Self-consciousness and self-determination have not yet developed. As a result of the style of life at this stage, the self re-

[63] *Ibid.*, p. 41; S.V., vi, 30.   [64] *Ibid.*, p. 42; S.V., vi, 30.

[65] Here Kierkegaard pokes fun at the Hegelian jargon of *an sich
und für sich*. Lowrie, the translator of the English edition, incorrectly
claims that the reference is to Kant's thing-in-itself.

[66] *Stages on Life's Way*, p. 39; S.V., vi, 27.

mains a multifarious collection of disconnected experiences. Time is experienced as a perpetual going-by, or an infinite succession of present moments of experience from which both past and future are excluded. Regarded in light of the two ways in which we have understood Kierkegaard's stages of existence, the immediate aesthetic characterizes, on the one hand, the life of the infant and, on the other hand, the life of the grown person who is controlled by desires or by his social world.

C. The Emergence of Reflection

In the second volume of *Either-Or*, Kierkegaard writes: "There comes a moment in a man's life when his immediacy is, as it were, ripened and the spirit demands a higher form in which it will apprehend itself as spirit."[67] The immediate aesthetic is only the first pole of the first stage of Kierkegaard's dialectic of existence. The second pole is the reflective aesthetic. Our present purpose is to examine the manner in which the movement from immediacy to reflection is accomplished. As the above quotation indicates, this involves a higher expression of the self.

Put in its most basic form, "reflection is the negation of immediacy."[68] The two poles of the aesthetic stage, therefore, stand in tension. Exactly how Kierkegaard understands reflection to be a negation of immediacy is rather involved, but is essential to understand if the movement of his dialectic is to be grasped. The following passage from an early work is especially helpful.

"Cannot consciousness then remain in immediacy? This is a foolish question, for if it could, no consciousness would exist. If this immediacy be identical with that of an animal, then the problem of consciousness is done away with. But what would be the result of this? Man would be an animal,

[67] *Either-Or*, II, p. 193; S.V., II, 170.
[68] *The Point of View*, p. 73; S.V., XIII, 562.

or in other words, he would be *dumb*. That which annuls immediacy, therefore, is language [*Sproget*]. If man could not speak then he would remain in immediacy. J. C. [Johannes Climacus] thought that this might be expressed by saying that immediacy therefore is reality [*Realiteten*] and language is ideality [*Idealiteten*]. . . . Reality I cannot express in language, for to indicate it, I must use ideality, which is a contradiction, an untruth. But how is immediacy annulled? By mediacy, which annuls immediacy by presupposing it. What, then, is immediacy? It is reality. What is mediacy? It is the word [*Ordet*]. How does the word annul actuality? By talking about it. For that which is talked about is always *presupposed*. Immediacy is reality. Language is ideality. Consciousness is opposition and contradiction."[69]

This extremely rich passage is repeatedly reflected in Kierkegaard's later works. The most important point to notice is that Kierkegaard argues that immediacy is annulled by the capacity to use language: "That which annuls immediacy is, therefore, language."

It will be helpful again to begin by regarding the stages of existence as the phases through which the developing self passes. We have seen that the immediate aesthetic represents the initial stage of life (infancy) which is pre-reflective, and in which the infant is fully governed by sensuous inclination. Immediacy begins to break down with the development of the child's capacity to use language. It must be underscored that Kierkegaard is not, at this point, drawing any major distinction between language and thought. Again relying on Hegel, Kierkegaard comments: "Whereas the philosophy of the recent past had almost exemplified the idea that language exists to conceal thought (since thought simply cannot express *das Ding an sich* at all), Hegel in any case deserves

---

[69] *Johannes Climacus or, De Omnibus Dubitandum Est*, pp. 148-149; *Papirer*, IV, 146. Consider the following parallel with Hegel: "Time is the negative element in the sensuous world. Thought is the same negativity, but its deepest, its infinite form." "Reason in History," *op.cit.*, p. 93.

credit for showing that language has thought immanent in itself and that *thought is developed language*. The other thinking was a constant fumbling with the matter."[70] Language and thought are two sides of the same coin. Therefore we can see that the foregoing claims can also be expressed by saying that the immediate aesthetic begins to break down with the development of the capacity for cognitive reflection. As long as one remains within the immediate aesthetic, language and thought are foreign: "There the sensuous has its home, there it has its own wild pleasures, for it is a kingdom, a state. In this wild kingdom, language has no place, nor sober-minded reflection. There sound only the voice of elemental passion, the play of appetites, the wild shouts of intoxication; it exists solely for pleasure in eternal tumult. The first born of this kingdom is Don Juan."[71] Don Juan, as the infant, "has not yet advanced to words, but moves always in an immediacy."[72]

The major reason for the annulment of immediacy by language and reflection is that through the exercise of these capacities self-consciousness develops. Self-consciousness involves two fundamental aspects: the distinction of the self from its surroundings, and the distinction of the self from itself. We have already seen that at the first stage of the immediate aesthetic, the self is completely undifferentiated from the environment. Gradually through the loss of the object of desire, the process of differentiation begins on an affective level. With the development of the self's cognitive capacities, however, clear distinctions begin to be made: "Language [*Sproget*] involves reflection, and cannot, therefore, express the immediate. Reflection destroys the immediate, and hence it is impossible to express the musical in language; but this apparent poverty of language is precisely its wealth. The immediate is really the indeterminate, and therefore language

---

[70] *Journals and Papers*, no. 1590; *Papirer*, III A 37.

[71] *Either-Or*, I, p. 88; S.V., I, 71.

[72] *Ibid.*, p. 55; S.V., I, 40. Compare: "The crucial point in the interpretation of Don Juan has already been indicated above: as soon as he acquires speech [*Replik*], everything is altered," p. 104; S.V., I, 86.

cannot properly apprehend it; but the fact that it is indeterminate is not its perfection but an imperfection."[73]

The most important distinction that cognition and the ability to use language make possible is, of course, the conscious distinction between the self and the world: "Here there is in fact a certain degree of self-reflection, and so a certain degree of observation of oneself. With this certain degree of self-reflection begins the act of discrimination [*Udsondrings-Akt*] whereby the self becomes aware of itself as something essentially different from the environment, from externalities and their effect upon it."[74]

The second aspect of self-consciousness depends upon the first. After having clearly differentiated the self from the not-self, one is able to distinguish oneself from one's own self. In other words, one can grasp possibilities that might be realized. With the use of language, the ability to articulate possibilities or to specify goals develops: "If one will compare the tendency to run wild in possibility with the efforts of a child to enunciate words, the lack of possibility is like being dumb [*stum*]."[75] The delineation of possibilities establishes a distinction between what the self is and what the self might be. The self distinguishes itself from itself by differentiating the real and the ideal selves. For this reason Kierkegaard claims that "Language has time as its element; all other media have space as their element."[76] With the development of the consciousness of possibility, one becomes aware of the future, and, in turn, of the past and of the present. This line of argument is implicit in the pivotal quotation examined at the outset of this section when Kierkegaard states: "Language is

[73] *Ibid.*, p. 69; S.V., I, 52. Here one should recall the comments made above concerning the manner in which music ideally represents the immediate aesthetic. Music consistently excludes word. Language, more especially prose, is the medium for the expression of the reflective aesthetic.

[74] *The Sickness Unto Death*, p. 188; S.V., XI, 166.

[75] *Ibid.*, p. 170; S.V., XI, 150. The Danish word *"stum"* can also be translated "mute."

[76] *Either-Or*, I, p. 67; S.V., I, 51.

ideality." The point is that with the capacity to use language, the self is enabled to envision an ideal toward which one can strive. The ideal is a possibility for the self, and as such represents to the self the future into which it can move.[77]

The immediate aesthetic is, therefore, annulled through the emergence of reflection. With the ability to use language and to cognize, self-consciousness develops. Self-consciousness involves both the distinction of the self from its world, and the distinction of the self from the self through the imagination of possibilities that might be realized. By the recognition of possibility, the self becomes *aware of* the future, and simultaneously of the present, as the time in which possibilities might be actualized, and of the past, as representative of the actuality of the self.[78]

An important qualification must be added at this juncture. It is the *consciousness* of the self that emerges at the reflective aesthetic. We have seen that consciousness is chiefly concerned with possibility. Therefore, what we have at this stage is the self in a state of potentiality. This might seem strange, for we have noted that one of the components of the self is

[77] Diem's comment is quite perceptive: "As soon as the reflecting subject performs this act of self-awareness, it automatically differentiates itself as such a subject from its empirical reality as object. It does not make this differentiation without keen interest: rather, in making it, it measures the empirical subject against a conceptual ideal subject. By this act, the ego becomes conscious of itself as an existing ego. It does not thereby become the ideal ego, but neither does it remain the empirical ego; the position is rather that as the ego which is interested in its own existence it is a mediator between the two." *Kierkegaard's Dialectic of Existence, op.cit.,* p. 21.

[78] In the course of discussing the Genesis account of the fall, Kierkegaard makes another interesting comment concerning the importance of language. As will be seen in chapter six, he interprets original sin in terms of dread. Dread is, moreover, directly related to the self's possibilities. The following lines give Kierkegaard's demythologization of the serpent in the Genesis story. "The imperfection in the account, the doubt how it could have occurred to anyone to say to Adam what he cannot understand, is eliminated when one reflects that the speaker is language, and hence it is Adam himself who speaks." *The Concept of Dread,* p. 43; S.V., IV, 43.

actuality. Furthermore, this very actuality dominates the immediate aesthetic. Now it is claimed that the self, in its entirety, is in a state of potentiality. This difficulty can be overcome by recognizing that Kierkegaard thinks that freedom, exercised through decision, is constitutive of the self's actuality. The self must first of all become conscious of itself: of its actuality, of its possibility, of its freedom, and of its dependence upon God. However, as long as one is only *conscious* of oneself, the entire self remains potential.[79] For the self to be actualized, and hence for the process of individuation to be carried further, freedom must be exercised. The self must freely accept the structure of its being — its actuality (the past), its possibility (the future), the freedom to realize possibilities (the present), and dependence upon God. The development of the capacity for language, and for reflection, is a necessary condition of the possibility of decision. As such, it represents an integral stage in the self's development.

Up to this point in this section, we have been considering the stages of existence as phases in the development of the self. The reader might suspect that the argument that has been presented encounters problems when one employs the other view of the stages presupposed in this book—the stages as representative of ideal personality types. After all, the two sorts of persons characterized as immediate aesthetes were both adults, and certainly were able to speak and to cognize. One was a person who lived his life in search of pleasure, and the other was the well-established bourgeois citizen whose life was governed by his social world. Surely these two types, whatever shortcomings they may have, are not babbling infants. How then can the foregoing argument be applied to such persons? The problem posed by this argument is only apparent, and is resolved when one realizes that the importance of the development of language and of reflection is to make possible *self*-consciousness. The ability to use language

[79] Kierkegaard's comment about irony is applicable to this point: "Its [irony's] actuality is sheer possibility." *The Concept of Irony*, p. 296; S.V., XIII, 351.

and to think is the necessary condition of the development of the awareness of oneself as distinct from all else that is. A portion of a quotation that was used above is helpful in clarifying this point: "With this certain degree of self-reflection begins the act of discrimination whereby the self becomes aware of itself as something essentially different from the environment, from externalities, and their effect upon it."[80]

But, as has been seen, such a differentiation of the self from its environment is precisely what neither the sensuous man nor the crowd-man has achieved. Although he may be in possession of the capacity to use language and to reflect, these powers have not been turned back on his own self so that self-consciousness properly so-called has developed. Such self-recognition is necessary before genuine action is possible, and hence before further self-development can occur. Here again the sensuous person and the crowd-man, though grown, remain children.

Having established that immediacy is annulled by the emergence of the correlative capabilities to use language and to reflect, which make possible self-consciousness, it is now necessary to examine the second pole of the aesthetic stage: reflection.

D. Reflection: Life in Possibility

While the most general characteristic of the aesthetic stage is the absence of decision, we have noted that Kierkegaard distinguishes different ways of foregoing decision: by the immersion in sensuous inclination, by the identification of oneself with the social-natural environment, or by infinite reflection. Immediacy represents the first two of these alternatives, and the reflective aesthetic represents the third.

Before we proceed to examine the reflective aesthetic in detail, it is necessary to make an important qualification about the word "reflective." It should be recognized at the

[80] *The Sickness Unto Death*, p. 188; S.V., xi, 166.

outset that Kierkegaard is highly critical of the mode of reflection that characterizes the reflective aesthetic. His criticisms are not, however, directed to all reflection. If this were so, it would be difficult to understand why he poured his life's energy into the composition of highly sophisticated reflective writings. It is, therefore, a particular sort of reflection of which Kierkegaard is so critical and which he represents as the reflective aesthetic. He criticizes reflection that is directed away from the self, or that does not intend to arrive at the self-clarification requisite for purposeful activity. Kierkegaard's writings are efforts to encourage the reader to reflect upon his own self for the purpose of better understanding his situation in existence. This form of reflection is not only useful, but is essential for the development of mature selfhood. There is, however, another mode of reflection that directs attention away from the self. The primary center of concern might be certain objects, as in the natural sciences; the historical process, as in the historical sciences or speculative philosophy; or simply interesting possibilities that one entertains but that one has no interest to enact, as in myths or fairy tales. This form of reflection distracts attention from the self and has, according to Kierkegaard's analysis, very negative effects. The following comment puts this point quite succinctly:

"It is one thing to think in such a way that one's attentiveness is solely and constantly directed towards the object as something external; it is something else to be so turned in thought that constantly at every moment one himself becomes conscious of one's own condition or how it is with oneself under reflection. But only the latter is essentially what thinking is: it is, in fact, transparency [*Gjennemsigtighed*]. The first is unclear thinking which suffers from a contradiction: that which in thinking clarifies something else is itself basically unclear. Such a thinker explains something else by his thought, and lo, he does not understand himself; eternally in the direction of the object he perhaps utilizes his natural talents very penetratingly but in the direction of inwardness he is very superficial, and therefore all his thought however fundamental it seems to be, is still basically superficial."[81]

While "subjective reflection turns its attention inwardly to the subject, and desires in this intensification of inwardness to realize the truth,"[82] objective thinking [*objektive tænkning*] is directed away from the self and hinders further self-development. It is the latter form of reflection that Kierkegaard considers at the reflective aesthetic stage of existence.

In defining the reflective aesthetic, Kierkegaard makes a sharp distinction between thought and decision. This distinction is the basis of the difference between the reflective aesthetic and the ethical stages. As will be seen in detail below, the ethical stage is the domain of decision. The reflective aesthetic is the stage at which one assumes the stance of reflection or observation. As the etymology of the word "aesthetic" indicates,[83] at the reflective pole of the aesthetic stage, one is fundamentally an observer whose primary goal is objective comprehension. In order to arrive at such comprehension, it is necessary to turn attention away from oneself and toward the object under investigation. In a general way, the distinction that Kierkegaard makes between the reflective aesthetic and the ethical stages parallels Kant's distinction between the theoretical and the practical employment of reason.[84]

[81] *Works of Love*, pp. 331-332; S.V., IX, 342. It will be helpful to recall the discussion of objectivity (as distinguished from subjectivity) at the beginning of chapter two. Many of the points raised in that context apply to the present discussion.

[82] *Postscript*, p. 175; S.V., VII, 164.

[83] Stephen Crites points out that " 'The Aesthetic' in its most comprehensive sense, is derived from the Greek verb ἀισθάναμαι, which means literally 'perceive,' 'apprehend by the senses,' 'learn,' 'understand,' 'observe.' " "Introduction" to *Crisis in the Life of an Actress, op.cit.,* p. 21.

[84] For indications of certain parallels between Kierkegaard and Kant with respect to the speculative (theoretical) and the subjective (practical), see Emil Brunner, "Das Grundproblem der Philosophie bei Kant und Kierkegaard," *Zwischen den Zeit*, vol. II, no. 6, 1924, pp. 31-47; Stephen Crites, "Introduction" to *Crisis in the Life of an Actress, op.cit.,* pp. 19ff.; *In the Twilight of Christendom, op.cit.,* Part I, ch. I; Jerry H.

A second important dimension of the reflective aesthetic that Kierkegaard emphasizes is that reflection so conceived is unending: "Reflection has the remarkable property of being infinite [*Uendelig*]. But to say that it is infinite is equivalent, in any case, to saying that it cannot be stopped by itself; because in attempting to stop itself it must use itself, and is thus stopped in the same way that a disease is cured when it is allowed to choose its own treatment, which is to say that it waxes and thrives. But perhaps the infinity thus characterizing reflection is the bad infinite [*den slette Uendelighed*]."[85] This reflection can be stopped only by the engagement of the will in decision. But such an exercise of freedom is precisely what is not accomplished at the reflective aesthetic.

Third, whereas at the immediate aesthetic there is an over-emphasis on the actuality or necessity of the self, at the reflective aesthetic the self's possibility is inordinately emphasized. This stress on possibility is an essential aspect of the reflective aesthetic, for, as Kierkegaard states, from this point of view, "possibility is higher than actuality. . . ."[86] Possibility is sought and actuality is feared, for it can only limit one's possibilities.

Finally, it is necessary to recall that Kierkegaard includes both Hegelianism[87] and romanticism[88] in the reflective

---

Gill, "Kant, Kierkegaard, and Religious Knowledge," *Essays on Kierkegaard, op.cit.*, pp. 58-73; Louis Mackey, "The Loss of World in Kierkegaard's Ethics," *op.cit.*, pp. 602-620; and Walter Sikes, *On Becoming the Truth, op.cit.*, p. 71.

[85] *Postscript*, p. 102; S.V., vii, 91. The term "*den slette Uendelighed*" calls to mind Hegel's "*die schlechte Unendlichkeit*." Lowrie, however, misleadingly inserts the German in the Danish text when Kierkegaard gives no warrant for doing so.

[86] *Ibid.*, p. 514; S.V., vii, 506.

[87] Whenever we consider Kierkegaard's criticisms of Hegel, or of the System, we should remember that his attacks are aimed as much (or perhaps more) at Danish Hegelians such as Heiberg and Martensen as at Hegel himself. For a detailed analysis of Kierkegaard's relation to these Danish Hegelians, see Niels Thulstrup, *Kierkegaards forhold til Hegel og til Spekulative Idealisme Intil 1846, op.cit.*; and Paul Sponheim, *Kierkegaard on Christ and Christian Coherence, op.cit.*, pp. 51ff.

[88] For a consideration of many of the currents in Romanticism of the

aesthetic. Although there are substantial differences between these two movements of thought, and in Kierkegaard's views of them, there are fundamental factors that unite the two when Kierkegaard turns his attention to criticism.

Kierkegaard develops his understanding of the reflective aesthetic in two basic ways. The first is by the presentation of a particular figure, Johannes the Seducer, whose "Diary" is published in the first volume of *Either-Or*.[89] However, in keeping with the overall dialogical character of Kierkegaard's authorship, one can also learn much about the reflective aesthetic from the criticisms made of Johannes by the representative of the ethical stage, Judge William. The second way in which Kierkegaard develops his analysis of the reflective aesthetic is by more general comments, many of which are critical of Hegel and of the Hegelianism of Kierkegaard's time. These are most evident in *Concluding Unscientific Postscript*. In light of this, it will be most efficient to begin the analysis of the reflective aesthetic by considering the "Diary of a Seducer" and some of Judge William's comments about it, and then briefly to turn our attention to Kierkegaard's major criticisms of romanticism and Hegelianism.

It is significant that Kierkegaard selects a seducer, and the intrigue of a seduction, for presenting his analysis of the re-

---

late eighteenth and early nineteenth centuries that were in Kierkegaard's mind, see Irving Babbit's discussion of "The Romantic Genius," *Rousseau and Romanticism* (New York: The World Publishing Co., 1962), pp. 39ff.; Anna Paulsen, "Kierkegaard in seinem Verhältnis zur deutschen Romantik Einfluss und Ubervindung," *Kierkegaardiana*, ed. Niels Thulstrup, vol. 3 (København: Munksgaard, 1959), pp. 38-47; James Collins, *The Mind of Kierkegaard, op.cit.*, ch. iii; Jean Wahl, "Kierkegaard et le Romantisme," *Kierkegaard Symposion* (København: Munksgaard, 1955), pp. 297-302; and Jean Wahl, *Études Kierkegaardiennes, op.cit.*, pp. 58ff.

[89] Geoffrey Clive points out that Laclos' *Viscomte de Valmont* and Stendahl's *Julien Soral* were very similar to Kierkegaard's "Diary of a Seducer" in both form and content. "The Teleological Suspension of the Ethical in Nineteenth Century Literature," *Journal of Religion*, 1954, p. 77.

flective aesthetic. By so doing, he establishes a conscious parallel with the "first born" of the kingdom of immediacy, Don Juan. The two seducers represent the tension between the immediate and the reflective poles of the aesthetic stage. Kierkegaard often muses over this distinction under the guise of his consideration of the differences between Don Juan and Faust. In many ways Faust is a clear example of the reflective aesthete. There is no doubt that much of the inspiration for Kierkegaard's Johannes is derived from the figure of Faust. Although both Don Juan of the immediate aesthetic and Johannes of the reflective aesthetic are seducers, the similarity in their erotic adventures ends here. Don Juan, as we have seen, is the embodiment of the power of sensuality. He conquers women by the sheer strength of his eroticism, rather than by a carefully developed and skillfully executed plan of seduction. Only music is able to express the power of his immediacy. Johannes, on the other hand, seduces only one woman. He brings about this seduction by a long and detailed plan that is described in tortuous detail in his diary. The prosaic form of the diary is most appropriate for recording Johannes' endless reflection and plotting. The basic difference between Don Juan and Johannes creates a different interest for the reader. "The immediate Don Juan must seduce 1,003; the reflective need only seduce one, and what interests us is how he did it. The reflective Don Juan's seduction is a sleight-of-hand performance, wherein every single little trick has its special importance; the musical Don Juan's seduction is a handspring, a matter of an instant, swifter done than said."[90] In the case of Don Juan, the immediate fact of his sex-

[90] *Either-Or*, I, p. 98; S.V., I, 80. In view of the above comment about the role of Faust in the development of Kierkegaard's thinking on this point, consider the following: "There is evidently something very profound here, which has perhaps escaped the attention of most people, in that Faust, who reproduces Don Juan, seduces only one girl, while Don Juan seduces hundreds; but this one girl is also, in an intensive sense, seduced and crushed quite differently from all those Don Juan has deceived, simply because Faust, as reproduction, falls under the category of

ual conquests arrests our attention, while in that of Johannes, the long and involved reflection in which he engages is of interest to us.

Johannes selects as the victim of his plan a young girl by the name of Cordelia. The reader, however, learns very little about Cordelia herself, for he constantly sees her through the plotting eyes of Johannes.[91] Johannes views Cordelia, as he does the other characters in the intrigue, as an *object* to be manipulated for his own purposes. His aim is to fashion her into the sort of a person that he wishes her to be. In the course of carrying out this plan, he seeks to bring about *interesting* situations that he can observe but to which he does not become a party: "Life is for him a drama, and what engrosses him is the ingenious unfolding of this drama. He is himself a spectator even when performing some act."[92] He seeks the interesting and avoids the boring.[93]

---

the intellectual. The power of such a seducer is speech, i.e., the lie." *Either-Or*, 1, p. 98; S.V., 1, 80. Compare *Journals and Papers*, no. 1180; *Papirer*, 1 A 227.

[91] Grimsley's comment is very insightful: "It is even doubtful whether Cordelia was ever a real person to Johannes, as he admits at one stage, his 'image' of her hovers uncertainly between her real and her ideal form. As he gazes steadfastly at the image mirrored in his own consciousness — and in his draft Kierkegaard significantly compares Johannes to Narcissus, the man who fell in love with his own reflection — the dividing line between reality and imagination becomes blurred. Detaching himself more and more from outward things, in order to contemplate the imaginative possibilities of his own inner being, he moves uncertainly between the two 'worlds' of fact and phantasy: as a seducer he certainly 'has to do' with reality (since he needs a victim) but he does not belong to it. As he admits, he does not want Cordelia for her own sake: he merely wishes to see whether 'one might be able to poetize oneself out of a girl.' She is only one moment in the elaboration of a subtle personal mood, the occasion for a personal experiment in poetic reflection." *Søren Kierkegaard and French Literaure: Eight Comparative Studies* (Cardiff: University of Wales Press, 1966), p. 36.

[92] *The Concept of Irony*, p. 300; S.V., XIII, 355.

[93] Whereas the categories of "pleasure" and "pain" are characteristic of the immediate aesthetic, the categories of "interesting" and "boring" are especially important for the reflective aesthetic.

The thing Johannes most fears is the commitment of himself to any binding relationship. He constantly tries to keep open as many possibilities as he can, a fact that considerably complicates his method of seduction. He wants to possess Cordelia, but he does not want to make any personal commitment to her that would limit him. Therefore he has to manipulate her in a way that forces her to take all of the decisive steps. His conduct must always remain ambiguous. As Judge William says of Johannes: "You are constantly hovering [*svæve*] over yourself, and however decisive every step may be, you retain a possibility of interpretation which with one word is able to alter everything."[94] Even during the closest periods of their relationship, Johannes remains enigmatic to Cordelia. Johannes recognizes this, and is pleased by it. He states, "The only thing about me that she cannot understand is that I am nothing [*ingen Ting*]."[95]

The desire to keep multiple possibilities open, and the correlative aversion to relationships, leads Johannes to try to avoid making any decisions. This consistent avoidance of decision is one of the points about which Judge William is most critical: "And now as for you — this phrase [either/or] is only too often on your lips, it has almost become a byword with you. What significance has it for you? None at all."[96] "But in reality you have not chosen at all, or it is in an improper sense of the word you have chosen. Your choice is an aesthetic choice, but an aesthetic choice is no choice."[97] From the reflective aesthetic viewpoint, decisions of any sort are regarded as restrictive. Because of this, Johannes retreats from the world of concrete actuality and enters a world in which the free play of his imagination rules.[98]

---

[94] *Either-Or*, ii, p. 11; S.V., ii, 11.

[95] *Either-Or*, i, p. 349; S.V., i, 323.

[96] *Either-Or*, ii, p. 162; S.V., ii, 144.

[97] *Ibid.*, p. 171; S.V., ii, 151.

[98] R. D. Laing (*The Divided Self, A Study in Sanity and Madness*, London: Tavistock Publications, 1959) has presented an analysis of a state of mind remarkably similar to that described by Kierkegaard in the "Diary of a Seducer." There are indications that Laing recognizes some

It is necessary to offer some more general comments about Johannes and the mode of life he represents. Kierkegaard himself gives a very helpful analysis of Johannes: "The *first* part [of *Either-Or*] represents an existential possibility that cannot win through to existence, a melancholy that needs to be ethically worked up. . . . It is an imagination-existence [*Phantasie-Existents*] in aesthetic passion, and therefore paradoxical, colliding with time; it is in its maximum despair; it is therefore not existence, but an existential possibility tending toward existence, and brought so close to it that you feel how every moment is wasted as long as it has not yet come to a decision."[99]

At the beginning of this section it was stated that while the component of actuality dominates the self at the immediate aesthetic, possibility is foremost at the reflective pole of the aesthetic stage. As we have seen in several contexts, imaginative reflection is most closely related to possibility, for through such reflection one envisions various alternatives that might be enacted. But this reflection on possibilities can never be confused with the actualization of those possibilities, because "If the content of thought were actuality, the most perfect possible anticipation of an action in thought before I had yet acted, would be the action. In that manner, no action would ever take place."[100] Decision, the free exercise of the will, is the means by which possibilities are actualized. The actualization of possibility through decision always involves the limitation of possibility. Once a decision is made, certain alternatives are no longer open to the individual. Such a foreclosing of possibility is what the reflective aesthete avoids.

The desire to remain open to possibility not only leads the reflective aesthete not to decide, but also encourages him not to recognize the actuality of his own self. Of such a person

---

kinship between his argument and that of Kierkegaard, but he is not sufficiently aware of how deep-going the similarities are. See esp. pp. 70ff.

[99] *Postscript*, p. 226; S.V., VII, 213.
[100] *Ibid.*, p. 302; S.V., VII, 293.

Kierkegaard thinks it must be said that ". . . the misfortune is that the man did not become aware of himself, aware that the self he is, is a perfectly definite something, and so is the necessary. On the contrary, he lost himself, owing to the fact that this self was seen fantastically [*phantastisk*] reflected in the possible."[101] The reflective aesthete does not acknowledge his particular given self with certain talents, certain capacities, and therefore only certain possibilities. By failing to do so, he is being self-deceptive: "That the self looks so and so in the possibility of itself is only half truth; for in the possibility of itself the self is still far from itself, or only half itself. So the question is how the necessity of the self determines it more precisely. . . . Instead of summoning back possibility into necessity, the man pursues the possibility — and at last he cannot find his way back to himself."[102] The reason for his refusal to acknowledge his actuality is again that this would impose limitations on the self.

Two closely related consequences follow from the persistent turning from actuality and the incessant playing with possibility. In the first place, "history is over and myths begin."[103] Life becomes "so ethereal and light that actuality is to a large degree lost sight of."[104] There develops a complete confusion of "poetry and actuality, truth and romance"[105] in the "dream"[106] of the reflective aesthetic. The second consequence involves the effect of such conduct on the self at the

[101] *The Sickness Unto Death*, pp. 169-179; S.V., xi, 149. Note the etymological parallel between *phantastisk* and *Phantasie* (imagination).

[102] *Ibid.*, p. 170; S.V., xi, 150. Kierkegaard's discussions of "The Despair of Finitude is Due to the Lack of Infinitude" (166-168; S.V., xi, 146-148) and "The Despair of Necessity is Due to the Lack of Possibility (170-175; S.V., xi, 150-155) are important for the immediate aesthetic, and his arguments in the sections entitled "The Despair of Infinitude is Due to the Lack of Finitude" (163-165; S.V., xi, 143-146) and "The Despair of Possibility is Due to the Lack of Necessity" (168-170; S.V., xi, 148-150) are important for the reflective aesthetic.

[103] *Either-Or*, i, p. 435; S.V., i, 408.

[104] *Ibid.*, p. 422; S.V., i, 395.   [105] *Ibid.*, p. 387; S.V., i, 359.

[106] *Ibid.*, p. 376; S.V., i, 348.

reflective aesthetic stage of existence. The reflective aesthete's self is "not really an actuality, but a possibility of everything."[107] The two following quotations are Kierkegaard's clearest statements about the self at the reflective aesthetic stage:

"In such a dream of imagination, the individual is not an actual figure but is a shadow, or rather the actual figure is invisibly present and therefore is not content with casting one shadow, but the individual has a multiplicity of shadows [*Mangfoldighed af Skygger*], all of which resemble him and for the moment have an equal claim to be accounted himself. The personality [*Personligheden*] is not yet discovered, its energy announces itself only in the passion of possibility [*Mulighedens Lidenskab*]; for it is true in the life of the spirit as it is in the case of so many plants that the germinal sprout comes last. . . . So does the possibility of the individual stray at random amongst its own possibilities, discovering now one and now another."[108]

"Possibility then appears to the self ever greater and greater, more and more things become possible, because nothing becomes actual. At last it is as if everything were possible — but this is precisely when the abyss has swallowed up the self. . . . At the instant something appears possible, and then a new possibility makes its appearance, at last this phantasmagoria moves so rapidly that it is as if everything were possible — and this is precisely the last moment, when the individual becomes for himself a mirage [*Luftsyn*]."[109]

We have seen that reflection is, on its own terms, infinite; it cannot put a stop to itself. As one continues to reflect, the possibilities that one envisions are multiplied. The more one is caught up in possibility, the less one has to do with actuality, either the actuality of one's own self or of the world around one. Furthermore this multiplication of possibilities

---

[107] *Postscript*, pp. 262-263; S.V., vii, 253.

[108] *Repetition*, pp. 58, 59; S.V., iii, 194, 195. Compare *Either-Or*, ii, pp. 17, 203; S.V., ii, 16, 179.

[109] *The Sickness Unto Death*, p. 169; S.V., xi, 149.

leads to a multifariousness of the self similar to that which was seen to characterize the immediate aesthetic. At the reflective aesthetic stage, the self becomes a bundle of unordered possibilities. Each possibility seems, "for the moment [to] have an equal claim" on the self. However, as long as one does not "summon back possibility into necessity" he "has lost himself." The end result is that such a person "becomes for himself a mirage." The only way for this infinite reflection to be stopped is by a resolution of the will. Through such a resolution, the self's component of actuality is asserted. But this process involves the exercise of freedom in decision, and with that development the self moves out of the aesthetic stage and into the ethical stage.

Up to this point, we have been interpreting the reflective aesthetic stage as a possible life-view, or as an ideal personality type. Before we move to a brief consideration of the way in which some of Kierkegaard's criticisms of romanticism and of Hegelianism are related to the issues we have been examining, it is necessary to consider the reflective aesthetic as a phase in the development of the self. As with the immediate aesthetic, Kierkegaard's reflective aesthetic parallels an aspect of the development of the self specified by later psychologists. Our task at this juncture is greatly simplified by the foregoing analysis of Kierkegaard's understanding of the emergence of reflection. Two principal points need to be made explicitly.

In the first place, many psychologists argue that the process of differentiating the child and its world that was begun by the frustration of desire is carried further, and gradually reaches the level of self-consciousness during the early phases of the anal stage. The fundamental distinction entailed in self-consciousness is the clear recognition of the difference between subjective and objective reality. This awareness develops with the differentiation of the ego from the id. Whereas the id, in the stage of immediate gratification, fails to discriminate between inwardness and externality, the frustration of desire engenders a distinction between inward desire and the outward means of fulfilling that desire. Since desire is no longer immediately satisfied, the self must seek the desired in the surrounding world. For this process of gratification of desire to take place, there must be a clear distinction between the desiring self and the particular desired object. The ego is the means by which inward desire is related to the outward reality that will satiate desire. By virtue of the ego, anti-cathexes restrain the id impulses until a proper direction for the object-cathexis is established. Through the ego, a plan is formed or a possible object is envisioned that will accomplish the purpose of fulfilling desire. Such intentional activity is greatly facilitated by the ability of the child to use language to articulate goals. Although the conditions requisite for voli-tion are present, the will has not actually been asserted at this point. Ego and id are clearly distinguished, and intentional activity is posited as a possibility. Quite evidently, the stage in the development of the self that has been summarized here is parallel to what Kierkegaard understands to take place in the movement from the immediate to the reflective pole of the aesthetic stage. In the second place, much of the life of a young child is an "imagination existence." Many psychologists stress the importance of the imagination in the process of so-cializing the child.[110] The centrality of the imagination for the development of the child is evident in the child's play. The child pretends to assume different roles with which his world presents him. Often the child is unable to distinguish clearly between the real and the imaginary.[111] In this imaginative playing, the child tries to see how the world looks from "in-side" a certain perspective. His world seems to be an infinite array of possibilities into any of which he can imagine him-self. Of course, for the child actually to appropriate an imag-ined role, a consistent exertion of the will would be necessary.

---

[110] The reader is again referred to the works of Erik Erikson cited above (p. 141).

[111] This explains, in part, the fascination of children with fairy tales. Kierkegaard stresses the interest of many of the romantics in myths and fairy tales.

This comes only at a later stage of life. Such imaginative playing is an important step in the self's maturation, and makes further development possible.

Kierkegaard's reflective aesthetic stage can, therefore, also be understood as descriptive of a phase in the development of the self. Here, as in other cases, problems are created if the characteristics of a particular phase of development become determinative for the entire life-view of an adult. This is, in large measure, what happens to Johannes. He, as the child, lives an existence of imagination, for his world is an unordered range of possibilities. Because Johannes never assserts his will, he never actualizes his own self.

We must now turn our attention to Kierkegaard's evaluation of romanticism and Hegelianism. Within the context of this book, it is impossible to conduct a detailed investigation of Kierkegaard's relationship to these two complicated movements of thought. Our purpose is to try to understand the reflective aesthetic stage more clearly by considering some of Kierkegaard's criticisms of these two schools of thought.

The most useful source for understanding Kierkegaard's response to some of the currents in nineteenth-century romanticism is his master's thesis, *The Concept of Irony*. It is, no doubt, too broad a statement to claim that he engages in a criticism of the romanticism of his day. More specifically, he focuses his attention on romantic irony as it is presented in the work of Friedrich Schlegel,[112] Tieck,[113] and Solger.[114] Kierkegaard himself, however, understands his remarks about irony to be applicable to romanticism as a whole.[115] In his discussion of the work of these thinkers, there are many

---

[112] See *The Concept of Irony*, pp. 302-316; S.V., XIII, 357-370.

[113] *Ibid.*, pp. 316-322; S.V., XIII, 370-376.

[114] *Ibid.*, pp. 323-335; S.V., XIII, 376-387.

[115] He comments in a note to his argument: "Throughout this discussion I use the expressions: *irony* and the *ironist*, but I could as easily say: *romanticism* and the *romanticist*. Both designate the same thing. The one suggests more the name with which the movement christened itself, the other the name with which Hegel christened it." *The Concept of Irony*, p. 292; S.V., XIII, 347.

anticipations of Kierkegaard's later views as expressed in the "Diary of a Seducer." Furthermore, many of Judge William's criticisms of Johannes are foreshadowed in Kierkegaard's consideration of romanticism.

Schlegel's novel *Lucinde* serves as a point of departure for many of Kierkegaard's arguments. In the course of analyzing the concept of irony as presented by Socrates and by Hegel, Kierkegaard accepts Hegel's definition of irony as "infinite negativity," which he explains as follows: "If we return to the general designation of irony given above as infinite absolute negativity, this will sufficiently indicate that irony no longer directs itself against this or that particular phenomenon, against a particular thing, but that the whole of existence has become alien to the ironic subject, that he in turn has become estranged from existence, and that because actuality has lost its validity for him, so he, too, is to a certain extent no longer actual. The word 'actuality' must primarily be taken to mean historical actuality, that is to say, the actuality given at a certain time under certain conditions."[116]

Kierkegaard directly echoes this passage when, at another point, he offers a general criticism of romanticism: "The calamity of romanticism is that what it grasps is not actuality."[117] The ironist (or the romanticist) seeks to maintain infinite freedom, or unlimited possibility by denying historical actuality. The actual with which the ironist is confronted is denied, and in its place is put a world that has been freely imagined by him. Foremost among the actualities that must be negated is the past, which is regarded as a limitation of one's possibilities. Therefore he endeavors to sever all connection with the past. By so doing, the ironist believes himself "in possession of the power to begin from the beginning whenever [he] pleases, for nothing in the past is binding upon [him]."[118]

Here is a pattern of conduct that is identical to that analyzed in connection with Johannes. With respect to the com-

[116] *The Concept of Irony*, p. 276; S.V., XIII, 333.
[117] *Ibid.*, p. 319; S.V., XIII, 372.   [118] *Ibid.*, p. 296; S.V., XIII, 351.

ponents of the self, actuality is denied and possibility is inordinately affirmed. One lives one's life within the realm of the imagination. Kierkegaard sees this as one of the dominant motifs in Schlegel's *Lucinde*: "That the imagination alone rules is repeated throughout the whole of *Lucinde*. Now who is such a monster that he is unable to delight in the free play of the imagination? But it does not follow from this that the whole of life should be given over to the imagination. When the imagination is allowed to rule in this way it prostrates and anaesthetizes the soul, robs it of all moral tension, and makes of life a dream. Yet this is exactly what *Lucinde* seeks to accomplish...."[119]

Through the play of his imagination, the ironist, as Johannes, seeks a situation in which "all things are possible"[120] for him. But as we have seen in connection with Johannes, when all seems possible, "the abyss has swallowed up the self" or, as Kierkegaard has put it above, the ironist "is to a certain extent no longer actual." The ironist "renounces all understanding and allows the phantasy alone to rule."[121] The world becomes dream-like, and his self becomes a bundle of conflicting possibilities: "Because the ironist poetically produces himself as well as his environment with the greatest possible poetic license, because he lives completely hypothetically and subjunctively, his life finally loses all continuity. With this he wholly lapses under the sway of his moods and feelings."[122]

As we turn our attention from Kierkegaard's comments on

[119] *Ibid.*, p. 308; note; S.V., XIII, 362.

[120] *Ibid.*, p. 299; S.V., XIII, 354. Babbit's discussion of the "Romantic Imagination" (*Rousseau and Romanticism, op.cit.*, pp. 67ff.) is illuminating when considering Kierkegaard's analysis at this point.

[121] *Ibid.*, p. 308; S.V., XIII, 362.

[122] *Ibid.*, pp. 300-301; S.V., XIII, 355. Croxall comments: "In Romanticism, the 'interesting' person is much what S.K.'s aesthetic person is — uncommitted, bored, supercilious. Indeed Grillparzer had in 1808 sketched a type of 'interesting' person calling him a 'person who is no person,' which is about what S.K. says of his 'Seducer.'" *Johannes Climacus, or De Omnibus Dubitandum Est*, p. 87.

romantic irony to his criticism of Hegelianism, two points are important for us to consider. First, Hegelian philosophy is a *speculative* science; second, its fundamental orientation is retrospective.

The main thrust of Kierkegaard's repeated criticism of Hegelianism for its consistently speculative stance has been indicated in what has gone before. In speculation, as the etymology of the word suggests, the individual is related to the world in a way similar to a spectator of a drama. The attention of the observer is directed away from himself and toward an object (or objects) that manifests itself to him. The aim of speculation is not self-knowledge, but a clear knowledge of the object being examined. In order to attain this goal, one's idiosyncratic interests must, as far as possible, be overcome. For Kierkegaard, however, such speculation prevents one from coming to terms with his individual existence: "Their [Hegelian philosophers'] thought is tranquilized, the objective logical thought is brought to rest in its corresponding objectivity, and yet they are in despair even though they find distraction in objective thinking; for a man can find distraction in many ways, and there is hardly any anaesthetic so powerful as abstract thinking, because here it is a question of behaving as impersonally as possible."[123] Speculative philosophy's propensity to turn one's attention away from the self makes it "treacherous."[124] The comment that Kierkegaard makes of Johannes might well be applied to speculative philosophy as a whole: "[He] keeps existence away by the most subtle of all deceptions, by thinking; he has thought everything possible, and yet he has not existed at all."[125]

Not only does Kierkegaard criticize Hegelian philosophy for its speculative stance, but he is also critical of its constant orientation toward the past. Taking Hegel's own historical writings as their point of departure, many Hegelians considered the task of philosophy to be the interpretation of the

[123] *Postscript*, p. 280; S.V., VII, 271.
[124] *Either-Or*, II, p. 8; S.V., II, 8.
[125] *Postscript*, p. 226; S.V., VII, 213.

world historical process as it had unfolded up to the present time. Philosophy could understand the past, but it could not deal with the future. From this point of view, an event could be understood within the context of the world historical process only *after* it had occurred. Kierkegaard is very critical of this procedure, and argues that speculative philosophy's understanding is always "behind-hand":[126] "Philosophy turns toward the past, toward the whole enacted history of the world, it shows how the discrete factors are fused into a higher unity, it mediates and mediates. On the other hand, it seems to me to give no answer to the question I put to it, for I ask about the future."[127]

By constantly contemplating the past, speculative philosophy distracts one's attention from the future and from the present. Since Kierkegaard thinks that authentic human existence requires one to attend to his future as he strives to realize imagined possibilities through present decisions, he argues that speculative philosophy abstracts from existence: "Speculation looks away from existence; in its eyes, the fact of existing amounts to having existed (the past), existence vanishes and is nullified in the pure being of the eternal. Speculation as the abstract can never be contemporary with existence and cannot grasp existence as existence, but can only see it retrospectively. This explains why speculative philosophy prudently holds itself aloof from ethics, and why it becomes ridiculous when it makes a trial at it."[128]

The result of the tendency to contemplate the past is the same as other aesthetic tendencies that we have considered. The self fails to actualize itself and, in effect, vanishes: "He stares at the historical spectacle until he is lost in it; he dies and leaves the scene, and nothing of him remains, or rather, he himself remains like a ticket in the hands of the usher, an indication that the spectator has gone."[129]

---

[126] *Ibid.*, p. 139; S.V., VII, 128.
[127] *Either-Or*, II, p. 174; S.V., II, 155.
[128] *Postscript*, p. 506; S.V., VII, 497. Compare p. 131; S.V., VII, 121.
[129] *Ibid.*, p. 142; S.V., VII, 131.

Kierkegaard's comments about the attitude of speculative philosophy toward the past direct our attention to the problem of time at the reflective aesthetic stage. Since much of what has gone before indicates the way in which time is experienced at this stage, only a summary is required here. We have seen that at the immediate pole of the aesthetic stage of existence, time is experienced as incessant flux and the person is immersed in the pleasure of the passing moment. In such immediacy, there is no clear recognition of past or future. At the reflective aesthetic, the situation is quite different. Either there is a concentration on the past to the exclusion of the present and the future, or on the future to the exclusion of the past and the present. In an essay that takes as its point of departure Hegel's discussion of the "unhappy consciousness" in the *Phenomenology*, Kierkegaard comments: "The unhappy person is one who has his ideal, the content of his life, the fullness of his consciousness, outside of himself. He is always absent, never present to himself. But it is evident that it is possible to be absent from oneself either in the past or in the future."[130] When one engages in reflection, one's concentration on either the past (in memory) or the future (in anticipation) can become so acute that one forgets the other tenses of time. Since for Kierkegaard, human existence is fundamentally related to all three tenses of time, he thinks that no tense can be excluded.

Quite clearly, speculative philosophy is an example of the way in which an individual can become "absent" from himself through reflection on the past. But Kierkegaard gives other interesting examples. In his essay entitled "Shadowgraphs" in the first volume of *Either-Or*, he analyzes three women whose lives are spent reflecting on their past. This is a concrete illustration of the implications of speculative philosophy's procedure for the existing individual. Each woman has been the victim of a broken love affair, and each is engaged in infinite (unending) reflection on her past.[131] Al-

---

[130] *Either-Or*, I, p. 220; S.V., I, 196.

[131] It is interesting to note that this is the only place where Kierke-

though there are significant differences among the three cases, for our purposes their similarity is more important. For each woman, reflection on the past closes them to the future and makes them absent from their present. The image of the shadow is carefully chosen by Kierkegaard. We have seen that life at the reflective aesthetic stage is "shadow existence" in which the "individual is not a real figure but is a shadow."[132] By constant reflection on the past, these women become shadows. However, Kierkegaard's comments about the persons depicted in the "Shadowgraphs" are fully applicable to speculative philosophy. The "Shadowgraphs" are only the development of the existential implications of the basic orientation of speculative philosophy.

But Kierkegaard argues that "it is possible to be absent from oneself either in the past or in the future." The analysis of Johannes that has been given above represents an individual who is absent from himself in the future. We have seen that Johannes is engaged in reflection upon his multiple possibilities. Possibilities are most basically related to the future, for they represent that which now is not, but which might become. Johannes' ideal is to keep open a maximum number of possibilities. To do so he has to deny actuality in a twofold way. First, because he thinks that the past can only bind and limit a person, he refuses to acknowledge his personal past. Second, he declines to make decisions in the present, for such decisions would again impose limitations and close possibilities. This form of existence concentrates on the future and excludes the past and the present.

Thus at the aesthetic stage of existence, one lives either fully in the passing moment, in the past, or in the future. There is no interrelationship or coinherence of the tenses of time. From Kierkegaard's point of view, this mode of experi-

---

gaard considers the broken love affair from the point of view of women. In all other instances (e.g., "Diary of a Seducer," *Stages on Life's Way,* and *Repetition*), the problem is considered from the male point of view.

[132] *Repetition,* p. 58; S.V., III, 194. See above p. 172.

encing time is not appropriate for authentic human existence. He believes that to be in time is to be faced with the either-or of decision. The present, the moment of decision in which freedom can be exercised, decisively differentiates the past and the future. Furthermore, decision draws together the three tenses of time: in *present* decision, future possibilities are related to *past* actualities. At the reflective pole of the aesthetic stage, the self becomes aware of its possibilities and its actuality through the emergence of cognitive processes. This is a necessary stage of development through which the self must pass. However, throughout the aesthetic stage there is an absence of decision as a result of the determination of the self by sensuous inclination, of the identification of oneself with the social-natural environment (the immediate aesthetic), or of the evaporation of the either-or of decision in infinite reflection (the reflective aesthetic). At the aesthetic stage, the self has not yet become temporalized: "He [the aesthete] has no contemporary time to support him; he has no past to long for, since his past has not yet come; he has no future to hope for, since his future is already past. . . . He cannot become old, for he has never been young; he cannot die, for he has not really lived; in another sense he cannot live, for he is already dead. He cannot love, for love is in the present, and he has no present, no future, and no past. . . . He has no time for anything, not because his time is taken up with something else, but because he has no time at all."[133] On this basis, Kierkegaard argues that "aesthetics does not trouble itself greatly about time."[134] The aesthete, be he immediate or reflective, is not concerned with, or engaged in the process of temporal becoming: "Time flows, life is a stream, people say, and so on. I do not notice it. Time stands still, and I with it."[135] "Time stands still" because there is no movement from

---

[133] *Either-Or*, I, p. 224; S.V., I, 199-200.

[134] *Fear and Trembling*, p. 95; S.V., III, 133.

[135] *Either-Or*, I, p. 25; S.V., I, 10. The aesthetic view of time influences Kierkegaard's method in writing the "Diary of a Seducer." "It is true that the dates [in the diary] are lacking, but even if I had them it

the past, through the present, into the future. The self lives exclusively in the past, the present, or the future.

In the final analysis, time becomes the enemy of aesthetic experience. This happens in one of two ways, depending on whether one is considering immediacy or reflection. For the immediate aesthete, the unalterable flow of time means the necessary negation of the present moment of pleasure. The pleasurable moment in which the immediate aesthete seeks to immerse himself always passes. His efforts are then directed to finding another moment in which to lose himself. But here too the moment passes. For the reflective aesthete, the transition from the realm of imaginative idealities to temporal actuality involves the movement into the realm of historical travail in which ideals are only gradually and partially realized. For the temporal individual, the ideal remains a goal that his existence approximates: "For the imaginary picture [*Indbildnings-Billedet*], that is, the picture which the imagination presents and fixes, is after all, in a certain sense, unreality, it lacks the actuality of time and duration and of the earthly life with its difficulties and sufferings."[136] The aesthete, either through sensual enjoyment or through imaginative reflection, is engaged in what Kierkegaard calls "killing time."[137] He avoids decision.

The consequences of aesthetic existence for the self have already been explored. At each pole of the aesthetic stage, there is an imbalance within the self. While immediacy stresses the self's actuality to the exclusion of possibility, reflection stresses the self's possibility to the exclusion of actuality. In both cases, there is a failure of the self to exercise free-

---

would not help much, since the Diary as it progresses becomes more and more sparing of dates, until at last it is a marked exception when one is given, as if the story in its progress becomes qualitatively significant to such a degree that, although historically real, it comes nearer to being idea [*Idee*], and for this reason the time-designations become a matter of indifference." *Either-Or*, I, pp. 306-307; S.V., I, 282.

[136] *Training in Christianity*, p. 186; S.V., XII, 174.

[137] See *Papirer*, VII¹ A 237 and VIII¹ A 40, A 75.

dom in decision. The result of such a form of existence is that the self becomes "multifarious" either as an array of conflicting sensual desires, or as a collection of incompatible possibilities. The only way for the self to break out of the control of sensuous inclination or of the infinity of reflection is through the engagement of the will in purposeful decision. With this, however, the self moves from the aesthetic to the ethical — the next stage in the self's development and in Kierkegaard's dialectic of existence.

CHAPTER FIVE

THE ETHICAL STAGE
OF EXISTENCE

A. THE LEVELS OF DECISION

While the primary characteristic of the aesthetic stage is the absence of the exercise of the self's freedom in decision, the fundamental characteristic of the ethical stage is the emergence of decision.[1] The category of decision is, moreover, quite important for the two major themes of this book — Kierkegaard's views of time and of the self. As we have seen, Kierkegaard argues that temporality is the process by which possibilities are actualized through decision. To be in time is to be faced with the either-or of decision. With respect to the self, decision is constitutive of individuality. Because of this, the self's development of responsible decision (and with it the transition of the ethical stage) marks a significant step in the process of individuation.

Kierkegaard's understanding of the phenomenon of decision is, however, quite involved. In order to present his views, he constructs a poetic personality who is, significantly, a judge — Judge William. The Judge's point of view is presented in three lengthy essays: "Aesthetic Validity of Marriage"; "Equilibrium between the Aesthetic and the Ethical in the Composition of Personality," which together comprise the second volume of *Either-Or*; and "Various Observations about Marriage, In Reply to Objections," which is part of *Stages on Life's Way*. In each case, the Judge is engaged in a dialogue with a representative of the aesthetic point of view. Our examination of the ethical stage will, therefore, re-

[1] In keeping with Kierkegaard's own practice, I shall use the words "decision" and "choice" interchangeably throughout this chapter.

185

quire frequent reference to issues that were considered in connection with the aesthetic stage. Because of the care with which Kierkegaard constructs the personality of Judge William, it will be most useful to begin the study of the ethical stage by understanding the stages as ideal personality types, and later to explore the implications of the Judge's comments for the understanding of the stages as phases in the development of the self.[2]

If we are to appreciate the importance of the category of decision for the ethical stage of existence, we must at once recognize that for Kierkegaard there are two clearly distinguished but closely related levels of decision. The first level involves what Kierkegaard calls the choice of oneself. The second level, for which the first is a necessary condition, is what is more commonly associated with decision—the deliberate resolution to strive to achieve a goal. Taken together, these two forms of decision are constitutive of an individual's self.

We must begin our investigation of the ethical stage by trying to understand Kierkegaard's category "to choose oneself," a term that causes commentators considerable difficulty. The Danish phrase is: *at vælge sig selv*. Judge William refers to this pivotal term as "a somewhat modernized Greek category,"[3] which he explains as follows: "The ethical individual knows himself, but this knowledge is not a mere contemplation (for with that the individual is determined by his necessity), it is a reflection upon himself [*Besindelse paa sig selv*] which itself is an action, therefore I have deliberately preferred to use the expression 'choose oneself' instead of know one-

---

[2] Although the limitations of this book do not allow the detailed development of historical influences on Kierkegaard's thought, the reader should at least be aware of the fact that in his understanding of the ethical stage, Kierkegaard is heavily dependent on both Kant (especially the second *Critique*) and Hegel (especially *Philosophy of Right*). Crites indicates some of the lines of influence. *In the Twilight of Christendom, op.cit.*, particularly part I.

[3] *Stages on Life's Way*, p. 124; S.V., VI, 116.

self."[4] Kierkegaard's use of "to choose oneself" is a variation of the Socratic maxim "know thyself." He complicates his argument by his repeated insistence that one must "choose oneself in his eternal validity."[5] The first level of decision is, therefore, designated as: "to choose oneself in his eternal validity."

Kierkegaard's understanding of the initial decision that the self must make is directly related to the structure of selfhood as it has been unfolded in chapter three. We have argued that for Kierkegaard the self is composed of actuality and possibility related to each other through freedom in the moment of decision. He continuously insists that the self is not an abstract X with unlimited possibility, and no actuality, but that it is concrete, endowed with certain actualities that condition the possibilities open to the self. Any understanding of Kierkegaard's analysis that contends that the self has unrestricted freedom is plainly incorrect. Kierkegaard's discussion of the choice of oneself in one's eternal validity depends upon his conception of the concreteness of the self's existence:

"He chooses himself, not in a finite sense (for then this 'self' would be something finite along with other things finite), but in an absolute sense; and yet, in fact, he chooses himself and not another. This self which he then chooses is infinitely concrete, for it is in fact himself, and yet it is absolutely distinct from his former self, for he has chosen it absolutely. This self did not exist previously, for it came into existence by means of the choice, and yet it did exist, for it was in fact 'himself.'

". . . that which is chosen does not exist and comes into existence with the choice; that which is chosen exists, otherwise there would not be a choice. For in case what I choose did not exist but absolutely came into existence with the choice,

---

[4] *Either-Or*, II, p. 263; S.V., II, 232. *"Besindelse paa sig selv"* implies collecting oneself, or gaining one's composure.

[5] *Either-Or*, II, p. 218; S.V., II, 192. The Danish form of this phrase is: *evige Gyldighed*.

I would not be choosing, I would be creating; but I do not create myself, I choose myself. Therefore, while nature is created out of nothing, while I myself as an immediate personality am created out of nothing, as a free spirit I am born of the principle of contradiction, or born by the fact that I choose myself."[6]

This long but important passage makes it clear that Kierkegaard's use of the phrase "to choose oneself in his eternal validity" is intended to steer a middle course between the knowledge of oneself (know thyself) and the creation of oneself (create thyself). Neither of these alternatives is correct: the former is too little, and the latter is too much.

That Kierkegaard does not think that the self creates itself has become apparent in the discussion of his analysis of the structure of selfhood. The self does not constitute itself, but is constituted by God. But there is another important fact that must be taken into account. The concretely existing self is always inextricably related to a social-natural environment that exercises constitutive influence on the self. The impact of the environment is, moreover, outside the control of the self. For example, both the physical and social influences of the parents on the child are givens in the self's being. But the impression of the environment upon the self extends far beyond one's parents. As will become increasingly evident, Kierkegaard argues that due to the close relationship between the individual and the human race, the historical development of the race affects the self in important ways. The immediate environment of the self is a conduit through which influences from the infinite expanses of time and of space reach the individual. Both the self's ontological dependence upon God, and the impact of the environment upon the self, are formative of the self's being. They are part of the self's actuality and, as such, are necessary components of the self. In these two ways, Kierkegaard thinks that the self is created and is not its own creator.

[6] *Ibid.*, pp. 219-220; S.V., ii, 193.

If it is too much to say that the self creates itself, it is too little to require the self only to know itself. The knowledge of oneself is a necessary but not a sufficient condition for the emergence of mature selfhood. We have seen in the foregoing chapter that immediacy is annulled with the emergence of self-consciousness. As reflection develops, one becomes increasingly aware of his particular distinctiveness. The goal of such self-reflection should be a deep penetration of one's concrete actuality. One must become aware of oneself as the product of a certain environment, and therefore endowed with certain talents, certain weaknesses, and certain possibilities: "The man we are speaking of discovers now that the self he chooses contains an endless multiplicity, inasmuch as it has a history, a history in which he acknowledges identity with himself. This history is of various sorts; for in this history he stands in relation to other individuals of the race and to the race as a whole, and this history contains something painful, and yet he is the man he is only in consequence of this history...."[7]

The self always becomes aware of itself as already-having-been.[8] From the first moment of self-awareness, one must acknowledge a past, an actuality, which, though it belongs to one, he has no part in forming. This is what Kierkegaard means when he says "... that which is chosen exists, otherwise there would not be a choice."[9] Before any further development of the self can take place, it is necessary to comprehend one's concrete actuality. "Eternal validity" in the phrase "to choose oneself in his eternal validity" refers to the given dimension of selfhood that is part of the self's constitution, but that has not resulted from the action of one's own self. After following the Socratic command to "know thyself," one must proceed to *choose* one's self: "... I have deliberately

---

[7] *Ibid.*, p. 220; S.V., II, 193.

[8] Compare Heidegger, *Being and Time, op.cit.*, part II, chapter 5, "Temporality and Historicality."

[9] For the full text, see above p. 187.

preferred to use the expression 'choose oneself' instead of know oneself. So when the individual knows himself, he is not through; on the contrary, this knowledge is in the highest degree fruitful, and from it proceeds the true individual."[10] The concretely given self must first be understood, and then be chosen. To choose oneself in this sense is to accept responsibility for oneself. It means acknowledging that the actuality of oneself has resulted from forces beyond the control of the self, but not, for this reason, refusing to be the self that one is:

"The individual thus becomes conscious of himself as this definite individual, with these talents, these dispositions, these instincts, these passions, influenced by these definite surroundings, as this definite product of a definite environment. But being conscious of himself in this way, he assumes responsibility for all of this. . . . Thus at the instant of choice he is in the most complete isolation, for he withdraws from the surroundings; and yet at the same moment he is in absolute continuity, for he chooses himself as product; and this choice is the choice of freedom, so that when he chooses himself as product he can just as well be said to produce himself."[11]

Kierkegaard foresees a possible problem in his argument, and tries to take steps to solve it. On the one hand, the self that is so chosen must have existed prior to the choice, or it could not, Kierkegaard argues, have been chosen but would have to be created. On the other hand, a significant change must come about as the result of this choice of oneself, or else it is difficult to see the importance of such a choice. The language that Kierkegaard uses to try to solve this problem is often confusing. Prior to the self's choice of itself, the self (understood to include all of the components analyzed in chapter three) remains in a state of immediacy. We have seen that immediacy can mean unmediated either by reflection or decision. The first stage of immediacy is annulled

[10] *Either-Or*, II, p. 263; S.V., II, 232.
[11] *Ibid.*, p. 255; S.V., II, 225.

when reflection develops. In this process, as has been noted, the self becomes *self*-conscious. But as has now become evident, self-knowledge is insufficient for mature selfhood. Decision is necessary. Therefore, the self that is known must be chosen. In one sense, one remains the same self after the choice of oneself as one had been before the choice. It is, after all, *himself* that one chooses. In another sense, however, one becomes a different self than one had been prior to the choice, for with the choice of oneself, the self emerges as a self-conscious, responsible individual. We can now understand more clearly an important part of the quotation with which this discussion began:

"In this case choice performs at one and the same time the two dialectical movements: that which is chosen does not exist and comes into existence with the choice; that which is chosen exists, otherwise there would not be a choice. For in case what I chose did not exist but absolutely came into existence with the choice, I would not be choosing, I would be creating; but I do not create myself, I choose myself. Therefore, while nature is created out of nothing, while I myself as an immediate personality am created out of nothing, as a free spirit [i.e., self] I am born of the principle of contradiction, or born by the fact that I choose myself."[12]

The paradox connected with the choice of oneself is that the self both is and is not prior to the choice. As a concrete self with given actualities and with the potential for purposeful decision, the self is. As clearly self-conscious and fully responsible for oneself, though one has not actively formed his entire self, the self is not. The choice of oneself in his eternal validity is the movement from the former to the latter situation.

The reader might be somewhat confused by the preceding argument. At the outset of the discussion of Kierkegaard's notion of choosing oneself, it was stated that his argument is directly related to the structure of selfhood as it had been de-

[12] *Ibid.*, pp. 219-220; S.V., ii, 225.

veloped in chapter three. Of the components there discussed, the choice of the self has been seen to be most closely related to the self's actuality, or to those aspects of the self's being that belong to it necessarily, i.e., that are not a function of the individual's own decisions. Now it appears as if one of the components of the self system, possibility, has engulfed all of the others. Even the self's actuality (or its necessity) that had been set in tension with its possibility appears to be subordinate to the component of possibility. In a sense, this is correct, but serious qualification is necessary. It should be fully evident that the self, for Kierkegaard, is not unlimited possibility. Possibilities are always restricted by actualities of two sorts. The first involves the *general* structure of selfhood. According to Kierkegaard, this structure cannot be changed, but must be acknowledged and accepted. The second dimension of the self's actuality is that which has resulted from the influences of the environment upon the self.[13] These factors are *particular* givens that the self has not determined, but that cannot be escaped. Kierkegaard argues, however, that if there is to be a development of mature selfhood, one's concreteness must be recognized and appropriated as part of one's being. Because of this, the actualities are, in a sense, transmuted into possibilities: the actuality (i.e., facticity) of the self is a possibility to be chosen. Kierkegaard argues: "This concretion is the individual's actuality, but as he chooses it in accord with his freedom one can also say that it is his possibility, or (to avoid an expression so aesthetic) that it is his task [*Opgave*]. For he who lives aesthetically sees only possibilities everywhere, he who lives ethically sees tasks everywhere."[14] By calling the self's actuality a possibility, Kierkegaard surely does not dissolve its concreteness, but

---

[13] To help to avoid confusion in the use of the word "actuality," it might be helpful at some points in our argument to use the terms "concreteness," "givenness," and "facticity" to refer to the particular givens within the self that result from the influence of the environment upon the self.

[14] *Either-Or*, II, p. 256; S.V., II, 225-226.

stresses that one's particular self must be penetrated through self-reflection and appropriated through free decision. Only on the basis of such self-knowledge and such self-acceptance can responsible decision be carried out.

Rather than making possibility the sole component of the self, the foregoing argument makes perfectly clear the way in which Kierkegaard understands the self's possibilities to be limited by actuality. Both the structure of selfhood and the formative influences of the environment on the self restrict the self's possibilities. For example, because of the concreteness of the self, it is impossible for the self to will its existence. Only God has the power of being, and the self depends upon God. In a similar way, one's historical situation renders certain things impossible for the self. For example, it was impossible for Socrates to be a Christian. Again, not every person has the natural endowments to become an accomplished scholar or a professional athlete. By a recognition of the self's actuality, one comes to a clearer awareness of what possibilities might be open to him. Therefore:

"This self which the individual knows is at once the actual and the ideal self [*virkelige selv og ideale selv*] which the individual has outside himself as the picture in the likeness to which he has to form himself and which, on the other hand, he nevertheless has in him since it is the self. Only within him has the individual the goal after which he has to strive, and yet he has this goal outside him, inasmuch as he strives after it. . . . Hence the ethical life has this duplex character, that the individual has his self outside himself and in himself."[15]

In the self's exercise of freedom, possibilities must always be related to and conditioned by actuality (givenness).

One further point remains to be made in connection with the first level of decision that Kierkegaard specifies. This concerns the phenomenon of repentance. In the process of coming to know itself, the self becomes aware of elements in its being that it would rather were otherwise: "Now when the

[15] *Ibid.*, p. 263; S.V., II, 232.

self with a certain degree of self-reflection wills to accept itself, it stumbles perhaps upon one difficulty or another in the composition of the self. For as no human body is perfection, so neither is any self. This difficulty, be it what it may, frightens the man away shudderingly."[16]

Furthermore we have seen that in coming to awareness of itself, the self becomes conscious of its intimate connection with the rest of the human race and its history. Along with that history must be included the wrongdoings of previous generations. As a matter of fact, the self recognizes that many of its own characteristics are the result of the errors of others. Therefore, the self becomes acutely aware of its own weaknesses and of the weaknesses of the human race of which it is a member and a product. In some instances, "weakness" is not a strong enough word to express what the self finds in itself. There are aspects of the self's facticity and of the life of the race as a whole to which the self is bound, which are nothing less than evil. This evil, however, is a part of the self's concreteness, and must be accepted in an appropriate way. The self repents of the evil that it finds within itself. For this reason, Kierkegaard repeatedly insists that the choice of oneself involves the repentance of oneself. "Only when in his choice a man has assumed himself, is clad in himself, has so totally penetrated himself [*giennemtrængt sig selv*] that every movement is attended by the consciousness of a responsibility for himself, only then has he chosen himself ethically, only then has he repented himself [*angret sig selv*], only then is he concrete, only then is he in his total isolation in absolute continuity with the reality to which he belongs. I cannot often enough repeat the proposition, however simple it may be in itself, that to choose oneself is identical with to repent oneself. For upon this everything turns."[17] The self cannot selectively appropriate some aspects of its givenness and exclude others. The totality of the self's concrete existence must be

---

[16] *The Sickness Unto Death*, p. 188; S.V., XI, 167.
[17] *Either-Or*, II, pp. 252-253; S.V., II, 222-223.

accepted. The evil dimensions of one's being are accepted in repentance.

It is important to notice in this connection, however, that the evil of which the self repents at this point has not resulted from the self's own action. It is evil, or weakness, that the self has suffered but that remains a part of the self. Such evil is the visitation of the sins of the fathers upon the sons: "There will come a moment in his life when his spirit will be ripened by the instant of choice, then he will choose himself, then also he will repent what guilt of mine may rest upon him. And it is a beautiful thing for a son to repent his father's fault, and yet he will not do this for my sake but because he only thus can choose himself."[18] The fact that there is evil and weakness within the self as a result of factors over which one has no control does not reduce the pain of recognition and acceptance. It is just this cognizance that makes the act of choosing oneself so difficult: "Here is the reason why it is so painful for men to choose themselves, it is because absolute isolation is in this case identical with the profoundest continuity, because so long as one has not chosen oneself there is, as it were, the possibility of being somewhat different either in one way or another."[19]

The first level of decision that Kierkegaard isolates is, therefore, the "choice of oneself in his eternal validity." This is the permeation of the self's concrete actuality through self-reflection and the acceptance of that self as one's own. It involves the self's recognition of one's strengths, weaknesses, evil, and one's close connection with the surrounding world. Only if the self so understands itself and accepts itself can one proceed to the second level of decision.

The second level of decision is what is more usually associated with decision — the deliberate resolution to attempt to

[18] *Ibid.*, p. 221; S.V., II, 195. Compare: ". . . if it be not cowardice, it is at least faint-heartedness not to be willing to repent the guilt of the forefathers; if not paltriness, it is at least pettiness and lack of magnanimity." P. 222; S.V., II, 195.

[19] *Ibid.*, p. 221; S.V., II, 195.

realize one's possibilities, or to strive to achieve some goal. The choice of oneself is a necessary condition of this second level of choice. The self's possibilities are always conditioned by one's facticity: ". . . when one has attained clarity about oneself, when one has had courage to will to see oneself, it by no means follows that now the history [of the self] is finished, for now it begins, now for the first time it acquires real significance for the fact that every individual moment experienced leads on to this total view."[20] Decision is the determination to try to actualize those potentialities that are commensurate with one's actuality.

Within the limited range of one's possibilities, decisions must be made concerning which options will be enacted and which ones will not be realized. A guiding principle that will enable the ethical person to choose among his possibilities is therefore necessary. Stated in general terms, the ethical person seeks to embody in his life those moral obligations which he understands to be universally binding upon mankind: "He who regards life ethically sees the universal [*Almene*], and he who lives ethically expresses the universal in his life, he makes himself universal man, not by divesting himself of his concretion, for then he becomes nothing, but by clothing himself with it and permeating it with the universal."[21]

In many of the formulations of this characteristic of life at the ethical stage, Kierkegaard alludes to Kant's categorical imperative by which the morality of a proposed action is determined by its ability to be universalized, i.e., to be applied under any circumstance.[22] However, when developing the meaning of universal principles of morality, Kierkegaard is much more specific than Kant. Moral obligation, as conceived at the ethical stage, consists of little else than the conscientious fulfillment of civic obligation — securing a good posi-

---

[20] *Ibid.*, p. 120; S.V., II, 107.   [21] *Ibid.*, p. 260; S.V., II, 229.
[22] As will become apparent as this chapter progresses, there are important differences between Kant's understanding of ethical obligation and Kierkegaard's argument as presented at the ethical stage.

tion in society, marrying, and raising a family.[23] The ideal of the ethical point of view is well-expressed in the following lines: ". . . I will here pronounce at once my view of what an extraordinary [*ualmindelige*] man is. The truly extraordinary man is the truly ordinary [*almindelige*] man. The more of the universal-human an individual is able to realize in his life, the more extraordinary he is. The less of the universal he is able to take up into his life, the more imperfect he is. He is then an extraordinary man to be sure, but not in a good sense."[24]

The two levels of decision that Kierkegaard distinguishes are, therefore, closely related. The person must first become aware of, and accept, the actuality of his particular self. Upon the basis of his concreteness, he must imagine possibilities that he might try to enact. He then proceeds to choose among his various possibilities according to universal laws of moral obligation. With these insights in mind, we must turn our attention to the implications of Kierkegaard's interpretation of decision for the self and for time.

B. The Actualization of the Self

Kierkegaard is often his own best commentator. In *Concluding Unscientific Postscript*, originally intended to complete the pseudonymous authorship, Kierkegaard includes a section entitled "A Glance at a Contemporary Effort in Danish Literature," in which he reviews the pseudonymous production up to that point. In the course of this review, Kierkegaard makes the following comment on *Either-Or* that is ex-

[23] Marriage is the paradigmatic instance of ethical obligation. Each of the Judge's treatises is concerned with marriage. Compare Hegel's discussion of marriage: *Philosophy of Right*, especially par. 161-169.

[24] *Either-Or*, II, p. 333; S.V., II, 294. Certain nuances of Kierkegaard's word play do not come through in English. The Danish word "*almindelige*" can be translated "universal" as well as "ordinary" or "common." Kierkegaard argues that the extraordinary (*ualmindelige*) person is the person who embodies universal (*almindelige*) obligation. Therefore, the extraordinary person is the ordinary (*almindelige*) person.

tremely helpful in understanding Kierkegaard's view of the
ethical stage of existence and its distinction from the aesthetic:

"The *second* part [of *Either-Or*] represents an ethical individual [Judge William] existing by virtue of the ethical. It is
also the second part which brings the first part into the open.
. . . The ethicist has *despaired* (the first part *was* despair); in
this despair he has *chosen himself*; in and by this choice he
reveals himself [*han blive aabenbar*] (the expression that
sharply differentiates between the ethical and the aesthetic
is this: 'it is every man's duty to reveal himself' — the first
part was concealment [*Skjultheden*]); he is a husband ('A'
[Johannes] was familiar with every possibility within the
erotic stage, and yet not actually in love, for then he would
instantly, in a way, have been in course of consolidating himself [*consolidere sig*]) and collects himself [*samler sig*],[25]
precisely in opposition to the concealment of the aesthetic, for
marriage is the deepest form of life's revelation [*Livets
Aabenbarelse*], by which time is taken into the service of the
ethically existing individual, and the possibility of gaining a
history [*Muligheden af at faae Historie*] becomes the ethical
victory of continuity [*Continueerlighedens*] over concealment, melancholy, illusory passion, and despair. Through
phantom-like images of mist, through the distractions of an
abundant thought-content, whose elaboration, if it has any
value, is absolutely the merit of the author, we arrive at an
entirely individual human being [*naars der hen til et ganske
enkelt Menneske*], existing in the strength of the ethical. This
then constitutes the change of scene; or rather, now the scene
is there: instead of a world of possibilities, glowing with
imagination and dialectically organized, we have an individual — and only the truth which edifies [*opbygger*] is truth for
you; that is, the truth is inwardness [*Inderligheden*], but
please to note, existential inwardness [*Existents-Inderlighed*],
here qualified as ethical."[26]

---

[25] Lowrie's translation of *samler sig* as "concentrates" is rather confusing in this context.

[26] *Postscript*, p. 227; S.V., VII, 214. The italics in this text are Kierkegaard's own.

From this long and involved passage, four issues can be defined that are important for this essay. In the words of the text, at the ethical stage of existence, one: first, "arrives at an entirely individual human being"; second, attains the "possibility of gaining a history," or "reveals himself"; third, "collects himself," or achieves "the ethical victory of continuity over concealment"; fourth, takes time up "into the service of the ethically existing individual." Each of these must be examined in turn. As the analysis proceeds, it will become apparent that taken together these points indicate Kierkegaard's contention that the movement from the aesthetic stage of existence to the ethical involves the actualization of the self.

Because Kierkegaard understands decision to be constitutive of individuality, the movement from the aesthetic (in which decision was absent) to the ethical is a very important step in the progressive individuation of the self. This movement involves nothing less than the "coming into being of the self." However, it is necessary to clarify what Kierkegaard means when he says that at the ethical stage the self is actualized, or that it comes into being.[27] The important claim in the above quotation in this connection is that at the ethical stage, one "arrives at an entirely individual human being." In another context Kierkegaard puts the same point in more graphic terms: "By the individual's intercourse with himself he impregnates himself and brings himself to birth."[28]

Since we have argued that the aesthetic stage is the first phase of the development of the self, it might seem problematic to contend that the self comes into being at the ethical stage. However, it will be recalled that Kierkegaard thinks that one must first choose himself in his eternal validity, and then strive to actualize those possibilities which are commensurate with his facticity. The problem faced by Kierkegaard at this point is that it surely seems that the self "is" prior to the act of choosing, and yet he is unwilling to grant that it is proper to speak of an actual self apart from self-

[27] In this context, these terms are equivalent for Kierkegaard.
[28] *Either-Or*, II, p. 263; S.V., II, 232.

defining decision. The following passage from the "Interlude" of the *Philosophical Fragments* deals with this problem. The title of the section from which it is taken is: "Coming into Existence [*Tilblivelse*]":

"In what sense is there change in that which comes into existence? Or, what is the nature of the coming-into-existence kind of change (κίνησις)? All other change (ἀλλοίωσις) presupposes the existence of that which changes, even when the change consists in ceasing to exist. But this is not the case with coming into existence. For if the subject of coming into existence does not itself remain unchanged during the change of coming into existence, that which comes into existence is not *this* subject which comes into existence, but something else. . . . This coming-into-existence kind of change, therefore, is not a change in essence but in being and is a transition from not existing to existing. But this non-being which the subject of coming into existence leaves behind must itself have some sort of being. Otherwise 'the subject of coming into existence would not remain unchanged during the change of coming into existence,' unless it had not been at all, and then the change of coming into existence would for another reason be absolutely different from every other kind of change, since it would be no change at all, for every change always presupposes something which changes. But such a being, which is nevertheless a non-being, is precisely what possibility is; and a being which is being is indeed actual being or actuality; the change of coming into existence is a transition from possibility to actuality."[29]

As our analysis of the structure of selfhood has shown, Kierkegaard thinks that for man possibilities are actualized through the free exercise of the will in decision. Prior to free decision, the self is a possibility. Since decision is absent from the aesthetic stage, the self at the aesthetic stage remains in

---

[29] *Philosophical Fragments*, pp. 90-91; S.V., IV, 236-237. Kierkegaard's earlier wrestling with this problem is apparent in a Journal entry that is virtually identical with this text. See *Journals and Papers*, no. 262; *Papirer*, V B 15:1.

a state of potentiality. Even the facticity (i.e., the actuality) of the self is transmuted into possibility to the extent that it must be freely appropriated. On the basis of his conviction that decision emerges at the ethical stage, Kierkegaard argues that the movement from the aesthetic to the ethical stage is the actualization of the self. Since Kierkegaard holds that possibility is "a being which is nevertheless a non-being" and actuality is "a being which is a being," he thinks that "the change of coming into existence is a transition from possibility to actuality."[30] A more precise way of putting this would be to say that through responsible decision, which develops at the ethical stage, there is a further individuation of the self, or the self is differentiated to a higher degree. In the transition from the immediate and the reflective aesthetic to the ethical stage, there is a movement from the undifferentiated identification of the self with its world through the emergence of self-consciousness to the development of a self as a center of responsible decision. The decisions that the self makes are constitutive of the self, and result in one's self-definition.

The second issue raised in the above quotation that merits discussion is Kierkegaard's contention that at the ethical stage one attains the "possibility of gaining a history" or "reveals himself." At one point Kierkegaard writes: "Here I would recall the definition I gave a while ago of the ethical, as that by which a man becomes what he becomes. The ethical then will not change the individual into another man but makes him himself, it will not annihilate the aesthetic but transfigures it. It is essential to a man who is to live ethically that he become so radically conscious of himself that no adventitious trait escapes him. This concretion the ethical would not obliterate but it sees in this task, it sees what it has to build upon and

---

[30] Diem's comment is quite accurate: ". . . in the process by which the concretely existing ego becomes a self and acquires a history, it is a question of the transition from possibility to reality, from non-being to being, from failure to exist to fullness of existence." *Kierkegaard's Dialectic of Existence, op.cit.,* p. 126; cf. p. 34.

what it has to build."[31] In the choice of oneself, one accepts one's givenness as that "upon which [one] has to build." But this initial exercise of freedom in decision is only the beginning of the self's development. When the self becomes aware of and appropriates its concreteness, the possibility of further development is established. Apart from the choice of oneself, everything appears to be possible, because nothing is actual. However, with the acknowledgment of the self's facticity, live options and dead options can be distinguished. When one's live options have been envisioned, one can decide which of these one will seek to actualize. The effort to actualize possibilities is the process in which "a man becomes what he becomes" and, as such, is the means by which the self "gains a history." The actualization of possibilities through decision is the historical becoming of the self. In this process, the self constitutes its actuality, and in so doing further defines itself. Furthermore, these decisions condition future possibilities insofar as choice irrevocably closes some possibilities and opens others. Kierkegaard goes so far as to hold that "man's eternal dignity consists in the fact that he can have a history."[32] His point in this claim is that man's dignity consists in the fact that within certain limits he is free to define his historical actuality through his own decisions.

Kierkegaard argues that the process of actualizing possibilities in which the self gains a history is the self's revelation of itself (*at blive aabenbare*): "So his [the ethical man's] ethical task is to develop out of his concealment and to reveal himself in the universal. Hence whenever he wills to remain in concealment, he sins and lies in temptation out of which he can come only by revealing himself."[33] Kierkegaard does not mean by this that one has an inner essence that only gradually becomes manifest. He is pointing to the fact that through historical becoming one gradually defines himself. Another translation of *aabenbare* is "to make known." This might con-

---

[31] *Either-Or*, II, pp. 257-258; S.V., II, 227.
[32] *Ibid.*, p. 254; S.V., II, 224.
[33] *Fear and Trembling*, p. 91; S.V., III, 130.

vey his meaning more accurately. By taking on a history through decisions, one makes known his self.

The process of gaining a history through the realization of possibilities is, of course, another step in the individuation of the self. After appropriating one's facticity, one proceeds to define oneself further through one's decisions. The decisions constitute one's history, and one's unique history differentiates one from other selves.

The third issue raised in the opening quotation involves "the ethical victory of continuity over concealment," or the process in which the self "collects itself." We have seen that at the aesthetic stage the self becomes multifarious either as a bundle of conflicting desires or as a collection of incompatible possibilities. In neither instance is there any unity of the self. From the standpoint of ethical existence, such a multiplicity of the self is "frightful": ". . . can you think of anything more frightful than that it might end with your nature being resolved into a multiplicity, that you really might become many, become, like those unhappy demonics, a legion, and you thus would have lost the inmost and holiest thing of all in a man, the unifying power of personality [*Personlighedens bindende Mægt*]?"[34]

For the ethical man, "the difficulty facing an existing individual is how to give his existence the continuity without which everything simply vanishes."[35] That the achievement of the unity of the self is of paramount importance to the ethical person is indicated by the contention that it is "the holiest thing of all in a man." This affirmation is underscored in a quotation, part of which has been previously cited: "For a man's eternal dignity consists in the fact that he can have a history, the divine element in him consists in the fact that he himself, if he will, can impart to this history continuity, for this it acquires only when it is not the sum of all that has happened to me or befallen me but is my own work, in such a

[34] *Either-Or*, II, p. 164; S.V., II, 146.
[35] *Postscript*, p. 277; S.V., VII, 268. See Reidar Thomte, *Kierkegaard's Philosophy of Religion, op.cit.*, pp. 38ff.

way that even what has befallen me is by me transformed and translated from necessity to freedom."[36] Because the unity of the self is not a given, it must be achieved by the self. Initially the self *is* a bundle of conflicting desires and an array of contradictory possibilities. The self's unity is a function of its own decisions. How this is so needs to be explained.

Let us first consider each of the sources of the self's multiplicity at the aesthetic stage: conflicting desires and contradictory possibilities. Kierkegaard argues that the stages of existence are dialectically related insofar as each succeeding stage displaces its predecessor from a position of centrality, while at the same time taking it up within itself, giving the former stage a relativized status. He expresses this view of the relationship of the stages by the Danish term *ophæve*, which is his rendering of Hegel's *aufgehoben*: "In the ethical the personality is concentrated in itself, so the aesthetic is absolutely excluded or is excluded as the absolute, but relatively it is still left. In choosing itself the personality chooses itself ethically and excludes absolutely the aesthetic, but since he chooses himself, and since he does not become another by choosing but becomes himself, the whole of the aesthetic comes back again in its relativity."[37]

In the context of the present discussion, this means that when one moves to the ethical stage of existence, the desire of the self is not fully eliminated, but is put in its proper place so that the self is no longer completely the creature of desire. Desire comes under the control of the individual's will: "He who lives ethically does not annihilate mood [*Stemningen*], he takes it for an instant into consideration, but this instant saves him from living in the moment, this instant gives him mastery over the lust for pleasure, for the art of mastering lust consists not so much in annihilating it, or entirely renouncing it, as in determining the instant. Take whatever lust you will, the secret of it, the power in it, consists in the fact that it is absolutely in the moment. . . . If he is capable of say-

[36] *Either-Or*, II, pp. 254-255; S.V., II, 224.
[37] *Ibid.*, p. 182; S.V., II, 161.

ing to himself, 'this instant I will not do it, in an hour I will,' he is cured. This hour is the *continuity* [*Continueerligheden*] that saves him. When a man lives aesthetically his mood is always eccentric because he has his center in the periphery. Personality has its center within itself, and he who has not this self is eccentric. . . . What he labors for is *continuity*, and this is always master over mood."[38]

Continuity is achieved when the multiplicity of the self's desires can be controlled by the assertion of the individual's will.

The assertion of the will also brings continuity to the otherwise contradictory possibilities of the self. We have seen that Kierkegaard argues that as long as one simply reflects on different possibilities, all things appear possible, because nothing is actual. Such an imagination existence ends in the self's becoming a mirage. However, once the will is asserted, the possibilities of the self start to lose their conflicting multiplicity, and begin to assume a general coherence. For example, the decision to do *A* might eliminate possibilities, *B*, *C*, and *D*, but open possibilities *X*, *Y*, and *Z*. In this way, both the sources of the self's multiplicity characteristic of aesthetic existence can be overcome through the self's decisions at the ethical stage.

In order to understand more completely how the unity of the self is achieved at the ethical stage, it might be helpful to examine briefly some of Judge William's observations about marriage. Throughout all of the Judge's lengthy, and often eloquent, discussions of marriage, one theme dominates: in marriage, love becomes a *duty*: "For me, duty is not one climate and love another, but for me duty makes love the true temperate climate, and for me love makes duty the true temperate climate, and perfection consists in this unity."[39] Since the immediate aesthete primarily seeks the sensual satisfaction of the passing moment, marriage and love are contradictory. Marriage turns one's attention from the present moment

[38] *Ibid.*, pp. 234-235; S.V., II, 206.
[39] *Ibid.*, p. 150; S.V., II, 134.

205

and obligates one to remain faithful to a partner even when immediate sensual enjoyment has passed. Therefore, marriage is to be avoided.

From the ethical point of view, the fact that aesthetic existence is in the moment is its shortcoming. When a person lives according to momentary desire, his self is dissolved into multiplicity. For the ethical man, the unity of the personality is an ideal for which he strives, and marriage is the paradigmatic instance of the manner in which this unity is achieved. The ethicist understands that love begins as an accidental infatuation that excites momentary desire. But for the ethical person, a resolution of the will must be added to the first stirring of love, if love is to assume its proper proportions. In one of his more poetic passages, Kierkegaard writes: "Love is the unfathomable bottom which is hidden in obscurity, but resolution [*Beslutningen*] is the victor which like Orpheus fetches love out to the light of day, for resolution is love's true form, its true transfiguration, hence marriage is holy and blessed by God. It is civic, for thereby the lovers belong to the state and the fatherland and the concerns of their fellow citizens. It is poetic, ineffably poetic, as love is, but resolution is the conscientious translator who translates enthusiasm into reality, and is so precise, oh, so precise! Love's voice 'sounds like that of fairies from the grottoes of midsummer-night,' but resolution has the earnestness of perseverance which resounds through the fleeting and the transitory. Love's gait is light as the feet which dance upon the meadow, but resolution holds the tired one till the dance begins again. Such is marriage."[40]

In the marriage vow, one assumes the responsibility for making love a duty. While for the aesthetic man to make love a duty is to cancel it, for the ethical man duty is love's fulfillment. When love is an obligation, it is no longer subject to momentary desire. Through marriage, love becomes self-determining. As long as love is subject simply to desire, it is not

[40] *Stages on Life's Way*, p. 121; S.V., VI, 113. *"Beslutningen"* can also be translated "decision." For another good statement of this point, see *Works of Love*, pp. 46-47; S.V., IX, 34.

actually within the power of the person to achieve. One cannot will desire. In addition to this, we have seen that the sensuous moment is transitory — the sheer succession of time holds its annulment. With the "transfiguration" of love in marriage, one gains the "earnestness of perseverance which resounds through the fleeting and the transitory." One wills to love another person even during those moments when desire is not at its height. Such "resolution holds the tired one till the dance begins again." The resolution to love another in marriage expresses the intention to remain constant in one's love, and not to let that love be determined by passing moods.

Through the marriage vow, the self achieves unification. Kierkegaard comments that marriage "brings melody into a man's eccentric movements."[41] The self is no longer resolved into a multiplicity of moods and possibilities: "By duty the way is cleared for the lovers, and I believe it is for this reason that duty is expressed by the future tense, to suggest its historical implication."[42] The "historical implication" of duty is that it states an intention of a person that must be worked out over a period of time. This decision bestows continuity on the self. Although the example of ethical obligation that Kierkegaard consistently uses is marriage, his analysis of marriage can be applied to ethical obligation in general. By committing oneself to ethical ideals, one assumes the obligation of remaining loyal to those goals throughout temporal duration. With this decision, the self gains a certain continuity. Some possibilities are excluded, and others are opened. Furthermore, one becomes the master over one's inclinations, for desires are controlled in light of the goal for which one strives. The continuity that is won is not, of course, achieved once-and-for-all, but must be repeatedly worked out in daily life. This is the historical element in duty and, in the final analysis, in the self. The self, through its decisions, has the possibility "of gaining a history." Depending on the nature of the decisions made, one has the possibility of giving to that history a con-

[41] *Either-Or*, II, p. 65; S.V., II, 59.
[42] *Ibid.*, p. 152; S.V., II, 136.

tinuity. As we have noted, from the ethical point of view, "a man's eternal dignity consists in the fact that he can have a history, the divine element in him consists in the fact that he himself, if he will, can impart to this history continuity."[43]

Throughout the discussion in this chapter, we have been concerned chiefly with the ethical stage as representing an ideal personality type. The ethical person, as presented through Judge William, is one for whom the significance of life lies in the strife to accomplish one's duty. Duty is viewed in terms of universal obligation, which, when more concretely defined, is the execution of civic responsibilities. With these insights, we see what Kierkegaard means by decision and the implications of such decision for the self. The preceding comments, however, are closely related to the other view of the stages of existence — phases in the maturation of the self. Before we proceed to examine the problem of time at the ethical stage, it will be helpful to look at Kierkegaard's arguments in light of the latter view of the stages.

When the ethical stage of existence is understood as a phase in the development of the self, two correlative factors must be stressed: the emergence of the will as formative of the personality and the development of a sense of morality. After the initial differentiation of the self from its world through the emergence of reflection, the next significant stage in the process of individuation is the child's assertion of his will. Through the increasing awareness of one's ability to assert the will, a more definite distinction is drawn between the self and the not-self. For example, the young child soon comes into conflict with his parents as a result of his own will. With the development of self-consciousness and the beginning of the assertion of the will, the child recognizes that he is not merely a reflex of the desires and the deeds of those around him, but can be a self-determining center of decision. In addition to this, the child becomes a formative factor in his own being. Prior to the development of decision, the child is

[43] *Ibid.*, p. 254; S.V., ii, 224.

what his parents and the surrounding world make him. When the child begins to act, however, he no longer is *fully* determined by his world, but becomes partially self-determining. Decisions are made that are constitutive of the self's being. These decisions, that start at this stage in the child's development, begin the formation of a personal history that over the years defines his self.

We have also seen that at the ethical stage the will is not randomly asserted but is guided by moral principles. At the time when the child is beginning to exercise his will, he is also being taught the moral standards of his society. These ethical principles direct the child's will by indicating which possibilities are most fitting to seek to accomplish. But, in addition to this, the acquisition of a sense of morality helps the child to gain a mastery over sensuous inclination. As we have seen, Kierkegaard contends that: "He who lives ethically does not annihilate mood, but he takes it for an instant into consideration, but this instant saves him from living in the moment, this instant gives him mastery over the lust for pleasure, for the art of mastering lust consists not so much in annihilating it, or entirely renouncing it, as in determining the instant."[44] The emergence of a will that is guided by moral precepts and that can control sensuous inclination is, therefore, an important phase in the development of the self.

Again we can recognize important similarities between Kierkegaard's analysis and the arguments of later psychological theorists. By stressing the significance of the emergence of the will as formative of the personality and the appropriation of moral codes as guides to the will and as checks on sensuous inclination, Kierkegaard points to developments that Freudian psychologists believe to take place during most of the anal and the early genital stages.[45] Freud contends that

[44] *Ibid.*, p. 235; S.V., II, 206.

[45] We have already seen that the differentiation of the ego from the id that takes place early in the anal stage is included under Kierkegaard's reflective aesthetic. Other than this process, the major part of the developments characteristic of the anal stage take place at Kierkegaard's ethical stage.

the exercise of the individual's will clearly develops at the anal stage. During the process of toilet training, the child has the first clear experience of regulating instinctual impulses. This is the beginning of the child's capacity to exercise his will, and thereby partially to control his development. Pleasure is volitionally postponed. With the development of willful activity, the child becomes more clearly distinguished from his parents (i.e., his world) by the fact that he becomes increasingly aware of his ability to defy their wishes. The early development of the will in connection with bodily functions advances as the child becomes capable of more complex volition. The child gradually is able to entertain various possibilities and to choose among them. At first such intentional activity is quite simple, but in time both the nature and the scope of possibilities become more sophisticated. As the options for action open to the child become more numerous and more complex, a means of selecting among them is required. This function is served by the superego which is formed by the internalization or introjection of the traditional values of the society. By means of the superego, the young person constructs an ego ideal that serves as the basis for selecting which possibilities will be realized. Of course, the id forces remain and are not destroyed, but their complete domination of the personality is overcome by the capacity of the ego, guided by the superego, to mediate inward desire and outward environment. In this process, there is an increasing differentiation of the self from its world and an increased individuation or further definition of the personality of the child. The maintenance of a healthy personality depends upon the ability to achieve a stasis among the three components of the self system (i.e., id, ego, and superego) during the process of self-actualization through volitional activity.[46]

[46] For other indications of some of the themes here discussed, see J. Preston Cole, "The Function of Choice in Human Existence," *op.cit.*, p. 203; *The Problematic Self in Kierkegaard and Freud, op.cit.*; T. H. Croxall, *Kierkegaard Studies, op.cit.*, p. 28; and George Price, *The Narrow Pass, op.cit.*, p. 38. Again it is necessary not to push the parallels

From these insights, it is apparent that in addition to presenting an ideal personality type at the ethical stage, Kierkegaard is also describing a phase in the development of the self. It is, moreover, a very important stage, for it involves the emergence of the self as a self-conscious center of responsible decision.

We began this section of the essay with a long quotation from which we derived four themes that are central to the ethical stage: the emergence of an "entirely individual human being," the self's "possibility of gaining a history," "the ethical victory of continuity over concealment," and the process by which the self takes time up "into the service of the ethically existing individual." We have seen that the first three of these involve the actualization of the self. Through responsible decision, the self moves from a state of potentiality (non-being) to actuality (being). As further decisions are made, the self gains a history upon which one can, through conscious effort, bestow a continuity. We must now turn our attention to the final issue raised in the opening quotation — the problem of time at the ethical stage.

C. Time as a Medium of Self-Definition

At the ethical stage of existence, time is regarded as a medium of self-definition. Over the course of time, one makes decisions that form one's personal history, and thereby define one's self. The problem of time at the ethical stage is, however, quite complicated. One reason for this is that at this point, Kierkegaard draws a distinction between internal history (or time) and external history (or time):

---

between Kierkegaard and Freudian psychology too far. In the detailed reflections of each, there are surely very significant differences. The point of this discussion is to indicate a few views that the two perspectives have in common. In this way, we gain a clearer understanding of the implications of Kierkegaard's stages when they are regarded as phases of the self's development.

211

"The Hegelian philosophy culminates in the proposition that the outward is the inward and the inward is the outward. With this Hegel virtually finishes. But this principle is essentially an aesthetic-metaphysical one, and in this way, the Hegelian philosophy is happily finished, or is fraudulently finished by lumping everything (including the ethical and the religious) indiscriminately in the aesthetic-metaphysical. Even the ethical posits opposition of a sort between the inward and the outward, inasmuch as it regards the outward as neutral. Outwardness, as the material of action, is neutral, for what the ethical accentuates is purpose; the result, as in the outwardness of action is indifferent, for what the ethical accentuates is purpose, and it is simply immoral to be concerned about the result; outwardness proves nothing at all ethically; outward victory proves nothing at all ethically, for ethically a question is raised only about the inward...."[47]

At the ethical stage of existence, Kierkegaard places the primary emphasis on inwardness. When he argues that the ethical stage is characterized by the exercise of the will in free decision, he understands decision as the person's inward resolution (his purpose), and not as the outward accomplishment of the resolution (the achievement of the purpose). Because Kierkegaard thinks that the outer consequence of one's deed is not within one's power, he holds that the individual is responsible only for his purpose, or his intention, and not for the outward result of his conduct. One must, in fact, remain fully indifferent to the results of his decision, and concentrate complete attention on his inner intention: "A truly great ethical personality would seek to realize his life in the following manner. He would strive to develop himself with the utmost exertion of his powers; in so doing, he would perhaps produce great effects in the external world. But this would

---

[47] *Postscript*, pp. 263-264, note; S.V., vii, 254; compare pp. 123-124; 139-141; and 418f.; S.V., vii, 112-113; 128-130; 276-278; and 407f. Kierkegaard goes on to say that there is a more decisive split between the inner and the outer at the religious stage. This will be considered in chapter seven.

not seriously engage his attention, for he would know that the result is not in his power, and hence that it has no significance for him, either *pro* or *contra*. He would therefore *choose* to remain in ignorance of what he had accomplished, in order that his striving might not be retarded by a preoccupation with the external, and lest he fall into the temptation which proceeds from it."[48] The inner intention is of central importance, and this only the actor himself can know.[49]

Having recognized that it is not with the outer time of the results of the self's actions, but with the inner time of purposeful decision that the ethical stage of existence has to do, we can proceed to examine in more detail the characteristics of this inner ethical time. Because Kierkegaard thinks that time is so closely related to man's intentional activity, he argues that the movement to the ethical stage involves the emergence of life-time. As distinguished from the aesthetic stage in which there is a concentration on one tense of time to the exclusion of the other two, in ethical existence there is an interpenetration or a coinherence of the three tenses of time. For the ethicist, past, present, and future are all significant, and are held together in a unity. Judge William, addressing Johannes, states: "You with your great powers of observation will certainly grant that I am right in making the general observation that men are divided into two great

[48] *Postscript*, p. 121; S.V., VII, 111. At some points Kierkegaard argues that Providence weaves a pattern from the consequences of individual's actions.

[49] Not only does this position mean that a person should not concern himself with the results of his actions, but it also means that one person cannot know another person from the other's actions (see *Postscript*, p. 284; S.V., VII, 275). The inner intention and not the outer action is constitutive of one's self. This is another basis of Kierkegaard's criticism of Hegel. Hegel *observes* world history from the outside. He has no access to the intentions of the actors in the world-historical process. Therefore, Hegel has to do only with outer history. Outer history is, as we have seen, of no interest ethically. Since Kierkegaard's chief concerns are ethical-religious, he regards Hegel's whole effort to interpret world history as fundamentally misdirected.

classes: those who predominantly live in hope, and those who predominantly live in recollection. Both have a wrong relation to time. The healthy individual lives at once both in hope and in recollection, and only thereby does his life acquire true continuity."[50] From other comments directed to Johannes, it is evident that Judge William is equally critical of the effort to live fully in the passing moment. One's aim should be to unify the past and the future in the present. At another point, the Judge argues that the "true present" is a "unity of hope and recollection."[51] For the ethical person, the past, the present, and the future coinhere and mutually condition one another, thereby forming an inseparable unity.[52]

In chapter three, we saw that Kierkegaard's understanding of life-time is related to his analysis of the structure of selfhood. The connection between the self and time is especially evident at the ethical stage, and helps us to see the way in which time is regarded from the ethical viewpoint. As has been demonstrated, the three tenses of time are correlated with the components of the self: the past is related to the self's actuality (its history); the future to the self's possibilities; and the present to the self's moment of decision. In this chapter it has been argued that the ethical ideal is to impart to the self a continuity through its decisions. The self must recognize and acknowledge its actuality (facticity), and in light of this givenness make decisions concerning which possibilities to enact. The actuality of the self conditions its possibilities, and the possibilities that are realized constitute the

[50] *Either-Or*, II, pp. 144-145; S.V., II, 128-129.

[51] *Ibid.*, p. 146; S.V., II, 130.

[52] The characteristic of ethical time that Kierkegaard is here presenting is what Heidegger calls the "ecstatic character of time." Although Kierkegaard initially perceives this aspect of time in human existence, Heidegger is usually given credit for the insight. Heidegger's analysis, though not clearly acknowledged, depends on Kierkegaard's arguments. *Being and Time, op.cit.*, esp. Part II, par. 65. Schrag's discussion in *Existence and Freedom: Towards an Ontology of Human Finitude, op.cit.*, pp. 126ff. is quite good on this subject.

self's actuality. All of this is accomplished through the self's decisions. When the parallel between the components of the self and the modes of time is recognized, it becomes evident why there is an interpenetration of the tenses of time at the ethical stage. The decisions that one makes in the present must take into account the self's past, and are directed toward the self's future. In the moment of decision (the present), the self's actuality (the past) and the self's possibilities (the future) are joined. The unity of the tenses of time and of these three components of the self is an ideal for which the ethical person strives. While for the aesthete there is no unity of self and no coinherence of time's tenses, the ethical person, by present decisions, seeks to achieve self-unity through establishing an interrelationship between past and future.

Directly related to these comments is Kierkegaard's understanding of the significance of time for an ethical person. For the aesthete time was seen as the enemy which either annulled the sensuous present or involved the imperfect embodiment of an imaginative ideal. For the ethical person, "Internal history is the only true history, but true history contends with that which is the life principle of history, i.e., with time. But when one contends with time, then the temporal and every little moment of it acquires for this fact immense reality."[53] The reason for the great importance of time for the ethical person is that time becomes for him a means of self-definition. Although such definition always takes place within given limits, the self's decisions constitute its history. Time is the medium in which the self defines itself. As a matter of fact, time is *necessary* for the ethical person. From the ethical point of view, the self realizes itself in purposeful decision. The continuity that the self is able to confer upon itself is the result of the perseverance of the self in its endeavors. For such purposeful striving and perseverance, time is required. Because the ethicist understands the significance of life to be the bestowal of unity on his personality through the accom-

[53] *Either-Or*, II, p. 137; S.V., II, 122.

plishment of his duty, "time has acquired for him such a beautiful significance."[54] Judge William says of the ethical person, "He is married, contented with his home, and time passes swiftly for him, he cannot comprehend how time might be a burden to a man or be an enemy of happiness; on the contrary, time appears to him a true blessing."[55]

The ethical person understands all phases of temporal development to be significant, for all are constitutive of the self. Kierkegaard presents this aspect of the ethical understanding of time in his discussion of the difference between aesthetic and ethical views of beauty. For the aesthete, a woman's beauty is most essentially the momentary beauty of her youth, which the aesthete tries to exploit in his erotic adventures. To the momentary beauty of the woman corresponds the momentary enjoyment of the aesthete. The ethical view of beauty differs significantly. Commenting on *Stages on Life's Way*, Kierkegaard writes: "Nevertheless he [the ethicist in *Stages*] brings forward a new aspect, and emphasizes a new aspect, and emphasizes particularly the category of time and its significance, as the medium for the beauty that increases with age; while from the aesthetic point of view, time and existence in time is more or less a regress."[56] For the ethicist, the beauty of a woman is not simply the first beauty of youth which, like the aesthete's moment of pleasure, is bound to pass. Rather, beauty lies in the whole course of development through which the woman proceeds. The ethicist "understands historical beauty":[57]

"By this I [Judge William] have indicated in what direction I am disposed to seek womanly beauty. Alas, even honest men have helped to give currency to the tragic mistake which reckless young girls accept, unfortunately, with only too much eagerness, without reflecting that it means despair: that woman's only beauty is the first beauty of youth, that she

[54] *Ibid.*, p. 311; S.V., II, 274.
[55] *Ibid.*, p. 310; S.V., II, 273-274. Compare p. 312; S.V., II, 275.
[56] *Postscript*, p. 262; S.V., VII, 253.
[57] *Either-Or*, II, p. 310; S.V., II, 273.

blooms but once, that this instant is the season of love, that one loves but once. That one loves but once is true, but woman's beauty increases with the years, and so far is it from falling off that there is about the first beauty something dubious in comparison with the subsequent beauty. Who, unless it were a madman, has ever beheld a young girl without a certain sense of sadness, because the fragility of life is here made evident in terms of the strongest contrast — vanity as fleeting as a dream, beauty as fair as a dream. But fair as the first beauty is, it is nevertheless not the truth, it is as a husk, a mantle, out of which only in the course of years, the true beauty develops before the husband's grateful eyes."[58]

The aesthete does "not think historically."[59] Therefore he sees woman's beauty only in the moment of youth. For the ethicist, historical development is of central importance, because with it one "becomes what he becomes." Through the years a woman further defines herself as she "gains a history" through her decisions. Each stage in this process has a form of beauty peculiar to it, and all stages are necessary for her being as a person. For the ethicist, the belief that a "woman's beauty increases with the years" is an expression of his perception of the significance of time for the development of the self.

Through decisions, one defines one's self, and by means of pledging loyalty to goals, one confers a unity upon one's personal history. In intentional activity, the three tenses of time are joined together, and time becomes the medium of self-definition.

D. DREADFULNESS

The sophistication of Kierkegaard's understanding of decision and the far-reaching consequences that he conceives such decision to have should by now be evident. However, one further element must be examined before all of the aspects of

[58] *Stages on Life's Way*, pp. 133-134; S.V., VI, 126-127. See also pp. 135-150; S.V., VI, 128-145.
[59] *Either-Or*, II, p. 130; S.V., II, 116.

Kierkegaard's analysis of decision have been considered: dread. The phenomenon of dread has become a particularly popular topic of consideration in the writings of Existentialist thinkers. Kierkegaard is commonly acknowledged to have isolated dread as a dimension of experience to be studied, and to have set the basic direction that later philosophical and psychological discussions of dread would take. Our concern here is to see how Kierkegaard's view of dread emerges from his understanding of the issues with which we are concerned: time and the self.

It is well to begin a consideration of Kierkegaard's understanding of dread by recognizing two important distinctions. The first distinction is between objective and subjective dread.[60] As has been seen in a previous context, Kierkegaard thinks that the individual is closely related to the race. Objective dread refers to the influence of the race upon the individual, and subjective dread refers to the individual's response to that influence. A self never begins *de novo*, but is always situated within the human race. This race has a history comprised of the collective acts of individuals. The individual person is both conditioned by and contributes to the history of the race. Throughout this history, Kierkegaard argues, there is a quantitative increase in dread. This argument is presented in the course of discussing inherited sin, and will be considered in chapter seven. We are here concerned with subjective dread, which is the expression for the manner in which the individual subject experiences dread. This dread is, it is true, part of the dread of the human race—objective dread. But the focus of attention is different. One is not so much concerned with the development of dread throughout the human race, but interested in exploring the way in which an individual self experiences dread. Such an understanding of subjective dread is actually necessary before one can comprehend what Kierkegaard means by the increase in objective dread throughout the human race.

[60] See *The Concept of Dread*, chapter II.

The second distinction that Kierkegaard makes, and that should be noted here, has become commonplace since his time — the distinction between dread[61] and fear.[62] Fear is characterized by its relation to something particular. What I fear is always quite concrete, and therefore can be indicated very specifically: "One almost never sees the concept dread dealt with in psychology, and I must therefore call attention to the fact that it is different from fear and similar concepts which refer to something definite [*noget bestemt*]. . . ."[63] Dread, on the other hand, is distinguished by the fact that it is not related to any definite thing. Kierkegaard argues that dread is the result of nothing: "In this state [the state of innocence] there is peace and repose; but at the same time there is something different, which is not dissension and strife, for there is nothing to strive with. What is it then? Nothing [*Intet*]. But what effect does nothing produce? It begets [*føder*] dread."[64] Kierkegaard's contention that dread results from nothing is better understood if we recognize that by "nothing" he means "no actual thing." That this is so becomes clear when the problem of dread is related to Kierkegaard's analysis of time and the self.

Dread is associated with three closely related issues that we have discussed in some detail: the future, the self's possibilities, and the self's freedom. Kierkegaard offers many alternative definitions of dread that stress, more or less, one of these three elements. For example, to indicate the close connection between dread and the future, he at one point writes:

[61] Both within philosophical and psychological discussions in general, and in Kierkegaard scholarship in particular, there is disagreement concerning the word appropriate to the phenomenon under discussion. The Danish word is *"Angest"* (German: *Angst*). Lowrie translates this "dread," while Hong insists that "anxiety" is better. Here I must side with Lowrie. "Anxiety" is not a strong enough word to express the terrifying aspect of the experience that Kierkegaard is discussing.

[62] The Danish word is *"Frygt."*

[63] *The Concept of Dread*, p. 38; S.V., IV, 313.

[64] *Ibid.*, p. 38; S.V., IV, 313.

"What is dread? It is the next day."[65] The relationship between possibility and dread is shown in many ways. Kierkegaard comments, for example, that dread is "the anxious possibility of *being able*."[66] Even more clearly, he argues that dread is connected with the "nothingness of possibility,"[67] or dread "is the first reflex of possibility."[68]

Dread is, however, most commonly associated with the self's freedom. In countless passages, Kierkegaard indicates dread's close relation to freedom.[69] The most succinct statement of this point is: "Dread is the possibility of freedom."[70]

---

[65] "The Anxiety [*Bekymring*] of Self-Torment," *Christian Discourses*, p. 80; S.V., x, 81-82. Compare Tillich's comment: "It is the future that awakens us to the mystery of time. Time runs from the beginning to the end, but our awareness of time goes in the opposite direction. It starts with the anxious anticipation of the end. In the light of the future we see the past and present." "The Eternal Now," *The Eternal Now* (New York: Scribner's Sons, 1963), p. 123.

[66] *The Concept of Dread*, p. 40; S.V., iv, 315. The Danish reads: "*den ængstende Mulighed af at kuune*." Lowrie's translation of "*ængstende*" as "alarming" is most misleading. It should be noted that in another context, while discussing the relation between dread and possibility, Kierkegaard equates possibility and capability: "Possibility is to be able." [*Muligheden er at kuune*]. P. 44; S.V., iv, 320.

[67] *Ibid.*, p. 69; S.V., iv, 345.

[68] *Journals and Papers*, no. 102; *Papirer* x² A 22.

[69] It is interesting to realize that there is a remarkable anticipation of Kierkegaard's view of dread in Kant's work: "He [man] discovered in himself a power of choosing for himself a way of life, of not being bound without alternative to a single way, like the animals. Perhaps the discovery of this advantage created a moment of delight. But of necessity, *anxiety* and alarm as to how he was to deal with this newly discovered power quickly followed; for man was a being who did not yet know either the secret properties or the remote effects of anything. He stood, as it were, at the brink of an *abyss*. Until that moment instinct had directed him toward specific objects of desire. But from these there now opened up an infinity of such objects, and he did not yet know how to choose between them." "Conjectural Beginning of Human History," *On History*, trans. by Lewis White Beck (New York: Bobbs-Merrill Co., 1963), p. 56; italics added.

[70] *The Concept of Dread*, p. 139; S.V., iv, 422.

Or as he puts it in another place: "The possibility of freedom announces itself in dread."[71] Dread is experienced when the self confronts its own freedom. By his repeated stress on freedom, however, Kierkegaard does not mean to undercut dread's relation to the future and to possibility. The future, possibility, and freedom are inextricably related.

Kierkegaard's analysis of dread, therefore, rests on his view of the structure of the self and the nature of time. We have seen that he defines three major components of the self: actuality, possibility, and freedom. Dread arises as a result of the self's recognition of its freedom to actualize its possibilities.[72] Furthermore, our analysis has made it apparent that the component of the self's being that Kierkegaard calls possibility is related to the future. For the self, the future is the range of possibilities that might be enacted through present decisions. Because of this close connection between the self's possibilities and the future, it can also be said that dread is the consequence of the self's awareness that in the present it faces a future toward which it can freely move. Therefore, if we combine the three phenomena with which Kierkegaard associates dread, we arrive at the following definition: Dread is the self's confrontation with its *future*, comprised of various *possibilities*, which can be actualized through the self's *freedom* to decide.

These insights make it easier to understand what Kierkegaard means when he argues that dread is of nothingness. This is more accurately stated by saying that dread is the self's encounter with its own nothingness. We have seen that at the ethical stage, the self moves from a state of possibility to actuality. But possibility, Kierkegaard holds, is a "being which is nevertheless a non-being." When the self comes into contact with its possibilities, it encounters its own non-being, its own nothingness. Kierkegaard insists on calling the self's

[71] *Ibid.*, p. 66; S.V., IV, 343.
[72] It is helpful to compare Heidegger's discussion of dread. *Being and Time, op.cit.*, par. 40, pp. 228ff.

possibility its nothingness because he equates being with actuality, and for the self decision is constitutive of actuality. One's possibility is that about which one has not yet decided and is, therefore, non-actual. Kierkegaard puts this rather complex point quite concisely when he says: "Dreamingly the spirit projects its own actuality [*Virkelighed*], but this actuality is nothing. . . ."[73] In reflection, one imagines his possibilities (i.e., projects his actuality). However, apart from a resolution of the will, such possibilities remain nothing — remain non-actual.

Dread engenders an ambiguous feeling in the self: it both attracts and repels. One "cannot flee from dread, for he loves it; really he does not love it, for he flees from it."[74] For this reason, Kierkegaard claims that "Dread is a *sympathetic antipathy and an antipathetic sympathy*."[75] This simultaneous attraction and repulsion enable one to "liken dread to dizziness."[76] The basis of dread's ambiguity lies in the fact that there is both something attractive and something repulsive about one's nothingness. As has become clear in the discussion of the immediate aesthetic, there is something intrinsically attractive about the multiple possibilities of one's self. As long as one remains in the realm of imaginary possibilities, everything seems to be possible. There is, moreover, something painful about acknowledging one's facticity. As soon as one recognizes one's concreteness, one's possibilities are limited. Furthermore, insofar as one's decisions constitute one's actuality, and thereby restrict possibilities, there is a deliberate aversion to decision. Although it may be correct to say that possibility is nothingness, this non-being exerts an attraction, for it enables one to sense his "infinitude" in a form not restricted by his "finitude." And yet this nothingness of possibility also has a repulsive aspect. The more deeply one perceives that his life is made up of an array of possibilities, the

[73] *The Concept of Dread*, p. 38; S.V., IV, 313.
[74] *Ibid.*, p. 40; S.V., IV, 315. [75] *Ibid.*, p. 38; S.V., IV, 313.
[76] *Ibid.*, p. 55; S.V., IV, 331.

more one sees that his self has no actuality. As has been noted previously: "Possibility then appears to the self ever greater and greater, more and more things become possible, because nothing becomes actual. At last it is as if everything were possible — but this is precisely when the abyss has swallowed up the self. . . . At the instant something appears possible, and then a new possibility makes its appearance, at last this phantasmagoria moves so rapidly that it is as if everything were possible — and this is precisely the last moment, when the individual becomes himself a mirage."[77] The lack of the self's actuality, its nothingness as it is experienced through dread, is disconcerting to the self. One recognizes that the price of self-actualization is the limitation of one's possibilities, but the pain of such self-limitation might be judged to be less than that of the continued nothingness of the self. At this point, the self stands ready to exercise freedom through decision.

Dread is, therefore, connected with the self's recognition of its freedom to actualize future possibilities. To the extent that one's possibilities remain undetermined, the self experiences both the attractiveness and the repulsiveness of its own nothingness. Because the possibility of decision is established at the reflective aesthetic, but is realized only at the ethical stage, dread emerges on the boundary between the aesthetic and the ethical stages of existence. Of course, the self continues to experience dread throughout life as one moves from the past into the future through present decisions.

Before we complete our analysis of the ethical stage of existence, it is necessary to explore one further topic: ethical religiosity. The consideration of this problem will at once bring to final clarity the nature of the ethical stage, and will show the reasons why Kierkegaard does not think that this form of existence achieves an equilibrium among the components of the self. In this way, our discussion of ethical religiosity points toward the third stage: Christianity, the culmination of Kierkegaard's dialectic of existence.

[77] *The Sickness Unto Death*, p. 169; S.V., XI, 149.

E. ETHICAL RELIGIOSITY[78]

From within the ethical standpoint, religion is understood to play an important part in one's life. This does not mean, however, that we have advanced to the religious stage. What develops at the ethical stage is a form of religiosity that, from the religious perspective, remains within the bounds of ethics.

In *Concluding Unscientific Postscript*, Kierkegaard stresses that: "Whenever the ethical is present, attention is directed entirely to the individual himself and his mode of life."[79] The import of this statement is implicit in what has gone before. We have seen that from the ethical point of view: ". . . man's eternal dignity consists in the fact that he can have a history, the divine element in him consists in the fact that he himself, if he will, can impart to this history continuity, for this it acquires only when it is not the sum of all that has happened to me or befallen me, but is my own work, in such a way that even what has befallen me is by me transformed and translated from necessity to freedom."[80]

Kierkegaard's point is that for the ethicist, the primary focus of concern is his own self. This might seem to stand in tension with the importance of moral obligation at the ethical stage. In other words, the ethicist might be interpreted as giving final devotion to a moral law that transcends his particular self, and that therefore requires him to turn away from himself. Although Kierkegaard is indebted to Kant in developing his interpretation of the ethical stage, he does depart from Kant's point of view in a significant way. For Kierkegaard's ethicist, moral devotion always has as its fundamental aim the self-realization of the individual. He holds that at the ethical stage, "Personality manifests itself as the absolute

---

[78] It is important to recognize that "ethical religiosity" is not to be confused with what Kierkegaard calls "Religion *A*." The latter will be discussed in the next chapter, and its difference from the former will then become evident.

[79] *Postscript*, p. 350; S.V., VII, 339.

[80] *Either-Or*, II, pp. 254-255; S.V., II, 224. See above p. 204.

which has its teleology in itself."[81] One seeks to fulfill the universal principles of morality in order to achieve a more concrete self-definition. In elaborating the understanding of moral obligation at the ethical stage, Kierkegaard argues: "The individual has his teleology in himself, has inner teleology, is himself his teleology. His self is thus the goal toward which he strives. This self of his, however, is not an abstraction, but is absolutely concrete. In the movement towards himself the individual cannot relate himself negatively towards his environment, for if he were to do so, his self is an abstraction and remains such. His self must be opened in due relation to his entire concretion; but to this concretion belong factors that are designated for taking an active part in the world. So his movement, then, is from himself through the world to himself. Here the movement is a real movement, for it is immanent teleology. . . ."[82] For the ethicist, it remains the case that "His self is . . . the goal towards which he strives." Therefore, ". . . to be concerned ethically about another's reality is also a misunderstanding, since the only question of reality that is ethically pertinent, is the question of one's own reality."[83]

As these passages indicate, and as we have seen in more detail in the second section of this chapter, while for the ethicist, his "eternal dignity" lies in his capacity to gain a history, his "divinity" resides in his ability to bestow upon that history a continuity. The means by which such continuity is attained is through continued loyalty to goals. In connection with the effort to achieve a unified self, the notion of the eternal, and correlatively of God, comes into play at the ethical stage. In

[81] *Ibid.*, p. 267; S.V., II, 236. Compare: ". . . I myself am the absolute." P. 217; S.V., II, 191. "What is the absolute? It is myself in my eternal validity." P. 218; S.V., II, 192.

[82] *Ibid.*, p. 279; S.V., II, 246.

[83] *Postscript*, p. 287; S.V., VII, 278. As will be seen in chapter seven, this is one of the major differences between the ethical and the Christian stages. The Christian is infinitely concerned about the reality of another — the reality of Christ.

analyzing the structure of selfhood,[84] we saw that one of the basic meanings of "eternal" in Kierkegaard's writings is "unchangeability." However, precisely how "unchangeability" is to be understood varies from stage to stage. At the ethical stage, unchangeability is associated with the individual's vow to remain ceaselessly loyal to certain ideals. In order to realize a unified self, one pledges to remain eternally (i.e., unchangingly) loyal: "The goal of movement for an existing individual is to arrive at a decision, and to renew it. The eternal is the factor of continuity; but an abstract eternity is extraneous to the movement of life, and a concrete eternity within the existing individual is the maximum degree of his passion."[85] A person's pledge to continue to strive for the goals that he envisions throughout the changing circumstances of his life gives the self a unity or a continuity that cannot otherwise be achieved. The task faced by the ethical person is to give adequate expression to the steadfastness of his intention.

The ethicist attempts to offer such an eternal commitment by referring his duty to God — the Eternal. At the ethical stage of existence, one comes into relation to God through one's relation to universal moral obligation. God is the means by which the ethical person secures his vow to remain loyal to his ideals. However, the primary concern remains one's own personality, and the effort to secure the continuity of one's self remains the ethicist's foremost interest. Even though God is introduced into the ethical situation, the ethical person still "has his teleology in himself, has inner teleology, is himself his teleology." In short, from the ethical perspective, God functions to certify, to justify, or to legitimate felt obligation. By way of anticipation, it should be recognized that this understanding of the relationship of God and the self stands in

[84] See chapter three, esp. pp. 90ff.

[85] *Postscript*, pp. 277; S.V., VII, 268. Walter Sike's discussion of this issue (*On Becoming the Truth, op.cit.*, pp. 117-118) is quite good. He argues that "the pathos of immanence is the pathos of self-realization," p. 117.

marked tension with Christianity. Having perceived the radical transcendence of God, the Christian does not understand his relationship to God to justify or to legitimate his relation to the world, but believes God to call into question or to relativize all obligation other than that incurred through the God relationship. The implications of this important difference between the ethicist and the person at the religious stage will become more apparent in the next two chapters.

For the moment, it is important to gain a deeper understanding of ethical obligation by again turning our attention to the paradigm of marriage. As we have seen, Judge William argues, in opposition to Johannes, that love, by its very nature, must develop into duty. Love does not consist of the immediate enjoyment of the momentary beauty of a young woman, but involves a long process of development during which two persons sustain a relationship: ". . . in marriage there is the law of motion. First love remains a non-actual *an-sich* which never acquires inward content because it moves only in an external medium; in the ethical and religious purpose, marital love possesses the possibility of an inner history and is distinguished from first love as the historical from the unhistorical."[86] At "this stage of love, the lovers wish to belong to one another *eternally*, in their resolution they resolve to be *everything* to one another."[87] During the marriage ceremony, love and duty are brought together as the two lovers take upon themselves the *task* of maintaining their relationship. "Love says, 'Thine forever'; the marriage service says, 'Thou shalt forsake all others and keep thee only to her. . . .' "[88]

No longer is love subject to capricious desire, for one *pledges* to maintain the relationship even when the heat of first passion has cooled. Because the marriage vow is taken before God (the Eternal), it is understood by the couple to be unbreakable. After they establish this permanent resolution to maintain their love by vowing before God, the life of

[86] *Either-Or*, II, pp. 95-96; S.V., II, 87.
[87] *Stages on Life's Way*, pp. 118-119; S.V., VI, 110.
[88] *Ibid.*, p. 165; S.V., VI, 160.

the married couple becomes the concrete execution of their stated intention: "The true idealizing resolution accordingly has this characteristic; it is signed in heaven and then it is countersigned in time."[89] The marriage vow before God is the signing of the lovers' resolution in heaven; their married life is the countersigning in time. In this entire process, nothing extraneous to love itself is added to the relationship. Rather, such a development is the perfection of love's fondest wishes:

"Already in the ethical and religious factors it [conjugal love] has duty in it, and when this appears before it, it is not as a stranger, a shameless intruder, who nevertheless has such authority that one dare not by virtue of the mysteriousness of love show him the door. No, duty comes as an old friend, an intimate, a confidant, whom the lovers mutually recognize in the deepest secret of their love. And when he speaks, it is nothing new he has to say; and when he has spoken, the individuals humble themselves under it, but at the same time are uplifted just because they are assured that what he enjoins they themselves wish, and that his commanding is merely a more majestic, a more exalted, a divine way of expressing the fact that their wish can be realized."[90]

With this understanding of God and eternity at the ethical stage, there is no tension between time and eternity. Quite to the contrary, eternity is the means by which one gives continuity to one's temporal becoming. There is a happy relationship between time and eternity, for the ethical man has his "eternity in time"[91] by virtue of his persistent commitment to the goals to which he has pledged himself.

Another way of making this point is to say that one's relationship to God grows *directly* out of one's perception of one's moral obligation. Insofar as the ethical man is concerned with religious matters, he is *immediately* related to God. At one point Kierkegaard comments: "The immediate relation to

---

[89] *Ibid.*, p. 116; S.V., VI, 108.
[90] *Either-Or*, II, pp. 148-149; S.V., II, 132.
[91] *Ibid.*, p. 142; S.V., II, 126.

God is paganism. . . ."[92] In an immediated (i.e., unmediated) relation to God, one relates oneself directly to God, and does not become related to God by means of a mediator. Briefly put, one has no relation with or concern about Christ.[93]

Another important consequence follows from the fact that the ethical relationship to God grows directly out of the sense of one's duty: there can be no conflict between ethical duty and religious obligation. As a matter of fact in the final analysis, ethical duty is itself divine: "The ethical is the universal [*Almene*] and as such it is again the divine [*Gyddommelige*]."[94] In the preceding analysis, we have seen that the ethicist believes that the ethical stage takes up into itself the aesthetic stage of existence.[95] Now it appears that the ethicist thinks that the religious stage of existence is also in harmony with the ethical. Ethical existence conceives the aesthetic, the ethical, and the religious dimensions of life to be harmoniously related, and to create no tensions among themselves. The Judge argues: "If you cannot reach the point of seeing the aesthetic, the ethical and the religious as three great allies, if you do not know how to conserve the unity of the diverse appearances which everything assumes in these diverse stages, then life is devoid of meaning, then one must grant that you are justified in maintaining your [Johannes'] pet theory that one can say of everything, 'Do it or don't do it — you will regret both.' "[96] To clarify his position on this central issue, Judge William again draws on his understanding of marriage: "Religion is not so foreign to human nature that a rupture is necessary in order to awaken it. But if the individuals in

[92] *Postscript*, p. 218; S.V., VII, 205.

[93] As will become apparent, this failure to become related to God through the mediator, Christ, is directly connected with the absence of a clear perception of sin at the ethical stage.

[94] *Fear and Trembling*, p. 78; S.V., III, 117.

[95] That is the point of the title (and the argument) of the Judge's essay, "The Aesthetic Validity of Marriage."

[96] *Either-Or*, II, p. 150; S.V., II, 134.

question are religious, then the power which encounters them in the wedding ceremony is not foreign to them. . . ."[97]

The continuity between the ethical and the religious as perceived from an ethical stance becomes evident in two of Judge William's discussions: one about the mystic in *Either-Or*, and the other about the religious exception in *Stages on Life's Way*. These arguments are especially important because, in large measure, the persons of whom the Judge is critical are understood from the viewpoint of the religious stage to be "knights of faith." The general characteristics of the mystic and of the religious exception are quite similar. There is, however, a difference in the Judge's argument in the two discussions. In *Either-Or*, the Judge is highly critical of the mystic. The mystic, the Judge thinks, is one who concerns himself solely with God to the exclusion of his relations with fellow men. "The whole world is a dead world for the mystic; he has fallen in love with God."[98] From the ethical perspective, it would, of course, be impossible for the love of God to cause one to become "dead to the world." The Judge accuses the mystic of "a certain intrusiveness in his relation to God," and continues by explaining that although one should love God: ". . . it by no means follows that the mystic is to disdain the reality of existence to which God has assigned him, for thereby he really disdains God's love or requires a different expression of it from that which God is willing to give."[99]

It becomes evident, however, that the primary criticism of the mystic from the ethical point of view is that his religious concern is distinguished from, and causes him to suspend, his ethical duty: "Finally, the life of the mystic displeases me because I regard it as a deceit against the world in which he lives, against the men to whom he is bound by obligations and with whom he might have come into relationship if he had not been pleased to become a mystic. . . . In choosing the solitary life he practices no deceit upon the others, for thereby he says to them in effect, 'I will have no relationship with

[97] *Ibid.*, p. 91; S.V., II, 82. [98] *Ibid.*, p. 247; S.V., II, 217.
[99] *Ibid.*, p. 248; S.V., II, 218.

230

you'; but the question is whether he has a right to say this, a right to do this. It is especially as a husband, as a father, that I am an enemy of mysticism."[100]

Judge William's opinion is somewhat more tempered in *Stages on Life's Way*, where he defines the religious exception as follows: "The religious abstraction desires to belong to God alone, for this love it is willing to disdain, renounce, sacrifice everything (these are the nuances); for this love it will not suffer itself to be disturbed, distracted, engrossed by anything else. . . ."[101] The Judge proceeds to outline the conditions that would have to be fulfilled for there to be such an exception. In so doing, he does admit the *possibility* of the religious exception. This is partly understandable in terms of the overall structure of *Stages on Life's Way*. The Judge's essay comes after *"In Vino Veritas,"* representative of the aesthetic stage, and before "Guilty/Not Guilty," descriptive of the religious stage. As such, Judge William both criticizes the aesthetic viewpoint and prepares the way for the religious stage. The main character of "Guilty/Not Guilty" fulfills the conditions laid down by William. Despite his willingness to admit the possibility of a religious exception, the Judge maintains: "I do not know whether there is such a justified exception, and if there be such a man, neither does he know it. . . ."[102] Furthermore, he reiterates the misgivings that dominate his consideration of the mystic when he writes that the religious exception's "inhumanity towards man is at the same time presumption towards God."[103]

---

[100] *Ibid.*, p. 249; S.V., II, 219. Compare: "He who devoted himself onesidedly to the mystical life becomes at last so alien to all men that every relationship, even the tenderest, the most heartfelt, becomes indifferent to him. It is not in this sense one is to love God more dearly than father and mother; God is not so self-loving as that, neither is He a poet who wishes to torment men with the most frightful collisions — and hardly could a more frightful thing be conceived than that there might be a collision between love for God and love for the persons for whom love has been planted by Him in our hearts," p. 249; S.V., II, 219.

[101] *Stages on Life's Way*, p. 169; S.V., VI, 165.

[102] *Ibid.*, p. 176; S.V., VI, 172.   [103] *Ibid.*, p. 169; S.V., VI, 165.

From the interpretation of the ethical stage that has been developed in this chapter, it should be clear that this form of existence presupposes, on the one hand, that man is able to understand his moral obligation: "The ethical is quite consistently very easy to understand, presumably in order that no time may be wasted, but a beginning made at once."[104] On the other hand, the ethicist holds that every person has the capacity to fulfill the obligation that has been understood: "Ethics points to ideality as a task and assumes that man is in possession of the conditions requisite for performing it."[105] In actual practice, however, the achievement of ideality proves to be very difficult. As a matter of fact, in striving to accomplish ideals, the ethical form of existence begins to break down, and the way is opened for the movement to the religious stage.

The first reason for the breakdown of the ethical stage is the fact that one is not successful in achieving a proper equilibrium among the various components of the self at this stage. Insofar as the self actualizes itself by free decision in which possibilities and actuality are dialectically related, the ethical stage represents a more authentic realization of selfhood than the aesthetic stage. But we have also seen that Kierkegaard believes the self to be constituted by God. Therefore, if the self is to establish an appropriate equilibrium, it must not only relate the components of possibility and actuality through freedom, but the whole self must relate itself, in dependence, to its constituting power. Here the shortcomings of ethical existence begin to appear. Because the primary concern of the ethicist is his own self-realization, it can be argued that his life is *self-assertion*: "If the individual is dialectical in himself inwardly in self-assertion [*Selvhævdelse*], hence in such a way that the ultimate basis is not dialectical in itself, inasmuch as the self which is at the basis

---

[104] *Postscript*, p. 350; S.V., VII, 339. See also *Journals and Papers*, no. 649; *Papirer*, VIII² B 81.
[105] *The Concept of Dread*, p. 15; S.V., IV, 288.

is used to overcome and assert itself, then we have the *ethical interpretation*."[106] At the ethical stage, the component of dependence on God, as the constituting and sustaining power, is not calculated sufficiently in the equation of selfhood.

The ethicist would respond that this is an unfair judgment, and would contend that the constant reference of duty to God is evidence of his recognition of the self's dependence upon God. Our analysis in this chapter should, however, make us suspicious of this argument. Self-realization remains the ethicist's primary interest, and God is subordinated to the self as the means by which one insures the permanence of one's intention, and thereby establishes the continuity of the self. The ethicist remains self-reliant. He believes himself able to understand his duty, and thinks that he has the capacity to fulfill it. From the ethical perspective, there is not an adequate sense of one's evil, and therefore no awareness of the need of a mediator through whom one might become related to God. Because ethical life is fundamentally an exercise of self-assertion in which dependence on God is not adequately acknowledged, the self remains in a state of disequilibrium.[107]

The second important reason for the breakdown of the ethical stage is the fact that the ethicist's optimism about his ability to achieve imagined ideals proves to be ill-founded. Ideals can never be fully translated into reality, but always remain goals that can be only gradually approximated. But ethics, by its very nature, continues to demand ideality: "Ethics would bring ideality into actuality [*Virkeligheden*]; on the other hand, its movement is not so designed to raise actuality up into ideality. Ethics points to ideality as a task and assumes that man is in possession of the conditions requisite for performing it. Thereby ethics develops a contradic-

---

[106] *Postscript*, p. 507; S.V., VII, 498.

[107] Malanschuk's comment is correct: "From the religious standpoint, it appears that even man's best endeavors in the human-ethical domain are basically an expression of self-assertion." *Kierkegaard's Way to the Truth, op.cit.*, p. 53.

tion, precisely for the fact that it makes the difficulty and the impossibility clear."[108]

By virtue of the very ideality built into ethical demands, the ethical stage of existence finally collapses. The standards that ethics sets are too ideal for man to fulfill. Yet the ethical person sees the fulfillment of these requirements as necessary for the achievement of his final *telos* — the realization of a unified self. With the failure to attain the ideality he had envisioned, the ethicist begins to perceive his own impotence. The self-confidence that had informed his efforts is called into question. Furthermore, as the ethicist recognizes his inability to achieve his aims, he assumes responsibility for his failure. With this development, the person begins to regard himself as guilty. But the ethicist understands his guilt analogously to the way in which error is understood in the process of knowing: "As all ancient thought and speculation were founded upon the assumption that thought had reality, so all ancient ethics was founded upon the assumption that virtue is realizable. Skepticism of sin is entirely foreign to paganism. For the ethical consciousness, sin is what error is in relation to knowledge, it is the particular exception which proves nothing."[109] Although the naive self-confidence that had once informed ethical striving is called into question by the ethicist's perception of his guilt, he still retains the conviction that his person is fundamentally good, and that he has the capacity to correct his errors.

But the ethicist soon discovers that the corruption of his self is more deep-going than he had first perceived. He is, in fact, a sinner: "In the fight to realize the task of ethics, sin shows itself not as something which only casually belongs to a casual individual, but sin withdraws deeper and deeper as a deeper and deeper presupposition, as a presupposition that goes well beyond the individual. Now all is lost for ethics, and ethics has contributed to the loss of all. There has come to the

<hr/>

[108] *The Concept of Dread*, p. 15; S.V., IV, 288.
[109] *Ibid.*, p. 17; S.V., IV, 292.

fore a category that lies entirely outside its province."[110] With the category of sin, one moves beyond the ethical stage of existence to the religious stage. Sin makes the ideality for which those at the ethical stage strive, and upon which all depends for the ethicist, impossible to accomplish: "Sin belongs to ethics only insofar as upon this concept it founders by aid of repentance. If ethics must include sin, all ideality is lost."[111]

For the reader sensitive to the theological background of Kierkegaard's reflection, the parallel with Luther's thought at this point should be evident. An explicit statement of the similarities between the two thinkers serves as a convenient summary of ethical religiosity and leads us toward the religious stage of existence. Kierkegaard indicates the background of his thinking when he writes: "What is said of the Law applies to ethics, that it is a severe schoolmaster, which in making a demand, by its demand only condemns, does not give birth to life."[112] Kierkegaard's understanding of the ethical stage and its relation to the Christian religious stage is in many ways congruent with Luther's understanding of the law and its relationship to the Gospel. Luther argues that the law makes unrelenting demands upon the one to whom it is addressed, which, if taken seriously, lead one to see one's own inability to conform to its dictates. This situation can cause one to despair. The law itself, however, cannot lead one beyond the point of recognizing weakness. To progress further, it is necessary to receive the Gospel. In this way, the law prepares the way for the Gospel. The law condemns; the Gospel forgives, and gives "birth to life."

We have seen that Kierkegaard argues that through the ideality of ethical demands one recognizes that one cannot completely accomplish one's duty. At first the ethicist insists that although he is guilty of not achieving the goals for which he had worked, his failure is the result of errors and can, with

[110] *Ibid.*, p. 17; S.V., IV, 292.   [111] *Ibid.*, p. 16; S.V., IV, 291.
[112] *Ibid.*, p. 15; S.V., IV, 288.

increased labor, be corrected. Further efforts, however, also prove to be of no avail. Here one reaches the limit of the ethical stage, and is pointed in the direction of the religious stage of existence. For this reason, Kierkegaard argues that "the ethical stage is only a transitional [*Gjennemgangssphære*] stage."[113] The requirement that ethics places upon the individual is "so infinite that the individual always goes bankrupt."[114] In his bankruptcy, the individual turns toward the religious stage of existence, for "the religious stage is that of fulfillment."[115]

[113] *Stages on Life's Way*, p. 430; S.V., VI, 443.
[114] *Ibid.*, p. 430; S.V., VI, 443.   [115] *Ibid.*, p. 430; S.V., VI, 443.

CHAPTER SIX

PROPAEDEUTIC TO CHRISTIANITY: RELIGION *A*

A. GOD'S TRANSCENDENCE — MAN'S BLESSEDNESS

The movement from the ethical to the religious stage of existence is rather complex. Part of the reason for this lies in the nature of the religious stage itself. Unlike the ethical, but like the aesthetic, the religious stage is bipolar. Kierkegaard includes under the general category of the religious stage religion *A* and Christianity, religion *B*.[1] At this point in our argument, we must consider the manner in which religion *A* functions within Kierkegaard's dialectic as a propaedeutic to Christianity. Before we do so, however, it will be helpful to try to define the general characteristics of the religious stage shared by religion *A* and Christianity that differentiate it from other stages of existence.

The first important feature of the religious stage is that a clear distinction is established between God and the world (or the self). At the aesthetic stage, where one's primary concern is enjoyment, the question of God is not raised at all. As a matter of fact, there is not even enough differentiation of the self from its surroundings for the self to be able to identify itself over against the not-self (God, for example). At the ethical stage, the chief interest is the realization of one's individual self. It is true that the ethicist invokes God. But when the ethical stance is examined, it becomes apparent that God functions as the means by which one attempts to secure the continuity or the unity of the self. In the final analysis, the ethicist does not distinguish God from the ethical order. "The

---

[1] This distinction is most clearly articulated in *Philosophical Fragments* and *Concluding Unscientific Postscript*.

ethical is the universal, and as such, it is again the divine."[2] The failure to differentiate adequately between God and world is closely associated with what Kierkegaard regards as the principal shortcoming of the ethical stage: the failure to recognize the total dependence of the self upon God.

From a religious perspective, the equation of God with the ethical order is actually a denial of God. Ethical principles are products of man, even though one may perceive their binding power only by referring them to God. Since ethical mandates are man's creations, one does not, through his relation to duty, become related to God. In ethical obligation, one remains within the human realm. "If I say in this connection that it is my duty to love God, I am really uttering only a tautology, inasmuch as 'God' is in this instance used in an entirely abstract sense as divine, i.e. the universal, i.e. duty. So the whole existence of the human race is rounded off completely like a sphere, and the ethical is at once its limit and its content. God becomes an invisible vanishing point, a powerless thought. His power being only the ethical which is the content of existence."[3]

For the religious person, God and the world are "absolutely different": "But as between God and a human being (for let speculative philosophy keep *humanity* to play tricks with) there is an absolute difference. In man's absolute relationship to God, this absolute difference must therefore come to expression, and any attempt to express an immediate likeness becomes impertinence, frivolity, effrontery, and the like."[4] There is, however, a difference in the exact manner in which religion *A* and Christianity specify the distinction between God and the world. Religion *A* defines the difference between God and man (the world) as the difference between the Creator and the creature. Christianity recognizes and accepts this distinction, but also finds a deeper difference between God and man. God is holy, and man is sinful. This insight

---

[2] *Fear and Trembling*, p. 78; S.V., III, 117. See above, p. 229.
[3] *Ibid.*, p. 78; S.V., II, 117.   [4] *Postscript*, p. 369; S.V., VII, 357.

leads Christianity to a more profound awareness of the self's dependence on God. While religion *A* understands God to be the Creator, Christianity, by the recognition of sin, also acknowledges that God is man's Re-Creator. For the Christian, God reestablishes the possibility of the self's salvation, a possibility that the self forfeited through sin. The mention of the problem of salvation leads directly to the next point to be made in this connection.

The second general characteristic of the religious stage that is important to notice for our purposes is the self's concern about its eternal blessedness.[5] This is closely related to the recognition of the difference between God and the world. With the development of the belief that God and the world are absolutely different, there is a shift in the fundamental *interest* of the self. The conviction arises that one's proper end lies not in the world but with God. Because the religious stage frequently expresses the difference between God and the world in terms of the difference between eternity and time, the claim is made that one's dominant interest is not the *temporal* self but is *eternal* blessedness. But here again there is a distinction between religion *A* and Christianity. Each views time and its relation to eternity differently. Consequently, there is a different understanding of the self and of the self's relationship to eternal blessedness at each pole of the religious stage. To begin to understand this difference, and hence to prepare the way for the discussion of religion *A*, it will be helpful to try to define what Kierkegaard means by "eternal blessedness."

Kierkegaard's use of "eternal blessedness" is highly ambiguous. It is, therefore, rather difficult to establish his primary meaning. One reason for much of the confusion regarding the definition of "eternal blessedness" is that Kierkegaard often

[5] It will be recalled (p. 8 above) that "blessedness" is used in this essay as the translation of the Danish *Salighed*. Most English translations use "happiness" at this point. Blessedness (or salvation) is, however, more in keeping with Kierkegaard's intention.

seems to use "eternal" or "truth" interchangeably with this phrase. The issue is further complicated by Kierkegaard's equation of God with the Eternal. In many instances, one is uncertain whether Kierkegaard is referring to eternal blessedness or to God. In addition to this, Kierkegaard's detailed consideration of the nature of religious truth makes the interchange of "eternal blessedness" and "truth" quite confusing.[6] We are not helped by the lack of an explicit discussion of this important term in Kierkegaard's works. He takes the individual's interest in eternal blessedness as the point of departure for both *Philosophical Fragments* and *Concluding Unscientific Postscript* to the *Fragments*. It is as if Kierkegaard assumes that the reader knows what he means by "eternal blessedness." We are, therefore, forced to discern Kierkegaard's meaning from his indirect comments on the subject.

It seems that a most important feature of eternal blessedness for Kierkegaard is eternal life or immortality. There is one point at which he equates eternal blessedness and immortality: "Existing religiously, one can express one's relationship to an eternal blessedness [*evig Salighed*] (immortality [*Udødelighed*]), outside of Christianity. . . ."[7] Eternal blessedness is very closely associated with personal immortality. There are, of course, other dimensions of eternal blessedness. Most notably, Kierkegaard believes that in one's immortality the self abides with God. However, as the necessary condition of any other aspects of eternal blessedness, immortality remains the central feature of *evig Salighed*. Especially at the Christian stage of existence, eternal blessedness (*evig Salighed*) is quite closely associated with one's salvation (*Salighed*). Kierkegaard argues that eternal blessedness is the self's eternal salvation. This salvation involves, most importantly, the eternal life or immortality of the self.

---

[6] See above chapter two, sections A and B.

[7] *Postscript*, p. 496; S.V., VII, 488. It should be pointed out that in many of his comments about eternal blessedness, Kierkegaard is indirectly criticizing the notion of an impersonal immortality as expressed by Spinoza and Hegel.

It becomes apparent that two of the primary characteristics of the religious stage as a whole are: (1) the distinction between God and the world; and (2) the self's interest in eternal blessedness, salvation, or immortality. We have suggested that the two poles of the religious stage, religion *A* and Christianity, understand these issues differently. We must now turn our attention to religion *A*. It will be argued that while religion *A*'s understanding of the implications for the self of the distinction between God and the world represents an advance on the ethical stage of existence, its view of the self's relation to eternal blessedness is, for Kierkegaard, deficient and represents the point at which Christianity advances beyond religion *A*.

B. Religion *A*

Much of the difficulty in arriving at a satisfactory understanding of religion *A* results from Kierkegaard's ambiguous presentation of the phenomenon. Although the term "religion *A*" is devised in the *Postscript*, the form of religiosity that it represents is evident throughout many of Kierkegaard's earlier writings. It seems that in the case of religion *A*, Kierkegaard's thinking is somewhat unclear. There are certain inconsistencies in the manner in which he characterizes this form of existence. Furthermore, the exact way in which he wishes to distinguish it from Christianity is not always evident. Part of the reason for this is that he is less interested in this form of existence for its own sake than he is in any other. His concern is not to describe a distinct stage of existence, but to delineate a point of view that brings into sharp focus the peculiarities of the Christian understanding of time and of the self.

Kierkegaard's imprecision in discussing religion *A* has led to great confusion among commentators. It is common to follow one of three courses: (1) to ignore religion *A* completely, and to move directly from the interpretation of the ethical stage to the Christian stage; (2) to identify religion *A* with a variation of what has been described in the previous chapter as "ethical religiosity"; or (3) to confuse religion *A* and Christianity. None of these alternatives is satisfactory. Certainly one cannot ignore religion *A*, for Kierkegaard repeatedly refers to it, and in his mind it has an important place in the dialectic of existence. Neither can it be confused with the ethical stage or with the Christian stage of existence. We will try to understand religion *A* by focusing on the general features of the religious stage defined above: the relation between God and the world, and the self's interest in eternal blessedness. From our analysis, it will become clear that these two issues are very closely related to the two themes that we have been discussing throughout our study: time and the self. Kierkegaard's argument about religion *A* paves the way for his final discussion of time and the self at the Christian stage.

Let us begin by exploring the way in which the person at the stage of religion *A* understands the relationship between God and the world.[8] As we have seen, at the ethical stage of existence there is no clear distinction drawn between God and the world. The ethicist's chief interest is his personal self-realization, in which he seeks to give continuity to his self by referring his duties to God. The result of this is that, in the final analysis, God is identified with the ethical order. The lack of a clear awareness of the difference between God and the world results in the failure of the ethical stage of existence adequately to comprehend the self's dependence upon God, a shortcoming that leads to a disequilibrium within the self. Religion *A* expresses the awareness of the absolute difference between God and man, and the ontological dependence of the self upon God, by believing that God is the Creator and man is a creature. Insofar as religion *A* recognizes the dependence of the self upon God, it represents an advance upon the ethical stage. There is, for Kierkegaard, a more adequate understanding of the structure of selfhood at

---

[8] Given the strictures of this book, our chief concern within the more general problem of the relation between God and the world is the relationship between God and the self.

the stage of religion *A*. Religion *A* does not, however, stop with the knowledge of the self's dependence upon God, but proceeds to try to embody this awareness in existence. How this is done should be considered, for it forms one of the distinguishing marks of religion *A*.

If there is an "absolute difference" between God and man, then one's obligation to God must be distinguishable from one's obligation both to his own self and to his fellow man. Speaking in terms of the more general issue of which the relation between God and man is a part, we can argue that because God and the world are absolutely different, one's responsibility to God can be distinguished from one's obligation to the world. Such a distinction cannot, of course, arise at the ethical stage, where ethical obligation and duty to God always coincide. In light of the distinction between God and the world made at the religious stage, it is sheer folly to devote one's highest interests to the world, for the world is not absolute. Kierkegaard comments that: ". . . it is precisely the most general expression for madness that the individual has an absolute relationship to that which is relative."[9] Yet from the religious point of view, it is just such an absolute devotion to the relative that characterizes both aesthetic and ethical existence.

The understanding of the relationship of dependence between the self and God poses a task for the self. At the stage of religion *A*, ". . . the maximum of attainment is simultaneously to sustain an absolute relationship to the absolute end, and a relative relationship to relative ends."[10] God is absolute, and the world is the relative. A person who lives at the stage of religion *A* attempts to devote himself absolutely to his Creator and relatively to the creation. Through absolute dedication to God, the self seeks to overcome one of the chief problems of ethical existence: the absence of a sufficient recognition of one's ontological dependence on God.

It is, however, quite difficult to embody the double relationship of an absolute relation to the absolute and a relative

[9] *Postscript*, p. 378; S.V., VII, 366. [10] *Ibid.*, p. 371; S.V., VII, 359.

relation to the relative. In the following passage, Kierkegaard makes a sharp distinction between religion *A* and the forms of existence that have preceded it in his dialectic of existence:

"In the immediate consciousness there is rooted the wish to have the power to do everything, and ideally its faith is that it can do everything, its factual inability being apprehended as due to an obstacle which comes from without, and from which it therefore essentially abstracts, just as it abstracts from misfortune; for the immediate consciousness is not dialectical in itself. Religiously it is the task of the individual to understand that he is nothing before God, or to become wholly nothing and to exist thus before God; this consciousness of impotence he requires constantly to have before him, and when it vanishes, the religiosity also vanishes."[11]

For religion *A*, God is the omnipotent source of all being upon whom the self depends absolutely. Therefore, "the religious individual lies fettered with the absolute conception of God present to him in human frailty."[12] This situation causes him to suffer "his annihilation in his nothingness."[13]

The precise mode in which the individual expresses his nothingness before God, and thereby accomplishes the simultaneous absolute relationship to the absolute and relative relation to the relative, needs further specification. With the consideration of the manner in which the self expresses absolute devotion to God, we begin to see some of the diversity in Kierkegaard's understanding of religion *A*. The form of religiosity that Kierkegaard later labels religion *A* makes its first appearance in *Fear and Trembling*. The general characteristic of the religious stage that we have been examining, the distinction between God and the world, is helpful in discerning the main thrust of Kierkegaard's argument. We have seen that while for the ethicist, ethical obligation and duty to God coincide, at the religious stage, devotion to God and duty to the world are clearly distinguishable. In order to make this point as sharply as he is able, Kierkegaard raises the possi-

[11] *Ibid.*, p. 412; S.V., vii, 401.   [12] *Ibid.*, p. 432; S.V., vii, 420.
[13] *Ibid.*, p. 386; S.V., vii, 365.

bility that one's duty to God and his duty to the world may come into conflict.[14] He does this by considering the possibility of what he calls "a teleological suspension of the ethical [*en teleologisk Suspension af det Ethiske*]." Kierkegaard uses the story of God's command that Abraham sacrifice his son Isaac (Genesis 22) as an example of this phenomenon. Because ethical obligation and devotion to God can be distinguished, he thinks that it is possible for them to come into conflict. If such a conflict emerges, a person at the stage of religion *A* believes that the ethical mandate must be "suspended" because of one's absolute relation to a higher *telos* — to God. In this situation, there is a teleological suspension of the ethical. By a consideration of Kierkegaard's analysis of Abraham, the meaning and the implications of his argument become considerably clearer.

Abraham believes that God asks him to sacrifice his only son, Isaac. Such a command does not cancel Abraham's ethical obligation to his son: "Abraham's relation to Isaac, ethically speaking, is quite simply expressed by saying that a father shall love his son more dearly than himself."[15] This is based on Kierkegaard's conviction that a later stage of existence does not abolish an earlier stage, but takes the earlier stage up into itself while giving it a relativized status. As the ethicist argues that the aesthetic is taken up into the ethical, so, from the viewpoint of religion *A*, the ethical is taken up into the religious: "So when in this connection it is said that it is a duty to love God, something different is said from that in the foregoing; for if this duty is absolute, the ethical is reduced to a position of relativity. From this, however, it does not follow that the ethical is to be abolished...."[16]

The fact that the ethical obligation for Abraham to love Isaac remains even in the face of God's command to kill his

---

[14] Kierkegaard discusses the same problematic, though with different implications, in "Guilty/Not Guilty?" the third part of *Stages on Life's Way*.

[15] *Fear and Trembling*, p. 67; S.V., III, 107.

[16] *Ibid.*, p. 80; S.V., III, 119.

son is precisely what creates the "fear and trembling" in the situation. The ethical demand is no longer an ideal to be realized but a temptation. Abraham is tempted to forego the demand of God and to repent himself back into the ethical, acknowledging that the whole episode was a terrible mistake. The situation is complicated by the fact that Abraham cannot fully understand the command, and he cannot make himself understood to others.[17] We have seen in a previous context[18] that ethical obligation is by nature universal, and hence is understandable for all persons. Thus when the tragic hero must sacrifice his daughter for the welfare of the whole state, people comprehend his duty and respect him for the courage to carry it through.[19] With Abraham the case is different.[20] He stands in what Kierkegaard calls an "absolute relation to the absolute."[21] This might be better expressed by saying that he stands in a wholly individual (or private) relationship to God. His sacrifice of Isaac has no higher ethical *telos*. It is carried out for the sake of no larger social whole, but is done for the sole reason that God commands it. What, then, does Kierkegaard think can be accomplished by a situation that

[17] This is the reason that Kierkegaard continually stresses the theme of "silence" throughout the work. Abraham *cannot* speak (or think) about his duty to God, for to do so would require the use of the universal categories of thought or language. Because his is an *individual* relationship to the absolute, Abraham's situation cannot be subsumed under universal categories. This is the reason he speaks neither to Sarah nor to Isaac. Kierkegaard consistently compares this form of silence to what he calls the demonic. A chief characteristic of the demonic is that it *willfully* remains in silence. The demonic is able to reveal itself, but chooses not to do so. Abraham cannot speak in order to reveal himself even if he so desires.

[18] See above p. 196.

[19] Upon this basis, Kierkegaard argues that the ethical offers one a certain "security." "He [the person at the stage of religion *A*] knows that it is refreshing to become intelligible to oneself in the universal so that he understands it and so that every individual who understands him understands through him in turn the universal, and both rejoice in the security of the universal." *Fear and Trembling*, p. 86; S.V., III, 124.

[20] See *Fear and Trembling*, pp. 67ff; S.V., III, 107ff.

[21] *Ibid.*, p. 66; S.V., III, 106.

would "transform a murder into a holy act well-pleasing to God"?[22]

The major point that Kierkegaard wishes to make in this part of his analysis of the Abraham-Isaac story is that at the stage of religion *A* ethical obligation is relativized as the result of the awareness of the distinction between God and the world. One's primary concern is believingly to offer absolute devotion to God. Abraham does this by his willingness to sacrifice his son simply because he thinks that God has commanded it. In *Fear and Trembling* Kierkegaard calls the movement exemplified by Abraham's readiness to sacrifice Isaac "infinite resignation [*uendelige Resignation*]," and one who makes this movement a "knight of infinite resignation." Through infinite resignation, one seeks to acknowledge his total dependence on God by resigning the things of the world completely. One recognizes that it is not from one's own self, or even from the world as a whole, that one has one's being. God, the one who is absolutely different from the world, is the power that constitutes and sustains the self (and all else). The case of Abraham is well-suited to Kierkegaard's purpose. Isaac is Abraham's most precious possession. As his only son, Isaac is Abraham's sole hope for personal extension in the world of space and time. The willingness to resign Isaac indicates Abraham's readiness to relinquish the totality of the worldly sphere. However, as should be evident from the preceding comments concerning Abraham's relation to Isaac, this does not mean that one completely ignores his life in the world at the stage of religion *A*. One's obligation to the world is relativized by devotion to God. In this way, the self seeks simultaneously "to sustain an absolute relation to an absolute end, and a relative relationship to relative ends." To resign the world infinitely is to believe that one's life comes not from oneself or from the world, but comes from the One to whom he gives absolute devotion — from God.[23]

---

[22] *Ibid.*, p. 64; S.V., III, 103.

[23] It should be noted that throughout *Fear and Trembling* Kierkegaard contrasts infinite resignation with faith. He argues that although

The implications of the distinction between God and the creature at the stage of religion *A* become more evident when it is recognized that there are two other terms that Kierkegaard uses virtually interchangeably with "infinite resignation" in his later works: "renunciation" [*Forsagelsen*] and "to die away from" [*afdø*]. In order to maintain an absolute relation to God, the individual must infinitely resign, renounce, or die away from the world. In religion *A*, one ". . . begins by exercising himself in the absolute relationship through renunciation. . . . In order that the individual may sustain an absolute relationship to the absolute *telos*, he must first have exercised himself in the renunciation of relative ends, and only then can there be a question of the ideal task: the simultaneous maintenance of an absolute relationship to the absolute, and a relative relationship to the relative. But not before, for before this the individual is always to some degree immediate, and is involved absolutely in relative ends."[24]

In each form of existence prior to religion *A*, the self does not adequately recognize its dependence on God, and therefore is not devoted absolutely to God but to some relative good. Such a person must first renounce that to which he had given allegiance; he must die away from the world. Kierkegaard most frequently expresses this requirement of religion *A* by saying that it is necessary "to die away from the self."[25] This means that the self must see that it is not self-sufficient but fully dependent on God. One must die away from his reliance on himself, and on anything of the world, i.e., anything other than God. Because the self must renounce completely

---

infinite resignation is the last stage prior to faith, it is not faith itself. In the final analysis, Abraham is a "knight of faith" who makes the second movement of faith after having made the first one of infinite resignation. What is involved in faith will become more evident in the next chapter.

[24] *Postscript*, pp. 386-387; S.V., VII, 374-375.

[25] *Ibid.*, p. 422; S.V., VII, 410. Notice the difference between this aspect of religion *A* and ethical religiosity as defined in the foregoing chapter (pp. 224ff.).

that in which it had had its life, such infinite resignation, renunciation, or dying away from the self is very difficult, and brings suffering to the individual: "This suffering has its ground in the fact that the individual is in his immediacy absolutely committed to relative ends; its significance lies in the transposition of the relationship, or the dying away from immediacy, or in the expression existentially of the principle that the individual can do absolutely nothing of himself, but is as nothing before God; for here again the negative is the mark by which the God-relationship is recognized, and self-annihilation [*Selvtilintetgjørelsen*] is the essential form of the God-relationship."[26] This suffering is not physical but the inward suffering that arises with the effort to reevaluate and to reorient one's entire life.

It becomes evident that one's absolute relationship to the absolute and relative relation to the relative are dialectically related. Through the infinite resignation of the world one expresses one's absolute relation to God. It is, therefore, necessary to remain in the world, but constantly to renounce the world as the source of one's being, and to recognize God as the sole Creator and Sustainer. Kierkegaard offers his most illuminating analysis of religion *A* in the following lines: "The edifying element at the stage of religiousness *A* is essentially that of immanence, it is the annihilation [*Tilintetgjørelse*] by which the individual puts himself out of the way in order to find God, since precisely the individual himself is the hindrance. Quite rightly the edifying is recognizable here also by the negative, by self-annihilation, which in itself finds the God relationship, is based upon it, because God is the basis when every obstacle is cleared away, and first and foremost the individual himself in his finiteness, in his obstinacy against God."[27]

[26] *Ibid.*, p. 412; S.V., vii, 401.

[27] *Ibid.*, pp. 497-498; S.V., vii, 487. Compare Kierkegaard's revealing remark: "And this is the miracle of creation, not the creation of something which is nothing over against the Creator, but the creation of something which is something, and which in true worship of God can

From our analysis, it is clear that at the stage of religion *A* there is a more complete recognition of the difference between God and the self, and therefore a deeper awareness of the self's ontological dependence upon God. This perception is embodied in the individual's life through the infinite resignation, renunciation, or dying away from the world and from the self as the source of one's being. The more usual religious expression for this form of existence is "Humility . . . the humility that frankly admits its human lowliness with humble cheerfulness before God, trusting that God knows all this better than man himself."[28]

We have seen that while one general characteristic of the religious stage of existence is the distinction between God and the world, a second of its major features is the self's interest in eternal blessedness. Religion *A*'s understanding of the self's dependence on God is the chief advance upon the ethical stage. But its view of the self's relation to eternal blessedness represents the point at which a Christian perspective is most critical of religion *A*. We must now examine how religion *A* sees the self to be related to its eternal blessedness. It will be recalled that Kierkegaard understands eternal blessedness to be salvation, the principal feature of which is the self's eternal life or immortality.

One of the points that Kierkegaard repeatedly makes in discussing religion *A* is that from this viewpoint the self is, by nature, immortal. In the course of distinguishing religion *A*

---

use this something [i.e., the self itself, or the self's freedom] in order by its true self to become nothing before God," p. 220; S.V., VII, 207.

[28] *Ibid.*, p. 440; S.V., VII, 428. It should be recognized that although Kierkegaard always presents religion *A* in dialectical relation with Christianity, he does hold that the former can exist independently of the latter. For example: "Existing religiously, one can express one's relationship to an eternal blessedness (immortality, eternal life) outside of Christianity, and this has surely been done; for of religiousness *A* one may say that, even if it has not been exemplified in paganism, it could have been, because it has only human nature in general as its assumption . . . ," p. 496; S.V., VII, 486.

and religion *B*, he comments: "The problem constantly dealt with here is this: how there can be an historical starting-point [for an eternal blessedness]. In religiousness *A* there is no historical starting-point. The individual merely discovers in time that he must assume he is eternal. The moment in time is therefore *eo ipso* swallowed up by eternity. In time the individual recollects that he is eternal. This contradiction lies exclusively in immanence."[29]

Kierkegaard most frequently uses Socrates as an example of a person who represents religion *A* through the conviction of the immortality of the soul. Many of Kierkegaard's arguments try to define the peculiarity of Christian religiousness by contrasting it with religion *A* as presented by Socrates. As the above quotation states, in religion *A*, "the individual merely discovers in time that he must assume he is eternal." The basis for this claim is Kierkegaard's understanding of the Socratic doctrine of recollection. As is well-known, in the *Meno* Socrates argues that all knowing is remembering.[30] This argument is based on the conviction that one can seek neither what one knows (for if one knows it, one does not need to seek it), nor what one does not know (for if one did not know, one would be incapable of seeking it). Thus the truth[31] that an individual seeks must once have been known, but subsequently forgotten. Insofar as one seeks a more complete knowledge of "eternal truth" one must at one time have had a knowledge of that truth, or else one could not inquire about it. In order to explain this implicit "knowledge" of truth, it must be presupposed that the soul is immortal. In the doctrine of recollection: ". . . the Truth is not introduced into the individual from without, but was within him. This thought receives further development at the hands of Socrates, and it

[29] *Ibid.*, p. 508; S.V., VII, 500.

[30] For Kierkegaard's account of Socratic recollection, see *Philosophical Fragments*, ch. I, pp. 11-27; S.V., IV, 179-191.

[31] Unfortunately much confusion is caused by Kierkegaard's repeated failure to specify exactly what he means by "Truth" or by "eternal truth" in this context.

ultimately becomes the point of concentration for the pathos of the Greek consciousness, since it serves as a proof for the immortality of the soul; but with a backward reference, it is important to note, and hence as proof for the soul's pre-existence."[32]

If eternal blessedness is to be understood in terms of the self's immortality, then, based on the preceding arguments, religion *A* would contend that the self is in possession of eternal blessedness. This does not, however, mean that temporal existence does not pose a problem for the self from religion *A*'s perspective. Indeed, the very immortality of the self is a source of the individual's dilemma. One is at once immortal and temporal. Yet within this tension, it is thought that one's real destiny lies in his immortality — in the relation to the eternal God. The sheer fact of temporal existence separates the self from its proper *telos*.

The belief that the self is immortal has significant implications that distinguish religion *A* from Christianity. We can define the major aspects of the differences by turning directly to the two primary themes of this essay: the self and time.

We have argued that in comparison to the aesthetic and the ethical stages, religion *A* represents a more adequately realized self to the extent that the self's ontological dependence on God is acknowledged. However, further implications of the structure of selfhood as conceived by religion *A* now become apparent. From the perspective of religion *A*, the self is regarded as *inherently* immortal. Religion *A* sees two primary dimensions of selfhood: an immortal soul and life in the temporal world. In the context of the discussion of Kierkegaard's view of the structure of selfhood, it was argued that he contrasts time and eternity in terms of being and becoming. With respect to selves, time is a process of becoming that is generated by decision. One of the chief characteristics of eternity was seen to be its unchangeability. At this stage of Kierkegaard's dialectic the distinction between temporality and

[32] *Philosophical Fragments*, pp. 11-12; S.V., IV, 180.

eternity again becomes important. When he argues that the self is a synthesis of the temporal and the eternal, we have seen that he means that the self's unchanging (eternal) component is freedom, while its changing (temporal) dimension is the interrelationship of its various possibilities and actualities.[33] The case is quite different for religion *A*. Here too the self is understood to include both temporality and eternity. In this instance, however, "temporal" designates the totality of the self's life in time, and "eternal" refers to an essential, inner, immortal soul that is opposed to, and stands in tension with, the temporal life of the self. Although immersed in the flux of temporal becoming, the self retains an essential core exempt from temporality. This immortal soul is "eternal," or unchanging.

The understanding of the structure of selfhood as conceived by religion *A* will be illuminated if we recall the previous discussion of the historical context in which Kierkegaard develops his understanding of the self.[34] It was noted that a common way to conceive the self is as comprised of substance and accidents. The accidents refer to the changing experiences of the self. Substance, as that which exists in and through itself, is the permanent, unchanging aspect of the self that unites ever-changing accidents. The notion of the self held by religion *A* is analogous to the substantialistic conception of selfhood.[35] The self is made up of an immortal soul and constantly changing temporal experiences. The soul itself suffers no change.

The belief in the immortality of the soul does not negate the conviction that the self is dependent upon God. As a matter of fact, the immortal soul is the "point of contact"[36] be-

---

[33] See above chapter three, section B, 3.

[34] See above chapter three, section B, 2.

[35] It can be argued that the substantialistic views of selfhood derive from earlier doctrines of the soul and its immortality. For an analysis of this point, see: Sydney Shoemaker, *Self-Knowledge and Self-Identity*, *op.cit.*

[36] This term, of course, is very important in the debates of neoortho-

tween the self and the absolutely different God. The self's immortality is its participation in the realm of the Eternal, or of God. The manner in which Kierkegaard expresses this for religion *A* is by saying that the self retains a knowledge of the Eternal or of eternal truth that is a function of the relationship to the Eternal prior to the self's temporal existence. Although coming to be in the temporal world obscures this knowledge and weakens the relationship, it never causes the severance of the connection between the Eternal God and the immortal soul. The bond remains and need only be made explicit.

Therefore, religion *A* conceives the two major aspects of the self to be an immortal soul and a changing temporal life. We must now examine the relationship between these two dimensions of selfhood. For our purposes, the most important fact to note is that the self's life in the world does not affect its essential immortal soul. To put it in more Kierkegaardian terms, the self's eternal blessedness is not influenced by its existence in time. Because religion *A* believes the soul to be immortal *by its very nature*, one's life in the world does not change the fact of the soul's immortality. Temporality must be endured, but has no final significance for the self, whose chief concern lies with the Eternal from which it has come and to which it desires to return. This makes apparent another aspect of the self's infinite resignation, dying away from the world, or renunciation. Not only does such resignation signify the self's recognition of its dependence on God, but it also indicates the self's thoroughly negative relationship to the entire temporal world. The world can be resigned because, in the final analysis, the immortal soul (the self's chief interest) is indifferent to life in the world. The ideal is to escape time and to return to eternity.

The criticisms that Kierkegaard makes of religion *A*'s view

---

doxy concerning the possibility of natural theology that dominated the first half of this century. Kierkegaard's criticism of religion *A* from the point of view of religion *B*, is similar to the neoorthodox criticism of natural theology.

of the self are implicit in our previous comments concerning his understanding of the self. Certainly he agrees with religion A's comprehension of the self's dependence upon God. But Kierkegaard cannot accept the contention that the self is immortal by nature. He refuses to acknowledge that there is an essential, immortal soul of the self that is indifferent to and unaffected by the self's temporal duration. One can argue that at this point religion A represents a regression in relation to the ethical stage with respect to the realization of the self. As has become apparent, Kierkegaard argues that decision is constitutive of individual selfhood. While it is true that the self has a definite structure, an immortal soul is not a component of selfhood. Within the general structure of selfhood, decision is the means by which the self defines itself. These decisions are not merely associated with an unessential aspect of the self that does not penetrate to the all-important core of selfhood. Religion A's conviction of the soul's immortality manifests a failure to recognize that decisions are thoroughly definitive of the self, or that the self is what it becomes through its decisions.

We have also seen that religion A's conviction that the self has an immortal soul represents the belief in an unalterable "point of contact" between God and man. Though strained by the fact of existence, this point of contact is never lost. Because of this, though religion A can understand that the self might become guilty, it cannot grasp the possibility of sin. Here religion A is in substantial agreement with the ethical stage, though the terms in which this is expressed differ significantly. Kierkegaard maintains that the difference between guilt and sin is difficult to discern. The basis for the distinction is given in the following text: "In the consciousness of guilt, it is the same subject that becomes essentially guilty by keeping guilt in relation to an eternal blessedness, but yet the individuality of the subject is such that guilt does not make the subject a new man, which is characteristic of the breach [i.e., of sin]."[37]

[37] *Postscript*, p. 474; S.V., vii, 464.

The important point to underscore in this text is the contention that guilt does not make one a "new man." When the self is regarded as guilty, it is viewed as making occasional errors that can, with effort, be corrected. From the perspective of religion A, it is again the lack of a clear awareness of the significance of decisions that leads to this consequence. For religion A, decisions do not transform the deepest dimensions of selfhood, making one a "new man." Because Kierkegaard sees sin as radical, he does not think that a recognition of the self's sinfulness can emerge from the viewpoint of religion A. When sin is fathomed, the self loses its "point of contact" with God that religion A seeks to retain.

The absence of a clear sense of the centrality of decision for the life of the self is also closely related to a second major problem of religion A. We have seen that time is understood (and experienced) differently at the different stages of existence. While for aesthetic existence there is always a concentration on one tense of time to the exclusion of the other two, for ethical existence, the past and the future are joined with the present in the moment of decision. Interestingly enough, religion A's view of time comes closest to that of the immediate aesthetic, where time is regarded as an infinite succession of disjoined "nows." The basis for this view of time is, however, quite different in each case. Religion A does not arrive at the view of time as a series of disconnected nows as the result of the immersion in sensual immediacy that seeks to exclude the disruption of the past and the future. Rather, it conceives time in this manner because time has no final importance for religion A. Time is the flux in which the unchangeable immortal soul has become ensnared, and from which it seeks to extricate itself.

Furthermore, it has been argued that for religion A the soul's immortality represents the self's essential relationship with the Eternal. Because of this essential, immutable kinship with the Eternal, the self does not have to establish its relationship with God through the decisions of its own life. Indeed, the self could not so constitute a relationship with God,

256

for the temporal life of the self is inconsequential for its eternal destiny. Kierkegaard comments on the implications of the conviction of the immortality of the soul for one's view of time when he states that for religion *A*, ". . . existence in time does not have any decisive significance, because the possibility of taking oneself back into eternity through recollection [*erindrende*] is always there. . . ."[38]

Kierkegaard's polemic against a "retrogressive" or "backwards" relation to Eternity runs throughout *Philosophical Fragments* and *Concluding Unscientific Postscript*. It is always contrasted with Christianity's claim that one must become related to God prospectively or forwards. By this Kierkegaard means that because of the conviction of the self's immortal soul, religion *A* does not think that the self must define itself in the most fundamental way through the decisions of one's lifetime. What is most essential to the self it has by nature: an immortal soul that establishes the self's unchangeable relationship with God. Christianity, however, denies that there is such an essential soul, and understands decision to be thoroughly definitive of selfhood. Therefore if one is to become related to God, it must be as a result of being the person that one becomes through one's decisions. Another way of putting this matter is to say that while religion *A* thinks that the self is implicitly in possession of its eternal blessedness, Christianity thinks that one's eternal blessedness is determined by the individual's decisions in time. From this difference, Kierkegaard derives one of the most fundamental distinctions between the two forms of religiosity. "Religiousness *A* makes the thing of existing as strenuous as possible (outside the paradoxical-religious stage), but it does not base the relation to an eternal blessedness upon one's existence, but lets the relation to an eternal blessedness serve as basis for the transformation of existence. From the individual's re-

[38] *Ibid.*, p. 184; S.V., vii, 172. Compare: "From the standpoint of the Socratic thought every point of departure in time is *eo ipso* accidental, an occasion, a vanishing moment." *Philosophical Fragments*, p. 13; S.V., iv, 181.

lation to the eternal, there results the how of his existence, not the converse, and thereby infinitely more comes out of it than was put into it."[39]

One further consequence of religion *A*'s predication of an immortal soul of the self needs to be made explicit. From the perspective of religion *A*, the self is understood to have an immediate relationship to God. We have seen that this is also characteristic of ethical religiosity. Moreover, it has been noted that Kierkegaard argues: "The immediate relationship to God is paganism, and only after the breach has taken place can there be any question of a true God-relationship."[40]

For neither ethical religiosity nor religion *A* is there an apprehension of the need for a mediator. To say that one has an "immediate relation to God" is to say that one is related to God without passing through a mediator (Christ). There is both a similarity and a difference in the reasons for ethical religiosity's and religion *A*'s conviction of the self's immediate relation to God. The similarity lies in the fact that neither of the two positions recognizes man's sinfulness. Although both perceive guilt, this guilt is not radical, and therefore does not effect a qualitative breach between God and man that would render impossible an immediate relation to God. The difference lies in the precise meaning that each life-view gives to the immediacy of the relation to God. For ethical religiosity to be immediately related to God means that one is related to God directly through the execution of one's moral duty. One's relation to God (who is not clearly distinguished from the world) grows immediately out of the relationship to duty itself. For religion *A*, the immediacy of the God-relationship is expressed by the conviction that the self has an immortal soul that is a link between the individual and God (who is totally different from the world). This connection with the realm of the Eternal is part of the self's constitution. However, because religion *A* perceives the difference between God and man, and therefore the dependence of man on God,

[39] *Ibid.*, p. 509; S.V., VII, 500.
[40] *Postscript*, p. 218; S.V., VII, 205.

the God-relationship is understood to be a paradox. For the Eternal God to be related to the individual man is, from the viewpoint of religion *A*, a paradox. Therefore, although both ethical religiosity and religion *A* regard the self's relation to God as immediate, religion *A* views this as a paradox, while ethical religiosity's failure clearly to recognize the difference between God and the world leads to no understanding of the paradox entailed in one's relation to God. An important qualification must be made at this point. While religion *A* recognizes the paradox involved in the Eternal God being related to a temporal man, there is no cognizance of the Absolute Paradox that is central for Christianity's understanding of God, the self, and the relation of the two. For the Absolute Paradox to be effected, the Eternal God must actually enter time (become incarnate), thereby establishing a relationship with a self whose qualitative difference from God lies not merely in his creatureliness but in his sinfulness.

With these remarks, we are brought to the conclusion of our consideration of religion *A*. At the outset of this chapter, we noted two general features of the religious stage as a whole: (1) the clear distinction between God and the world; and (2) the self's interest in eternal blessedness, salvation, or immortality. In the succeeding analysis, it has been argued that religion *A*'s understanding of the implications of the former insight represents an advance beyond the view of the self at the ethical stage, and religion *A*'s stance on the latter issue is regarded from the Christian perspective to involve certain misunderstandings about the self and time. For Kierkegaard, the most complete realization of the self and the fullest recognition of the significance of time for the life of the self are reached at the stage of Christianity. Here the process of individuation that we have been following throughout the dialectic reaches its *telos*. Before we turn our attention to a detailed exploration of Kierkegaard's interpretation of Christianity, a comment about the way in which the stages of existence are to be understood in our consideration of Christianity is required.

C. TRANSITIONAL REMARKS

Throughout the discussion we have seen that the stages of existence can be regarded both as the phases through which a self passes in coming to maturity, and as ideal personality types or as representations of different life-views. In a sense, these two interpretations of the stages come together at the Christian religious stage of existence. The Christian stage clearly represents a definite life-view, a stance, that the self can assume in daily conduct. However, as the culmination of Kierkegaard's dialectic of existence, it also represents the final phase of the development of the self, or the most complete individuation of the self.

But we have also observed significant ways in which Kierkegaard's argument anticipates insights of later psychologists. The merging of the two interpretations of the stages does not result in an end to these parallels. In order to bring into sharper focus the relationship among the stages when they are regarded as phases through which the self passes in the course of maturing, and to see how the Christian stage marks the culmination of this process, it will be helpful, by reviewing our foregoing analyses, to reconsider the way in which Kierkegaard's understanding of the development of the self anticipates later psychological theories of personality development.

It will be recalled that the first pole of the aesthetic stage, immediacy, is comprised of three subdivisions. At the outset of its development, the neonate, as the fetus, exists in a pre-reflective state in which there is no differentiation between self and not-self. The world is experienced as a ceaseless flux of impressions. The person cannot distinguish various perceptions clearly, and is unable to discriminate between his own self and the world that he experiences. World and self are fully indefinite. There is not even enough differentiation to distinguish between the self and the object of desire. The initial stages of differentiation entail the gradual emergence of a distinction between desire and its object. As we have seen,

Kierkegaard charts this development in great detail. At the third stage of the immediate aesthetic, desire and its object are clearly distinguished. The infant becomes aware of the particular object of desire.

Kierkegaard insists, however, that there is never cognition in immediacy. The distinction between self and object is purely affective, and consciousness has yet to emerge. Furthermore, the infant is not yet a centered individual, but remains a reflex of the desire whose embodiment it is. Life in immediacy is ruled by the principles of pleasure and pain.

This stage of Kierkegaard's dialectic parallels Freud's analysis of the oral stage of personality development. For Freud, as for Kierkegaard, the beginning of life is marked by the absence of self-consciousness and by the domination of the person by desire. In precise Freudian terminology, the id rules the personality, i.e., the pleasure principle has ascendancy. Furthermore, there is no differentiation between the infant and its world. The separation of self and world develops slowly as the result of the frustration of desire. The immediate gratification of desire that characterizes the prenatal state ends with birth. The development of an interval between desire and its satisfaction marks a significant point in the process of individuation. For further development to take place, the infant must pass from the state of immediacy to self-consciousness.

Kierkegaard argues that the child begins to move beyond the immediate aesthetic with the development of cognition through the ability to use language. As long as one remains in immediacy, the capacity to use language does not develop. However, as one acquires the capability to use language, self-consciousness begins to take form. Self-consciousness entails, first, the distinction of the self from its surroundings, and, second, the distinction of the self from itself. The differentiation between the self and its world that had begun on an affective level at the immediate aesthetic reaches further clarity as one is able to use language to designate particular objects in the sensational flux, and to recognize himself as distinguishable from those objects. Moreover, the cognizing subject can turn reflection back on himself, becoming an object to himself. When this occurs, it is possible to draw a distinction between the real self and the ideal self. Through the delineation of possibilities, one distinguishes what he is from what he might be. In short, purposeful activity is a possibility that might be realized.

Again Kierkegaard and Freud seem to be analyzing similar dimensions of the self's development. For Freud, the process of differentiating self and not-self that was begun at the oral stage with the frustration of desire gradually reaches the level of self-consciousness during the early phases of the anal stage. The loss of the object of desire engenders a recognition of the difference between subjective and objective reality. This awareness Freud describes in terms of the differentiation of the ego from the id. Since desire is no longer immediately fulfilled, inward desire must seek satisfaction in outward reality. The ego is the mechanism by which inwardness and outwardness are mediated. By means of the ego, a plan is formulated to satisfy the cravings of the id. At this point, the ego and the id are clearly distinguished, and volitional activity is posited as a possibility. But the will still has not been asserted. The engagement of the will in purposeful becoming marks the next phase of the individual's development.

The fundamental characteristic of Kierkegaard's ethical stage of existence is the development of the self as a center of responsible decision. It becomes apparent that the aesthetic stage prepares the way for the ethical. Before there can be any responsible decision, the self must be self-conscious and must be able to apprehend possibilities that can be realized through its decisions. We have seen that Kierkegaard believes decision to be constitutive of selfhood. But decision is, for Kierkegaard, rather complex. We have defined two basic levels of decision. The first is the choice of oneself, which involves the penetration and the appropriation of one's concrete actuality. The second, which depends upon the first, is the deliberate resolution to strive to actualize envisioned possibilities. At the ethical stage of existence, one seeks to actualize imagined possibilities through the free exercise of one's will. However, possibilities are not randomly selected for realization. The deciding self is guided by the moral standards of the society of which one is a member. The importance that Kierkegaard attaches to morality in guiding individual decisions is indicated by his designation of this phase of the self's development as the "ethical" stage. From the ethical norms that one internalizes, a conception of an ideal self takes form. One then endeavors to realize this ideal self through one's decisions. Not all of those possibilities that one's actuality enables one to realize ought to be sought. Moral codes help one to choose among one's live options. Furthermore, in this process of purposeful decision, desires are controlled. Kierkegaard does not think that the ethical stage abolishes the desires that rule immediate aesthetic existence. Deliberate decision does, however, enable one to manage one's desires, and frees one from the complete domination by desire.

This complex process of choosing oneself and trying to realize one's goals is another nodal point in the self's individuation. Through self-defining decision, one acquires a history that is, in the final analysis, a revelation of oneself. Personal decisions define one's actuality as distinct from all else that is, and thereby establish one's unique individuality.

Freud agrees with Kierkegaard's contention that the phase of the self's development toward maturity that follows the emergence of cognition is the development of the formative activity of the will. Freud believes this to take place primarily during the anal stage. With the ability to exercise one's will, and hence to control desire, the child becomes partially determinative of its own development. Such self-control more clearly defines the child as an autonomous center of consciousness and activity. Although the initial decisions of the self are quite simple, in time they become more complex. With the increasing complexity of the decision-making process, there is need of a means for selecting among various alternatives. Freud holds that this function is served by the superego. In a way similar to Kierkegaard, Freud argues that by means of the superego an individual constructs an ego ideal that serves as the basis for choosing among possibilities and for controlling the desires of the id. In making decisions with the guidance of the superego, a person reaches a higher stage of differentiation by giving himself further definition.

At this juncture, there emerges an important difference between Kierkegaard's and Freud's conceptions of the development of the self. While both thinkers agree that the maintenance of a healthy personality depends upon the ability to achieve an equilibrium among the various components of the self, they disagree about how such a balance is to be achieved. Freud understands the later years of a person's life in terms of conflicts engendered in early years. No significant development takes place after adolescence, and adult life is regarded as a repetition and further elaboration of infantile experience. Kierkegaard opposes this viewpoint. While he agrees that one's actuality always conditions one's possibilities, he disagrees with the contention that significant becoming is restricted to a particular period of life, or that any phase in the self's development is more decisive than another. Therefore, Kierkegaard extends his analysis of the development of the self to the entire course of one's life.

Many post-Freudian psychologists recognize the problems involved in Freud's failure to consider the whole life cycle. Erik Erikson is an example of the student of personality who attempts to improve Freud's analysis by expanding it to encompass the self's whole life. It is to Erikson that we must turn to see the psychological implications of Kierkegaard's religious stage of existence.

Erikson argues that there are eight stages in the life cycle. The eighth stage he describes by the polar terms "ego integrity and despair."[41] For our present purposes this final

[41] See *Childhood and Society* (New York: W. W. Norton, 1963),

stage is most important. At this point in the development of the self, the individual attempts to survey his life and to accept what he has become. Like Kierkegaard, Erikson calls the failure to accept oneself, or the desire to be rid of the self one has become, despair. The successful appropriation of oneself Erikson calls ego integration. However, he realizes that this acceptance of the self is frequently a difficult task. As Kierkegaard notices, there are aspects of the self that one wants to forget or to repress. Such repression, however, is detrimental to the self's health; neurosis or even psychosis can develop. Not infrequently the dis-ease with the self is so profound that it requires psychoanalytic treatment. The process of divulging, understanding, and accepting one's past through psychoanalysis is not functionally very different from understanding, confessing, and accepting one's past through the belief in the forgiveness of sins. In both instances, one seeks to regain a meaningful present and an open future by coming to terms with the past. Once attained, the goal of ego integration results in a sense of wholeness that is the hallmark of a healthy personality. At this stage, Erikson argues, one reaches "the most mature *faith* that an aging person can muster in his cultural setting and historical period."[42] Therefore, for Erikson, as for Kierkegaard, the final stage in the maturation process involves overcoming the despairing rejection of oneself by the faithful appropriation of the self that one has become throughout one's life-time.

In the next chapter we will explore Kierkegaard's view of the form of existence that represents the fullest realization of selfhood—Christianity. In the course of our analysis, the parallels with Erikson's insights will become apparent. Although we will be concerned primarily with Christianity as a lifeview or as ideally characterizing a certain stance of the self, it will become clear that Christianity also represents the final

---

pp. 247-269, and *Psychological Issues* (New York: International Universities Press, 1968), pp. 55-101.

[42] *Childhood and Society, op.cit.,* p. 272.

stage in the self's movement to maturity. In this way, the two interpretations of the stages with which we have been concerned throughout our study merge in Christianity to depict what Kierkegaard regards as the most authentic form of human existence.

CHAPTER SEVEN

THE CHRISTIAN STAGE
OF EXISTENCE:
THE MOMENT AND
THE INDIVIDUAL

Throughout this book we have emphasized that the Christian stage of existence is the culmination of Kierkegaard's dialectic. From the foregoing analysis, it has become apparent that a very definite understanding of the structure of selfhood and of the nature of time informs Kierkegaard's pseudonymous authorship. Furthermore, we have argued that the arrangement of the stages of existence and the primary characteristics of each stage depend on his conception of time and of the self. By making Christian existence the *telos* of his dialectic, Kierkegaard contends that this life-view is the most adequate form of self-realization, and most clearly comprehends the significance of time for the temporal individual. In the process of taking up the Christian form of existence, the self achieves the equilibrium among its components that eludes every other life-possibility.

Kierkegaard develops his understanding of the way in which the self realizes itself and in which the self attends to the significance of time in Christian existence by considering two principal Christian doctrines: sin and the incarnation.[1] For Kierkegaard the incarnation is the focus of his understanding of Christianity. But there is a double dimension of the incarnation according to his interpretation: "Thus our paradox [the incarnation] is rendered still more appalling,

---

[1] Kierkegaard virtually reduces the sum of Christian dogma to these two doctrines.

or the same paradox has the double aspect which proclaims it as the Absolute Paradox; negatively by revealing the absolute unlikeness of sin, positively by proposing to do away with the absolute unlikeness in absolute likeness."[2] On the one hand, God's act in Christ reveals the individual's sin. On the other, it discloses a possible resolution to the problem posed by the self's sinfulness. In our investigation of Kierkegaard's understanding of Christianity, we must focus on these two dimensions of the incarnation.

A. THE DILEMMA OF SINFULNESS

At no stage of existence other than Christianity does Kierkegaard think that the awareness of the self's sinfulness arises. The aesthete does not even raise the question of God and of the self's relation to God. Although aware of his failure adequately to achieve the ideals that he has envisioned, the ethicist believes his shortcomings to be the result of deviations from an otherwise correct course. There is no sense of pervasive evil within the self. Religion *A*'s persistent conviction that the self is, by nature, immortal and thereby inextricably bound to the Eternal testifies to its failure to apprehend the reality of sin. For Kierkegaard the absence of the awareness of sin at each of these stages of existence is not at all surprising for as the above quotation implies, a revelation from God is necessary before sin can be recognized: "Precisely the concept by which Christianity distinguishes itself qualitatively and most decisively from paganism is the concept of sin, the doctrine of sin; and therefore Christianity assumes quite consistently that neither paganism nor the natural man knows what sin is; yea, it assumes that there must be a revelation from God to make manifest what sin is."[3]

The reason that "no man by himself and of himself can ex-

[2] *Philosophical Fragments*, p. 59; S.V., IV, 214. See also *Postscript*, p. 517; S.V., VII, 508-509.

[3] *The Sickness Unto Death*, p. 220; S.V., XI, 200-201. Compare pp. 206-207; S.V., XI, 183-184.

plain what sin is, [is] precisely because he is in sin."[4] The recognition of the sinfulness of one's existence must come to man from without, by means of a revelation. This revelation Kierkegaard believes occurs in Christ, the Absolute Paradox.

In this section we will try to understand what Kierkegaard means by sin and to analyze the manner in which sin is related to his views of time and of the self. Working within the general framework of the history of Christian thought, Kierkegaard makes a distinction between "inherited sin"[5] and "actual sin."

1. Inherited Sin

Kierkegaard presents his most extended discussion of inherited sin in *The Concept of Dread*. He understands the doctrine of inherited sin to have been devised by Christian theologians to try to explain sin itself. The accounts that have been developed are, Kierkegaard argues, very unsatisfactory. Therefore when he constructs his own understanding of inherited sin, he is constantly polemicizing against traditional views of the problem within theological (especially Lutheran) circles. His discussion is further tangled in polemics by the fact that throughout his analysis of inherited sin he is criticizing Hegel's understanding of sin and redemption.[6] Within the context of his arguments about inherited sin, Kierkegaard clearly delineates what he understands to be many of the most substantial differences between his own thinking and

[4] *Ibid.*, p. 225; S.V., XI, 205.

[5] The Danish word that Kierkegaard uses is *"Arvesynden,"* which is properly translated as "inherited sin." We will use this term rather than the more usual "original sin" because "inherited sin" is more revealing of Kierkegaard's interpretation of the doctrine.

[6] For an excellent discussion of many of Hegel's views which Kierkegaard criticizes in his discussion of inherited sin, see: Stephen Crites, "The Gospel According to Hegel," *Journal of Religion*, vol. XLVI, no. 2, April 1966, pp. 246-263. This is a greatly abbreviated form of his argument in: *The Problem of the Positivity of the Gospel in the Hegelian Dialectic of Alienation and Reconciliation*, unpublished Ph.D. thesis, Yale University, 1961.

that of Hegel. Although his criticisms of both earlier theological formulations of the doctrine of inherited sin and of Hegel's argument are very interesting, and quite important in the genesis of his views, we cannot go into these issues in this context. We must be content with trying to discern Kierkegaard's meaning independently of the polemics in which he is involved.

The chief task that Kierkegaard sets for himself in his development of the doctrine of inherited sin is to give an account of sin that is at once consistent with the intention of the classical Christian doctrine, but in no way minimizes the freedom of the individual. The major error of both traditional Lutheran views of inherited sin and of the argument of Hegel is that the self's freedom is compromised in order to explain the doctrine. From Kierkegaard's perspective, this line of interpretation misunderstands the importance of the self's freedom, and in so doing denies the self's responsibility for sin.

Kierkegaard argues that inherited sin should be understood as a description of the mental state of the individual prior to his own act of sin. For this reason, he contends that the examination of inherited sin is a "psychological investigation":[7] "But the abiding state, that out of which sin constantly becomes (comes into being), not by necessity [as Kierkegaard claims Hegel argues], for a becoming by necessity is simply a state of being (as is, for example, the entire history of the plant), but by freedom—in this abiding state, I say, which is the predisposing assumption, the real possibility of sin, we have a subject for the interest of psychology. That which can concern psychology and with which it can concern itself is the question of how sin can come into existence, not the fact that it exists."[8] On the basis of his own "psychological investigation," Kierkegaard concludes that the mental state of the individual prior to sin is best described as "dread." In

[7] Hence the subtitle of *The Concept of Dread*: "A simple psychological deliberation oriented in the direction of the dogmatic problem of original sin."

[8] *The Concept of Dread*, p. 19; S.V., IV, 294.

other words, inherited sin can be understood in terms of dread. Kierkegaard comments: "The nature of inherited sin has often been examined, and yet the principle category has been missing — it is dread, that is what really determines it...."[9]

Because we have already analyzed Kierkegaard's understanding of dread,[10] it is not necessary to go into detail concerning this concept at this point. We need only specify the importance of our previous conclusions for the problem of inherited sin. We have seen that for Kierkegaard, dread is closely related to his understanding of both life-time and the structure of selfhood. More particularly, he associates dread with the future, the self's possibilities, and the self's freedom. Dread was defined as "the self's confrontation with its *future*, comprised of various *possibilities*, which can be actualized through the self's *freedom* to decide."[11] There is always an element of uncertainty, and therefore of risk, in the decision situation. Dread is the manner in which the self experiences the uncertainty of its future and the risk of its decisions.

The relationship between inherited sin and dread that Kierkegaard sees becomes more apparent when further connections between dread and the self are recognized. In the analysis of the ethical stage, we saw that he thinks that there is a very close connection between the individual and one's social-natural surroundings. The relation of the self to the social environment is especially important for Kierkegaard's interpretation of inherited sin. He argues that: "... man is an individual and as such is at once himself and the whole race, in such wise that the whole race has part in the individual, and the individual has part in the whole race [*Slægtens*]."[12] By this Kierkegaard means that the historical development of the entire human race exercises a determinative influence on the individual self. At this point, he does not regard selves

---

[9] *Journals*, ed. Dru, no. 402; *Papirer*, III A 233.
[10] See above chapter five, section D.
[11] See above p. 221.
[12] *The Concept of Dread*, p. 26; S.V., IV, 301.

as atomistically isolated individuals, but sees an important interrelationship among persons. Others with whom the self comes into direct contact serve as the conduits through which the life of the larger society flows into the individual self. Because Kierkegaard regards all selves in this manner, the influence of other persons upon the self is thoroughly extensive in both time and space.

The relationship between the individual and the race is, however, fully dialectical. We have seen that the race influences, and actually comes to live in and through, the individual. But the race is nothing apart from the individuals who make up that race. Furthermore, in the discussion of the ethical stage, we have seen that Kierkegaard thinks that the self defines its history through its decisions. Therefore, if the self is historical, and if the race is made up of individual selves, then the race must likewise have a history. Kierkegaard makes precisely this point: "Hence the individual has a history; but if the individual has a history, so also has the race."[13] The history of the race is made up of the histories of the individuals who comprise the race. Therefore while the history of the race surpasses any one individual *qua* individual, it does not surpass the totality of individuals who now are, or who have been. Thus Kierkegaard argues that persons are a synthesis of their own individuality and of the race as a whole. The race, as the individuals of the race, has a history.

Kierkegaard's view of the history of the human race, and the intimate connection between the individual and the historically developing race, is an important part of his argument about inherited sin. On the basis of his contention that the human race develops historically, he argues that dread itself has a history. To make his point, he consistently uses two terms throughout *The Concept of Dread*: "quantitative" and "qualitative." The term "quantitative" refers to the developing race as a whole, and the term "qualitative" refers to the individuals within the race. Kierkegaard holds that in the course of the development of the race, there is a quantitative

[13] *Ibid.*, p. 26; S.V., IV, 300.

increase in dread. This dread is, in turn, the "predisposing assumption, the real possibility of sin."[14] In this way, he is able to draw the connection between inherited sin and dread. Inherited sin refers to the mental state of the individual prior to the act of sin, and is not the same as the individual's sinful deed itself. This mental state Kierkegaard thinks is best described as "dread." The use of the qualifier "inherited" stresses his conviction that there is a quantitative increase in the predisposition to sin in the course of the historical development of the race. This increase, however, never causes the individual to sin. Sin is always posited by the qualitative leap of the individual himself.[15] This is Kierkegaard's way of saying that sin remains a function of the individual's *free* decision, and therefore is the individual's responsibility.

It should be recognized that Kierkegaard's conception of the relationship between the individual and the race leads him to assert a certain circularity in the connection between sin and dread. We have seen that for Kierkegaard, the history of the race both conditions the individual and is conditioned by the deeds of individuals. Insofar as there is a quantitative increase in dread that predisposes (but does not force) the individual to make the qualitative leap into sin, the history of the race influences the particular self. But by his individual act of sin, the self contributes to the history of the race. Furthermore, Kierkegaard thinks that the individual's leap into sin is both conditioned by dread and brings further dread with it. Therefore, he argues that "Sin entered by dread, but sin in turn brought dread with it."[16] Only by such a paradox does he think a satisfactory explanation of the relation between dread and sin can be offered.

[14] *Ibid.*, p. 19; S.V., IV, 294.

[15] To understand Kierkegaard's argument, it is necessary to recognize that his insistence that a quantitative increase can never lead to a qualitative change is set in direct opposition to Hegel's contention to the contrary. For Hegel's discussion of this point, see: *Science of Logic, op.cit.*, esp. pp. 365ff.

[16] *The Concept of Dread*, p. 47; S.V., IV, 323.

In order to grasp more fully the importance of Kierkegaard's concept of dread for his interpretation of inherited
sin, it is necessary to examine in more detail what he means
by a quantitative increase in dread. The quantitative increase
in dread results from man's nature as a derivative being and
from his situation in an historical nexus. Both of these points
must be considered. Each person is, of course, physically derived from those who precede him. This derivation, according to Kierkegaard, results in an increased disposition of the
derived individual to sin, and hence in an increase in dread.
He uses the Genesis account of Adam and Eve to make his
point: "Eve is the derived being [*det Deriverede*]. True, she
is created like Adam, but she is created out of a precedent
creature. True, she is innocent like Adam, but there is as it
were a presentiment of a disposition, which indeed is not yet
in existence, yet may seem like a hint of the sinfulness posited
by reproduction. It is the fact of being derived which predisposes the individual, without at all making him guilty."[17]

Kierkegaard argues that the increased disposition to sin is
a consequence of the greater sensuousness of the derived self.
Adam and Eve again serve as examples: "This derivation of
woman explains also in what sense she is weaker than man,
a fact which has been assumed in all time, whether it is a
pasha who speaks or a romantic knight. . . . The expression
for the difference is that dread is more reflected in Eve than
in Adam. That is due to the fact that woman is more sensuous
than man."[18]

In some ways the Genesis account is ill-chosen in light of
Kierkegaard's overall argument. Throughout his discussion
in *The Concept of Dread* he contends that the increase of sensuality in later individuals is due to the fact that at the moment of the procreative act, the two persons involved are
fully determined by their sensuous inclinations. Both the

[17] *Ibid.*, pp. 42-43; S.V., IV, 318.
[18] *Ibid.*, p. 57; S.V., IV, 333. This viewpoint is the basis for many of
Kierkegaard's very degrading remarks about woman and her relationship to man.

capacity for cognition and the capability of free decision are suspended as the individuals allow themselves to be ruled by their passions: "One thing, however, is sure, that in describing love, pure and innocent as they may represent it, all poets associate with it an element of dread. . . . But why this dread? Because in the culmination of the erotic the spirit [i.e., freedom] cannot take part. I will speak here with Greek candor. The spirit indeed is present, for it is this which constitutes the synthesis, but it cannot express itself in the erotic experience; it feels itself a stranger."[19]

Kierkegaard feels that an individual derived from the sexual act in which sensuality predominates is more likely to be controlled by his sensual passions. Such sensual domination is, of course, posited only as a possibility for the derived person. The individual is related to this possibility in dread. Whether or not he allows himself to be controlled by sensuality is a function of the individual himself. It is important to recognize that Kierkegaard is not simply identifying sin with sexuality. The precise reason that an increase in sensuality leads to an increased propensity to sin can only become clear when we have established what he means by actual sin. For the moment, suffice it to say that insofar as one is dominated by sensuous inclination, one's self is in disequilibrium.[20]

Kierkegaard's meaning of a quantitative increase in dread is further illuminated by considering the implications of the self's situation within an historical nexus. We have already seen that the self's relationship with the social world is, within limits, determinative of its being. This is so in two ways. In the first place, those around a person influence his actuality. In all kinds of ways, from the biological fact of heredity to the subtle inculcation of mental attitudes, those with whom one comes into contact become a part of one's being. But the social world also plays an important role in defining one's possibilities. The various roles that a person might choose to

[19] *Ibid.*, p. 64; S.V., IV, 341.
[20] We have considered some of the aspects of this problem in our examination of the immediate aestheic stage of existence.

enact are, in large measure, defined by the social world in which one participates. Kierkegaard is very sensitive to the power of example to shape one's possibilities. When imagined by the self, the lives of those around him become possibilities to be enacted. Therefore, to the extent that the lives of those around one are expressions of sin, the *possibility* of sin becomes increasingly evident to an individual. The subjective correlative of an increase in the sinfulness of the lives of men is an increase in dread. As there are increasing instances of sin with the development of the race, there is an increase in dread for the person who sees in the lives of others possibilities that he himself might actualize.

From the comments in this section, we can conclude that Kierkegaard understands the doctrine of inherited sin to be an effort to explain the manner in which sin arises by analyzing the mental state of the individual prior to the act of sin. In trying to arrive at an explanation that at once takes into account the positive aspects of the traditional theological formulation of the doctrine, but that does not compromise the freedom (and hence the responsibility) of the individual, he argues that inherited sin is best understood in terms of dread. Furthermore, because the human race as a whole has a history, there is a quantitative increase in dread. Such a quantitative increase in dread, however, never brings about the individual's qualitative leap into sin. This is always accomplished through the self's own free decision. With this understanding of Kierkegaard's view of inherited sin, we can turn our attention to his interpretation of sin itself, or of actual sin.

2. *Actual Sin*

Our analysis of actual sin[21] is greatly facilitated by previous parts of our discussion. While Kierkegaard's discussion of inherited sin is, for the most part, contained in *The Concept of Dread*, his most detailed consideration of sin is presented in

[21] The term "actual sin" is, quite evidently, intended to indicate a contrast with "inherited sin." This distinction having been noted, we will use only "sin" to indicate "actual sin."

The Sickness Unto Death. Here he characterizes sin as the "potentiation of despair [*Potensationen af Fortvivlelse*]."[22] Therefore, to come to terms with his view of sin, we must understand the meaning of "despair" and of "potentiation."

Kierkegaard's understanding of despair is fully dependent on his conception of the structure of selfhood as it has been developed in chapter three. Stated in the most general terms, despair is the failure (or the refusal) of the self to be itself. Based on his understanding of the self, Kierkegaard argues that despair can take two forms: "Such a derived, constituted, relation is the human self, a relation which relates itself to its own self, and in relating itself to its own self relates itself to another [i.e., to God]. Hence it is that there can be two forms of despair properly so called. If the human self had constituted itself, there could be a question of only one form, that of not willing to be one's own self, of willing to get rid of oneself, but there would be no question of despairingly willing to be oneself."[23]

The first form of despair is that of "not willing to be one's own self, of willing to get rid of oneself," which Kierkegaard calls "weakness" [*Svaghed*].[24] The second form is that of "despairingly willing to be oneself," which he calls "defiance" [*Trods*].[25] These expressions are, however, very closely related. Kierkegaard contends that: "To despair over oneself, in despair to will to be rid of oneself, is the formula for all despair, and hence the second form of despair (despair at willing to be oneself) can be followed back to the first (in despair at not willing to be oneself). . . ."[26] Thus both weakness and defiance are different forms of the self's refusal to be it-

---

[22] *The Sickness Unto Death*, p. 208; S.V., xi, 189. It is interesting to note that in Danish the adjectival form of *Fortvivlelse* is *fortvivlende*, which can be translated "hopeless." As will become evident in the next chapter, faith, the opposite of potentiated despair, is closely related to hope.

[23] *Ibid.*, pp. 146-147; S.V., xi, 129.

[24] *Ibid.*, p. 208; S.V., xi, 189.　　　　[25] *Ibid.*, p. 208; S.V., xi, 189.

[26] *Ibid.*, p. 153; S.V., xi, 144.

self. This becomes evident if we recall his analysis of the structure of selfhood.

We have seen that the self is comprised of possibilities and actualities that are related to each other through free decision. Furthermore, the entire self is constituted and sustained by God. Despair under the form of weakness refers to the first dimension of selfhood, and despair under the form of defiance refers to the second aspect of the self's being. The self is, for Kierkegaard, a concretely existing individual. As such it is endowed with a definite actuality, and thereby has open to it certain possibilities. Upon the basis of its given actuality, the self can, through free decision, strive to realize some of the possibilities available to it. Decisions further define one's actuality and condition possibilities. Kierkegaard contends that one must accept both the formal structure of the self, and the particular actualities and possibilities of his individual self. He regards the failure to do this as weakness for two reasons. In the first place, as soon as one recognizes and accepts the formal structure of one's self, one realizes that one has the possibility of freely making decisions. Since decision always involves uncertainty and risk, the willingness to make decisions requires a degree of courage. The unwillingness to make decisions is, consequently, viewed as weakness. In the second place, as we have seen above, the recognition and the acceptance by the self of its own concrete actuality is always painful either because of certain aspects of the self's actuality that one would rather were otherwise or because of the aversion to limiting one's possibilities.

However, this concrete self, as we have seen, is not constituted by itself, but is constituted by another — by God. This is a given in the self's being that, though it might be denied, cannot be negated. If the self is to accept itself, it must constantly acknowledge its ontological dependence on God. The failure to do so Kierkegaard holds to be defiance.

The nature of despair becomes more evident when the stages of existence that we have examined are considered in light of the foregoing comments on despair. Throughout our

278

analysis, we have seen that the goal of the self is to achieve a proper equilibrium among its various components. It has also been asserted, but is yet to be demonstrated, that this balance is achieved only at the Christian stage of existence. Therefore, at every other stage, the self remains in unbalance. This failure to achieve an equilibrium can now be seen to be despair. Each of the stages of existence that we have considered is, in the final analysis, despair. As such each stage must fall under the category of either weakness or defiance.

The immediate and the reflective aesthetic are modes of despair under the form of weakness, while the ethical and religion *A*, though in different ways, are defiance. The case is rather clear for both poles of the aesthetic stage. At the immediate pole of the aesthetic stage we have seen that there is an overemphasis on the actuality of the self. The self is primarily governed by sensuous inclination or fully determined by its natural and social environment. In each case the self neither takes cognizance of its possibilities nor acknowledges its freedom to decide to actualize those possibilities. At the reflective pole, the opposite situation obtains. Here the self is engaged in infinite reflection on its possibilities. This leads to the failure of the self to acknowledge its actuality, and therefore to recognize the manner in which its possibilities are limited by its actuality. Furthermore, because it is recognized that decision constitutes actuality and limits possibility, there is a consistent avoidance of decision. In neither of these forms of existence does the self will to be itself. Either there is a failure to recognize one's possibilities, or there is a refusal to acknowledge one's actuality. In both cases the freedom of the self to decide to actualize its possibilities is overlooked or ignored. Such forms of existence, according to Kierkegaard, represent the self's weakness of "not willing to be itself."

That the ethical stage of existence represents despair under the form of defiance should be evident from the discussion of chapter five. One of the chief shortcomings of ethical existence, as conceived by Kierkegaard, is the failure adequately to recognize the self's ontological dependence on God. Although the ethicist acknowledges God, God becomes a point of reference for ethical obligation. The primary interest is to achieve the continuity of the self by means of sealing one's resolution in the name of the eternal God. Here again the self does not will to be itself, for there is not a sufficient recognition of the self's dependence on God. The manner in which Kierkegaard expresses this is by saying that the self wills to be itself in self-assertion. But actually, willing to be one's own self (willing to constitute oneself and not willing to regard oneself as constantly constituted by another) is not willing to be oneself: "The self is its own lord and master, so it is said, absolutely its own lord, and precisely this is despair, but it is also what it regards as its pleasure and enjoyment. However, by closer inspection one easily ascertains that this ruler is a king without a country, he rules really over nothing; his condition, his dominion, is subjected to the dialectic that every instant revolution is legitimate."[27]

The reason that Kierkegaard understands religion *A* to be a form of defiance is less apparent. We have seen that religion *A*'s conviction that the soul is immortal represents both a misunderstanding of the significance of decision for the self and a lack of an awareness of the self's sinfulness. It might appear that this would make religion *A* a form of weakness, for neither the general structure of the self (i.e., the importance of decision) nor the particular actuality of the self (i.e., sin) seems to be accepted. But Kierkegaard insists that in this instance, there is an interchange in the meanings of "weakness" and "defiance": "Ordinarily weakness is: in despair not to will to be oneself. Here this is defiance; for here it is clearly defiance not to will to be the man one is, a sinner, and for this reason to will to dispense with the forgiveness of sins."[28] The conviction that the self retains a positive relation to God, regardless of the consequences of one's temporal life, is, for Kierkegaard, defiance.

We can now return to Kierkegaard's definition of sin with considerably more understanding. He argues: "Sin is this:

[27] *Ibid.*, p. 203; S.V., xi, 180.   [28] *Ibid.*, p. 244; S.V., xi, 223.

before God, or with the conception of God to be in despair at not willing to be oneself, or in despair at willing to be oneself. Thus sin is potentiated weakness or potentiated defiance: sin is the potentiation of despair."[29] Having discussed the meaning of despair, we must try to understand the adjective "potentiated." "Potentiated" refers to the fact that despair is "before God, or with the conception of God." Kierkegaard continues the foregoing quotation by saying: "The point upon which the emphasis rests is *before God*, or the fact that the conception of God is involved; the factor that dialectically, ethically, religiously, makes 'qualified' despair . . . synonymous with sin is the conception of God."[30]

For Kierkegaard, one constantly lives his life "before God" regardless of whether or not this fact is recognized by the individual. When it is realized, however, a significant alteration takes place in the self's understanding of itself. Commenting on the border between the previous stages of existence and the Christian stage, Kierkegaard writes: "The gradations in the consciousness of the self that we have hitherto been employing are within the definition of the human self, or the self whose measure is man. But this self acquires a new quality or qualification in the fact that it is the self directly in the sight of God. This self is no longer the merely human self but is what I would call, hoping not to be misunderstood, the theological self [*theologiske Selv*], the self directly in the sight of God. And what an infinite reality this self acquires by being before God!"[31] By "existing before God" Kierkegaard expresses his conviction that the God who is wholly different from man nevertheless has an intimate interest in man.[32] God

---

[29] *Ibid.*, p. 208; S.V., XI, 189.   [30] *Ibid.*, p. 208; S.V., XI, 189.

[31] *Ibid.*, p. 210; S.V., XI, 191.

[32] In making this argument Kierkegaard is using the model of a transcendent *personal* God. In the final analysis, this is the conception of God that dominates his work. However, due to his constant effort to relate religion *A* and Christianity, he often uses language that is more characteristic of Greek metaphysics than of a personal God. As a consequence his arguments sometimes sound as if his God is the Aristotelian Unmoved Mover. The Greek terminology is, however,

is concerned with what man becomes through his decisions. In this relation of God to man lies a possibility of offense.[33]

When one is aware of one's existence before God, one recognizes both the importance of one's decisions and the consequences of one's previous decisions. Decisions define the self that one is before God. Kierkegaard argues that when one's dependence on and responsibility to God become clear, despair is potentiated, i.e., becomes sin. Furthermore, one perceives that in any form of existence other than Christianity, the self does not will to be itself, and therefore remains in disequilibrium, in despair, or in sin.

Kierkegaard's analysis of sin falls into two dialectically related parts: inherited sin and actual sin. Inherited sin is understood in terms of dread and describes the mental state of the individual prior to the qualitative leap into (actual) sin. Sin is the failure of the self to will to be itself. This takes the form of either weakness — the refusal to accept one's possibilities and actualities, or to recognize the self's freedom to actualize possibilities — or defiance — the self's refusal to acknowledge dependence on God, or to accept one's sinfulness. With this understanding of Kierkegaard's view of sin, we must now consider what he sees as the consequences of sin.

3. The Consequences of Sin

With the recognition of one's sinfulness, another step is taken in the process of individuation. Kierkegaard comments: "The more conception of God, the more self; the more self, the more conception of God. Only when the self as this definite individual is conscious of existing before God, only then is it the infinite self; and then this self sins before God."[34] With the revelation of one's sinfulness, the self becomes

---

intended to be understood within the framework of a personal God. Whether Kierkegaard is successful in presenting a consistent view of God can be determined only after careful analysis. See below, section B, I.

[33] See *The Sickness Unto Death*, p. 214; S.V., XI, 194-195.

[34] *Ibid.*, p. 221; S.V., XI, 201.

aware of itself as existing before God. As the above passage indicates, "The more conception of God, the more self" or, as Kierkegaard says elsewhere, "the self is potentiated in the ratio of the measure proposed for the self, and infinitely potentiated when God is the measure."[35] The point of these rather cryptic remarks is that the awareness of existing before God involves a significant alteration in the self's understanding of itself. There is a much clearer apprehension of the importance of decision for the life of the self than at any previous stage of existence. It becomes apparent that one's decisions are *infinitely* important, for the self that one becomes through decision stands in relation to the eternal God.

Kierkegaard expresses the manner in which the awareness of sin affects one's understanding of the significance of decision for the self in various ways. The main point is, however, always the same: decision is constitutive of the self's being. In addressing the problem of the forgiveness of sins, Kierkegaard makes it evident that sin is not an occasional mistake, but that it is "radical" — it goes to the roots of one's being: "An immediate relation between immediacy and the forgiveness of sin means that sin is a single separate thing, and that this single thing forgiveness takes away. But this is not the forgiveness of sin. Thus a child does not know what the forgiveness of sin is, for a child believes of itself that fundamentally it is a nice child, 'if only that thing had not occurred yesterday,' and forgiveness takes that thing away. But if sin is something radical (a discovery due to repentance, which always precedes forgiveness), this means precisely that immediacy is viewed as invalid, but if so viewed, it is practically abolished."[36] Kierkegaard makes the same point when he contends that sin is "a new existence medium,"[37] a "transformation of existence,"[38] a "position,"[39] or a "state."[40]

<hr />

[35] *Ibid.*, p. 211; S.V., XI, 193.
[36] *Stages on Life's Way*, p. 434; S.V., VI, 447.
[37] *Postscript*, p. 516; S.V., VII, 508.
[38] *Ibid.*, p. 516; S.V., VII, 508.
[39] *The Sickness Unto Death*, p. 237; S.V., XI, 216.
[40] *The Concept of Dread*, p. 14; S.V., IV, 287.

A Christian perspective denies religion *A*'s contention that one has an immortal soul impervious to the decisions of the temporal self. The denial of this immortal soul means that the self is neither actually in possession of its eternal blessedness, nor has a positive and unalterable relationship to God. For the self to gain eternal blessedness, a proper relation to God must be maintained by the self's constant willing to be itself. As we have seen, the failure to establish such an equilibrium within the self (which is characteristic of every stage other than the Christian) is despair, and finally sin. Here more painfully than anywhere else, actuality limits possibility. The actuality of sin forecloses the possibility of a proper relation to God, and thereby renders impossible the attainment of eternal blessedness. At this juncture, there is *nothing* the self can do to regain the possibility lost by its own decisions. One cannot simply correct past errors, thereby setting matters straight between the self and God. The consequences of decision go more deeply than that, for decisions determine actuality, and *decisively* condition possibility. If the possibility of a proper relation to God (and hence of eternal blessedness) is to be regained by the self, an act of God is necessary. Kierkegaard comments on the manner in which the perception of one's sinfulness differs from the understanding of existence presented by religion *A*.

"But the more difficult it is made for him [the existing individual] to take himself out of existence by way of recollection, the more profound is the inwardness that his existence may have in existence; and when it is made impossible for him, when he is held so fast in existence that the back door of recollection is forever closed to him, then his inwardness will be the most profound possible . . . . If even Socrates understood the dubiety of taking himself speculatively out of existence back into the eternal, although no other difficulty confronted the existing individual except that he existed, and that existing was his essential task, now it is impossible. Forward he must, backward he cannot go."[41]

[41] *Postscript*, pp. 186-187; S.V., VII, 174-175.

After having sinned, the self can realize the possibility of eternal blessedness only by faithfully responding to God's act of forgiveness in Christ.

It should be apparent that a different understanding of both time and of the significance of decision develops with the awareness of sin. In aesthetic existence, there is no genuine decision, and time is regarded as an enemy that either cancels the enjoyment of the moment, or involves ideals in the travail of historical becoming. For the ethicist, time is a medium of self-definition, and decision is the means by which the temporal self establishes a history and seeks to bestow a continuity on that history. In so doing, the ethical person defines his identity in the world. Religion *A* does not view time and decision as having final significance for the self. The essential interest of the self is an immortal soul that is thought to be unaffected by decisions in time. With the Christian stage's recognition that one always exists before God, time and decision take on *eternal* significance. What one becomes through one's decisions determines what one is for all eternity. Decision, therefore, not only defines the temporal personality but establishes one's eternal being. There is no immortal soul within one that is exempt from this influence. It is in time that one establishes or fails to establish one's relation to Eternity, to God. With the recognition of the eternal importance of time and of decision for the self, Kierkegaard contends that the structure of the self, and the meaning of the self's existence in time, are more adequately conceived. To the extent that the self accepts the implications of sin, there is a further realization of selfhood, and the process of individuation advances another step. From the undifferentiated identification of the self with its surroundings, we have now moved to the individual, isolated from all of those around himself through his own decisions, standing before God as a convicted sinner. For this reason, Kierkegaard argues that "The category of sin is the category of the individual."[42]

A final consequence of sin needs to be noted. Through sin,

[42] *The Sickness Unto Death*, p. 250; S.V., XI, 228.

"existence has stamped itself upon the existing individual a second time"[43] by establishing a qualitative difference between man and God. Man is sinful, and God is holy: "The doctrine of sin, the doctrine that we are sinners, thou and I, which absolutely disperses the 'crowd,' fixes then the qualitative distinction between God and man more deeply than ever it was fixed anywhere. . . . As a sinner, man is separated from God by a yawning qualitative abyss [*Qvalitetens svælgend Dyb*]. And obviously God is separated from man by the same yawning qualitative abyss when He forgives sin."[44] With the recognition that the difference between God and man is sin, man's predicament is altered. No longer is his task only to recognize his ontological dependence upon God, the Creator and Sustainer. Man must now acknowledge that he himself has disrupted his relation to God by failing to be his own self. He must admit not only that he is a creature, but that he is a sinful creature. How can one respond to the actuality of one's sinfulness?

4. The Responses to Sin

Kierkegaard delineates three responses to sin: (1) a demonic response (dread of the good); (2) a repentant[45] response (dread of the evil); and (3) a faithful response (belief in forgiveness). Kierkegaard defines the demonic as "*det Indesluttede*."[46] This is an extremely difficult word to translate into English. Lowrie renders it "shut-upness." This is not

---

[43] *Postscript*, p. 186; S.V., VII, 174.

[44] *The Sickness Unto Death*, p. 252; S.V., XI, 231. See also pp. 253-259; S.V., XI, 232-237 and *Philosophical Fragments*, p. 58; S.V., IV, 214. Kierkegaard uses the qualitative difference between God and man in terms of sin as the basis for his rejection of any form of pantheism. See *The Sickness Unto Death*, pp. 227-228; S.V., XI, 207-208.

[45] The Danish word for repentance is "*Anger*." This can also be translated "remorse." Lowrie (especially in *The Concept of Dread*) uses repentance and remorse interchangeably with no indication that it is the same Danish word. This leads to confusion. To avoid such problems, we shall consistently use repentance.

[46] See *The Concept of Dread*, pp. 105-137; S.V., IV, 386-420.

incorrect, but some explanation is helpful in understanding Kierkegaard's intention. *Indesluttede* is composed of two words: *ind*, meaning "in," and *slutte*, meaning "to close." From this we can say that the demonic individual is one who closes in on himself, or who becomes locked up within himself, never opening himself to others or allowing others to become involved with him. In the present instance, the demonic person is one who closes in on his sin. By so doing, he closes himself off from the good: "It [the demonic] will have nothing to do with the good, will not be weak enough to harken once in a while to another sort of talk. No, it will hear only itself, have to do only with itself, shut itself in with itself, yea, enclose itself within one enclosure more and by despair over its sin secure itself against every assault of the good or every aspiration after it."[47]

In another context, Kierkegaard specifies what he means by "the good," thereby clarifying the above passage: "The good of course signifies to it [the demonic] the reintegration of freedom, redemption, salvation, or whatever name one would give it."[48] By closing in on one's sin, one dreads not one's sin, but the good, i.e., salvation, or the release from sin. The reason for this is that sin itself becomes a source of pleasure for the demonic individual. To become related to the good would require him to give up his sin, and thereby to lose the pleasure that he derives from it.

"Even if at this point God in heaven and all his angels were to offer to help him out of it [sin] — no, now he doesn't want it, now it is too late, he once would have given everything to be rid of this torment but was made to wait, now that's all past, now he would rather rage against everything, he, the one man in the whole of existence who is the most unjustly treated, to whom it is especially important to have his torment at hand, important that no one should take it from him — for thus he can convince himself that he is in the right.

---

[47] *The Sickness Unto Death*, p. 240; S.V., xi, 219.
[48] *The Concept of Dread*, p. 106; S.V., iv, 387.

This at last becomes so firmly fixed in his head that for a very peculiar reason he is afraid of eternity — for the reason, namely, that it might rid him of his (demonically understood) infinite advantage over other men, his (demonically understood) justification for being what he is."[49]

Kierkegaard believes this situation to be a complete reversal of the proper state of affairs. Evil is loved, good is hated. Instead of seeking release from sin through salvation, the demonic person closes himself in on his sin and ". . . must constantly regard everything which is of the nature of repentance and everything which is of the nature of grace not only as empty and meaningless but as its foe, as the thing which most of all it has to guard against. . . ."[50]

Repentance is the opposite of the demonic's positive relationship to sin. The repentant individual is fully aware of the consequences of his failure to maintain an appropriate equilibrium within his self and therefore to establish the proper relationship with God. This recognition engenders dread. However, dread, as always, is related to possibility.[51] In repentance, sin is recognized as a "possibility annulled."[52] The actuality of sin annuls the possibility of eternal blessedness. The repentant individual dreads the consequence of his action: "The posited sin is at the same time in itself a consequence. . . . This consequence announces itself, and dread is related to the future of this consequence, which is the possibility of a new state."[53] Such dread is of the possibility that is consistent with the self's actuality (i.e., sin). This possibility would have to be the opposite of eternal blessedness — eter-

[49] *The Sickness Unto Death*, pp. 205-206; S.V., xi, 183.

[50] *Ibid.*, p. 240; S.V., xi, 219.

[51] It seems that the specificity here given to what one dreads is greater than Kierkegaard's arguments in other contexts would allow. See above chapter five, section D.

[52] *The Concept of Dread*, p. 101; S.V., iv, 381. The word translated "annulled" is the problematic Danish word "*ophæve*." Here, as in other places, Lowrie insists on putting the German *aufgehoben* in the English text when Kierkegaard gives no warrant for doing so.

[53] *Ibid.*, p. 101; S.V., iv, 382.

nal damnation. What this entails for Kierkegaard can be inferred by recalling the close relation that he sees between the self's eternal blessedness and immortality. Eternal damnation would be the loss of the possibility of immortality, or the total obliteration of the self in nothingness.

The recognition of this drastic consequence of sin drives the self to sorrow over its sin. Speaking of the lesson to be learned from "The woman who was a sinner" (Luke 7:37ff.), Kierkegaard states: "First, we can learn to become, like her, indifferent to everything else, in absolute sorrow for our sins, yet in such a way that one thing is important to us, and absolutely important: to find forgiveness."[54] A repentant response to sin is the deep sorrow over one's sins that follows the apprehension of the consequences of sin. In this sorrow, one wants nothing more than to be rid of one's sin. One seeks forgiveness that would reopen the possibility of a proper relationship with God, and thus of eternal blessedness. But the further one penetrates one's sin in sorrow through repentance, the more clearly one sees that by oneself one is impotent to achieve forgiveness. Forgiveness must first be offered by another, in this instance by God. Kierkegaard again thinks that the woman who was a sinner is instructive: "Next, thou canst learn of the sinful woman, what she well understood, that in relation to finding forgiveness she herself could do nothing at all."[55] By repentance the individual "uses up absolutely all his strength":[56] " . . . repentance cannot neutralize sin, it can only sorrow over it. Sin goes forward in its consequence, repentance follows it step by step, but always an instant too late."[57]

The recognition of the consequences of one's sin and the

---

[54] "The Woman who was a Sinner," *Training in Christianity*, p. 262; S.V., xii, 250. This was an edifying discourse that accompanied *Either-Or*. Lowrie has translated it, and includes it with *Training in Christianity*.

[55] *Ibid.*, p. 262; S.V., xii, 250.

[56] *Fear and Trembling*, p. 109; S.V., iii, 147.

[57] *The Concept of Dread*, p. 102; S.V., iv, 383.

awareness of one's impotence to rectify the situation create in the individual a *need* for God and an *interest* in God's forgiving act in the incarnation.[58] Kierkegaard argues that in Christ, God acts to make available forgiveness, and thereby to reopen the possibility of the self's eternal blessedness.[59] The cognizance of sin brings the perception of the need of forgiveness that, Kierkegaard argues, is available only through the faithful response to God's act in Christ. In brief, the awareness of sin drives one to Christianity: "'But if the Christian life is something so terrible and frightful, how in the world can a person get the idea of accepting it?' Quite simply, and, if you want that too, in a Lutheran way: only the consciousness of sin can force one into this dreadful situation — the power on the other side being grace. And in that very instant the Christian life transforms itself and is sheer gentleness, grace, loving-kindness, and compassion. Looked at from any other point of view Christianity is and must be a sort of madness or the greatest horror. Only through the consciousness of sin is there entrance to it, and the wish to enter

---

[58] In a very interesting note in the *Postscript* (p. 179; S.V., vii, 167) Kierkegaard comments on the relation between the need of the self and God: "In this manner God certainly becomes a postulate [*et Postulat*] not in the otiose manner in which this word is commonly understood. It becomes clear rather that the only way in which an existing individual comes into relation with God, is when the dialectical contradiction brings passion [*Lidenskaben*] to the point of despair, and helps him to embrace God with the 'category of despair' (faith) [*Tro*]. Then the postulate is so far from being arbitrary that it is precisely a life-necessity [*Nødværge* — my translation here follows Lowrie. This word might also be rendered "self-defense."] It is then not so much that God is a postulate, as that the individual's postulation of God is a necessity [*Nødvendighed*]." Much of the interest in this passage results from recognizing the strong similarity between the argument presented by Kierkegaard and Kant's analysis of the connection between the postulate of God and man's moral needs as developed in *The Critique of Practical Reason*, trans. by Lewis White Beck (New York: Bobbs-Merrill, 1956). See esp. Book ii, ch. ii, part v, pp. 128-136.

[59] The possibility of a repeated failure to establish a proper relationship to God (i.e., to will to be oneself), of course, remains open.

in by any other way is the crime of *lèse-majesté* against Christianity."[60]

At the Christian stage of existence, the individual first becomes aware of his sinfulness, and therefore of his separation from God, the source of eternal blessedness. Insofar as the self willfully acknowledges its own sinfulness, there is a further realization of selfhood and a more profound apprehension of the significance of time for the life of the self. But the self can move beyond its sinful state only by faithfully responding to God's act of forgiveness in Christ. In his analysis of Christianity Kierkegaard defines two central moments: the incarnation and faith. According to him, at the stage of Christian faith there is the most complete individuation of the self and the strongest emphasis on the self's life-time. As we have stated throughout, Christian faith is the *telos* of Kierkegaard's dialectic of existence. To see exactly how this is so, we must examine his interpretation of both the moment of incarnation and the moment of faith.

B. The Moment and The Individual (I)

1. The Incarnation

God's atoning love as manifested in Christ not only discloses the self's sinfulness, but also makes newly possible a proper relation between the individual and God. Because the self's eternal blessedness is contingent upon such a proper relation to God, the possibility of eternal blessedness is reopened by God's act in Christ. At each previous stage of existence, the self, by not willing to be itself, constitutes itself a

[60] *Training in Christianity*, p. 71; S.V., xii, 64-65. Compare: "God is that of which each individual has infinite need and the passionate understanding of this is the true God-relationship." Swenson, *Something About Kierkegaard, op.cit.*, p. 125. And: "When every human hope has been eliminated or transformed itself into hopelessness, and the understanding confirms that there is no hope . . . the Spirit brings the hope of eternity." Thomte, *Kierkegaard's Philosophy of Religion, op.cit.*, p. 173.

sinner, and in so doing forfeits the possibility of salvation. If this possibility is to be reestablished for the temporal self, it cannot be merely the result of the action of that self. A prior act of God is required. According to Kierkegaard, the incarnation is just such a divine action. We must, therefore, examine his interpretation of the incarnation.

Kierkegaard understands the incarnation to be the Absolute Paradox in which God enters history in the person of Jesus. The presentation of the incarnation as the Absolute Paradox rests on Kierkegaard's persistent contention that God and man are absolutely and qualitatively different. As we have seen, this difference can be expressed in various ways. It can be understood as the difference between the Creator and the creature, or as the difference between the holy God and sinful man. When discussing the incarnation, however, Kierkegaard most often expresses the difference between God and man (or the world as a whole) in terms of eternity and temporality. At times this line of argument is somewhat confusing, for it appears that his God is more Greek than Christian.[61] Although there are a few points at which he seems to characterize God in a manner similar to Aristotle's Unmoved Mover, if this were Kierkegaard's final view of the matter, he would be involved in irresolvable contradictions. For Kierkegaard, God always remains preemi-

---

[61] Some authors argue that Kierkegaard has two different and conflicting views of God — the Greek Absolute and the Christian personal God. For arguments that stress this difference, see Torsten Bohlin, *Kierkegaards dogmatiska aaskaadning i dess historiska Sammenhang, op.cit.* Wyschogrod, *Kierkegaard and Heidegger: The Ontology of Existence, op.cit.*, esp. pp. 42ff; Richard Kroner, "Kierkegaard's Understanding of Hegel," *Union Seminary Quarterly Review*, vol. 21, no. 2, Jan. 1966, pp. 233-244; Robert L. Horn's rebuttal of Kroner's argument, "On Understanding Kierkegaard's Understanding . . . ," *Union Seminary Quarterly Review*, vol. 21, no. 3, March 1966, pp. 341-345; Robert Whittemore, "Pro Hegel, Contra Kierkegaard," *Journal of Religious Thought*, vol. 13, Spring-Summer 1956, pp. 131-144; and Henry Nelson Wieman, "Interpretation of Kierkegaard," *Christian Century*, 1939, p. 446.

nently a personal being. Distinguishing the Greek and the Christian views of faith and of God, he argues:

"In the Greek view, faith is a concept that belongs in the sphere of the intellect. . . . Thus faith is related to probability, and we get the progression: faith — knowledge."

"Christianly, faith is at home in the existential [*Existentielle*] — God has not made his appearance in the character of an assistant professor who has a few axioms that one must first believe and afterward understand."

". . . Faith is the expression for personality's relationship to personality. . . ."

"In this purely personal relationship between God as personality and the believer as *existing* personality lies the concept of faith. . . . Therefore the *obedience* of faith (i.e., Romans 1:5) is the apostolic expression: then faith is oriented toward will, personality, not toward intellectuality."[62]

The meaning of "eternal" with reference to the Christian notion of God can be understood by recalling the two fundamental dimensions of Kierkegaard's use of the word "eternal." We have noted that "eternal" is consistently associated with unchangeability and with possibility. Kierkegaard uses the word "eternal" of God to indicate that God's will remains unchanged: " . . . the Atonement . . . teaches that God has remained unchanged while men changed, or it *proclaims* to men-altered-in-sin that God has remained unchanged."[63] For

[62] *Journals and Papers*, no. 180; *Papirer*, xi[1] A 237. Compare: "God is a subject. . . ," *Postscript*, p. 178; S.V., vii, 167; and ". . . *for since God is a personal being*, thou canst well conceive how abhorrent it is to Him that people want to wipe His mouth with formulas, to wait upon Him with official solemnity, official phrases, etc. Yea, precisely because *God is personality in the most eminent sense, sheer personality*, precisely for this cause is the official religion infinitely more loathsome to Him than it is to a woman when she discovers that a man is making love to her . . . out of a book of etiquette," *Attack on Christendom*, p. 153, italics added. See also *Journals and Papers*, nos. 1349, 1382, and 1392; *Papirer*, vii[1] A 201; x[1] A 20; and x[1] A 629.

[63] *Journals and Papers*, no. 1348; *Papirer*, vii[1] A 143. Compare: "But God is unchanged love — a spring, cool every morning, is not more

Kierkegaard, the Christian God is a transcendent personal being, and is not the Greek Unmoved Mover. God's eterntiy is his unchangeable will in his love for man. Such unchangeability is set in tension with temporality that is characterized by changeability. In contrast to the unchanging will of God expressed in his unswerving love of man, man's will wavers, and his sin expresses an absence of love of God. Paradoxically, it is through one's awareness of sin and the perception of God's willingness to forgive sin that one becomes most acutely conscious of the unchangeable love of God. God's love is not altered by man's shortcomings, but remains constant. This brings into play the second characteristic of eternity — possibility. Because God's will is unchangeable, possibilities are open to sinful selves that would otherwise be closed. Most importantly, through the possibility of the forgiveness of sins, the self regains the possibility of eternal blessedness.

For the most part, however, Kierkegaard uses "temporal" and "eternal" in connection with the incarnation as a means to indicate as sharply as possible what he sees as the absolute absurdity of Jesus' claim to be God. Against the Hegelians of his day who tended to see in the incarnation the identification of the divine and the human that culminated in speculative philosophy's contention that God and the world are one, Kierkegaard constantly holds that God and the world are wholly different. Because God and the world are totally different and are not implicitly identical, it is, Kierkegaard argues, absolutely paradoxical to believe that a particular individual within the world is at the same time God. Kierkegaard repeatedly tries to evoke the radical nature of the claim that Jesus made about his person. According to him, and again in direct opposition to Hegelian philosophers, Jesus did not proclaim the

---

unchanged; the sun, warm every dawning day, is not more unchanged; the sea, every morning refreshing, is not more unchanged than God unchanged is love." No. 1379; *Papirer*, IX A 374. The implications of this part of Kierkegaard's argument will become more apparent in our discussion of the atonement.

identity of the human race with God. Rather, Jesus insisted that he himself, in his concrete individuality was at the same time God: "Man is not the unity of God and mankind. Such terminology exhibits the profundity of optical illusion. The God-Man is the unity of God and an individual man. That the human race is or should be akin to God is ancient paganism; but that an individual man is God is Christianity, and this individual is the God-Man."[64]

The Christian claim is that God, who is qualitatively different from man, entered the world at a *particular moment* in the form of a *particular individual*: "*The paradoxical religiousness* places the contradiction absolutely between existence and the eternal; for precisely the thought that the eternal *is* at a definite moment of time, is an expression for the fact that existence is abandoned by the concealed immanence of the eternal. In religiousness *A* the eternal is *ubique et nusquam*, but concealed by the actuality of existence; in the paradoxical religiousness the eternal is at a definite place, and precisely this is the breach with immanence."[65] For Kierkegaard, the Absolute Paradox is that this particular individual is at the same time God. The Absolute Paradox brings together that which is totally different in a coincidence of opposites. The two parts of the term "God-Man" refer to the two elements in the opposition. For this reason, Kierkegaard most often refers to the incarnation as the Absolute Paradox, or refers to Jesus as the God-Man.

As the term implies, the Absolute Paradox is, by all rational standards, completely absurd. Any attempt to comprehend this paradox rationally is bound to fail. Kierkegaard makes this point by arguing that the God-Man is an "offense" to reason, the "shipwreck" of reason, and the "crucifixion" of the understanding.[66] This does not mean, however, that reason

[64] *Training in Christianity*, p. 84; S.V., xii, 79. The theme of the absurdity of the claim made here runs throughout this work.

[65] *Postscript*, p. 506; S.V., vii, 497.

[66] See especially: *Philosophical Fragments*, pp. 46-67; S.V., iv, 204-221.

has *no* role to play in relation to the Absolute Paradox. Reason is dialectically related to the Absolute Paradox in a negative way. "The activity of reason is to distinguish the paradox negatively — but no more. . . ."[67] Kierkegaard's point is that the task of reason in relation to the God-Man is constantly to make clear the fact that the Absolute Paradox cannot be understood. One can be positively related to the incarnation only in faith. But before the faithful response to the Absolute Paradox is explored, some further dimensions of the incarnation itself must be discussed.

2. *Sacred History*: *The God-Man*

In the *moment* of the incarnation, God becomes incarnate in the *individual* person of Jesus. Because this event reestablishes the possibility of eternal blessedness, it is of infinite interest to the sinful self. Therefore, Kierkegaard calls this moment the "fullness of time": "And now the moment. Such a moment has a peculiar character. It is brief and temporal indeed, like every moment; it is transient like all moments are; it is past, like every moment in the next moment. And yet it is decisive, and filled with the Eternal. Such a moment ought to have a distinctive name; let us call it the *Fullness of Time* [*Tidens Fylde*]."[68] Kierkegaard constantly regards the incarnation as an *historical event*. In both the *Philosophical Fragments* and in the *Postscript* to the *Fragments*, he takes as his central problematic the following issue: "The eternal blessedness of the individual is decided in time through the relationship to something historical, which is, furthermore, of such a character as to include in its composition that which by virtue of its essence cannot become historical, and must therefore become such by virtue of the absurd."[69]

It soon becomes apparent, however, that the incarnation is an "historical" event of a very peculiar sort. In the first place, usually historical events are understood to stand in an

[67] *Journals and Papers*, no. 7; *Papirer*, x² A 345.
[68] *Philosophical Fragments*, p. 22; S.V., iv, 188.
[69] *Postscript*, p. 345; S.V., vii, 333.

ongoing historical process in which events grow out of previous events and condition events that are to come. This is not so for the incarnation. It is absolutely new, and therefore does not grow out of the previous development of the world historical process. Furthermore, this occurrence bears an ambiguous relationship to succeeding historical events. With respect to the incarnation, what is most important is the brute facticity of the event itself: "If the contemporary generation [i.e., the generation contemporary with the incarnation] had left nothing behind but these words: 'We have believed that in such and such a year the God appeared among us in the humble figure of a servant, that he lived and taught in our community, and finally died,' it would be more than enough. The contemporary generation would have done all that was necessary. . . ."[70] The negative relationship between the incarnation and later historical development is indicated by Kierkegaard's constant polemic against the "1800 years" of the history of Christianity. The historical development of Christendom, by which the incarnation is gradually assimilated and slowly rationalized, only minimizes the absurdity of Jesus' claim, and thereby is a hindrance to one who seeks to establish a proper relationship with the God-Man.

While Kierkegaard argues that the life of the God-Man is an historical event, he represents the incarnation as a moment that stands apart from the ongoing historical process. The reason for his isolation of this moment becomes evident when the second peculiarity of this "historical" event is examined.

The historical event of the incarnation is an "eternal fact [*et evigt Faktum*]" or an "absolute fact [*et absolute Faktum*]."[71] Because Jesus claimed to be God, the historical event

[70] *Philosophical Fragments*, p. 130; S.V., IV, 266.

[71] *Philosophical Fragments*, pp. 124-125; S.V., IV, 262-263. One might ask whether it makes any sense to talk about an "eternal" or an "absolute" historical fact. Kierkegaard would most likely reply: "Of course not. That's precisely the point!" This does not, however, resolve the problems in his position. These will become more evident as we proceed.

297

of the incarnation is different from other historical events. Insofar as Jesus was a man like all other men (Christ's manhood) his life formed a part of the ongoing historical process. The history of this life was fully apparent to all of his contemporaries. Furthermore, this history could be known by amassing historical data. Therefore, the closer to Jesus' historical epoch one is, the better is one's position to "know" Jesus. The person with the greatest advantage would be the one who was constantly with Jesus from the moment of his birth to the time of his death. But such "ordinary" historical knowledge is of no avail in adjudicating the claim that Jesus made about his person. That Jesus was at the same time God is open to no historical verification: "A contemporary may go where he can see the Teacher — and may he then believe his eyes? Why not? But may he also believe that this makes him a disciple? By no means. If he believes his eyes, he is deceived, for the God is not immediately knowable. But then perhaps he may shut his eyes. Just so, but if he does, what profit does he have from his contemporaneity?"[72]

As far as any observer could discern, Jesus was a man like other men; yet he claimed to be God. This is the Absolute Paradox. If there were any external sign by which Jesus could be *known* to be God, it would be unnecessary to *believe* it. Jesus' divinity was an inwardness that stood in absolute opposition to the outwardness of his humanity. Furthermore, it was an inwardness that *could not* become outward: "The God's servant-form, however, is not a mere disguise, but is actual; it is not a parasitic body, but an actual body; and from the hour that in the omnipotent purpose of his omnipotent love the God became a servant, he has so to speak imprisoned himself in his resolve, and is now bound to go on (to speak foolishly) whether it pleases him or not. He cannot betray himself. There exists for him no such possibility as that which is open to the noble king, suddenly to show that he is after all the king. . . ."[73] There was *nothing* that Jesus could say or do that would make his divinity perfectly evident.

[72] *Ibid.*, p. 78; S.V., IV, 228. [73] *Ibid.*, p. 68; S.V., IV, 221.

Kierkegaard often uses the term "incognito" to indicate the inwardness of Jesus' divinity. During his life on earth, Jesus maintained a strict incognito. His divinity remained hidden and was, in fact, contrary to his outward appearance:

"What is unrecognizableness [*Ukjendeligheden*]? It means not to appear in one's proper role, as, for example, when a policeman appears in plain clothes.

"And so unrecognizableness, the absolute unrecognizableness is this: being God, to be also an individual man. To be the individual man, or an individual man (whether it be a distinguished or a lowly man is here irrelevant), is the greatest possible, the infinitely qualitative remove from being God, and therefore the most profound incognito [*Incognito*]."[74]

These peculiar features of the "historical" event of the incarnation have far-reaching consequences. It becomes clear that if the incarnation is to be called an "historical" event, some qualification of "historical" is required. History, as it is usually understood, actually has nothing to do with what is most important in the Christ-event: "Can one learn from history[75] anything about Christ? No. Why not? Because one can 'know' nothing at all about Christ; He is the paradox, the object of faith, existing only for faith. But all historical communication is communication of 'knowledge,' hence from history one can learn nothing about Christ."[76]

Kierkegaard appears, therefore, to have involved himself in a contradiction. On the one hand, he argues that the incarnation is the historical event that is most important for man, because this event is the *historical* point of departure for man's eternal blessedness. On the other hand, he argues

---

[74] *Training in Christianity*, p. 127; S.V., xii, 118. Compare: ". . . God is pleased to walk here on earth in a strict incognito such as only an almighty being can assume, an incognito impenetrable to the most intimate observation. . . ," pp. 27-28; S.V., xii, 23-24.

[75] Kierkegaard's note: "By 'history' is to be understood throughout profane [*profane*] history, world-history, history as ordinarily understood, in contrast to sacred [*hellige*] history." This distinction will be analyzed in what follows.

[76] *Training in Christianity*, p. 28; S.V., xii, 24.

that "History . . . has nothing whatever to do with Christ.
. . ."[77] He tries to solve this dilemma by making a distinction
between sacred (*hellige*) and profane (*profane*) history:[78]
"With the everlasting contemplation of world-history and the
history of the human race, with the everlasting talk about universal history and its significance, etc., people have become
all too nimble in appropriating Christianity without more
ado as a part of world-history, they have come to regard it as
a matter of course that Christianity is a stage in the development of the human race. They have quite forgotten that
Christ's life on earth (and this is what Christianity is — a different thing entirely from the history of Christians, the lives
of Christians, their biographies, their fate, and so to speak of
the history of heretics and of science) is sacred history, which
must not be confused with the history of the human race."[79]

Profane history is, therefore, history as usually understood
— the course of events that develops as the result of the sufferings and actions of persons. To the extent that Christ was
fully man, he participated in and contributed to this historical
process. But, following the traditional Christological formulation concerning the person of Christ,[80] Kierkegaard regards
Jesus as at the same time fully God. Insofar as Jesus is divine,
he participates in sacred history. As the above quotation
makes clear, sacred and profane history are separated by an
abyss as great as the difference between God and man.

The most important dimension of the incarnation for the
sinful self is the fact that God enters the world. This is an
"historical" fact upon which the possibility of the self's eter-

[77] *Ibid.*, p. 33; S.V., xii, 28.

[78] For a contemporary statement of this distinction between sacred
and profane history which depends on Kierkegaard, see Rudolf Bultmann, *Jesus Christ and Mythology* (New York: Charles Scribner's Sons,
1958), pp. 6off.

[79] *Training in Christianity*, p. 216; S.V., xii, 203.

[80] Kierkegaard's use of the Chalcedonian formula is, however, quite
different from the tradition. This will become clear when we discuss
the manner in which the incarnation is related to Kierkegaard's view
of the self.

nal blessedness depends. It now appears, however, that this historical event is most essentially related, not to the history in which the self participates, but to a sacred history from which the self's daily life is excluded. While Christ was an historical figure, he was "not at all a merely historical person, since as the Paradox He [was] an extremely unhistorical person."[81]

Some of the problems raised by Kierkegaard's distinction between sacred and profane history emerge when we consider the implications of his interpretation of the incarnation. Two important points are implicit in the comments we have already made. In the first place, the historical details of Jesus' life are of no significance to the believer. Historical facts are concerned with profane history, and thereby pertain to Jesus' humanity, but not to his inward divinity: "A merely historical person, a human being, is present only historically—therefore every detail is of great importance. . . . But Christ is present in an entirely different way. Once again it is seen how strict orthodoxy really downgrades Christ. For however paradoxical it is, it is true that it is Christian that with regard to Christ the historical details are not nearly so important as

[81] *Training in Christianity*, p. 67; S.V., xii, 60. Bultmann's analysis is helpful: "The paradox of Christ as the historical Jesus and the ever-present Lord, and the paradox of the Christian as an eschatological and historical being is excellently described by Erich Frank (*The Role of History in Christian Thought*, pp. 74, 75) '. . . to the Christians the advent of Christ was not an event in the temporal process which we mean by history today. It was an event in the history of salvation, in the realm of eternity, an eschatological moment in which rather this profane history of the world came to its end. And in an analogous way, history comes to its end in the religious experience of any Christian who is "in Christ." In his faith he is already above time and history. For although the advent of Christ is an historical event which happened "once" in the past, it is, at the same time, an eternal event which occurs again and again in the soul of any Christian in whose soul Christ is born, suffers, dies and is raised up to eternal life. . . . The advent of Christ is an event in the realm of eternity which is incommensurable with historical time.' " *History and Eschatology* (New York: Harper and Row, 1957), pp. 152-153.

with Socrates and the like, simply because Christ is Christ, an eternally present one for he is true God."[82] With respect to the incarnation, all one needs to know is that at such-and-such a time, there appeared a man who claimed to be God. With this the object of faith, the person of the God-Man, is posited and the believer is called upon to respond.

The second consequence of Kierkegaard's view of the nature of the historical event of God's incarnation is that the historical development of Christianity is of no concern to the believer. For each individual, the problem presented by the incarnation is the same: to believe that Jesus is God. Because Kierkegaard thinks that the establishment of a Christian church and the growth of a body of believers minimizes the absurdity of the claim made by Jesus, he argues that the historical development of Christianity has a negative influence upon the individual who strives to be faithful. One must bypass the history of the church, and seek an immediate confrontation with the Absolute Paradox.

The third consequence of Kierkegaard's analysis of the nature of the historical event of the incarnation involves his notion of "contemporaneity" [*Samtidighed*]: "If our fact is assumed to be a simple historical fact, contemporaneity is a *desideratum*. It is an advantage to be a contemporary . . . , or to be as near to such contemporaneity as possible. . . . If the fact in question is an eternal fact, every age is equally near; but not, it should be noted, in faith; for faith and the historical are correlative concepts, and it is only by an accommodation to a less exact usage that I employ in this connection the word 'fact,' which is derived from the historical

[82] *Journals and Papers*, no. 318; *Papirer*, VIII[1] A 583. It should be pointed out that the problem of the historical Jesus had been thrust to the center of theological discussions during Kierkegaard's time by the publication of Strauss' *Leben Jesu* (1835). In opposition to those who, in the face of Strauss' argument, maintained that historical facts concerning Jesus' life were important for the Christian believer, Kierkegaard holds that all historical details are unimportant. He carries on a constant polemic against historical-biblical research. See *Postscript*, pp. 30-31; S.V., VII, 18-19.

realm. . . . If the fact in question is an absolute fact, or to determine it still more precisely, if it is the fact we have described, it would be a contradiction to suppose that time had any power to differentiate the fortunes of men with respect to it, that is to say, in any decisive sense."[83]

Since the incarnation is an eternal or an absolute fact, every age is equally near to, and distant from, the event. Because Christ's divinity is not open to external inspection, but is inward and participates in sacred history, temporal proximity to his earthly life is of no consequence for the believer. If the historical details of Jesus' life were decisive for the believer, those who lived during Jesus' time would have an incomparable advantage over those who lived later. If the historical development of Christianity were of importance for faith, those persons of later generations would have an advantage over those of earlier generations. However, due to the nature of the event, the God-Man exists only for faith, and faith comes about in the same manner for all persons, regardless of historical circumstance—by the non-offense at Jesus' claim to be God: "The God-Man (and by this, as has been said, Christianity does not mean that fantastic speculation about the unity of God and man, but an individual man who is God) — the God-Man exists only for faith; but the possibility of offense is just the repellent force by which faith comes into existence — if one does not choose instead to be offended [*vægler at forarges*]."[84] Insofar as the fact of the incarnation is proclaimed, all persons are equidistant from the event; all are contemporaries of the God-Man.[85]

Because our analysis of Kierkegaard's understanding of the incarnation and of the consequences of his view of the nature

---

[83] *Philosophical Fragments*, pp. 125-126; S.V., iv, 262-263. Compare *Postscript*, pp. 88-89; S.V., vii, 76-77.

[84] *Training in Christianity*, p. 122; S.V., xii, 114. See also *Philosophical Fragments*, p. 128; S.V., iv, 264.

[85] Kierkegaard's idea of contemporaneity is developed by Bultmann in *Jesus Christ and Mythology, op.cit.*, pp. 77ff. and *History and Eschatology, op.cit.*, pp. 152-153.

of this historical event has been involved, a brief summary of our discussion will be helpful. In view of his conviction that God and man are qualitatively different, Kierkegaard argues that the incarnation is the Absolute Paradox in which there is a *coincidentia oppositorium* — a coincidence of temporality and eternity. By virtue of his manhood, Jesus participates in profane history, and by virtue of his divinity, he participates in sacred history. The incarnation event might, therefore, be understood in the following manner:

Jesus Christ:	God	Eternity	Sacred History
	Man	Temporality	Profane History

Kierkegaard repeatedly stresses that God is incarnate in a particular *individual,* and that this event occurs at a particular *moment* in the historical process. Because the incarnation event reopens the possibility of eternal blessedness for the sinful self, Kierkegaard calls this moment the "fullness of time."

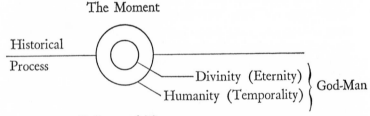

The Moment

Historical Process

Divinity (Eternity)
Humanity (Temporality) } God-Man

Fullness of Time

What makes this moment ultimately significant is Jesus' divinity. But this is inward and cannot be discerned by external observation. It must be believed and, in believing, the fact of the coincidence of God and man in the person of Jesus, is established *for the believer.*

A clarification needs to be made at this point concerning the nature of the inwardness of Jesus' divinity. From our analysis of the ethical stage of existence, we have seen that Kierkegaard argues that there is a distinction between one's inward intention and his outward action. Furthermore, it is the inner intention and not the outer action that is invested with ethical significance. One can never be certain that another person's outward actions are congruent with his inward intentions. For this reason, persons must relate to one another in belief: "Personality is not a sum of axioms nor is it an immediate accessibility; personality is a bending-into-itself, a *clausum* . . . . personality is the 'in-there,' because of which the word *persona* (*per-sonare*) is suggestive, the 'in-there,' to which one, himself a personality, must relate himself believingly [*maa forholds sig troende til*]. Between personality and personality, no other relationship is possible."[86]

To the extent that Jesus is regarded as fully human, he shares the inwardness of intentional activity. But this is not the inwardness of his divinity. Jesus' inner divinity is further removed from outwardness than even the inner intention of his actions.[87] Therefore, the belief by which one relates himself to another person is not the same as the faith by which one relates oneself to the God-Man. Faith in the God-Man is what Kierkegaard calls faith in the "strictest sense of the word." The precise nature of this faith will become clearer in what follows. For the moment, it is sufficient to recognize that in view of these considerations, a revision of the foregoing diagram is necessary. (See the following page.)

The contention that Jesus is God transforms his life into what Kierkegaard calls an "eternal" or an "absolute" event. But Kierkegaard maintains that this "eternal event" actually took place at a particular moment in time, and thereby is likewise an historical event. This creates the Absolute Paradox: "But the absolute fact is also an historical fact. Unless we

---

[86] *Journals and Papers*, no. 180; *Papirer*, XI[1] A 237. Kierkegaard makes no consistent *terminological* distinction between the faith by which persons relate to one another, and the faith in which one relates to Jesus' divinity. In both instances, he uses "*Tro*" or words derivative from "*Tro*."

[87] The analogy to this heightened inwardness in man is faith. This is discussed below.

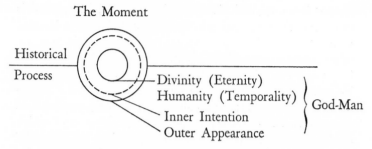

The Moment

Historical Process

—Divinity (Eternity)
Humanity (Temporality) } God-Man
Inner Intention
Outer Appearance

The Fullness of Time

are careful to insist on this point, our entire hypothesis is nullified; for then we speak only of an eternal fact. The absolute fact is an historical fact, and as such it is the object of faith. The historical aspect must indeed be accentuated. . . ."[88]

However, as we have seen, the consequence of the inwardness of Jesus' divinity is that the historical details relating to Jesus' life are of no importance for belief. If one hears the proclamation that at a particular moment in time there was a man named Jesus who claimed to be God, one is contemporary with the incarnation event. All persons are equidistant from God's act in Christ. Interestingly enough, this leads to a view of the incarnation and its relationship to the ongoing historical process (profane history) that might be diagrammed in the following manner:

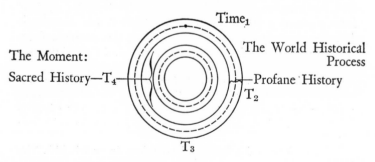

Time$_1$

The Moment:

Sacred History—T$_4$

The World Historical Process

—Profane History
T$_2$

T$_3$

[88] *Philosophical Fragments*, p. 125; S.V., IV, 262.

Because the incarnation is the Absolute Paradox, the problem is the same for each generation of believers: to have faith, or to take offense.[89]

3. Atonement: The Forgiveness of Sins

We have stated that the incarnation is God's act that establishes the possibility of resolving the dilemma in which man has involved himself. To understand Kierkegaard's argument at this point, it is necessary to recall the nature of the self's predicament as it was developed in the first part of this chapter. In brief, man's problem is that through his own decisions, he has become a sinner. Because man has not willed to be his own self, he has disrupted his relationship with God. Since eternal blessedness depends on the proper relation to God, man's sin renders impossible his attainment of eternal blessedness. Put in terms that are descriptive of the structure of selfhood, the self's (self-constituted) actuality as a sinner cuts off the possibility of the self's reaching a state of eternal blessedness. In relation to the possibility of eternal blessedness, the self is no longer free but is limited by the history that it has acquired through its decisions. The self's dilemma is, therefore, its sinfulness.

The resolution of man's dilemma must involve coming to terms with sinfulness. This possibility is opened by one's relationship to the God-Man:[90] "Moreover, the determination of

[89] The reader should have recognized that Kierkegaard's interpretation of the incarnation as a moment that does not grow out of preceding historical events, and that has no close connection with succeeding events, bears a certain resemblance to spatialized time as discussed in chapter three, and to the experience of time characteristic of immediate aesthetic existence. As should be evident, however, the basis for such a view of time is different in Christianity than in aesthetic existence. Furthermore, the similarity is not as great as it may appear at this point, for the faithful response of the incarnation event is the paradigmatic instance of life-time.

[90] When discussing the atonement, Kierkegaard most often describes Jesus as the Redeemer. He uses the etymology of the Danish word "Forløser" to develop his interpretation of the significance of the incarnation. "Forløser" derives from "løse" which means to loosen, or to

sin as a position involves also . . . the possibility of offense, the paradox. For the paradox results from the doctrine of the atonement. First Christianity goes ahead and establishes sin so securely as a position that the human understanding never can comprehend it; and then it is the same Christian doctrine which, in turn, undertakes to do away with this position so completely that the human understanding can never comprehend it. . . . But Christianity, which is the first discoverer of the paradoxes, is in this case also as paradoxical as possible; it works directly against itself when it establishes sin so securely as a position that it seems a perfect impossibility to do away with it again—and then it is precisely Christianity which, by the atonement, would do away with it so completely that it is as though drowned in the sea."[91] The incarnation of God in Christ establishes the possibility of atonement for the self. Kierkegaard consistently understands the atonement to be the forgiveness of the *individual's* sins. Curiously, this aspect of Kierkegaard's understanding of the incarnation has gone virtually unanalyzed by commentators. Yet it is of central importance for grasping his understanding of Christianity and of the self.

Because it is the actuality of one's sinfulness that limits the possibility of eternal blessedness, if one were able to come to terms with one's sin, the possibility of eternal blessedness might again be available. This possibility is posed by God's act in Christ. For Kierkegaard, Christ is the atoner for our sins.[92] The manner in which he develops his argument is quite

---

release. As we shall see, this is precisely what the incarnation makes possible — the loosening of man from his self-incurred sin. (The other term that Kierkegaard uses in this context is "Savior." Here the Danish word is "*Frelseren*," from the root "*frelse*," which means to save or to rescue.)

[91] *The Sickness Unto Death*, p. 231; S.V., XI, 210-211. Compare *Philosophical Fragments*, pp. 58-59; S.V., IV, 214.

[92] Here I differ substantially from a critic like Thomte, who holds that "In the writings of Kierkegaard Christ is presented primarily as the Pattern (*Vorbild*) or example to be followed, rather than as the atoner

common in the theological tradition. Jesus is the substitution for the sins of the individual: "For when He, when the suffering and death of the Atoner is the satisfaction [*Fyldestgjørelsen*] for thy sin and guilt — being a satisfaction it assumes in fact thy place, or He, the Substitute, steps into thy place, suffering in thy place the punishment for sin, that thou mightest be saved, in thy place suffering death for thee, that thou mightest live — did He not put Himself in thy place?"[93]

Kierkegaard's understanding of the atonement as the forgiveness of the individual's sins is dependent on the Lutheran tradition from which so much of his thinking derives. On the basis of I Peter 4:8 ("Love shall hide the multitude of sins"), Kierkegaard frequently uses the metaphor of Christ hiding the sins of the individual: "He [Christ] hides them [one's sins] quite literally. When a man places himself in front of another and covers him entirely with his body so that no one at all can get a sight of him who is hidden behind — so it is that Jesus Christ covers with his holy body thy sin. Though justice were to rage, what more can it want? For satisfaction has indeed been made. Though the repentance within thee be so contrite that it thinks it a duty to aid external justice to discover thy guilt — satisfaction indeed has been made, a satisfaction, a vicarious satisfaction, which covers thy sin entirely and makes it impossible to see it. . . ."[94]

---

for our sins." *Kierkegaard's Philosophy of Religion, op.cit.*, p. 174. In Kierkegaard's post-1848 writings, the theme of Christ as *Vorbild* is present. This can, however, be understood as the result of the *Corsair* affair. In carefully articulated theological statements, Christ is primarily the atoner for our sins.

[93] *Christian Discourses*, p. 368; S.V., x, 258. Compare: ". . . by his self-imposed bondage the learner has brought upon himself a burden of guilt, and when the Teacher gives him the condition and the Truth he constitutes himself an *Atonement* [*Forsoner*], taking away the wrath impending upon that of which the learner has made himself guilty." *Philosophical Fragments*, p. 21; S.V., IV, 187.

[94] "Love hides a multitude of sins," *For Self-Examination and Judge for Yourselves!*, p. 22; S.V., XII, 287. Compare *Journals and Papers*, no. 1859; *Papirer*, x² A 255.

While Kierkegaard argues that the incarnation makes forgiveness possible, he maintains that the individual must always be aware of his sin. Only in this manner can one understand oneself in one's concrete actuality as a forgiven sinner. Furthermore, only in this way can the decisive importance of one's previous life be appreciated. Forgiveness does not simply obliterate the self's past in one swift stroke. One retains his past, but now that past is forgiven. If a person were simply to forget his past sinfulness, he would not understand himself as a forgiven sinner. Kierkegaard argues:

"For Christ did not come into the world to make life easy in the light-hearted sense, nor yet to make it heavy in the sense of a mournful heart, but to lay the light burden on the believer. The light-hearted would allow all to be forgotten — he believes in vain. The mournful heart would allow nothing to be forgotten — he believes in vain. But he who believes, believes that all is forgotten, only in this wise, that he is bearing a light burden — for is he not bearing the memory that he has been forgiven? The light-hearted would let that memory be forgotten then — all is forgotten and forgiven! But faith says: All is forgotten; remember that it has been forgiven. One may forget indeed in many ways. One may forget, because one gets something else to think about. One may forget thoughtlessly and frivolously. One may consider that all has been forgotten because one has oneself forgotten — but the eternal righteousness can forget and will forget only in one way, through forgiveness. And so the believer himself must not forget, but on the contrary, must constantly remind himself, that all has been forgiven him."[95]

Before analyzing the individual's response to the incarnation, we must consider three important implications of Kierkegaard's argument. First, the atonement manifests God's unchangeable love. Here we find further confirmation of the fact that when Kierkegaard refers to God as Eternal, he is pointing to the unchangeability of God's will — His steadfast

[95] *The Gospel of Our Sufferings,* pp. 45-46.

love of man.[96] Although the incarnation took place at a particular moment in time, it expresses God's "eternal resolve" to love man: "His [God's] resolve, which stands in no equal reciprocal relation to the occasion, must be from eternity, though when realized in time, it constitutes precisely the *Moment*. . . . The moment makes its appearance when an eternal resolve comes into relation with an incommensurable occasion."[97] Through the incarnation, the individual sees that a change has developed in his own self, and not in God's person. While God's love remains constant, the individual, by his refusal to be his own self, *becomes* a sinner:

"What the Atonement expresses is therefore directly opposed to the objection; it teaches that God has remained unchanged while men changed, or it *proclaims* to men-altered-in-sin that God has remained unchanged. Every objection attacks essentially the last clause (that men are changed by sin), but slyly assumes the appearance of profundity by speaking about the first clause, that God must have been changed. We transform the whole thing into a phantom-battle about the predicates of God, instead of simply asking the objector whether or not he has become changed from what he eternally must be assumed to be. If he actually has been changed, then *eo ipso* the proclamation of God's unchangeableness is his most urgent need. For a reconciliation it is by no means necessary that both parties be changed, for if the one party is in the right, it would be madness for him to be changed. But if his unchangeableness (as proclaimed in the Atonement) is an abstract something, then there is another reason for its not being a reconciliation, for then one party is not a part to it at all but is an abstract something and there is only an impersonal relationship between them. . . . The relationship must be between the two reconciled parties, so that the change of one party (the man in sin) has a relationship to the unchangeableness of the other party (God). Here it is

---

[96] See above pp. 292ff.
[97] *Philosophical Fragments*, p. 30; S.V., IV, 193-194.

311

again evident that it is especially the significance of the change of sin and the reality of this change which must be maintained if everything is not to be confused."[98]

Second, in the atonement, the sinful individual is related to God through the Mediator, the God-Man. The relation to God passes through no other channel than Jesus. For example, Kierkegaard does not think that the atonement effects an ontological change in the human race as a whole in which the individual person shares by virtue of his participation in the race. Furthermore, he does not hold that the benefits of Christ's incarnation are mediated to the self through the church, so that one is related to Christ, and hence to God, only to the extent that he is related to the church. The atonement is a transaction between the sinful *individual* and the holy God that is mediated through the person of the God-Man.

Third, the event of God's incarnation in Jesus does not by itself accomplish the forgiveness of the sinner. For forgiveness to transpire, there must be both the willingness of the offended party to forgive and the belief of the offending party in the forgiveness offered to him. God's act in Christ calls for a response from the sinful self. A negative response is offense (further sin). A positive response is faith and entails both the belief that Jesus is God, and the believing acceptance of the forgiveness offered by the God-Man. Forgiveness, as the Absolute Paradox, can be appropriated only through faith:

"Let us take the paradox of the forgiveness of sins. Forgiveness is a paradox in the Socratic sense, insofar as it involves a relationship between the eternal and an existing individual; it is a paradox *sensu strictiori*, because the existing individual is stamped as a sinner, by which existence is accentuated a second time, because it purports to be an eternal decision in time with retroactive power to neutralize the past, and because it is linked with the existence of God in time. The individual existing human being must feel himself a sinner; not

<hr />

[98] *Journals and Papers*, no. 1348; *Papirer*, VII[1] A 143.

objectively, which is nonsense, but subjectively, which is the most profound suffering. With all the strength of his mind . . . he must try to understand the forgiveness of sins, and then despair of the understanding. With the understanding directly opposed to it, the inwardness of faith must lay hold of the paradox; and precisely this struggle on the part of faith, fighting as the Romans once fought, dazzled by the fierce light of the sun, constitutes the tension of its inwardness."[99]

Having considered the moment of God's incarnation in the individual person of Jesus, we can now examine the individual believer's response to the incarnation event in the moment of faith.

C. THE MOMENT AND THE INDIVIDUAL (II)

1. Faith

Although Kierkegaard uses the term "faith" in a variety of ways, faith *sensu eminentiori* always refers to the Christian stage of existence: "And faith belongs essentially at the stage of the paradox-religious, as has constantly been asserted . . . all other faith is only an analogy, which is no faith, an analogy, which may serve to call attention, but nothing more, and the understanding of which therefore is revocation."[100]

As might be expected, Kierkegaard's interpretation of faith is very closely related to his understanding of the God-Man: faith is the positive response to God's act of forgiveness in Christ. However, as our analysis proceeds, it will become clear that in Kierkegaard's view the two central moments of Christian existence, the incarnation and faith, are formally parallel and constitute inverse images of one another.

We can begin to understand what Kierkegaard means by

[99] *Postscript*, p. 201; S.V.; VII, 187. Compare: "It is to be remembered that the forgiveness of sin is the paradoxical satisfaction by virtue of the absurd," p. 479, note; S.V., VII, 470.

[100] *Ibid.*, p. 505, note; S.V., VII, 496. Throughout the remainder of the book, "faith" will be used to indicate Christian faith, unless otherwise specified.

faith by recognizing that he associates it most fundamentally with the will.[101] But even this most basic point seems to be problematic. Working as self-consciously within the Lutheran tradition as Kierkegaard does, he has to come to terms with the issue of grace and works in relation to his view of faith. At some points, he places a strong emphasis on the role of grace in the development of the individual's faith. But for the most part, he recognizes that such a position is not consistent with his overall understanding of the self. It is of central importance for Kierkegaard's argument that man himself be responsible for faith. As we have seen in the context of studying his view of sin, he holds that the correlative of responsibility is the individual's free assertion of his will. Therefore, any notion of grace that renders impossible or unnecessary man's volitional activity in faith, cannot be acceptable for him.

However, because of Kierkegaard's keen sense of the dilemma that man's sinfulness poses for the existing self, he does not feel comfortable with an outright Pelagian view. He concludes that faith is a function of *both* God's grace and of man's willful activity. Kierkegaard argues that man's sin removes the possibility of his eternal blessedness, *unless* there is an act of God that reopens this possibility. As we have seen, he believes that this is accomplished in the incarnation. The incarnation is God's act of grace. Had not God first acted in the incarnation, man would remain bound in sin, and excluded from blessedness. God's act in Christ is a necessary,

[101] The division of man's capacities into thinking, willing, and feeling, which is made by faculty psychology serves as a useful tool for classifying various views of faith. Faith can be associated primarily with man's cognitive capacities, with his affectional sensibilities, or with his volitional capability. Of course, as we shall see, no radical disjunction can be made among these capacities. But it is correct so say that different views of faith often stress one capacity more than others. Considering Kierkegaard's argument, it is most surprising to note that Van Harvey quite incorrectly contends that Kierkegaard's "own view basically hangs on the identification of faith with propositional belief. . . ." *The Historian and the Believer: The Morality of Historical Knowledge and Christian Belief* (New York: Macmillan Co., 1966), pp. 286-287.

but not the sufficient condition of the individual's salvation. For the final realization of blessedness, the individual must respond to the incarnation in faith. Faith in God's atoning action is a function of the individual's determination of his will. In this way, Kierkegaard tries to hold that faith involves both the grace of God and the will of the self.

Both the importance of the will in faith, and the role afforded to the cognitive and affectional dimensions of the self become more apparent when faith is related to its object — Jesus Christ. We have seen that Kierkegaard repeatedly emphasizes the absurdity of Jesus' claim to be God by speaking of the incarnation as the Absolute Paradox. With such expressions, he stresses as strongly as he can that in the move of faith, there is *absolutely no rational certitude offered to the individual.* There are no logically compelling reasons to acknowledge that Jesus was God. Furthermore, because Jesus' divinity was inward and was not outwardly manifested, there was no way for contemporaries of Jesus to *know* that Jesus was God. As we have seen,[102] the only role that cognition can play in relation to the God-Man is constantly to make clear that the Absolute Paradox cannot be understood. There is nowhere for the individual to turn for support in the movement of faith. The Absolute Paradox poses for the sinful individual the task of making an "absolute decision."[103] Were the fact with which the individual must come to terms in faith any less paradoxical, the role of the will would be lessened. Reasons could be deduced, or evidence offered, and the movement of faith would not be a radical venture or a decisive leap. One believes in the God-Man not because of discernible evidence or ascertainable reasons, but by the sheer strength of his own will by which he *wills* to believe that which cannot be understood.[104] For this reason, Kierkegaard's

[102] See above p. 297.

[103] *Philosophical Fragments,* p. 125; S.V., IV, 262.

[104] Compare Crites' point: "The project of faith in which the stages culminate, spirit becoming spirit, is the maximum of that responsibility. It is a venture without visible means of support, unsupported by pre-

dominant metaphor for the movement of faith is the leap — *det Spring*. The emphasis on paradox in relation to the incarnation is the means by which he brings into clear focus the necessity of *willing* to believe that Jesus was God.

One might ask what could move a person to believe an absurdity such as the Absolute Paradox. Kierkegaard's answer is that the self's *interest* in its eternal blessedness moves the will to believe that Jesus was God's act of forgiveness. We have seen that with the awareness of the difference between God and the world that emerges at the religious stage of existence, there is a shift in the self's interest from worldly achievement to eternal blessedness. But at the Christian stage, the self becomes aware that it has forfeited the possibility of eternal blessedness by the actuality of its sinfulness. This creates a desperate[105] situation for the self. The individual is infinitely interested in, but decisively separated from, eternal blessedness. Only if God first acts to forgive the self's sins can the possibility of eternal blessedness be reopened. The desire for salvation creates in the self an interest in, or concern about, the person of Jesus: ·

"Here we may clearly note the difference that exists between faith *sensu strictissmo* on the one hand . . . and the ethical on the other. To ask with infinite interest [*uendeligt interesseret*] about an actuality that is not one's own, is faith, and this constitutes a paradoxical relationship to the paradoxical. Aesthetically it is impossible to raise such a question except in thoughtlessness, since possibility is aesthetically higher than actuality. Nor is it possible to raise such a question ethically, since the sole ethical interest is the interest in one's own actuality. The analogy between faith and the ethical is found in the infinite interest, which suffices to distinguish the believer

---

dictable consequences or by a socially defined role, or even by the most legitimate ethical claims: every ground is paradox, because spirit is its only support." *In the Twilight of Christendom, op.cit.*, p. 74.

[105] I intentionally use the word "desperate" at this point because of its etymological connection with "despair."

absolutely from an aesthete or a thinker. But the believer differs from the ethicist in being infinitely interested in the actuality of another (in the fact, for example, that God has existed in time)."[106]

The interest in the God-Man is a function of the self's interest in regaining the possibility of eternal blessedness. The combination of an infinite interest in salvation and the awareness that sin closes the possibility of eternal blessedness moves the individual to accept that which is absurd, the Absolute Paradox.

These insights enable us to see that Kierkegaard conceives faith and knowledge to be antithetical — where there is knowledge, there can be no faith, and vice versa. With respect to faith, knowledge can only understand that it cannot understand. Faith is, for Kierkegaard, a movement of the will, motivated by the self's interest in its eternal blessedness. It is always a desperate movement, a movement of one who has perceived the depth of the dilemma in which sin has involved him. It is the movement of one who recognizes that humanly speaking he has exhausted his possibilities, and if further possibilities (particularly the possibility of eternal blessedness) are to be reestablished, it must be through God himself. Only such a keen awareness of the predicament in which one involves oneself through one's own decisions could move one to believe something as absurd as Jesus' claim to be God, and the claim that the life and death of this person atone for one's sins. When no other possibility remains open, one believes.

The major thrust of Kierkegaard's argument might be better grasped by recalling his view of indirect communication. Because he thinks that in religious matters truth is subjectivity, Kierkegaard employs an indirect method of communication in which he withdraws himself from the works in order to present the reader with a situation calling for decision. In relation to the pseudonymous writings, the reader's task is to

---

[106] *Postscript*, pp. 287-288; S.V., VII, 278-279. Compare pp. 290-291 and 514; S.V., VII, 281-282 and 506.

reflect what he has understood in his own existence by means of personal decisions: "Indirect communication can be produced by the art of reduplicating the communication. This art consists in reducing oneself, the communicator, to nobody, something purely objective, and then incessantly composing qualitative opposites into unity. This is what some of the pseudonyms are accustomed to call 'double reflection.' An example of such indirect communciation is, so to compose jest and earnest that the composition is a dialectical knot — and with this to be nobody. If anyone is to profit by this sort of communication, he must himself undo the knot for himself."[107]

However, in the course of analyzing the God-Man, Kierkegaard argues that ". . . indirect communication can be brought about also in another way, by the relationship between the communication and the communicator. Whereas in the former case the communicator was left out of account, here he is a factor, but (be it noted) with a negative reflection."[108] The person of Jesus Christ necessitates the employment of indirect communication: "When one says directly, 'I am God, the Father and I are one,' that is a direct communication. But when he who says it is an individual man, quite like other men, then this communication is not perfectly direct; for it is not perfectly clear and direct that an individual man should be God — although what he says is perfectly direct. By reason of the communicator, the communication contains a contradiction, it becomes indirect communication, it puts to thee a choice, whether thou wilt believe Him or not."[109]

As we have seen, the most fundamental characteristic of indirect communication is that it poses a choice to its recipient. Both Kierkegaard's pseudonymous works and the life of Christ, though in different ways, call for a decision. But the decision is brought about only by the resolution of the indi-

[107] *Training in Christianity*, pp. 132-133; S.V., XII, 124-125.
[108] *Ibid.*, p. 133; S.V., XII, 125.   [109] *Ibid.*, p. 134; S.V., XII, 126.

vidual's will.[110] While God reveals himself to man in Christ, man reveals (i.e., defines) himself *to God* in the moment of faith. With respect to God's indirect communication to man through Christ: ". . . an altogether different sort of reception is required — that of faith. And faith itself has a dialectical quality — and the receiver is the one who is revealed [*bliver aabenbar*], whether he will believe or be offended."[111]

Kierkegaard's understanding of the role of the will in faith underscores his conviction that from a Christian perspective, the entire life of the self is a period of decision: "Suppose it [Christianity] accentuates existence so decisively that the individual becomes a sinner, Christianity the paradox, existence the period of decision."[112]

We have seen in previous chapters that Kierkegaard regards decision as constitutive of the self's actuality. What Christianity makes perfectly clear is that one is *eternally* what he becomes through his decisions in time: "Christianity is the frightful earnestness that your eternity is decided in this life."[113] Regardless of the degree to which the self is deter-

---

[110] "What is it to believe? It is to will (what one *ought* and because one *ought*), God-fearingly and unconditionally obediently, to defend oneself against the vain thought of wanting to comprehend and against the vain imagination of being able to comprehend." *Journals and Papers*, no. 1130; *Papirer*, x^1 A 368.

[111] *Training in Christianity*, p. 140; S.V., XII, 130. It is important to emphasize that it is *to God* that one becomes revealed in faith. As we shall see below, faith does not manifest itself to other persons within the sphere of ordinary human intercourse.

[112] *Postscript*, p. 192; S.V., VII, 180.

[113] *Journals and Papers*, no. 547; *Papirer*, xi^1 A 91. Compare: "This is how Christianity presents it. Before you lies an eternity — your fate is decided in this life, by how you use it. You have perhaps 30 years left, perhaps 10, perhaps 5, perhaps one, perhaps only one month, one day: Frightful restlessness." At the time of the writing of this book, two of the projected five volumes of the Hongs' translation of Kierkegaard's *Journals and Papers* have been published. The Hongs have, however, been kind enough to make available to me the entries pertaining to this study that will be included in later volumes. This is one of those texts. It is from Kierkegaard's *Papirer*, xi^1 A 399.

mined by factors over which one has no control, the individual's awareness of existing before God expresses the self's consciousness of complete responsibility for one's own self. Kierkegaard argues that Christianity emphasizes the eternal significance of the self's decisions through its two principal doctrines: sin and the incarnation. By not willing to be its own self (i.e., by sin), the self disrupts its relation to God and loses the possibility of eternal blessedness. But Christianity does not stop here in emphasizing the importance of the self's decisions. Having established that one has lost the possibility of eternal blessedness through decisions in time, Christianity proceeds to reopen this possibility by claiming that God acts in time to forgive man's sins. According to Kierkegaard, the basic tenet of Christianity is expressed in the following lines: "That an eternal blessedness is decided [*afgjøres*] in time through the relationship to something historical [i.e., the God-Man] was the content of my experiment,[114] and what I now call Christianity. I scarcely suppose that anyone will deny that it is the Christian teaching in the New Testament that the eternal blessedness of the individual is decided in time, and is decided through the relationship to Christianity as something historical. . . . To avoid distraction again, I do not wish to bring forward any other Christian principles; they are all contained in this one, and may be consistently derived from it, just as this determination also offers the sharpest contrast with paganism."[115]

Since the possibility of eternal blessedness has been lost through decisions that make one sinful, it must be regained through decisions that make one faithful. The incarnation presents an opportunity for faith, and thus establishes anew

[114] "My experiment" refers to *Philosophical Fragments*. In this work, Kierkegaard conducts what he calls "an experiment in thought." He describes the general characteristics of Christianity as a possibility, but nowhere mentions Christianity by name. In the *Postscript* to the *Fragments*, he makes the explicit identification of Christianity and the content of his thought experiment.

[115] *Postscript*, p. 340; S.V., vii, 319.

the possibility of eternal blessedness. It is, therefore, an historical point of departure for the self's eternal blessedness. We have seen, moreover, that eternal blessedness is equated with salvation and necessarily involves the immortality of the individual self. Unlike religion *A*, Christianity does not believe that the self is inherently immortal, but holds that one's immortality is decided in time by the relationship to something historical — the God in time:

"The problem constantly dealt with here is this: how there can be an historical starting point, etc. In religiousness *A* there is no historical starting point. The individual merely discovers in time that he must assume that he is eternal. The moment in time is therefore *eo ipso* swallowed up by eternity. In time the individual recollects that he is eternal. This contradiction lies exclusively within immanence. It is another thing when the historical is outside and remains outside, and the individual who was not eternal now becomes such, and so does not recollect what he is, but becomes what he was not, becomes, be it observed, something which possesses the dialectic that as soon as it is, it must have been, for this is the dialectic of the eternal. This proposition inaccessible to thought is: that one can become eternal although one was not such."[116]

It will be helpful to specify precisely what is entailed in the individual's faithful response to the incarnation. Faith[117] in the strictest sense of the word is, as we have noted, related to the God-Man. But according to the analysis of the foregoing section, there are two primary dimensions of the God-Man. In the first place, there is the "fact" that the particular historical person of Jesus was at the same time God. In the second place, there is the claim that God's act in Christ makes forgiveness available to the sinful individual, and thereby reopens the possibility of eternal blessedness. These two aspects

[116] *Ibid.*, p. 508; S.V., VII, 500.

[117] I intend no distinction between faith and belief, but use the words interchangeably. The Danish word is the same in both instances: *"Tro."*

of the incarnation are correlative to the two principal characteristics of the eternal that we have noted throughout the essay and to the two aspects of the individual's response to the incarnation.

In the course of our discussion, we have found that from Kierkegaard's various uses of "eternal," two overriding characteristics can be discerned: eternity is consistently associated with unchangeability and with possibility. However, even the significance of these two characteristics changes from stage to stage, and from context to context. At the Christian stage of existence, Kierkegaard frequently uses "eternal" to refer to God. In this connection, the first aspect of eternal — unchangeability — involves the steadfastness of God's will. Regardless of the changes within himself wrought by man, God's love stands fast. This unchangeability involves the first aspect of the incarnation — the fact that Jesus was God. God's steadfast love leads him to humble himself in the form of a particular human being. The second aspect of eternity — possibility — is closely related to the first. God, moved by his unchanging love, acts in the incarnation in such a way that the possibility of the forgiveness of sins is opened for man. This has the effect of reopening the possibility of man's eternal blessedness. The incarnation, therefore, opens again a possibility that man, through his own decisions, had closed. But both the divinity of Jesus and the forgiveness of the individual's sins are paradoxical. The task of the sinful individual is to apprehend both of these in faith. To understand the dynamics of faith from within the stance of faith itself, we must first consider the relationship between the incarnation event and the self's eternal blessedness.

Kierkegaard consistently associates faith with possibility and with God, the ground of possibility: "In as much as for God all things are possible, it may be said that this is what God is, viz. one for whom all things are possible. The worship of the fatalist is, therefore, at its maximum an exclamation, and essentially it is dumbness, dumb submission, he cannot pray. To pray is to breathe [*aande*],[118] and possibility is to the self what oxygen is for breathing. But for possibility alone or for necessity alone to supply the conditions for the breathing of prayer is no more possible than it is for a man to breathe oxygen alone or nitrogen alone. For in order to pray there must be a God, a self, and possibility, or a self and possibility in the pregnant sense; *for God is that all things are possible, and that all things are possible is God*; and only the man whose being has been so shaken that he became spirit [*Aand*] by understanding that all things are possible, only he has had dealings with God. The fact that God's will is the possible makes it possible for me to pray; if God's will is only the necessary, man is essentially as speechless [*umælende*] as the brutes."[119]

Kierkegaard's point in this passage is that from the perspective of the faithful individual, belief in God is the belief in possibility. But the possibility in which the believer believes has the peculiar quality of being an impossible possibility — an absurdity. One believes that Jesus was God and that he (the sinner) is forgiven. We have already seen that as a coincidence of opposites, the God-Man is the Absolute Paradox. To understand how God, the ground of infinite possibility, relates to the self by opening an impossible possibility, it is necessary to recall Kierkegaard's view of the structure of selfhood.

It has become clear that Kierkegaard understands the self in terms of purposeful becoming. The self is an activity in which possibilities are actualized through free decision. In this process, possibility and actuality always condition one another. Kierkegaard does not think that the self is immortal or that it inherently possesses eternal blessedness. Eternal

[118] Note the etymological relationship between "breathe" [*aande*] and "spirit" [*Aand*].

[119] *The Sickness Unto Death*, pp. 173-174; S.V., xi, 153. Italics added. In light of earlier discussions, it is important to recognize the connection between language and possibility that is implicit in this text.

blessedness is a possibility that can be realized by the self's maintenance of a balance among its components. The failure to achieve an equilibrium is sin. According to Kierkegaard, the self inevitably, but not necessarily, becomes sinful. Because of the dialectical relationship between actuality and possibility, the actuality of the self's sinfulness closes the possibility of eternal blessedness and opens the possibility of eternal damnation (i.e., the total obliteration of the self). Left to oneself, the self can expect no other future. Genuine human becoming ceases, and the remainder of the self's life is the further outworking of the actuality of its own sin.

In this situation, there are two alternatives open to the self: one can resign oneself to the loss of one's eternal blessedness; or one can cling to the possibility of one's eternal blessedness in spite of one's recognition of its impossibility. The former option is despair, the latter is faith: "Faith is essentially this — to hold fast to possibility. This is what pleased Christ so much in the sufferer, that after suffering for many, many years, he persistently believed with the same originality and youthfulness that in God help was possible. The demoralizing aspect of suffering is the paralysis of foundering in hopelessness: It is too late now; it is all over, etc."[120]

What is essential to recognize in this context is that the possibility in which the faithful person believes is at odds with his own actuality. As such, it is an impossible possibility or an absurdity. In one place Kierkegaard makes this point quite explicitly and succinctly: "in the Ethics, Book III, where Aristotle develops the distinction between wishing and moral purpose, he says one cannot make the impossible his moral purpose but one can indeed wish it; 'there is such a thing as wishing for the impossible, as for example, for immortality.' "[121] The only way one can believe such an absurdity is to believe that for God, the ground of infinite possibility, possibility is not fully conditioned by actuality. In a very important passage, Kierkegaard argues:

[120] *Journals and Papers*, no. 1126; *Papirer*, IX A 311.
[121] *Ibid.*, no. 115; *Papirer*, X⁵ A 31.

"The decisive thing is, that for God everything is possible. This is eternally true, and true therefore at each instant. In a way, this is commonly recognized, and commonly affirmed; but the decisive affirmation comes first when a man is brought to the utmost extremity [*Yderste*], so that humanly speaking, there is no possibility. Then the question is whether he will believe that for God everything is possible — that is to say, whether he will *believe*. But this is completely the formula for losing one's understanding; to believe is precisely to lose one's understanding in order to win God. . . . Thus salvation is humanly speaking the most impossible thing of all; but for God all things are possible! This is the struggle of faith, which struggles madly (if one would so express it) for possibility. For possibility is the one salvation. When one swoons, people shout for water, Eau-de-Cologne, Hoffman's drops; but when one is about to despair, the cry is, Procure possibility, procure possibility! Possibility is the only salvation; given a possibility, and with that the desperate man breathes once more, he revives again; for without possibility a man cannot, as it were, draw breath. Sometimes the inventiveness of a human imagination suffices to procure possibility, but in the last resort, that is, when the point is to *believe*, the only help is this, that for God all things are possible."[122]

Through the awareness of sin, the self realizes that the possibility of eternal blessedness is lost. By belief in God as the ground of infinite possibility, the possibility of eternal blessedness is regained. Further specification of precisely how this is so is necessary.

The possibility of eternal blessedness is reopened for the self by the belief that God's act in Christ is undertaken for the purpose of forgiving the individual's sins. This belief is the result of the willful acceptance by the self of that which is rationally absurd. Two aspects of this faith have been empha-

---

[122] *The Sickness Unto Death*, pp. 171-172; S.V., XI, 151. I have considered some of these issues in another context. See: "Kierkegaard as a Theologian of Hope," *Union Seminary Quarterly Review*, vol. XXVIII, no. 3, Spring 1973, pp. 225-233.

sized. In the first place, one must believe that the particular man, Jesus, was at the same time God. In the second place, one must believe that the incarnation is undertaken out of God's unchanging love for the purpose of forgiving the sins of individuals. Because both of these claims are contrary to reason, they must be accepted by the willful belief of the self. That which moves the self to believe these absurd claims is its interest in eternal blessedness. Because there is no means of verification, the venture of the will in the movement of faith is as great as can be imagined. Only the interest in eternal blessedness could move one to make such a leap.

We have argued, however, that the belief in Jesus as the God who offers man the forgiveness of sins reopens the *possibility* of man's eternal blessedness. The question naturally arises concerning the manner in which this possibility is actualized. It must be recognized that as long as the self exists, eternal blessedness remains a possibility that can never be fully actualized: "In the life of time, the expectation [*Forventningen*] of eternal blessedness is the highest reward, because an eternal blessedness is the highest *telos*. . . ."[123] The reason for this is that one's eternal blessedness is not a possibility that can be realized by a single decision of the self, but must be the result of one's *total* life. Until the end of the self's temporal existence, the chance remains that the self's efforts will fall short of what is required for the actualization of the possibility of eternal blessedness. For this reason, Kierkegaard argues that there is a close relationship between the eternal and the future:

"Is it not the case that eternity is for an existing individual not eternity, but the future, and that eternity is eternity only for the Eternal who is not in the process of becoming? But where everything is in the process of becoming, and only so much of eternity is present as to be a restraining influence in the passionate decision where *eternity* is related as *futurity* to the individual in the process of becoming, there the abso-

[123] *Postscript*, p. 360; S. V., vii, 349.

lute disjunction belongs. Where I put eternity and *becoming* together, I do not get rest, but coming into being and futurity. It is undoubtedly for this reason that Christianity has announced eternity as the future [*det Tilkommende*], namely, because it addresses itself to existing individuals, and it is for this reason also that it assumes an absolute either-or."[124]

That Kierkegaard sees such a close relationship between the eternal and the future should not be surprising. We have seen that the future is associated with possibility. It now becomes apparent that the self's eternal blessedness remains a possibility as long as the self temporally exists. Since Kierkegaard understands eternal blessedness to entail the self's immortality, if the self were fully to realize its eternal blessedness, it would no longer be a temporally existing self, but would be immortal. As long as temporal existence continues, eternal blessedness remains a possibility.

Because the self's eternal blessedness continues to be a possibility, and hence in the future, during temporal existence one is related to it in *hope*. The following rather lengthy quotation is extremely important for understanding Kierkegaard's view of the self's relationship to eternal blessedness:

"Eternally the eternal is the eternal; in time the eternal is possibility, the future. Therefore we call tomorrow the future, but we also call eternal life the future. Possibility as such is always a duality and the eternal relates itself in possibility equally to this duality . . . when the man to whom the possibility is relevant relates himself equally to the duality of the possibility we say: he *expects*. To expect contains in it the same duality that possibility has, and to expect is to relate oneself to the possible simply and purely as such. Thereupon the relationship divides, inasmuch as the expecting person chooses. To relate oneself expectantly to the possibility of the

[124] *Ibid.*, p. 271, and 272-273; S.V., VII, 262, and 263-264. Compare: "The future is the guise in which eternity will make itself present." George C. Bedell, "Kierkegaard's Conception of Time," *The Journal of the American Academy of Religion*, vol. XXXVII, no. 3, Sept. 1969, p. 268. See also Jean Wahl, *Études Kierkegaardiennes, op.cit.*, p. 327.

good is to *hope*, which therefore cannot be some temporal expectancy but rather an eternal hope. To relate oneself expectantly to the possibility of the evil is to fear. But one who hopes is just as expectant as one who fears. But as soon as the choice is made, possibility is altered, for the possibility of the good is the eternal. It is only in the moment of contact that the duality of possibility is equivocal. Through the decision to choose hope, one thereby chooses infinitely more than is apparent, for it is an eternal decision. Only in pure possibility, consequently for the purely or indifferently expectant, is that possibility of the good or of the evil equivocal. In the differentiation (and the choice is indeed differentiation) the possibility of the good is more than possibility, for it is the eternal."[125]

For Kierkegaard, hope must itself be chosen. Furthermore, the previous quotation points out that when eternity and becoming are put together, the result is not rest, but coming into being. In these difficult texts, Kierkegaard is arguing that since one's eternal blessedness is contingent upon one's decisions, it cannot be fully actualized during the self's life-time. It is always something future. As future, it is the possibility that the self's entire existence seeks to actualize. Through the self's decisions, hope is chosen. Put in other terms, the unrest that results by bringing together the self's eternal blessedness and temporal life is the movement whereby the self seeks to actualize the possibility of its eternal blessedness through its own decisions.

This hope is expressed by the self's belief that Jesus was God, and that the incarnation is a manifestation of God's unchanging love and consistent intention to forgive man's sins. Therefore, the incarnation reopens the possibility of the self's eternal blessedness, and the self's faithful response to the incarnation is the actualization of that possibility. But faith is, according to Kierkegaard, a constant battle. It is not accomplished once-and-for-all, but is the function of the entire life-

---

[125] *Works of Love*, pp. 233-234; S.V., IX, 238. See also pp. 236-237 and 241; S.V., IX, 240-241, and 245.

time of the individual. For Kierkegaard, as for Luther, in faith, the task is *semper a incipere*. In the struggle for faith, there is no gradual and progressive growth in the Christian life. The task of belief is always the same, and is always of equal difficulty. The strife of faith is, most basically, a constant repetition of one's positive appropriation of the incarnation and of its implications for the life of the self.

2. Repetition

From the perspective of the faithful Christian, the Christ event effects a repetition [*en Gjentagelse*]. "Repetition" is one of Kierkegaard's most troublesome categories. In this context, he uses the term to refer to the believer's conviction that as a result of the incarnation, he regains his self: "The dialectic of repetition is easy; for what is repeated has been, otherwise it could not be repeated, but precisely the fact that it has been gives repetition the character of novelty."[126] We have seen that Kierkegaard holds the self to be a system that, while dependent on God, possesses the capacity to actualize possibilities through the freedom of decision. However, with respect to the most important possibility that the self faces — salvation — the freedom to realize possibility has been lost through sin. When this possibility is reopened, the self again has the freedom to constitute itself saved through its own decisions. The individual thereby feels that he has regained himself. One receives again what one nevertheless possesses — one's own self:

"I am again myself. This self that another would not pick up from the road, I possess again. The discord in my nature is resolved, I am again unified. The terrors that found support and nourishment in my pride no longer enter to distract and to separate.

"Is there not then a repetition? Did I not get myself again, precisely in such a way that I must doubly feel its significance? And what is repetition of earthly goods that are of no conse-

[126] *Repetition*, p. 52; S.V., III, 189.

quence to the spirit — what are they in comparison with such a repetition."[127]

Having experienced the despair of losing the possibility of eternal blessedness through sin, the self feels doubly the significance of this possibility. Such a repetition can occur, however, only when one has thoroughly penetrated the actuality of one's sin. By so doing, it appears that a repetition is fully impossible, and yet, just at this point, the repetition takes place: "So then there is such a thing as a repetition. When does it come about? Well, that's not so easy to say in any human language. When did it come about for Job? When all *conceivable* human certitude and probability pronounced it impossible. Little by little he loses everything; therewith hope vanishes gradually in proportion as actuality, far from being mollified, makes heavier and heavier claims upon him."[128]

Kierkegaard argues that repetition involves the "rebirth" of the self.[129] This is a "birth within a birth."[130] By saying that the self is reborn, or that there is a repetition in which the self gets itself back, he means that the possibility of the self's attainment of eternal blessedness that had been closed by the self's own sin is reopened by God's act in the incarnation. To have this possibility reestablished is like getting oneself back, or being reborn. The difficult point to grasp in Kierkegaard's argument is that this rebirth *does not* completely cancel what the self had been prior to the repetition. He does not think that the self's actuality as a sinner is fully obliterated — the self remains a sinner. What God's act in Christ opens is the possibility of the forgiveness of sins.

Because the self's actuality as a sinner remains, the possi-

---

[127] *Ibid.*, pp. 125-126; S.V., III, 253-254.

[128] *Ibid.*, pp. 117-118; S.V., III, 245-246.

[129] *Philosophical Fragments*, p. 23; S.V., III, 187. The Danish word is *Gjenfødelsen*. (Note the etymological similarity of *Gjentagelse*.) Hong translates this word as "New Birth." In the context of Kierkegaard's argument, however, "Rebirth" seems to be a more accurate rendering of the Danish.

[130] *Ibid.*, p. 122; S.V., IV, 260. Compare *The Concept of Dread*, p. 95; S.V., IV, 374.

bility of eternal blessedness is discontinuous with its actuality. This possibility can be regained only through God's action. However, after this action has taken place, the possibility of eternal blessedness is actualized by the self's faith in the God-Man.

Through the awareness of rebirth at the Christian stage of existence there develops a deeper recognition of the self's dependence on God than is present at any other stage. Not only must one realize that God is the Creator, but one must also acknowledge God as the Re-Creator: God recreates the possibility for the self to attain salvation. According to every canon of human justice, the appropriate response of the offended party (i.e., God) would be the withdrawal of his sustaining power. But God, out of steadfast love, offers forgiveness, and with it effects the rebirth of the self. Kierkegaard believes that no greater emphasis of the self's radical dependence upon God is possible.

Throughout the book, we have claimed that the Christian stage of existence is the *telos* of Kierkegaard's dialectic where there is the fullest realization of individual selfhood and the clearest recognition of the significance of the self's life-time. Furthermore, it has been stated that the Christian doctrines that Kierkegaard selects for detailed consideration are intended to illuminate his understanding of human existence. The support for these contentions is implicit in the argument of this chapter, and must now be made explicit. Let us first consider the manner in which Kierkegaard's analysis of Christian doctrines elucidates his conception of the self and of the importance of time for the life of the self.

As we have seen, Kierkegaard understands the self to have a very definite and definable structure. It is, of course, true that each self exists concretely, and is thereby a particular embodiment of the general structure of selfhood. Kierkegaard's works present both more general discussions of the structure of the self, and concrete depictions of particular instances of this structure. From the vast array of details and descriptions, we have seen that, for him, the self is composed of various components that must be interrelated and kept in equilibrium. First, because the self is always concrete, it suffers a certain actuality that precedes any action of the self. Second, this concrete self has possibilities that are not infinite but that are conditioned by its actuality. However, unlike the entire non-human world, the self does not remain determined by its given actuality. This leads to the third aspect of the self: the freedom to actualize possibilities. Although certain of the self's actualities are given, the self can, through the free assertion of its will in decision, further define its actuality. Such self-definition, in turn, conditions one's possibilities. The final dimension of selfhood that needs to be specified to complete Kierkegaard's analysis is the dependence of the self on God as the constituting and sustaining power.

The doctrines of sin and of the incarnation are the central foci of Kierkegaard's interpretation of Christianity. His use of each of these doctrines is directly related to the understanding of the self that has just been summarized. Through the insights expressed in these two tenets of Christianity, the self comes to the most complete self-realization by recognizing the degree to which one's decisions are constitutive of one's individuality, and by grasping the eternal significance of the self's life-time. As we saw in the first part of this chapter, Kierkegaard divides his analysis of sin into two parts: inherited sin and actual sin. By this distinction he attempts to indicate that although one's temporal-spatial setting is of decisive importance for the actuality of the self, it does not relieve one of the responsibility for becoming one's own self. A person cannot deny responsibility for something because of the influences of others, but must accept responsibility even for what he suffers. Kierkegaard stresses this by interpreting inherited sin in terms of dread. Dread is the manner in which one is related to possibilities that might be realized through decision. Insofar as there is an increase in examples of human sinfulness or a proliferation of instances of inauthentic human existence as the human race develops, there is a quantitative increase in dread. Such an increase in dread, however, never leads necessarily to the qualitative leap of the individual into sin. No matter how much one's surroundings conspire to influence the self, the self retains the possibility of acting freely to actualize any of a variety of possibilities. With the recognition that in constituting oneself a sinner the possibility of eternal blessedness is forfeited, there is a profound recognition of the significance of decision for the self and of the importance of the individual's life-time.

Kierkegaard's interpretation of the incarnation functions in a similar way to illuminate his understanding of the self and of time. As we have seen, while sin closes the possibility of eternal blessedness, the incarnation reopens this possibility: "That an eternal blessedness is decided in time through the relationship to something historical was the content of my experiment, and what I now call Christianity. I scarcely suppose that anyone will deny that it is the Christian teaching in the New Testament that the eternal blessedness of the individual is decided in time, and is decided through the relationship to Christianity as something historical. . . ."[131] From the Christian point of view, if the self is to realize eternal blessedness, it must be the result of its life in time: "Christianity is the frightful earnestness that your eternity is decided in this life."[132]

Kierkegaard argues that faith is a function of the individual's exercise of his will in response to God's act in Christ. The very nature of the object of faith — the Absolute Paradox — requires a maximum assertion of the will. Both the God-Man's person and what his life seeks to accomplish (the forgiveness of sins) are paradoxical. There is no rational evidence by which one can demonstrate the divinity of Christ and the forgiveness of sins. This can be held only if the individual *wills* to believe it. In the movement of faith, the self, cognizant of its self-incurred plight of sinfulness and passionately interested in its eternal blessedness, wills to believe the absurd claims of Jesus. The repeated reassertion of this

---

[131] *Postscript*, p. 340; S.V., vii, 330.
[132] *Ibid.*, p. 192; S.V., vii, 180.

faith is the manner in which the possibility of one's eternal blessedness is actualized. According to Kierkegaard: "Existence can never be more sharply accentuated than by means of these determinations."[133]

From this analysis, it becomes apparent that there are two central moments in the Christian understanding of existence: the moment of the incarnation, and the moment of faith. In the moment of the incarnation, there is a coincidence of the temporal and the eternal: God becomes man. Faith is the positive response of the sinful individual to the incarnation event. Through faith, the individual gains eternal blessedness. But we have seen that eternal blessedness entails immortality.[134] Therefore, in the moment of faith, the temporal individual becomes immortal. Here too there is a coincidence of the temporal and of the eternal. In an important passage, Kierkegaard argues: "But the Paradox unites the contradictories, and is the historical made eternal and the Eternal made historical."[135] The incarnation is "the Eternal made historical" — God becomes man. In this act, the possibility of the self's eternal blessedness is reopened. By the repeated faithful response of the self to this event, the self can actualize this possibility. However, because the self's eternal blessedness involves the individual's immortality, in the moment of faith, the "historical [is] made eternal."

Kierkegaard makes explicit the conclusion to which his argument leads him: "But in that case is not Faith as paradoxical as the Paradox? Precisely so; how else could it have the Paradox for its object, and be happy in its relation to the Paradox?"[136] The moments of the incarnation and of faith are both paradoxical, for in both there is a coincidence of the temporal and the eternal. However, this coincidence is, as it were, from opposite directions. In the incarnation God (the

---

[133] *Ibid.*, p. 187; S.V., VII, 175.
[134] The reader is again referred to the important passage in the *Postscript*, p. 508; S.V., VII, 500.
[135] *Philosophical Fragments*, p. 76; S.V., IV, 226.
[136] *Ibid.*, p. 81; S.V., IV, 230.

Eternal), out of his love for man, enters time. In the moment of faith, man, through his faithful response to the moment of the incarnation, becomes immortal.

With the moments of the incarnation and of faith, we have reached the *telos* of Kierkegaard's dialectic of existence. One of our major contentions has been that as one moves through the stages of existence there is an increasing emphasis on time and a further realization of the self. At the Christian stage of existence, time and the self are most radically emphasized. Christianity involves the individual self's response to the moment of the incarnation in the moment of faith. Through this response the individual constitutes himself either sinful or faithful. Here is the strongest emphasis on the significance of time for the self that Kierkegaard can imagine. It is in time, by one's relationship to something historical (i.e., something in time), that one's eternal destiny is decided. Eternal blessedness is not an inherent possession of the self, but can be gained only as a consequence of one's life in time. In the *moment* of the incarnation, God becomes incarnate in the *individual* person of Jesus. In the *moment* of faith, one realizes the possibility of eternal blessedness by constituting himself a faithful *individual*. In this way, Kierkegaard brings together time and the self at the *telos* of the dialectic through the categories that he regards as central to the Christian understanding of human existence: the moment and the individual. Kierkegaard argues that the tenses of time are correlated with the components of the self: the past represents the self's actuality, the future its possibility, and the present its time of decision. In the moment of decision, one takes on a past, or acquires an actuality, which conditions his future, or his possibilities.

By placing such a strong emphasis on the moment and the individual, Christianity makes perfectly clear the eternal consequences of the self's decisions in time. In the moment of faith, one sees that his decisions in time define his eternal being. One is eternally what he becomes through his decisions in his life-time. By comprehending and accepting the implications of the Christian understanding of human existence, the self can attain the equilibrium within itself that eludes one at every other stage of existence. From the aesthetic stage in which there is no clear differentiation between the self and the not-self and in which time as tensed is not clearly defined, we have moved to the most radically individualized self and the most emphatically stressed temporal moments at the Christian stage of existence.

3. Sacred History: The Faithful Individual

Before leaving the analysis of Christianity, we must point out one more aspect of faith. The comments that are developed in this section will be especially important for the criticisms that are made of Kierkegaard's position in the following chapter.

In the course of analyzing Kierkegaard's interpretation of the incarnation, we saw that in order to distinguish Jesus' divinity and humanity, he makes a distinction between sacred and profane history. Ostensibly Jesus was a man like all other men. During his life-time, he undertook different actions with various intentions. One could not, it is true, definitely discern Jesus' intentions from his outer deeds. If Jesus chose to disclose his intentions, one would have to relate to the revelation of his purposes believingly. All of this, however, remains characteristic of Jesus' humanity, and could be said with equal justice of any human being. As such, it represents Jesus' participation in profane history.

But, in addition to being a man, Jesus claimed to be God, and therefore participated in sacred history. The divinity of Jesus was not discernible in his outward actions. As a matter of fact, there was no possible way for Jesus' divinity to manifest itself outwardly. His divinity was more deeply inward than even the intentions of his actions. While one has to relate believingly to the statement of another's intentions, faith in the strictest sense of the word is required if one is to acknowledge the divinity of Christ. Christ's Godhood was, as Kierkegaard repeatedly asserts, his incognito. It was hidden in the inwardness of sacred history with no evident manifestation in the world of profane history in which men live their lives. Interestingly enough, a similar situation obtains in the life of the believer. Again there is a parallel between the moment of faith and the moment of the incarnation. Kierkegaard argues that faith is an inwardness that cannot become outward. Here too the inwardness about which he is speaking is deeper than the inwardness of the intention of one's actions: "Another author (in *Either-Or*) has properly carried the ethical back to the determination of self-revelation; that it is every man's duty to reveal himself. Religiosity on the other hand is the secret inwardness, but not, please note, an immediacy that needs to be brought out into the open, not an unclarified inwardness, but an inwardness whose clarifying determination it is to be hidden."[137]

Kierkegaard consistently argues that there is no outward manifestation of one's faith. Faith "forbids the direct expression, forbids the outward difference by which recognition could be effected, protests against the assumed commensura-

[137] *Postscript*, pp. 446-447, note; S.V., VII, 434-435, note. It must be recognized that in later writings (most notably the Journals and the popular publications of the "Attack on Christendom") Kierkegaard's contention that faith is inward undergoes a change. In these writings, he associates faith more with actual suffering at the hands of other persons. The faithful individual is the "*extraordinarious*" or the "*heterogeneous*" who is singled out to suffer. This view is, however, at odds with the analysis of the self and of faith that is so carefully developed in the pseudonymous works. It seems that the only way this shift can be explained is to view it as the result of the attacks that Kierkegaard suffered at the hands of journalists and of the general society of Copenhagen that grew out of his criticism of the *Corsair*. Kierkegaard never, however, carefully articulates the view of faith in which faith is outwardly discernible. Neither does he seem to be aware of the tension between his later comments on faith and its consequences and the view of faith in the pseudonymous works. Valter Lindström also suggests that the *Corsair* affair might have been decisive in Kierkegaard's shift away from viewing faith as inward. See: "La Théologie de l'imitation de Jesus-Christ chez Søren Kierkegaard," *Revue d'Historie et Philosophie Religieuse*, vol. 35, 1966, pp. 379-392.

bility of the external. . . ."¹³⁸ Kierkegaard goes so far as to use the same term of the believer as he uses of Jesus: "Is it not his [the believer's] *incognito* [*Incognito*] that there is absolutely nothing that marks him off from the others, absolutely nothing that could serve as a hint of his secret inwardness, not even so much as the humoristic?"¹³⁹

In many different contexts, Kierkegaard tries to show the difference between inwardness and outwardness. Often his arguments are directed against the Hegelian contention that there is a commensurability between the inner and the outer. Kierkegaard begins his first major work of the pseudonymous authorship by writing: "Dear Reader: I wonder if you may not sometimes have felt inclined to doubt a little the correctness of the familiar philosophic maxim that the external is the internal, and the internal the external."¹⁴⁰

Perhaps Kierkegaard's most sustained effort to indicate the disparity between the inward and the outward is carried out in the two diaries of the pseudonymous authorship — "The Diary of a Seducer" in *Either-Or*, and "Guilty/Not Guilty?: A Passion Narrative" (or "Quidam's Diary") in *Stages on Life's Way*. Outwardly there is a marked similarity between the conduct of the two persons. Each is involved in discontinuing a love relationship. However, the diary form enables the reader to assume a perspective that makes it clear that Johannes and Quidam represent two very different problematics. Johannes is involved in an elaborate aesthetic intrigue, while Quidam is in the midst of an apparent religious crisis. Nevertheless, the outward conduct of the two remains virtually identical. In faith, the discontinuity between the inward and the outward is most decisively posited. Making direct reference to Hegel, Kierkegaard argues: "In the Hegelian philosophy *das Aussere* (*die Entäusserung*) is higher than *das Inner*. This is frequently illustrated by an example. The child is *das Innere*, the man *das Aussere*. . . . Faith, on

¹³⁸ *Ibid.*, p. 151; S.V., vii, 140.
¹³⁹ *Ibid.*, p. 447, italics added; S.V., vii, 435.
¹⁴⁰ *Either-Or*, i, p. 3, S.V., i, 5.

the contrary, is the paradox that inwardness is higher than outwardness. . . . The paradox of faith is this, that there is an inwardness which is incommensurable for the outward, an inwardness, be it observed, which is not identical with the first, but is a new inwardness."[141]

The life of the believer is, therefore, an analogue to the life of Christ. As Christ's divinity is his incognito and does not issue in an external manifestation, so too faith is the believer's incognito for which there is no clear evidence in the external world. Furthermore, the incognito of Christ and the incognito of the believer are very closely related. It is by constantly appropriating the incognito of Christ (and the consequences of that incognito for the self) that the self assumes the incognito of a believer. The diagram by which the person of Christ was represented (p. 304 above) can now be paralleled by a diagram of the person of the faithful individual.

Faithful Individual:	Life of Faith	Eternal Blessedness	Sacred History
	Life in World	Temporality	Profane History

However, as has been argued, the moment of faith is occasioned by and is a response to the moment of the incarnation. Therefore, if Kierkegaard's final view of the matter is to be accurately represented, the two pivotal moments in the Christian interpretation of existence must be brought together. This can be depicted by a modification of the previous diagram of the incarnation event and its relationship to the ongoing historical process. (See the following page.)

With the examination of Christianity, we are brought to the conclusion of Kierkegaard's dialectic of existence. As we have seen, in Christianity the self reaches the highest degree of individuation and the deepest awareness of the significance of its life-time. For Kierkegaard, the quest of genuine selfhood ends with Christianity. Through a faithful response to the Christ event, an individual is able to establish the equilib-

---

[141] *Fear and Trembling*, p. 79; S.V., III, 118.

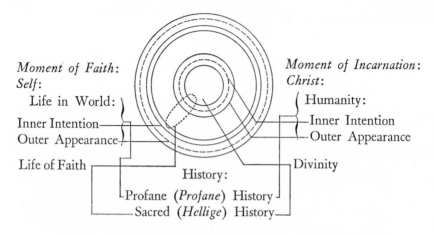

Moment of Faith:
Self:
   Life in World:
Inner Intention
Outer Appearance
Life of Faith

Moment of Incarnation:
Christ:
   Humanity:
Inner Intention
Outer Appearance
Divinity

History:
Profane (*Profane*) History
Sacred (*Hellige*) History

rium among the different components of his self that is absent from every other form of existence. Such an equilibrium is the most authentic form of existence that a person can actualize. However, the reader might have suspected that there are some problems with Kierkegaard's understanding of human fulfillment. Our purpose in the concluding chapter is to consider some of these problems in an effort to clarify both the weakness and the strength of his interpretation of time and of the self.

PART III

A CORRECTIVE

CHAPTER EIGHT

THE SOLITARY SELF

Throughout our study, we have seen that Kierkegaard's purpose in composing the complex pseudonymous authorship is to engage his reader in a Socratic dialogue that will issue in a more profound self-awareness and a more complete realization of selfhood. Kierkegaard's communication is not one-way but constantly calls for the reader's personal contribution. In the preceding chapters we have been concerned to clarify precisely what Kierkegaard is saying through the various personae of his authorship. From Kierkegaard's perspective, that means that we are now ready *to begin* to come to terms with his work. He persistently maintains that the most important aspect of his writings is the change that they occasion in the lives of his readers. Such personality modification is, of course, the task of each individual reader. Kierkegaard can only be the midwife who assists in the birth of the truthful self.

Given the nature and the intention of the pseudonymous writings, we would be delinquent if we only allowed Kierkegaard to speak, and ourselves remained listeners. To be sure, we must listen to his pseudonyms. But it is also our responsibility to speak — to respond to Kierkegaard. We must offer our contribution to his Socratic dialogue. Quite naturally this involves a risk, the risk of misunderstanding and of being misunderstood. But not to respond is a greater risk and a deeper misunderstanding of Kierkegaard's writings.

A. The Self: Inwardness and Isolation

The analysis in the previous chapter has shown that for Kierkegaard the resolution of the dilemma posed by the self's sinfulness arises from the faithful response to God's act in Christ. However, we have also noted that the faith which characterizes the positive response to the God-Man is completely inward. According to Kierkegaard, faith is an inwardness that not only is not, but that cannot be outwardly expressed: "The religious lies in inwardness [*i det Indvortes*]. In this case, the result *cannot* be shown outwardly [*Her kan da Resultatet ikke vise i det Udvortes*]."[1] As we have seen, Kierkegaard holds that there is *no* other manifestation of the self's faith, for faith "forbids the direct expression, forbids the outward difference by which recognition could be effected, protests against the assumed commensurability of the external. . . ."[2] He goes on to argue: "Is it not his [the believer's] incognito that there is absolutely nothing that marks him off from the others, absolutely nothing that could serve as a hint of his secret inwardness, not even so much as the humoristic?"[3] The faith of the believer, as the divinity of Christ, is an incognito that remains hidden in inwardness.

Several important consequences follow from Kierkegaard's conviction that faith is inward. By regarding faith as an inwardness that cannot become outward, he maintains that when the decision of faith is made, there is no ostensible alteration of the self's life: "The less outwardness, the more inwardness. There is something strangely profound and wonderful in the fact that the most passionate decision of human life can transpire in a man without anything external bearing witness to it. . . ."[4]

Kierkegaard's view that there is no *clearly discernible* effect of faith on the life of the believer leads to the problematic conclusion that there is no noticeable difference between the lives of the believer and the non-believer. In a long, but important passage, Kierkegaard argues that:

"The knights of the infinite resignation are easily recognized: their gait is gliding and assured. Those on the other

[1] *Stages on Life's Way*, p. 399; S.V., vi, 411, italics added.
[2] *Postscript*, p. 151; S.V., vii, 140. [3] *Ibid.*, p. 447; S.V., vii, 435.
[4] *Ibid.*, p. 341; S.V., vii, 331.

hand who carry the jewel of faith are likely to be delusive, because their outward appearance bears a striking resemblance to that which both the infinite resignation and faith profoundly despise . . . to Philistinism.

". . . if I knew where there was such a knight of faith, I would make a pilgrimage to him on foot, for this prodigy interests me absolutely. I would not let go of him for an instant, every moment I would watch to see how he managed to make the movements. I would regard myself as secured for life, and would divide my time between looking at him and practising the exercises myself, and thus would spend all my time admiring him. As was said, I have not found any such person, but I can well think him. Here he is. Acquaintance made, I am introduced to him. The moment I set eyes on him I instantly push him from me, I myself leap backwards, I clasp my hands and say half aloud, 'Good Lord, is this the man? Is it really he? Why, he looks like a tax-collector!'[5] However, it is the man after all. I draw closer to him, watching his least movements to see whether there might not be visible a little heterogeneous fractional telegraphic message from the infinite, a glance, a look, a gesture, a note of sadness, a smile, which betrayed the infinite in its heterogeneity with the finite. No! I examine his figure from tip to toe to see if there might not be a cranny through which the infinite was peeping. No! He is solid through and through."[6]

In the final analysis, Kierkegaard's argument "establishes the possibility that no one is religious and the possibility that everyone is religious. . . ."[7] Only God can know!

To put this important point in terms that are more in keeping with this essay: Kierkegaard's view of faith as inward entails the conviction that there is no definite *outward* distinction among selves at different stages of existence. The aes-

[5] Recall Kierkegaard's emphasis on the fact that Jesus appeared to be a man like other men.

[6] *Fear and Trembling*, pp. 49-50; S.V., III, 89-90. See the rest of this passage.

[7] *Postscript*, p. 457; S.V., VII, 445.

thete, the ethicist, and the Christian cannot be distinguished by the lives they live in the world. An apparently aesthetic person might be the most devout Christian, and vice versa. Kierkegaard discusses both of these alternatives in his writings. The first concerns his own life and work as an author. We have seen[8] that during the period in which he was most intensely involved in developing the pseudonymous authorship, Kierkegaard constantly undertook various actions that were intended to make himself appear to his fellow Copenhageners as an aesthetic dandy. The façade of aesthetic existence, however, concealed the actual religious intention of his undertaking. Although he appeared to others to be a perfect representative of aesthetic existence, he regarded himself as preoccupied with religious matters. The religious concerns were not, however, expressed in his outward conduct, but were reserved for his individual inwardness. The apparent aesthetic life was, in fact, an expression of religious interest. Kierkegaard argues that the second alternative was represented by the Christendom of his day. With the development of the state-related church in Denmark, all Danes had come to consider themselves Christian. But such Christianity resulted from the fact of one's birth into a Christian country, and was not a function of the personal appropriation of God's act in Christ. While the Danes of Kierkegaard's time professed to be Christians, the lives they lived were, according to him, fully aesthetic.

The reader who has followed the argument of this essay should notice that a problem emerges at this point in Kierkegaard's analysis. The conception of faith that he so carefully develops in the pseudonymous writings is inconsistent with his well-known attack on Christendom. If faith is inwardness, as Kierkegaard argues, there would seem to be no way for him to know that the lives of the apparent Christians in nineteenth-century Denmark were actually aesthetic. Whether or not one is faithful cannot be discerned by another person, and

---

[8] See above, chapter two.

can be believed only by the faithful individual himself. This would seem to undercut the basis of Kierkegaard's attack on the church.

As the *telos* of Kierkegaard's dialectic of existence, Christianity represents the most complete realization of the individual self. However if faith, which is the primary accomplishment of the Christian stage of existence, remains inward, there is no evident difference between the most complete and the most incomplete actualizations of selfhood. The difference remains inward. At the most basic level, it seems that the chief difference between the fullest and the least realizations of the self lies in the *attitudes* of the two selves. Kierkegaard's argument entails the possibility that two persons can live lives that are, for all intents and purposes, identical, but that represent completely different stages of existence because of the different attitudes the selves assume toward their lives. As we have seen, this is the point of the carefully contrived outward similarities between the lives of the individuals represented in Kierkegaard's two great diaries — Johannes of "Diary of a Seducer" and Quidam of "Guilty/Not Guilty?" Although the actions of the two persons involved in severing a love relationship are quite similar, the different attitude of each of the persons toward his actions marks one as an aesthetic and the other as a religious person.

Here a very interesting consequence emerges from Kierkegaard's argument. In analyzing his notion of religious truth[9] we saw that he criticizes Hegel for identifying thought and being. For the existing individual, to think and to be are clearly distinguished. Between thought and being lies the assertion of the will in decision. But if one follows the course of the argument presented in the pseudonymous authorship, it seems that Kierkegaard comes perilously close to making an identification of thought and being that is rather similar to the point of view that he so ardently opposes. If, as we have seen, it is one's *inward attitude* toward one's actions that is

[9] See above, chapter two.

347

finally determinative of the self's form of existence, then it would appear that the self's being is virtually identified with its thought. The way in which one thinks about one's actions, and not the actions themselves, seems to be decisive for the self.

Kierkegaard's identification of faith with inwardness is the consistent conclusion of a point of view that establishes a sharp difference between inner intention and outer action. He understands decisions to be constitutive of the self. But he identifies the self's decisions with the inward resolution of the will. In Christian faith, one comes to the clearest understanding of the significance of decision for the life of the self. Furthermore, due to the nature of the object of faith, the God-Man, faith itself is the most radical instance of decision that one can encounter. The claim of Jesus to be God contradicts every canon of rational judgment. If one accepts this assertion, it must be the function of the sheer exercise of the will to believe what is fully absurd. This decision transpires at the deepest level of the self's inwardness; no outward manifestation of such a decision is possible. While intentions that inform all ethical conduct lie within the self's subjectivity and cannot, as it were, be "read off" the action itself, the inwardness of the decision to believe that Jesus is at the same time God, acting to forgive the individual's sins, lies even more deeply hidden within the self's inwardness.

It would, of course, be foolish to deny the distinction that Kierkegaard draws between one's intention and the outcome of one's action. It does seem, however, that major problems arise when this distinction is drawn too sharply. The result of Kierkegaard's argument is the establishment of two fully discrete identities of the individual self — an inward one and an outward one. Furthermore, these two identities bear no necessary relationship to one another. One's inner and outer identities can be either consistent or at odds with each other.

Many of the problems involved in Kierkegaard's position on the inwardness of faith might be overcome by a point of view that both recognizes the validity of the distinction between inner intention and outer action, and yet is able to maintain a connection between the two. A more satisfactory resolution of this issue can be achieved by reconsidering the term "action." Three major elements are included in all purposeful activity:

1. *Imaginative representation* of a purpose to be enacted or an ideal to be pursued.

2. *Desire* to accomplish the purpose or to achieve the ideal.

3. *Resolution of the will.*

a) *Decision* or self-conscious resolution to fulfill one's purpose or to seek one's ideal.

b) *Efficacious effort* or actual labor to embody in actuality the desired possibility for which one has decided.

These components must be present in any form of intentional activity, no matter how simple or how complex. We must notice how these factors are related. The second element (desire) mediates the first (imaginative representation) and the third (resolution of the will). For any purposeful action to take place, one must first imaginatively represent to himself the purpose to be sought, or the ideal to be achieved. Clearly, however, such an imaginative representation is only the initial step in the process; the purpose or the ideal remains an unrealized possibility. For the imagined possibility to be translated into actuality, a resolution of the will is required. Up to this point, Kierkegaard would agree with us. But he seems to identify the resolution of the will with the self's inward decision. Against this point of view, it must be argued that the exercise of the will has two dimensions that might be distinguished as subjective and objective. The subjective aspect of the resolution of the will is the self's decision to work for a particular purpose. The objective element is the persistent and laborious effort to embody the purpose or the ideal in the world of actuality. It is evident that efficacious effort presupposes decision. But it must also be stressed that decision requires efficacious effort before we have a genuine assertion of the will. Inner decision and outer efficacious effort together constitute the resolution of the will. The imaginative representation of the purpose and the resolution of the will to strive to achieve that purpose are related to each other through a third element: desire. Desire is the spring of action that moves the will to decide upon and to work to accomplish an imagined ideal. Through desire we single out those purposes that we strive to achieve.

If all of these factors are included in the understanding of action, the sharp separation that Kierkegaard makes between inward intention and outward action would be overcome. Intention and striving to achieve one's purpose are dialectically related. The intention appropriated in one's decision consistently informs actions. But in addition to this, one's actions constantly act back on, and thereby condition, the actor's intentions.

Another important consequence of Kierkegaard's argument that faith is inward must be made explicit. Since he regards Christianity as the most complete realization of individual selfhood, and because he understands Christian faith to be an inwardness that cannot become outward, he argues that the fullest realization of selfhood is to be found in isolated individuality rather than in community with other selves. Since he sees faith as lying within the inwardness of the self, Kierkegaard must contend that at the deepest level, the level of one's faith, persons cannot communicate with one another. Each individual is locked up within the inwardness of his own subjectivity. Selves are discrete and isolated, and where the most profound issue of the self's life is concerned, there is no possibility of relating to other selves. This is the point of his repeated emphasis on silence. Although this is a theme that runs through much of his writing and all of his personal life, it is most explicitly discussed in *Fear and Trembling*.

Here Kierkegaard stresses that in the trial of faith Abraham could communicate with no one. It is significant that the two persons who are most frequently discussed in connection with Abraham's silence are Sarah, his wife, and Isaac, his son: "It was early in the morning, Abraham arose betimes, he had the asses saddled, left his tent, and Isaac with him, but Sarah looked out of the window after them until they had passed down the valley and she could see them no more. They rode in silence for three days. On the morning of the fourth day, Abraham said never a word, but he lifted his eyes and saw Mount Moriah afar off."[10] Sarah and Isaac were the persons closest to Abraham. Yet even in relation to them, the inwardness of faith lay too deep to be communicated: "Silence is the snare of the demon, and the more one keeps silent, the more terrifying the demon becomes; but silence is also the mutual understanding between Deity and the individual."[11]

Because faith can be achieved only in a private relation to a transcendent God that isolates one from all other persons, Kierkegaard maintains that any form of existence in which one remains in community with other selves is less authentic than the existence of the individual in isolation from others: "The Christian combat is always waged by the individual; for this precisely is spirit, that everyone is an individual before God, that 'fellowship' [*Fælledsskab*] is a lower category than 'the single individual' [*den Enkelte*], which everyone can and should be."[12] From the standpoint of Christian existence, "the single individual" is more highly esteemed than "fellowship" or community because it is understood that: ". . . intercourse with God is, in the deepest sense, absolutely non-social [*ubetinget uselskabelig*]."[13]

Two significant points follow from Kierkegaard's contention that the self's relationship to God is "absolutely non-social." In the first place, one must seek isolation from others: "The spiritual man differs from us men in being able to endure isolation, his rank as a spiritual man is proportionate to his strength for enduring isolation, whereas we men are constantly in need of 'the others,' the crowd; we die, or despair if we are not reassured by being in the crowd, or of the same opinion as the crowd, etc. But the Christianity of the New

[10] *Fear and Trembling*, p. 27; S.V., iii, 61.
[11] *Ibid.*, p. 97; S.V., iii, 135.
[12] *Training in Christianity*, p. 218; S.V., xii, 204.
[13] *Christian Discourses*, p. 334; S.V., x, 25.

Testament is precisely reckoned upon and related to this isolation of the spiritual man. Christianity in the New Testament consists in loving God, in hatred to man, in hatred to oneself, and thereby of other men, hating father, mother, one's own child, wife, etc., the strongest expression for the most agonizing isolation."[14]

The second point is a necessary correlate of the first, and is implied in the foregoing quotation. Community with other selves is to be avoided. Rather than being the fulfillment of selfhood, life in social community with other selves is a concession to the human weakness of not being able to endure the isolated individuality that is characteristic of genuine selfhood: "Right at this point the real meaning of religious sociality is to be found — that is, when the ideality of the God-relationship has become too strong for an individual . . . , he must now have another person to discuss it with. From this we see that sociality is not the highest, but is really a concession to human weakness. Here, also, is the significance of the idea that God related himself to the whole race. The idea of the race, of sociality, is then a middle term between God and the single individual. . . . There is alleviation . . . in making use of sociality. It is not good for man to be alone, it is said, and therefore woman was given to him for community. But it is true that being alone, literally alone with God, is almost unendurable for a man, is too frightfully strenuous — there-

[14] *Attack Upon Christendom*, p. 163; S.V., xiv, 196. The last point made by Kierkegaard in this passage has far-reaching implications that will become more evident in what follows. For the moment, it is sufficient to compare these texts: "Thus it was the Apostle forsook all, broke with everything that binds a man to the earth. Out of love for Christ, or out of hatred for the world, he forsook all things, his position in life, livelihood, family, friends, the human language, love to father, and mother, love for the fatherland, the faith of the fathers, he forsook the God he had hitherto worshiped." *Christian Discourses*, p. 193; S.V., x, 186. And: "Then there is the question whether the principle of hating oneself, which belongs to Christianity, is not so asocial that it cannot constitute community." *Journals and Papers*, no. 2057; *Papirer*, xi[1] A 190.

fore man needs community. God and man are separated by an infinite qualitative difference; when the relationship becomes too frightfully strenuous, the category of community must come between as a middle term. . . ."[15]

Kierkegaard brings his dialectic to rest with the isolated individual standing before a God to whom the self is absolutely responsible. For Kierkegaard, this is the strongest conceivable emphasis on the significance of an individual's decisions and on the importance of the self's life-time. Kierkegaard's consistent polemic against the "crowd" or the "herd" is directed against the loss of the radical individuality that he sees to be so closely related to one's recognition of one's responsibility for the self that one becomes through one's decisions. Others (i.e., the crowd) are always those behind whom one hides in the flight from responsibility.

A major problem with Kierkegaard's argument at this point is his refusal to acknowledge the possibility of a form of human community that enhances and does not abolish responsible individuality. Certainly he is correct in criticizing the mode of human association in which individuals are differentiated neither from one another nor from their surroundings. To exist primarily as a reflex of the influences of others rather than as a self-conscious center of responsible decision is to fail to achieve the full potentiality of selfhood. But Kierkegaard errs in the opposite direction. While the mindless identification of the self with others cannot be accepted as the most complete realization of the self, neither can a form of existence that puts primary emphasis on the self's life of iso-

[15] *Journals and Papers*, no. 1377; *Papirer*, IX A 315. Compare: "This is how we save religion in our day. We acknowledge with humor the world of actuality. . . , and thus we keep it (religion) healthy. We do not enter the monastery, but become fools in the world. One is reminded of Christ's words: 'When you fast. . . , anoint your head and wash your face so that your fasting may not be seen by men.' With these words, all this chittering and chattering about community and living for the idea of community is abolished. The first thing the religious man does is to lock his door and talk in secret." *Journals and Papers*, no. 2111; *Papirer*, IV A 86.

lated individuality to the exclusion of participation in genuine human community be accepted as the fulfillment of the self.

A possible way out of Kierkegaard's either-or of isolated individuality versus undifferentiated identification with the social group is opened by recognizing that human community is, in an important sense, a unique form of existence. Unlike non-human forms of interrelationship, human community cannot arise from the *mechanical* relationship of thoughtless entities. This is precisely the fault of the type of association to which Kierkegaard refers as the crowd. Here selves exist in a manner analogous to the non-human world. What is peculiar about human community is that it is comprised of self-conscious individuals who freely act within the bounds of the social whole of which they are a part. Genuine human community can be constituted only by individuals who are self-conscious about their idiosyncratic nature and about their own freedom to act within the social whole to which they are integrally related. Therefore if there is to be genuine human community, there must be a complete recognition by the self of its own individuality. For this reason, there is great value in Kierkegaard's analysis of the development of the self. He charts the process by which a self comes to an awareness and an actualization of its own individuality. The problem with his argument is that it stops at this point. After considering the differentiation of the self from its surroundings, and thereby arriving at a sophisticated comprehension of the nature of the self's individuality, he does not proceed to reintegrate the self into the social and natural whole from which it has been distinguished. He seems to make the error of identifying all forms of social interrelationship with a non-human form of mechanical association. What he has not done is to develop the manner in which selves, by participation in social communities, can further realize the individuality of which they have become aware.

The movement from the undifferentiated identity of the self and the not-self to the fully individuated self of Christian existence is necessary for the maturation of the self. However, it seems problematic to hold that the most complete realization of selfhood involves the self standing in isolation from all other selves before a God who transcends the world of time and space. Against Kierkegaard's position, it might be argued that the fullest actualization of selfhood is the individual self in community with other mature selves who are fully conscious of their individuality. After the movement of differentiation or of individuation has taken place, a second movement of reintegration must be accomplished. Surely the mature self must be definitely distinguished from the social and natural matrix of which it is a part. But it must also be reintegrated into this larger whole. The point that should be stressed in this context is that the reintegration of the self into the larger social-natural whole does not necessarily involve the loss of individuality. Individuality is maintained and in fact enhanced by interaction with other selves that have likewise undergone the long and laborious process of individuation. Human community consists of the interrelation of mature individuals all of whom are self-conscious of their own peculiarity and all of whom are intent on not violating the individuality of the other members of their social community. In this manner, one's participation in a social whole does not entail the loss of responsible individuality, but is a more complete realization of that individuality. The uniqueness of each individual is defined by his particular position within the social whole of which he is a member. According to this interpretation, the self is most fully realized by actively interrelating with other mature individuals within social communities.

When these implications of Kierkegaard's argument are recognized, it becomes evident that his understanding of faith as inwardness leads to a veneration of the individual's isolation from other selves. Furthermore, because the inwardness of faith cannot be outwardly expressed, faith seems to have virtually no relationship to one's life in the world. At the Christian stage of existence, the self recognizes its sinfulness and seeks forgiveness by the faithful response to God's act in Christ. But such faith is hidden from the world in one's inner subjectivity and has primary significance not for one's life in the world, but for eternal blessedness, or for life after death. The self's attention is turned toward individual salvation and away from other persons and from involvement with "ordinary" historical development. At this point we begin to see more clearly the questionable ethical implications of Kierkegaard's interpretation of Christian faith and of his analysis of the most complete realization of selfhood. However, here, as in so many other places, the problem of the self is very closely related to the problem of time. Therefore before the ethical implications of Kierkegaard's argument can be fully grasped, some critical comments concerning his understanding of the significance of time must be developed.

B. Time: The Moment and History

We have seen that Kierkegaard maintains that from a Christian perspective, there is a perception of the eternal significance of one's life-time. Through the recognition of sin and the awareness of God's act in the incarnation, one realizes both that he stands before a God to whom he is absolutely responsible, and that his eternal destiny is the result of the decisions that he makes during the time of his own existence. If one does not actualize the possibility of eternal blessedness during his own life-time, he will never acquire the salvation that is his most passionate interest. By this argument, Kierkegaard endeavors to give the strongest possible emphasis to the significance of time for the life of the self. It is necessary, however, to examine somewhat more closely the precise nature of the importance that Kierkegaard attributes to time.

In the analytical part of the essay, we have seen that when Kierkegaard argues that at the Christian stage of existence time is radically accentuated, he means that two particular moments of time are singled out and emphasized. When he speaks of time in connection with the Christian form of existence, he does not mean the entire temporal process, but refers to the two moments of the incarnation and of faith. These are the temporal moments *par excellence*, and all other moments in the temporal process are of little or no concern to the Christian. Moreover, we have noted these moments to be correlative: the moment of the incarnation is God's act, and as such is the occasion of belief for the self to whom it is addressed; the moment of faith is the believing response of the self to Jesus' claim to be God and to the assertion that this act of God has been undertaken out of steadfast love for the purpose of forgiving the individual's sins. In this way, the moment of the incarnation and the moment of faith are brought into the closest proximity. The situation in which these two central moments confront one another Kierkegaard calls "contemporaneity." The following quotation indicates some of the implications of the notion of contemporaneity: "The Christian fact [i.e., the incarnation] has no history, for it is the paradox that God once came into existence in time. This is the offense, but also it is the point of departure; and whether this was eighteen hundred years ago or yesterday, one can just as well be contemporary with it. Like the polar star, this paradox never changes its position and therefore has no history, so this paradox stands immovable and unchanged; and though Christianity were to last for another ten thousand years, one would get no farther from this position than the contemporaries were. The distance is not to be measured by the quantitative scale of time and space, for it is qualitatively decisive by the fact that it is a paradox."[16]

By arguing that the Christian is not primarily interested in the historical process as a whole, but centers his attention on the two moments of the incarnation and of faith, Kierkegaard seems to lose any notion of the developmental nature of time. To put this important point in other terms, his view of time as presented at the Christian stage of existence has no sense of history as a *process*.[17] In a revealing remark, Kierkegaard

---

[16] *On Authority and Revelation*, pp. 60-61.

[17] The conception of time that characterizes the ethical stage is more

writes: "Out with history. In with the situation of contemporaneity."[18] The ideal of the believer is to disregard the historical development to which Jesus' life gave rise and to establish
a direct relationship with the fact that this particular man
claimed to be God. The intervening course of historical development only impedes the believer's direct relation to the
moment of the incarnation.

Kierkegaard does not, however, present an argument in
which he establishes the possibility of "overleaping" the 1800
years of Christian history. He simply assumes that such contemporaneity is possible. The root of this assumption seems
to be his failure to appreciate the processive nature of historical development. At the Christian stage, he is concerned exclusively with two moments that are extracted from the rest
of the historical process. What Kierkegaard does not sufficiently recognize is that the moment of the incarnation is
always filtered to the believer through the intervening events
of the historical process. Even if, as he holds, the awareness
of Jesus' claim to be God were sufficient to establish the possibility of faith, the historical development that has tran-
spired between that event and the response of the believer
remains determinative for the believer. For example, his own
understanding of God's act in Christ draws upon the history
of theological and philosophical reflection that grew out of
Jesus' life.

Kierkegaard does not come to an immediate relation with
the incarnation event in the moment of faith. He is related to
that event through 1800 years of Christian history. It is a fact
of the historical nature of man's existence, and of the processive quality of that history in which man is totally immersed,
that it is impossible to disregard the course of history since
the time of Christ. Kierkegaard's concentration on the mo-

in keeping with an understanding of history as a process, but Kierkegaard does not develop the implications of the ethical understanding of
time for history as a whole.

[18] *Journals and Papers*, no. 69; *Papirer*, IX A 76.

ments of the incarnation and of faith to the virtual exclusion of other moments in the historical process leads him to an inadequate understanding of historical development by causing him to overlook the processive quality of history.

This oversight is not accidental. Its basis is the nature of the two moments that Kierkegaard considers to be of central importance for Christian existence. In the previous chapter we established that the two pivotal moments of Christian experience are formally parallel. In both moments there is a coincidence of the temporal and the eternal. In the moment of the incarnation, the Eternal, God, becomes temporal (i.e., becomes man) in order to offer the forgiveness of sins. In the moment of faith, the temporal, man, becomes eternal (i.e., gains eternal blessedness, which necessarily entails immortality) by believing the claim of Jesus to be God and by accepting the forgiveness of sins thereby made available. This characteristic of these two moments means that when one speaks of them as temporal or as historical,[19] a certain qualification is necessary. These moments *are not* temporal in the ordinary sense of the word. They are events in "sacred time" or in "sacred history," and must be clearly distinguished from the "ordinary" or "profane" historical process. We have seen that Kierkegaard argues: ". . . With the everlasting contemplation of world-history and the history of the human race, with the everlasting talk about universal history and its significance, etc., people have become all too nimble in appropriating Christianity without more ado as a part of world-history, they have come to regard it as a matter of course that Christianity is a stage in the development of the human race. They have quite forgotten that Christ's life on earth (and this is what Christianity is — a different thing entirely from the history of Christians, or of the lives of Christians, their biographies, their fate, not to speak of the history of heretics and of science) is sacred [*hellige*] history, which must not be con-

---

[19] In the comments that follow, I intend no distinction between "temporal" and "historical."

founded with the history of the human race or of the world."[20]

Sacred history is inward and is at the farthest remove from the outwardness of historical development as it is usually understood. For this reason, sacred history has no clear and definable relationship to the ongoing historical process.

Kierkegaard's distinction between sacred and profane history has extremely important implications for one's theological-ethical estimate of his argument. With this distinction in mind, it is necessary to reconsider his contention that the Christian stage of existence represents the most profound recognition of the importance of time for the life of the self. When Kierkegaard argues that his dialectic discloses the eternal significance of the self's temporal life (i.e., life-time), he means that in the time of the self's own existence one determines his eternal destiny through personal decisions. As we have seen in many different contexts, he holds that in time one either attains or fails to attain eternal blessedness through the response to God's temporal act in Christ. In the passage cited above, Kierkegaard continues: "They [the members of Christendom] have entirely forgotten that Christianity is essentially related to eternity, that life here on earth . . . is the time of probation [*Prøvens Tid*] for every individual in particular among the countless millions who have lived or shall live."[21] This remark makes explicit what remains implicit in many of Kierkegaard's arguments. Time, the self's life in time, is most essentially a time of trial or of probation. The eternal significance of life in time results from the fact that during one's life-time, the individual's eternal destiny is decided. This eternal destiny is a consequence of the self's response to the God in time. But, as we have seen, the God in time is not an historical event in the usual sense of the term, but is an event in sacred history. The result of Kierkegaard's argument is that the significance of the self's life-time is the way in which it prepares one for life *beyond* time. Further-

[20] *Training in Christianity*, p. 216; S.V., xii, 203.
[21] *Ibid.*, p. 217; S.V., xii, 203.

more, the nature of the two moments that he sees as determinative of the individual's eternal blessedness directs the self's interest away from the ongoing historical process.

At the most basic level, the question arises of whether it makes any sense to talk of sacred time and sacred history as time and history. Kierkegaard repeatedly argues that the distinguishing feature of such time or history is that it is opposed to time or history as usually understood. However, he also consistently characterizes eternity as antithetical to temporality. This would seem to lead to an identification of sacred history or sacred time with eternity. But if this is the case, then to call sacred history "history" or sacred time "time" is most misleading, if not contradictory. By trying to maintain that both sacred and profane history are, in some sense, temporal or historical, Kierkegaard seems to involve himself in a very confusing contradiction. The dilemma is not resolved by holding that when considering these two moments of Christian existence, we are involved with paradoxes that cannot, by their very nature, be comprehended by human reason. The problem is one of making sense of the terms and concepts that Kierkegaard uses. With respect to sacred history, this task is virtually impossible.

We can, however, understand the implications of Kierkegaard's argument about sacred history for history understood as a process in which selves are interrelated by their common involvement in various projects. In other words, we can now see clearly the implications of his argument for one's life in the world. If one carefully analyzes his view of the self and of time as developed at the final stage of existence, he is driven to the conclusion that despite Kierkegaard's repeated assertions that his dialectic accentuates the *temporality* of selfhood, he maintains a negative attitude toward history and the temporal life of the self. His interest in the self's life-time does not involve the intrinsic valuation of the individual's life in the world. He is concerned with the self's temporal development *only insofar as it directs one to life beyond the world.* Kierkegaard certainly contends that one's salvation is the function of the decisions made during a person's life-time. To this extent, he sees one's temporal life as important. But the temporal self who seeks to attain eternal blessedness focuses on only one moment of the historical process — the incarnation. Moreover, the most important dimension of this moment, Christ's divinity, is radically distinguished from events in the "ordinary" historical process. The Christian believer has minimal concern for the total course of history, and for his diverse and complex life in the world. In addition to this, although the possibility of one's salvation is decided in time, by the relation to something in time, the fulfillment of the individual's salvation involves the extrication of the self from the temporal process. To be saved is to be removed from the vicissitudes of historical existence and to find peace by being at one with the Eternal God. Salvation does not entail the redemption of the historical process itself, but enables one to be freed from the strictures that this process places upon the self.

Kierkegaard holds that from a Christian viewpoint, one's fundamental interest cannot be the historical process, for the self's final destiny lies beyond history.[22] For Kierkegaard, salvation does not involve the reformation of the structures of the historical-natural process, but removes the self from historical travail to a realm that lies beyond the world of space and time. Life in the world is not valued for its own sake, but is most basically a time of probation during which the individual seeks eternal blessedness. Daniel Day Williams clearly perceives the heart of the issue when he writes: "So far at least I understand Kierkegaard and his followers [i.e., neo-orthodox theologians]. This standpoint represents the sharp-

[22] For more recent discussions that parallel Kierkegaard's position on this important issue, see: Karl Barth, *Church Dogmatics* (Edinburgh: T. and T. Clark), vol. II, part II, esp. "The Time of Revelation," pp. 45ff.; Rudolf Bultmann, *History and Eschatology, op.cit.*, esp. chapter x, "Christian Faith and History," pp. 138ff.; and Nicholas Berdyaev, *The Destiny of Man* (New York: Harper Torchbooks, 1960), pp. 260ff. and 296ff.

est possible challenge to liberal theology with its affirmation that the natural processes are the locus of God's redemptive work; and that the meaning of life is organically involved in the emergence of orders of value in history."[23]

Here a profound irony emerges. Much of Kierkegaard's dialectic is formulated in dependence on, and by criticism of, Hegel. One of the chief points in his persistent polemic against Hegel is that Hegel has forgotten the radical temporality of the existing self.[24] In his world-historical speculation, Hegel has thought himself out of existence and has aspired to assume a point of view that only God himself could approach.[25] Put in its briefest form, Kierkegaard holds that Hegel has not comprehended the temporal-historical situattion of the existing self. In opposition to this tendency in Hegel and his followers, Kierkegaard applies much of Hegel's own dialectic to the individual self. By so doing he attempts to stress as strongly as possible the significance of time for the life of the self. This point is reached only with the moments of faith and of the incarnation. But it is just at this juncture that one's concern with and involvement in the historical process becomes unimportant. History is of interest only to the extent that it points beyond itself to eternity. Time is of concern only insofar as it enables the self to gain eternal blessedness.

In the preceding section of this chapter, we saw that Kierkegaard interprets faith as an inwardness that is not outwardly manifest. In view of the implications of his conception of time at the Christian stage of existence, we can now understand more completely the consequences of his notion of faith. The moments of the incarnation and of faith are essentially concerned with sacred history. This "history" or "time"

[23] *God's Grace and Man's Hope* (New York, 1949), p. 121.

[24] This argument does, of course, seriously misrepresent Hegel's position.

[25] It is interesting to recognize that there are places where Kierkegaard indicates that although no existing self can be an Hegelian, God could be!

is inward and is removed from the ordinary historical process in which men conduct their lives. Only by holding fast to the absurd claims of Jesus, through the belief in Jesus' divine incognito, does the individual assume the incognito of a believer. The incognito of belief is the condition of actualizing the possibility of eternal blessedness. Both the divinity of Christ and the faith of the self are at levels of inwardness that preclude outward expression. As a result of the conviction that faith is inward, Kierkegaard argues that faith does not result in a more complete participation in the historical process, but prepares the self for a salvation that lies decisively beyond that process. Faith, therefore, does not lead to the effort to change the structures of the temporal-historical process that distort human life and that make the realization of genuine selfhood impossible: "Christianity's divine meaning is to say in confidence to every man, 'do not busy yourself with changing the shape of the world or your condition in life, as if you . . . , instead of being a scrub-woman, perhaps could be called *Madam*. No, make Christianity your own, and it will show you a point outside of the world by the help of which you shall move heaven and earth so quietly, so easily, that no one notices it.' "[26]

The result of Kierkegaard's argument that we have been following throughout its various stages is a very problematic distinction between Christian faith and ethical action. In Christian faith, the self is inwardly related to the inner divinity of Christ. Ethical conduct involves the self's active life in the "ordinary" historical process. It is certainly true that he would want to argue that the Christian stage of existence does not negate the ethical stage, but takes it up into itself, reducing the ethical stage to a position of relativity. However, in his effort to distinguish Christian faith from ethics, Kierkegaard concentrates on the way in which religious obligation can lead to the "suspension" of ethical duty. A fundamental problem with his argument is that he does not move beyond the negative relationship between faith and ethical obligation

[26] *Works of Love*, pp. 137-138; S.V., IX, 131-132.

to an articulation of the positive way in which Christian faith can inform and encourage ethical activity. In the final analysis, the view of faith that Kierkegaard develops does not give one an adequate basis upon which to establish a satisfactory ethical standard for life in the world. Faith lies in inwardness; ethics concerns outward change. Kierkegaard writes:

"In proportion to the capacities granted to me and also with various self-sacrifices I have diligently and honestly worked for the inward deepening of Christianity in myself and in others insofar as they are willing to be influenced. But simply because from the beginning I have understood Christianity to be inwardness and my task to be the inward deepening of Christianity, I have overscrupulously seen to it that not a passage, not a sentence, not a line, not a word, not a letter, has slipped in about a proposal for external change or suggesting a belief that the problem is lodged in externalities, that external change is what is needed, that external change is what will help us.

"There is nothing about which I have greater misgivings than all that even slightly tastes of this disastrous confusion of politics and Christianity...."[27]

There appears to be no germane connection between Kierkegaard's notion of Christian faith and ethical obligation. The inwardness of faith and the correlative disinterest in "ordinary" history mean that changing the injustices of the historical process is not a direct concern of faith: "To bring about likeness among men, to apportion the conditions of temporal existence equally, if possible, to all men, this is a task that preeminently occupies the secular world. Yet even what one may call well-intended secular striving along these lines never comes to an understanding with Christianity."[28]

But the consequences of Kierkegaard's dialectic are even more problematic than this conclusion suggests. Not only does his view of the most complete realization of selfhood at

[27] "An Open Letter," *Armed Neutrality*, p. 49. See also pp. 50-55, and *The Point of View*, pp. 107-108; XIII, 589-590.
[28] *Works of Love*, p. 82; S.V., IX, 81.

the Christian stage of existence give one no adequate basis upon which to construct an ethic for life in the world; it actually serves to discourage any effort to accomplish significant social change: "Rightly used, this category, 'the single individual,' will never be damaging to the existing order. Used in a time of peace its purpose will be to awaken inwardness into heightened life in the established order without making any external change; and in agitated times its purpose will be to support the established order more directly by leading the single individual to be indifferent to external change and thus to support the established order. Earthly reward, power, honor, and the like can never be associated with the proper application of this category, because what is rewarded in the world is, of course, only external changes and working for external changes. Inwardness does not interest this world."[29]

Since faith involves the inwardness of the self, there is no need to be concerned about one's outward life in the world. If the individual's inner relation to God is established, one's condition in the world does not matter. Here is one of the most devastating forms of the tranquilizing effect that religion can have. Rather than directing one to engage his energies to change the structures of the historical process so that greater justice can be achieved, such a form of religiosity holds that this historical process involves merely one's outward self and does not concern the all-important depths of an individual's inwardness. ". . . the religious man ought not so much to be concerned about external things, but rather seek the highest good, peace of mind, his soul's salvation: this always pleases God."[30]

It is important to recognize in the context of the present criticism of Kierkegaard that his generally negative evaluation of the self's obligation to the historical process is very

[29] *Papirer*, IX B 66. This is translated by Hong in *Armed Neutrality*, p. 80. Compare Thomte, *Kierkegaard's Philosophy of Religion, op.cit.*, p. 85 and Louis Mackey, "The Loss of the World in Kierkegaard's Ethics," *op.cit.*, p. 605.

[30] *Postscript*, p. 453; S.V., VII, 441.

closely related to his understanding of the extreme transcendence of God. We have seen that for Kierkegaard, God is infinitely and qualitatively different from the world. God's deepest involvement with the world is, of course, the incarnation. Other than this moment, however, Kierkegaard does not offer detailed consideration of the relationship of God to the temporal process. His concern is not to examine the manner in which God is involved in the historical process as a whole. Because God is totally different from the world, and is related to the world primarily in the person of the God-Man, one becomes related to God not through general involvement with the world historical process, but by a concentration on the moment of the incarnation to the exclusion of other persons and events. If one's engagement in the historical process is to have more fundamental significance for the self's religious life, the God to whom one devotes himself must have a closer relationship with the total world historical process. In other words, Kierkegaard's notion of the radical transcendence of God would have to be reconsidered. If God is more deeply involved in "ordinary" history than Kierkegaard allows, then devotion to God might include the individual's devotion to the world. Faith would no longer be limited to a private relationship to a transcendent God, mediated by a single historical act of God. Rather, faith would involve one ever more deeply in the historical process by urging one to strive to realize new values and a more just social structure.

At this juncture, all of the major criticisms of Kierkegaard's argument that have been developed in this chapter come together. For him, an individual assumes the incognito of faithfulness by believing that Jesus was God's act undertaken to forgive sins. The self's faith, as Jesus' divinity, is inward and cannot be outwardly expressed. Because he understands faith in this way, Kierkegaard does not think that Christianity encourages one to change the structures of the historical process, or directs one to other persons. At the stage where selfhood is supposed to reach its most complete realization, selves remain isolated individuals, closed in their own subjectivity. According to Kierkegaard, at the final stage of human existence, Christianity, one must: "Seek first the kingdom of God. But what am I supposed to do? Shall I seek an office in order to be influential? No, first you shall seek God's kingdom. Shall I give all my fortune to the poor? No, first you shall seek God's kingdom and his righteousness. Shall I go out in the world as an apostle and proclaim these? No, first you shall seek God's kingdom. But isn't this in a certain sense doing nothing at all? Yes, to be sure, in a certain sense this is what it is."[31]

[31] *Journals and Papers*, no. 478; *Papirer*, IX A 14. In order not to distort Kierkegaard's viewpoint on this crucial issue, it is necessary to call the reader's attention to remarks that he makes that stand in tension with the texts that have been quoted in this section of the essay. In some of his ethical and religious discourses, Kierkegaard makes very profound observations about ethical obligation and offers eloquent remarks about love. Commentators such as Howard Hong ("Introduction" to *Works of Love*) and Vernard Eller (*Kierkegaard and Radical Discipleship: A New Perspective, op.cit.*) perceptively analyze these dimensions of Kierkegaard's thought. The argument presented in this chapter surely does not intend to deny those aspects of Kierkegaard's writings to which Hong and Eller direct our attention. To the contrary, if a balanced view of the entire corpus is to be attained, it is necessary to recognize his positive statements concerning the religious import of ethical activity. The point that we wish to emphasize is that the carefully articulated analyses of time and of the self, as developed in the pseudonymous works, stand in tension with many of the ethically oriented comments of the edifying literature. Furthermore, Kierkegaard's understanding of the temporality of selfhood, as we have interpreted it throughout this book, seems to underlie many of the disturbing texts that have been quoted in this chapter. We have noted above (pp. 364-365) that Kierkegaard does not adequately consider the way in which the form of Christian faith presented in the pseudonymous works is positively related to ethical conduct. The argument of this chapter seeks to indicate a way in which this positive connection might be explicated without doing violence to his most profound insights. Such a reconciliation of Christian faith and ethical activity seems not only to lead to a more adequate theological and philosophical position, but also suggests a way in which some of Kierkegaard's ostensibly disparate arguments might be integrated.

C. Kierkegaard and our "Global Village"

At one point in his Journals, Kierkegaard comments: "My task has continually been to provide the existential-corrective by poetically presenting the ideals and inciting people about the established order, with which I collaborate by criticizing all the false reformers and the opposition who simply are evil — and whom my own ideals can halt."[32]

Throughout his entire authorship, Kierkegaard regards himself as a corrective to the times in which he was living. His writings are addressed to individual readers in nineteenth-century Denmark. His diagnosis of the ills of his age conditions the cure he prescribes. Kierkegaard maintains that the people of his day had forgotten what it means to be an existing individual. For the person on Copenhagen's streets, absorbed in newspapers and public affairs, as well as for philosophers, engrossed in world historical speculation, attention was directed away from the subjective problem of individual selfhood. For Kierkegaard, this self-forgetfulness manifested itself most clearly in the common conviction that one becomes a Christian by virtue of his birth into a Christian country. All sense of the significance of decision for the life of the self and of the importance of an individual's life-time in determining his eternal destiny had been lost. In this situation, Kierkegaard believes that Providence had singled him out to reawaken the age to the dynamics of selfhood and the meaning of time by reintroducing Christianity into Christendom. The pseudonymous authorship is the means by which he attempts to accomplish this task. In these works, he seeks to bring his reader to a clearer understanding of the character of his self and to a more profound awareness of the importance of his life-time. Only Christianity represents the complete realization of authentic selfhood. Kierkegaard tries to incite his reader to begin his own quest of selfhood. But he can do no more than show us the way. We have to undertake

---

[32] *Ibid.*, no. 708; *Papirer*, x⁴ A 15.

the journey ourselves, for each of us must work out our own salvation in "fear and trembling."

However, as we begin our quest of authentic selfhood, we soon discover that our age is not Kierkegaard's age. Because he sees himself as a corrective to his age, some of the problems to which he devotes such passionate attention are not currently critical. Furthermore, his historical situation made it impossible for him to consider problems that have arisen since his time and that today command our attention. Kierkegaard expresses his understanding of the relativity of his diagnosis and his cure when he writes: "It is an unhappy mistake if the person who is used to introduce the corrective becomes impatient and wants to make the corrective normative for the others, an attempt that will confuse everything."[33] Certainly this does not mean that Kierkegaard has little to teach our age. Ours is also a time in which people, in Erich Fromm's terms, seek an "escape from freedom." Individuality and subjectivity are all too frequently lost in the objectivity of public opinion and mass movements. Therefore, we too need to be reawakened to the depths of selfhood and to the enigma of our temporality. In seeking to rediscover ourselves, Kierkegaard remains our guide.

And yet our age and its problems are different from those of Kierkegaard. Although he would probably reassert many of his insights in our day, doubtless his remarks would be changed somewhat to fit our situation. At this point, we are called upon to respond to Kierkegaard's works by offering our own corrective. He would have it no other way.

In the decades of this century, modern technology has created what Marshall McLuhan has called a "global village." Richard R. Niebuhr perceives the significance of our altered situation when he writes: "With our communications technology we have extended our senses and our sensibilities in making the scope of our eyes and ears coterminous with the inhabited earth and its solar environment. There is no physi-

[33] *Ibid.*, no. 709; *Papirer*, x⁴ A 596.

cal horizon over which the enemy can vanish. Without physical horizons no social or psychological distances remain to
give credibility to the Psalmist's assurance: 'A thousand shall
fall at thy side, and ten thousand at thy right hand; but it
shall not come nigh thee.' Our electronic global nervous system relentlessly transmits the anger, fears, and hopes of every
emerging nation and pent-up ghetto to the sleepless mind of
the radio listener."[34]

We have all become members of one another. In Kierkegaard's own terms, the individual is at once himself and the
entire race. Actions that we perform reverberate throughout
our world. No longer can we afford a mode of religion that
too sharply distinguishes our inner intentions and our outer
actions. We must assume responsibility for both. If religious
faith is to retain significance in our new world, it must be of
such a nature that it does not simply involve an individual's
private inwardness, but informs his conduct in the world by
encouraging him to strive for a more just social system. In this
undertaking we have to cultivate our "fellow-feeling"[35] to an
unprecedented degree. Religion cannot drive us apart into
the isolation of our idiosyncratic inwardness, but must draw
us together in the laborious task of bringing to fuller expression our common humanity. Our purpose in seeking to
change social structures should remain the creation of a
world in which individual selfhood is as completely realized
as possible. The lessons that Kierkegaard teaches us concerning the nature of the self and the significance of time can help
us greatly on our way to this goal. We must listen to him,
learning from his insights, and respond to him, correcting his
errors. But we can never forget the inestimable debt we owe
this great student of time and of the self.

In this book, we have examined the way in which the
themes of time and of the self unify Kierkegaard's pseudony-

[34] Richard R. Niebuhr, *Experiential Religion* (Harper and Row,
1972), p. 3.
[35] This is Schleiermacher's term, and is repeatedly used by Niebuhr.

371

mous writings. We have followed his careful analysis of these problems from the point at which self and world are undifferentiated and time as tensed has not emerged, to the most radically individualized self standing alone before God in the most significant temporal moment. Through our contribution to Kierkegaard's Socratic dialogue, we have attempted to elucidate the significance of his views for our day and to indicate where a corrective must be offered to his viewpoint if his insights are to address contemporary problems. The Socratic dialogue in which we have been engaged is endless, for our reply calls forth a response from Kierkegaard and from his students. The dialogue goes on — and must go on, for to stop it would be to put an end to our quest of authentic selfhood. When we are wrestling with Kierkegaard, our end is always a new beginning.

BIBLIOGRAPHY

A. Primary Sources

1. Danish

Søren Kierkegaards Papirer, eds. P. A. Heiberg and V. Kuhr, København: Gyldendalske Boghandel, 1912.

Søren Kierkegaards Samlede Værker, eds. A. B. Drachmann, J. L. Heiberg, and H. O. Lange, København: Gyldendalske Boghandel, 1901ff.

2. English

Armed Neutrality and An Open Letter, trans. and edited by Howard and Edna Hong, New York: Simon and Schuster, 1969.

Attack Upon "Christendom," trans. by Walter Lowrie, Princeton: Princeton University Press, 1968.

Christian Discourses, trans. by Walter Lowrie, New York: Oxford University Press, 1962.

Concluding Unscientific Postscript, trans. by David F. Swenson and Walter Lowrie, Princeton: Princeton University Press, 1941.

Crisis in the Life of an Actress and Other Essays on Drama, trans. by Stephen D. Crites, New York: Harper Torchbooks, 1967.

Edifying Discourses, trans. by David F. and Lillian Marvin Swenson, 4 vols., Minneapolis: Augsburg Publishing House, 1943ff.

Edifying Discourses: A Selection, trans. by David F. and Lillian Marvin Swenson, New York: Harper Torchbooks, 1958.

Either-Or, vol. I trans. by David F. and Lillian Marvin Swenson, vol. II trans. by Walter Lowrie, Princeton: Princeton University Press, 1971.

Fear and Trembling, trans. by Walter Lowrie, Princeton: Princeton University Press, 1970.

For Self-Examination and Judge for Yourselves! trans. by Walter Lowrie, Princeton: Princeton University Press, 1968.

Johannes Climacus or, De Omnibus Dubitandum Est and A Sermon, trans. by T. H. Croxall, Stanford, Calif.: Stanford University Press, 1967.

Journals, trans. and edited by Alexander Dru, New York: Oxford University Press, 1938.

Journals and Papers, eds. Howard and Edna Hong, Bloomington: Indiana University Press, 1967ff.

On Authority and Revelation, trans. by Walter Lowrie, New York: Harper Torchbooks, 1966.

Philosophical Fragments, trans. by David F. Swenson, revised by Howard V. Hong, Princeton: Princeton University Press, 1967.

Purity of Heart Is To Will One Thing, trans. by Douglas V. Steere, New York: Harper Torchbooks, 1948.

Repetition, trans. by Walter Lowrie, New York: Harper Torchbooks, 1964.

Stages on Life's Way, trans. by Walter Lowrie, New York: Schocken Books, 1967.

The Concept of Dread, trans. by Walter Lowrie, Princeton: Princeton University Press, 1957.

The Concept of Irony, trans. by Lee M. Capel, Bloomington: Indiana University Press, 1968.

The Difficulty of Being a Christian, trans. by Jacques Colette, English trans. by Ralph M. McInery and Leo Turcotte, Notre Dame: University of Notre Dame Press, 1969, based on French translation.

The Gospel of Our Sufferings, trans. by A. S. Aldworth and W. S. Ferrie, Grand Rapids: William B. Eerdmans, 1964.

The Last Years, Journals of 1853-1855, trans. and edited by Ronald Gregor Smith, New York: Harper and Row, 1965.

The Point of View of My Work as an Author: A Report to History, trans. by Walter Lowrie, New York: Harper Torchbooks, 1962.

The Sickness Unto Death, trans. by Walter Lowrie, Princeton: Princeton University Press, 1970.

Thoughts on Crucial Situations in Human Life, Three Discourses on Imagined Occasions, trans. by David F. Swenson, Minneapolis: Augsburg Publishing House, 1941.

Training in Christianity, trans. by Walter Lowrie, Princeton: Princeton University Press, 1967.

Works of Love, trans. by Howard and Edna Hong, New York: Harper Torchbooks, 1962.

B. SELECTED SECONDARY SOURCES

The number of works about Kierkegaard is, of course, enormous. The following is a list of works that are especially relevant to the problems considered in this book. I have placed an asterisk before particularly useful studies.

Anz, Wilhelm, *Kierkegaard und der deutsch Idealismus*, Tübingen: J. C. B. Mohr, 1956.

Barth, Karl, "Kierkegaard and the Theologians," *Canadian Journal of Theology*, vol. 13, Jan. 1967, pp. 64-65.

Bedell, George C., "Kierkegaard's Conception of Time," *Journal of the American Academy of Religion*, vol. XXXVIII, no. 3, Sept. 1969, pp. 266-269.

Blass, Josef, *Die Endlichkeit der Freiheit: Untersuchungen zur Konstitution der existierenden Subjektivität bei Sören Kierkegaard*, Köln, 1962.

*Bohlin, Torsten, *Kierkegaards dogmatiska aaskaadning i dess historiska sammanhang*, Stockholm: Svenska Kyrkans Diakonistyrelses, 1925.

Bonifazi, Conrad, *Christendom Attacked: A Comparison of Kierkegaard and Nietzsche*, London: Rockliff, 1953.

*Broudy, Harry S., "Kierkegaard's Levels of Existence," *Philosophy and Phenomenological Research*, 1940-1941, pp. 294-312.

——, "Kierkegaard on Indirect Communication," *Journal of Philosophy*, 1961, pp. 225-232.

Brunner, Emil, "Das Grundproblem der Philosophie bei Kant und Kierkegaard," *Zwischen der Zeiten*, vol. ii, no. 6, 1924, pp. 31-44.

Buske, T., "Die Dialektik der Geschichte zur Theologie Kierkegaards," *Neue Zeitschrift für systematische Theologie und Religionsphilosophie*, vol. 5, no. 2-3, 1963, pp. 235-247.

Carnell, Edward J., *The Burden of Søren Kierkegaard*, Grand Rapids: William B. Eerdmans Publishing Co., 1965.

Cavell, Stanley, "Kierkegaard's *On Authority and Revelation*," *Must We Mean What We Say?* New York: Charles Scribner's Sons, 1969, pp. 163-179.

Clive, Geoffrey, "Teleological Suspension of the Ethical in Nineteenth Century Literature," *Journal of Religion*, 1954, pp. 75-87.

Cole, J. Preston, "The Function of Choice in Human Existence," *Journal of Religion*, vol. xlv, 1964, pp. 196-210.

——, *The Problematic Self in Kierkegaard and Freud*, New Haven: Yale University Press, 1971.

Colette, Jacques, "Kierkegaard et la categorie d'historie," *Kierkegaardiana*, vol. v, ed. Niels Thulstrup, København: Munksgaard, 1964, pp. 85-93.

*Collins, James, *The Mind of Kierkegaard*, Chicago: Henry Regnery, 1967.

*Crites, Stephen, *In the Twilight of Christendom: Hegel vs. Kierkegaard on Faith and History*, Chambersburg, Pa.: American Academy of Religion, No. 2, 1971.

——, "Introduction," *Crisis in the Life of An Actress and Other Essays on Drama*, New York: Harper Torchbooks, 1967.

BIBLIOGRAPHY

*———, "Pseudonymous Authorship as Art and as Act," *Kierkegaard: A Collection of Critical Essays*, ed. Josiah Thompson, New York, Doubleday and Co., 1972, pp. 183-229.

———, "The Author and the Authorship: Recent Kierkegaard Literature," *Journal of the American Academy of Religion*, vol. xxxviii, no. 1, March 1970.

*———, "The Gospel According to Hegel," *Journal of Religion*, vol. xlvi, no. 2, April 1966, pp. 246-263.

Croxall, T. H., *Kierkegaard Commentary*, London: James Nisbet and Co., 1956.

———, *Kierkegaard Studies*, New York: Roy Publishers, n.d.

Diem, Hermann, *Kierkegaard: An Introduction*, trans. by David Green, Richmond: John Knox Press, 1966.

*———, *Kierkegaard's Dialectic of Existence*, trans. by Harold Knight, London: Oliver and Boyd, 1959.

Dietrichson, Paul, "Kierkegaard's Concept of the Self," *Inquiry*, vol. viii, 1965, pp. 1-32.

Dupré, Louis, *Kierkegaard as Theologian*, New York: Sheed and Ward, 1958.

*———, "The Constitution of the Self in Kierkegaard's Philosophy," *International Philosophical Quarterly*, vol. iii, 1963, pp. 506-526.

Eller, Vernard, *Kierkegaard and Radical Discipleship: A New Perspective*, Princeton: Princeton University Press, 1968.

Fischer, Friedrich Carl, *Existenz und Innerlichkeit: eine Einführung in die Gedankenwelt Sören Kierkegaards*, München: Beck, 1969.

Geismar, E., *Sören Kierkegaard: seine Lebensentwicklung und seine Wirksamkeit als Schrift-steller*, 1929.

Gerdes, Hayo, *Das Christbild Sören Kierkegaards, verglichen mit Christologie Hegels und Schleiermachers*, Düsseldorf: Eugen Dietrichs, 1960.

Gill, Jerry H., "Kant, Kierkegaard, and Religious Knowledge," *Essays on Kierkegaard*, ed. Jerry H. Gill, Minneapolis: Burgess Publishing Co., 1969, pp. 58-73.

Grimault, Marguerite, *La Mélancholie de Kierkegaard*, Paris: Aubier Montaigne, 1965.

Heiss, Robert, *Die grossen Dialektiker der 19 Jahrhunderts*: *Hegel, Kierkegaard, Marx*, Köln: Kiepenheuer and Witsch, 1963.

*Henriksen, Aage, *Methods and Results of Kierkegaard Studies in Scandinavia*: *A Historical and A Critical Study*, Copenhagen: Ejnar Munksgaard, 1951.

*———, *Kierkegaards Romaner*, København: Gyldendal, 1969.

Hepburn, Ronald W., *Christianity and Paradox*, New York: Pegasus, 1966.

Himmelstrup, Jens, *Terminologisk Ordbog, Søren Kierkegaards Samlede Værker*, vol. 20, eds. Drachmann, Heiberg, Lange, København: Gyldendal, 1964.

*Hirsch, Emanuel, *Kierkegaard-Studien*, Gütersloh: C. Bertelsmann, 1930-1933.

Holm, Søren, "L'être comme catégorie de l'éternité," *Kierkegaard Symposion*, København: Munksgaard, 1955, pp. 84-92.

Holmer, Paul, "On Understanding Kierkegaard," *A Kierkegaard Critique*, eds. Howard A. Johnson and Niels Thulstrup, Chicago: Henry Regnery Co., 1962, pp. 40-54.

———, "Kierkegaard and Religious Propositions," *Journal of Religion*, 1955, pp. 135-146.

Jaspers, Karl, "The Importance of Nietzsche, Marx, and Kierkegaard in the History of Philosophy," *Hibbert Journal*, 1950-1951, pp. 227-234.

*Johnson, Howard A., and Niels Thulstrup, editors, *A Kierkegaard Critique*: *An International Selection of Essays Interpreting Kierkegaard*, Chicago: Henry Regnery Co., 1962.

Jolivet, Regis, *Introduction to Kierkegaard*, trans. by W. F. Barber, London: Frederick Muller Ltd., 1950.

Klemke, E. D., "Some Insights for Ethical Theory from Kierkegaard," *Philosophical Quarterly*, vol. x, 1960, pp. 322-330.

Kroner, Richard, "Kierkegaard on Hegel," *Revue Internationale de Philosophie*, 1952, pp. 79-96.

LeFevre, Perry D., "An Interpretation of Kierkegaard's Life and Thought," *The Prayers of Kierkegaard*, Chicago: University of Chicago Press, 1963.

*Lindström, Valter, *Stadiernas Teleologi, en Kierkegaard Studie*, Lund: Haakan Ohlssons, 1943.

———, "The Problem of Objectivity and Subjectivity in Kierkegaard," *A Kierkegaard Critique*, eds. Howard A. Johnson and Niels Thulstrup, Chicago: Henry Regnery Co., 1962, pp. 228-243.

Løgstrup, K. E., "Le Concept de l'existence chez Kierkegaard," *Studia Theologica*, vol. 19, no. 1-2, 1965, pp. 260-268.

Löwith, Karl, *From Hegel to Nietzsche*, New York: Doubleday and Co., 1967.

Lowrie, Walter, *Kierkegaard*, New York: Oxford University Press, 1938.

Mackey, Louis, "Kierkegaard and the Problem of Existential Philosophy, i," *The Review of Metaphysics,* vol. 9, no. 3, March 1956, pp. 404-419.

———, "Kierkegaard and the Problem of Existential Philosophy, ii," *The Review of Metaphysics*, vol. 9, no. 4, pp. 569-588.

———, "The Loss of the World in Kierkegaard's Ethics," *The Review of Metaphysics*, vol. XV, 1961-1962, pp. 602-620.

*———, *Kierkegaard: A Kind of a Poet*, Philadelphia: University of Pennsylvania Press, 1972.

Malantschuk, Gregor, *Frihends Problem I Kierkegaards Begrebet Angest*, København: Rosenkilde og Bagger, 1971.

BIBLIOGRAPHY

*Malantschuk, Gregor, *Kierkegaard's Thought*, Princeton: Princeton University Press, 1971.

McKinnon, A., "Kierkegaard and His Pseudonyms, A Preliminary Report," *Kierkegaardiana*, vol. VIII, ed. Niels Thulstrup, København: Munksgaard, 1968, pp. 64-76.

Miller, Libuse Lukas, *In Search of the Self: The Individual in the Thought of Kierkegaard*, Philadelphia: Muhlenberg Press, 1962.

Niedermeyer, Gerhard, *Sören Kierkegaard und die Romantik*, Leipzig: Quelle and Meyer, 1910.

Paulsen, Anna, "Kierkegaard in seinen Verhältnis zur deutschen Romantik Einfluss und Überwindung," *Kierkegaardiana*, ed. Niels Thulstrup, vol. III, København: Munksgaard, 1959, pp. 38-47.

Prenter, R., "L'homme, synthèse du temps et de l'éternité d'après Søren Kierkegaard," *Studia Theologica*, vol. II, 1948, pp. 5-20.

Price, George, *The Narrow Pass: A Study of Kierkegaard's Concept of Man*, New York: McGraw-Hill Book Co., Inc., 1963.

Ramsey, Paul, "*Existenz* and the Existence of God: A Study of Kierkegaard and Hegel," *The Journal of Religion*, vol. XXVIII, no. 3, July 1948, pp. 157-176.

Rohrmoser, Günter, "Kierkegaard und das Problem der Subjektivität," *Neue Zeitschrift für Systematische Theologie und Religionsphilosophie*, vol. 8, no. 3, pp. 289-310.

Schmied-Kowarzik, Wolfdietrich, "Marx, Kierkegaard, Schelling: zum Problem von Theorie und Praxis," 1: *Schelling Studien: Festgabe für Manfred Schiöter zum 85 Geburtstag,* München und Wien: Oldenbourg, 1965, pp. 193-218.

*Schrag, Calvin O., *Existence and Freedom: Towards an Ontology of Human Finitude*, Evanston: Northwestern University Press, 1961.

*Shmuëli, Adi, *Kierkegaard and Consciousness*, Princeton: Princeton University Press, 1971.

Sløk, Johannes, "Kierkegaard and Luther," *A Kierkegaard Critique*, eds. Howard A. Johnson and Niels Thulstrup, Chicago: Henry Regnery Co., 1962, pp. 85-101.

———, "Das existenzphilosophie Motiv in Denken von Kierkegaard," *Studia Theologica*, vol. IX, no. 2, 1955, pp. 116-130.

*———, *Die Anthropologie Kierkegaards*, København: Rosenkilde und Bagger, 1954.

Sontag, Frederick, "Kierkegaard and the Search for a Self," *Essays on Kierkegaard*, ed. by Jerry H. Gill, Minneapolis: Burgess Publishing Co., 1969, pp. 154-166.

*Sponheim, Paul, *Kierkegaard on Christ and Christian Coherence*, New York: Harper and Row, 1968.

Stack, George, "Kierkegaard and the Phenomenology of Repetition," *Journal of Existentialism*, vol. VII, 1966-1967, pp. 111-125.

Swenson, David, *Something About Kierkegaard*, ed. by Lillian Marvin Swenson, Minneapolis: Augsburg Publishing House, 1956.

Taylor, Mark C., "In Defense of Marriage," *American Ecclesiastical Review*, vol. 167, no. 3. March 1973, pp. 164-177.

———, "Kierkegaard as a Theologian of Hope," *Union Seminary Quarterly Review*, vol. XXVIII, no. 3, Spring 1973, pp. 225-233.

———, "Kierkegaard On The Structure of Selfhood," *Kierkegaardiana*, ed. Niels Thulstrup, København: Munksgaard, 1974.

———, "Of Space, Time, and God's Transcendence," *Iliff Review*, 1974.

———, "Review" of Crites' *In the Twilight of Christendom*, *Union Seminary Quarterly Review*, vol. XXVII, no. 4, Summer 1972, pp. 243-245.

———, "Time's Struggle With Space: Kierkegaard's Understanding of Temporality," *Harvard Theological Review*, July 1973.

Thomas, J. Heywood, *Subjectivity and Paradox*, New York: Macmillan and Co., 1957.

*Thompson, Josiah, *The Lonely Labyrinth*: *Kierkegaard's Pseudonymous Works*, Carbondale, Illinois: Southern Illinois Press, 1967.

——, *Kierkegaard*, New York: Knopf, 1973.

Thomte, Reidar, *Kierkegaard's Philosophy of Religion*, Princeton: Princeton University Press, 1948.

*Thulstrup, Niels, *Kierkegaards forhold til Hegel og til den spekulative idealisme intil 1846*, København: Gyldendal, 1967.

Tillich, Paul, "Kierkegaard as Existentialist Thinker," *Union Review*, 1942.

*Wahl, Jean, *Études Kierkegaardiennes*, Paris: Fernard Aubier, 1938.

——, "Kierkegaard und das Problem der Zeit," *Schweizer Monatshefte*, vol. XLIII, 1963-1964, pp. 197-198.

Whittemore, Robert C., "Of History, Time and Kierkegaard's Problem," *Journal of Religious Thought*, vol. II, 1954, pp. 134-155.

Widenman, Robert, "Some Aspects of Time in Aristotle and Kierkegaard," *Kierkegaardiana*, ed. Niels Thulstrup, København: Munksgaard, vol. VIII, 1969, pp. 7-21.

Wild, John, *Existence and the World of Freedom*, Englewood Cliffs: Prentice Hall, 1963.

——, "Kierkegaard and Contemporary Existentialist Philosophy," *Anglican Theological Review*, vol. 38, Jan. 1956, pp. 15-32.

Wolf, Herbert C., *Kierkegaard and Bultmann*: *The Quest of the Historical Jesus*, Minneapolis: Augsburg Publishing House, 1965.

INDEX

Library of Congress Cataloging in Publication Data

Taylor, Mark C   1945-
    Kierkegaard's pseudonymous authorship.

    Bibliography: p.
    Includes index.
        1. Kierkegaard, Søren Aabye, 1813-1855.   2. Self (Philosophy)
    3. Time.   I. Title.
    B4378.T5T39   198'.9   74-30005
    ISBN 0-691-07202-7